PENGUIN HANDBOOKS

MOUNTAINEERING

Alan Blackshaw was born in Liverpool in 1933 and educated at
Merchant Taylors' School, Crosby, and Wadham College, Oxford.
He began hill walking in 1948 and climbing in 1949, and has been
to most areas in Britain. He has done over fifty difficult alpine
climbs, including the first British guideless ascents of the North-
East Face of the Piz Badile and the North Face of the Aiguille de
Triolet. He was a member of two of Lord Hunt's expeditions: to
the Caucasus in 1958 and to north-east Greenland in 1960.

Alan Blackshaw is keenly interested in teaching mountaineering,
and first instructed at Glenmore Lodge in 1952. He was an
instructor in mountaineering with the Royal Marine Commandos
during his National Service, and has since continued this and ski-
training in the Royal Marines Reserve. He is President of the
British Mountaineering Council and a Vice-President of the
Climbers' Club; and has previously been Editor of the *Alpine
Journal* and of the Alpine Climbing Group *Bulletin*. He has written
articles for club journals and lectured and broadcast about his
expeditions.

He is an active skier and ski-mountaineer, and led the British
Alpine Ski Traverse 1972 which traversed the mountains along the
whole length of the Alps from the Gross Glockner area in Austria
to south of the Dauphiné in France. He is at present working on
a new Penguin handbook, *Skiing*, which aims to cover all aspects
of the sport.

An Under-Secretary in the Department of Energy, Alan Blackshaw
is currently at the Offshore Supplies Office in Glasgow; and lives
in Scotland with his wife and daughter.

ALAN BLACKSHAW

mountaineering

FROM HILL WALKING TO

ALPINE CLIMBING

Foreword by the Rt. Hon. Lord Hunt

With 176 photographic and line illustrations and four maps

*Approved by the British Mountaineering Council and the
Mountaineering Council of Scotland*

PENGUIN BOOKS

Penguin Books Ltd, Harmondsworth,
Middlesex, England
Penguin Books Inc., 7110 Ambassador Road,
Baltimore, Maryland 21207, U.S.A.
Penguin Books Australia Ltd, Ringwood,
Victoria, Australia
Penguin Books Canada Ltd, 41 Steelcase Road West,
Markham, Ontario, Canada
Penguin Books (N.Z.) Ltd, 182–190 Wairau Road,
Auckland 10, New Zealand

First published 1965
Revised edition 1968
Revised edition 1970
Reprinted with revisions 1973, 1975
Copyright © Alan Blackshaw, 1965, 1968, 1970, 1973, 1975

Printed in Great Britain by
Fletcher & Son Ltd, Norwich
Set in Monotype Baskerville

General design: John Slee-Smith, M.S.I.A.
Photographic design: Alan Blackshaw

FRONTISPIECE: *Alpine Heights*. On the Leiterspitzen, Zermatt

TO MY PARENTS

Contents

Mountain climbing is an adventure: an adventure open before our eyes and more or less accessible. There can be no adventure without uncertainty of its result, and in good adventure there is also an element of risk, even of danger to life. In climbing mountains, danger is a constant element, not remote as in other sports: it is always with us behind the veil of pleasant circumstances, and it can be upon us before we are aware. The mountaineer, therefore, has not only to know and observe the rules which govern the good playing of all games, he has to keep another set of values constantly in mind, values which involve the larger issues of life and death. To lose a game may be beneficial and is always educative; to be beaten on a mountain may incur the loss of a life or of our peace of mind.

Geoffrey Winthrop Young *Mountain Craft*

High proficiency in the sport is only attainable when a natural aptitude is combined with long years of practice, and not without some, perhaps much, danger to life and limb. Happily, the faithful climber usually acquires this skill at an age when the responsibilities of life have not yet laid firm hold upon him, and when he may fairly claim some latitude in matters of this sort. On the other hand he gains a knowledge of himself, a love of all that is most beautiful in nature, and an outlet such as no other sport affords for the stirring energies of youth: gains for which no price is, perhaps, too high. It is true the great ridges sometimes demand their sacrifice, but the mountaineer would hardly forgo his worship though he knew himself to be the destined victim. But happily to most of us the great brown slabs bending over into immeasurable space, the lines and curves of the wind-moulded cornice, the delicate undulations of the fissured snow, are old and trusted friends, ever luring us to health and fun and laughter, and enabling us to bid a sturdy defiance to all the ills that time and life oppose.

A. F. Mummery *My Climbs in the Alps and Caucasus*

Foreword

This book is an introduction to mountaineering for the thousands who will be hill walking and climbing in the third quarter of the twentieth century. The author is a man who is highly qualified by his experience and achievements to accept the great responsibility of writing it. He has done many fine climbs in the Western Alps, in addition to numerous hard routes on British crags, during the last fourteen years or so. He has served as Honorary Secretary of the Climbers' Club and on the Committee of the Alpine Club. His National Service as a Royal Marine gave him the opportunity to pass on his skill to the Marine Commandos on sea-cliffs, inland crags, and in the snow-filled corries of the Highlands; as a Reserve officer, he has continued with this important service since. Alan Blackshaw accompanied me to the Caucasus in 1958 and to the mountains of Scoresby Land in north-east Greenland in 1960. I know no one with whom I feel more confidence and comradeship on a rope.

My own introduction to mountaineering took place forty years ago. It was in 1924, when I was fourteen, that I was given as a Christmas present George Finch's *The Making of a Mountaineer*. In its turn this was a personal, vivid account of the making of one very distinguished member of the fraternity of mountaineers and I read it avidly. In that year George Leigh Mallory and Sandy Irving had died on Everest, probably not very far from the top; this dramatic event had stirred my youthful imagination anew, as had the story of Scott's last expedition ten years before. Although I had been walking and ski-ing in the European Alps since the age of ten, it was this book which started me off on my mountaineering career. Alan Blackshaw's sound, informative, and comprehensive book is a worthy successor to John Barford's *Climbing in Britain* (1946) in the Penguin Series, and I feel sure that it will start many others on their climbing careers in the future.

A great social revolution has taken place during the forty years since I started climbing and among its many benefits are the far wider opportunities now open to almost anybody to enjoy such adventurous, stimulating, and challenging activities as hill walking and mountain climbing, which were obvious but open to few people in my youth. In stressing the value, timeliness, and importance of this book as a contribution to the problems raised by the phenomenon of the prevailing human explosion into the mountains, I feel it is as well to begin at the beginning: to define the term 'mountaineering'. If you aspire, as I did, to become a mountaineer, you will be well advised to start by grasping what it is and what it is not. What makes a mountaineer?

Let me pose, and attempt to answer, some very simple questions. Are the people who inhabit mountainous areas mountaineers? Not necessarily. Not unless they travel from time to time up and down and through those mountains on their feet. So mountaineering implies a physical relation between a man and a mountain.

Is a man who climbs a rock route at 'VS' standard on a British cliff a mountaineer? I say again, not necessarily. At the lowest estimate this can be likened to a gymnasium technique. I write this with no disrespect whatever to any rock expert or any mountain dweller.

So mountaineering, though it can embrace them, is more than each of these things; indeed it is a symposium of them all. This is splendidly represented in this book. You can, of course, enjoy one, or more, without necessarily all, the parts; each can be sufficient unto itself. Take rock climbing. A French friend of mine with whom I used to climb on the boulders in the Forest of Fontainebleau was missing from our rendezvous one week-end. When we next met at the foot of one of these outcrops, a seventy-foot monster known as the Dame Jeanne, he told me he had just returned from an ascent of the West Face of the Drus at that time deemed to be one of the hardest and longest routes in Europe. I congratulated him. 'Yes,' he said and added, in all seriousness, 'and it was excellent training for the Dame Jeanne.' This is a valid point of view!

This book tells you where and how to begin and to progress – always supposing you want to get beyond the seventy-foot boulder stage. What it does not tell you is where and when to stop. Well, it may be some encouragement to know that you can carry on in this fascinating sport into advanced middle age, always provided that you keep going. The best age for high altitude ascents, when experience and stamina are at a premium, is nearer forty than twenty-five. And you can continue tackling technically hard climbs even at my age – I still do!

But in another sense, there is no need to give up. Mountaineering may come to mean something more than a sport; you may find in it a philosophy of living. If you do, and I hope you may, then you and the mountains will be inseparable through life.

I hope that many thousands of people who feel the call of adventure in the mountains, and others again who have already fallen under their spell, will enjoy and use this book as an aid to progress.

Good climbing!

21 January 1965   JOHN HUNT

Acknowledgements

This book could not have been written without a great deal of help from many fellow mountaineers and others, and I should like to express my appreciation to all who have so generously given their time and knowledge.

Those who have commented on the complete text in draft are: Peter Crew, John Jackson, John Neill, Tom Patey, Anthony Rawlinson, George Robertson, Hilary Sinclair (Hon. Sec., British Mountaineering Council), Jack Soper, and Geoffrey Sutton. In addition, I have had comments on individual chapters from Allan Austin, Eric Byne, Dick Cook, Len Frank, Ross Higgins, Dorothy McMaster, Barry O'Flynn, Joe Della Porta, Cecily Ramsey, Sean Rothery, and Jeremy Talbot. The Mountaineering Section of the Camping Club vetted chapter 4 and the British Mountaineering Council's Equipment Subcommittee chapters 3 and 7. The Mountain Rescue Committee gave a great deal of help with chapter 12, which is largely based on their handbook *Mountain Rescue and Cave Rescue*, and with the lists of rescue posts in chapter 13. The glossary of place names follows the similar one in J. E. Q. Barford's *Climbing in Britain* (Penguin Books, 1946) which was based on material by John Bartholomew & Sons Ltd (Gaelic and Norse names) and Emlyn Jones (Welsh names): it has been revised by Robert Grieve and Tom Patey, and by the Climbers' Club Subcommittee on Welsh Nomenclature. Barford's book had a profound influence on my own attitude to mountaineering and I am sure that much of his teaching will show through in this its successor in the Penguin series, though the text is completely new.

I should particularly like to express my appreciation to Sir John Hunt for his foreword.

The majority of the photographs have been taken by me. I am much indebted to 'Mac' McDermott, Cornwall Rock Climbing Guide, who acted as model for most of them, in Cornwall and the Alps, and also to Tom Patey [17, 114, 118, and 120c]* and Gerry Rogan [99]. The heavy work of developing and printing them was undertaken by Paul Diston, who has also been an invaluable source of advice on their design and layout. Frank Davies and Robert Lawrie loaned me equipment for some of them. I am grateful to the following for the other photographs: Alan Clarke [150], Dick Cook [3, 11], Basil Goodfellow [1, 5, 23, 36, 129, 131, 133, 135, 139, 141, 142, 149, 151], the Headmaster of Ullswater School [43], Sir John Hunt [128, 130], R.A.F. Mountain Rescue [126], Rosemary Soper [39, 40], B. J. Ward Ltd [31], Tom Weir [46, 47], and Alan Wright [149].

The diagrams were drawn by John and Jean Slee-Smith, those in chapter 12 being adapted from *Mountain Rescue and Cave Rescue* by courtesy of Roche Products Ltd [127] and the Mountain Rescue Committee [124, 125].

Unfortunately, space prevents me from mentioning individually the large number of others who have helped but my appreciation is none the less sincere because they are anonymous.

Finally, the writing has made heavy inroads into my private time in the past two years and this has been accepted with much understanding and patience by my wife and small daughter, for which I thank them.

London sw1

Alan Blackshaw
November 1964

*Square brackets are used in the text (but not in the captions) to refer to illustrations.

Introduction

The soundest way to become an all-round mountaineer is to begin with hill walking and scrambling and later on to branch out into rock climbing and snow and ice climbing. When you have a good knowledge of these, the way is open to alpine mountaineering and perhaps to the greater ranges outside western Europe. The pleasures of mountaineering are, however, personal to the individual and the extent to which you specialize must depend upon yourself, your tastes and ambitions. Ordinary hill walking can be tremendous fun in its own right and many would not wish to do more. For some, on the other hand, nothing less than mastery of all forms of mountaineering in distant ranges as well as at home is sufficient. While obviously the more experienced and proficient you become in the various aspects of mountaineering the more satisfaction you will derive, there is no reason why you should not stop short of roped climbing if you so wish and still obtain great pleasure and interest from the hills: the important thing is to go to them and to get to know and enjoy them in their very wide variety of conditions.

Unfortunately, the number of accidents to British hill walkers and climbers in the past decade has been high, partly no doubt as a result of the great increase in the popularity of the hills for recreation. All mountaineering involves an element of unavoidable risk – from such hazards as falling stones or ice, or bad rock – and this has been the cause of about one tenth of the accidents which have occurred in Britain, some of them involving very good mountaineers indeed (in the Alps, the proportion has been a good deal higher because of the greater objective dangers). Most accidents, however, have been due to ignorance or inexperience and could have been avoided if the victims had appreciated the hazards of hill walking and climbing better. In this book I have concentrated on safety in the hope that it will help to reduce the number of avoidable accidents in the future. But I have also attempted to show the way to fair enjoyment and full achievement in all aspects of mountaineering. Judgement built on experience is the crucial factor here, because everything depends on striking the right balance between prudence and boldness, safety and danger.

The scope of this book

This book aims to give factual information on the techniques and equipment needed for all forms of mountaineering that are normally undertaken in this country and the Alps or other European ranges. It is divided into three main parts:

Part one: Hill walking in Britain;
Part two: Climbing in Britain;
Part three: Alpine mountaineering.

Special attention has been paid to hill walking and scrambling, and in particular to winter conditions (chapter 2) and to navigation in the hills (appendix E), two aspects which are frequently neglected. It is assumed that the would-be climber will have gained experience of hill walking before starting climbing, and part two concentrates solely on climbing techniques and equipment. It covers all aspects of climbing as practised in this country, leaving to part three only the special techniques and equipment which are not required in Britain.

The second and third parts of the book describe advanced as well as more routine techniques since, even as a beginner, you will benefit by incorporating the skills of advanced climbing into your technique, so that your climbing is well directed and skilful from the start. Given this, however, it should be made clear that a progressive apprenticeship, starting on the easier routes and gradually improving your standard, is the only really sound way to become a good all-round mountaineer.

It is not suggested that the methods described here are the only methods; different people, with differing qualities and physiques, will inevitably do things in somewhat different ways, and in any case one of the pleasures of mountaineering lies in finding out your own personal way of doing things. But this book does set out to give a basis of good practice, which can be used safely and to good purpose. Other books should be read as well, to broaden your understanding, and a list of these is in the bibliography. Mountaineering can well be combined with other pursuits such as ski-ing, photography, ornithology, and botany, and some books on these subjects are included in the list.

Need for a companion

As a general rule, it is advisable to have a companion for any hill walking or scrambling you undertake. Even an experienced mountaineer might twist his ankle and be unable to move and, if there were no one with him, might lose his life through long exposure. The best number for a party is three or four (§ 2). A great deal depends however on the popularity and difficulty of the route, and its condition at the time: for example, you would be unlikely to come to harm in walking alone on an easy route such as the Llanberis track on Snowdon in good weather in summer when there are plenty of other people around, but it would be folly to do so in bad weather or in winter when the conditions are much more serious. The risks to the inexperienced *solo* rock climber or snow-and-ice climber are very great indeed since he rarely has a second chance if a well-tried hold gives way or if a falling stone dislodges him. You are definitely recommended not to climb alone at any time. *Unroped* climbing is occasionally practised by very experienced climbers who know the route well and who are climbing

very well within their capacities but there is no doubt at all that on any rock or ice where a falling climber might otherwise be held by the rope, unroped climbing is dangerous. It should certainly never be undertaken by novices, even on practice crags.

If you are a beginner, your companion should ideally be someone with experience who will be able to show you much of what follows in this book. If you cannot find such a person, get someone who will at least share the adventures and responsibilities equally. Be sure that he can be relied on under trying circumstances: bad weather, fatigue, and danger can strain nerve and temper badly and break up what under normal conditions is an agreeable friendship. These strains are part and parcel of mountaineering, and it is because of them that leaders of expeditions to the major ranges look for equable temperaments as well as climbing ability in their companions.

Equipment

There is a very wide range of equipment available at the climbing outfitters. Much of this is expensive and if you are bitten by the mountain bug your problem may be to avoid spending so much on equipment that you have to cut down on your week-ends or holidays in the hills! It is important to get the right equipment for whatever type of mountaineering you are doing, and the equipment chapters of this book have been linked with the technique chapters so that you can see what is required in each case.

When choosing equipment, look for its general suitability, including good design, robustness, and lightness. No matter how great the saving in cost you should never rely on unsafe equipment as your life itself may depend on it one day. For

1. *Snowdon and Crib Goch (North Wales).* From above Pen y Pass. Snowdon is the peak on the left (see also 11 and 12). North Wales gives excellent walking and climbing of all standards (§ 106).

example, the soles of your boots (§ 23) should always be in good condition so that they give a good grip, and you should not allow economy considerations to force you to use moulded rubber-soled boots without crampons (§ 77) on hard snow or ice in winter. The climber for his part would be foolish to use anything but a good nylon or perlon climbing rope of the requisite strength (§ 51), or to retain it when it is past its prime.

No two mountaineers would agree about the choice of kit, and you should defer buying most of it until you have gained some experience; on training courses (see p. 25) it is often possible to hire the essentials. It is however advisable to get boots, an anorak, a rucksack, and maps and a compass straight away. These are described in chapter 3, and a list of some of the shops which sell equipment is in appendix B.

How to start

Hill walking. When you have found a companion and have acquired the basic minimum of equipment, you can begin your hill-walking career without more ado. It is best to start gently, if possible in low hills near your home, where you can practise map and compass work (see appendix E) as well as walking. Make your first visit to one of the main mountain areas (see chapter 13) in the summer or autumn, when the hills are easier and safer than in the snow and ice of winter and late spring. Stay at a youth hostel where you can meet other hill walkers, or camp (chapter 4). If your companion is also a beginner, you must both recognize your inexperience and err always on the side of caution. Given this, there is no reason why you should not have a thoroughly enjoyable holiday finding your way about the hills, and practising the skills described in part one.

2. *Rock climbing.* A Very Difficult climb on Raven Crag, Langdale (Lake District). See also 3.

Rock climbing [2]. Try to get some general experience of hill walking and scrambling before starting on rock climbing proper, if only so that you can get to the more distant crags and find your way back from them if bad weather should develop. You are strongly recommended to get an introduction to the sport from an experienced climber, who can show you the basic skills and safety precautions. Rock climbing does not lend itself to experiments on a trial-and-error basis, and serious – even fatal – injuries can be caused by ignorance of some quite simple point. If you do not already know a climber who is prepared to take you with him, there may possibly be a mountaineering club near by whose members are prepared to help (not all clubs cater for beginners, however – see p. 27). Alternatively, you may meet an experienced climber at one of the mountain centres which you are using for hill walking, or at an outcrop or practice crag. If it is quite impossible to get someone experienced to show you the way, it is probably best to join one of the training courses organized by the various training organizations or mountain schools, or possibly to have a few days with a guide (see below). Alternatively a gentle start may be made at short outcrops where your colleague can walk round the side and secure the rope from above, so that no one actually leads a climb.

Snow and ice climbing. The basic techniques for snow and ice climbing can be learned while hill walking in winter and spring. The easier snow and ice routes are on the whole less technical than the rock routes, but they tend to be a good deal more serious because they are longer and higher (while the days are colder and shorter), and because it is difficult to secure the party adequately (chapter 11). It is again recommended that you should get an introduction from someone with experience who knows the area (if necessary by going on a course), but in addition you should already have learned to climb Difficult or preferably Very Difficult rock (see § 35 for standards of difficulty), since it is often necessary to negotiate iced-up rock pitches.

Alpine climbing. This requires a good all-round level of competence on rock and also (often overlooked by British parties) on snow and ice. It is discussed in detail in chapter 14.

Training organizations

There is an increasing number of organizations which run courses in the various aspects of mountaineering, from hill walking to alpine climbing (or even ski mountaineering), at a price. Details of the main ones are in appendices B and D. The courses are usually brief, but cover the basic essentials and would enable you to meet other people of about the same standard with whom you could walk or climb independently later. The courses in hill walking and elementary mountaineering cover the techniques described in part one, and should deal with mountain rescue (chapter 12) as well. Rock climbing and snow and ice climbing courses require a higher level of instruction and consequently tend to be rather more expensive. On any but the most elementary climbing, one instructor should ideally take not more than two, or at most three, students; but some organizations to reduce costs allow as many as six students per instructor with the result that the benefit to the individual is reduced and the inconvenience and possibly the risks to all concerned are increased (including to other parties which are held up by long 'caravans' on popular climbs).

In addition to the climbing instruction provided by the permanent mountain schools and mountain guides, certain local authorities arrange evening classes; several British travel organizations also run walking and climbing holidays and courses on the Continent, often in conjunction with the Continental alpine clubs or training organizations.

All these forms of instruction are valuable, but as they usually give instruction in groups or classes, they are best suited to people who can mix easily and who are prepared to share their pleasures (and pains) with others.

Professional mountain and rock-climbing guides

Britain. For most of the main centres there are mountain and rock-climbing guides who may be engaged by the day or the week by prior arrangement. The guides with the British Mountain Guide qualification have passed stringent tests organized by the Association of British Mountain Guides in consultation with the British Mountaineering Council (B.M.C.)* and the Mountaineering Council of Scotland (M.C. of S).* These include not only rock-climbing and mountaineering in summer and winter but also navigation, mountain rescue and first aid. Although the guides may specialize in one particular area, they are expected to be competent at guiding anywhere in the country. The certificates have to be renewed regularly. Guides usually charge about £8 a day plus certain expenses, with variations according to the number of clients and the difficulties of the climb requested. Reduced rates are normally available to young beginners. Ropes are to be provided by the guide. A list of B.M.C. guides is published in the Council's annual handbook, and there are also advertisements in some of the British mountaineering magazines (bibliography, 1). Not all B.M.C. guides are available on call because some of them have other regular jobs, and guide only at week-ends or on their holidays.

It would be very rare for someone in this country to engage a guide for all his early mountaineering, partly because of the expense and partly because there is so much that even the novice can do without full-time instruction (provided he and his companion are sensible); a good compromise on a fortnight's holiday would be to take a guide for two days or so to fill in the gaps in your knowledge of hill walking, or rather longer if you want him to introduce you to climbing.

*Explanations of abbreviations, and references to definitions in the text of common terms, are in the index.

The Alps. On the Continent, guiding is very much more organized than it is in Britain and a very good service is provided, though the price is high. The pros and cons of hiring guides for alpine climbing are discussed in § 113.

British mountaineering clubs

Some mountaineers do not believe in clubs, regarding them as a form of regimentation in a sport which is essentially an escape from the restrictions of civilization. But most find membership of a club useful as well as pleasant. British clubs usually issue a list of their members' addresses (useful for making contact with fellow members) and a journal; most of them run meets in mountain areas, and many have indoor evenings where members and guest lecturers show films or slides. Many clubs have huts in climbing areas; these are often very well-equipped cottages with a reasonable standard of comfort (§ 27). Members of certain clubs are able by prior arrangement to use the huts of other clubs. A list of clubs is in appendix C. Most of them fall into the following main categories:

1. *Senior clubs*. These were mostly formed around the turn of the century and have been closely linked with the development of British mountaineering. They usually require minimum standards of experience and competence, and stipulate that a candidate's application must be supported by two existing members. Moreover, some – but not all – of them are under such pressure of numbers that they have had to limit new admissions. One reason for this is that a club which became too large would tend to lose its informal atmosphere; a second reason is that the clubs are run by their own members on a voluntary basis, and too large a membership would impose an unduly heavy burden of administration. These clubs do a great deal for members and non-members alike in publishing guide-books to the main climbing areas (§ 35 and chapter 13) and journals

in which new developments are recorded, and by taking a lead in the laborious administrative work needed to safeguard the interests of mountaineers and to preserve access to the mountains. The Alpine Club (A.C.) has a special place, being the oldest mountaineering club in the world (it was founded in 1857). It has premises in London, a comprehensive library, lectures, and a series of alpine guide-books (chapter 19). Apart from the *Alpine Journal* (bibliography, 1), which gives an up-to-date account of mountaineering developments world-wide, members also receive free of charge *Alpine Climbing*, insurance against alpine rescue costs, and special rights in French, German, Italian and certain Austrian huts. Since 1974 the Club has been open to women meeting the same mountaineering qualification as men (about twenty alpine peaks and three seasons of experience); and there is also an Aspirant Membership for those alpine climbers not yet eligible for full membership.

2. *Local clubs*. With a few exceptions these are much more limited in size and scope than the senior clubs. Their number has multiplied many times since the Second World War as mountaineering has attracted more and more devotees, and most places in Britain have one within reasonable travelling distance. Some of these clubs are well established, with a steady membership and their own hut; some, on the other hand, are small, centring perhaps on a group of friends and possibly disappearing as they split up. With a few notable exceptions these clubs do not require any standard for participation in their activities, though they may do so for full membership. They are, therefore, the ideal type of club for the beginner, since they enable him to meet mountaineers from the same locality who can introduce him to the sport and possibly help with transport for week-end climbing in the mountains. Some of them are not listed in appendix c, and it is as well to make inquiries in your own area; the Y.H.A.'s local groups, for instance, sometimes have mountaineering sections.

3. *University clubs, etc.* There are also clubs peculiar to one section of the community, such as the universities, the teaching hospitals, the Services, and some business concerns. These clubs hardly ever require any standard for membership, and indeed often cater especially for beginners.

The British Mountaineering Council (B.M.C.) and the Mountaineering Council of Scotland (M.C. of S.)

Each climbing club in this country manages its own affairs, but for certain purposes they have since the Second World War combined together into the British Mountaineering Council and the Mountaineering Council of Scotland (formerly the Association of Scottish Climbing Clubs – A.S.C.C.). These two bodies have a membership of about 160 clubs and 30 clubs respectively (see appendix c). The two organizations work closely together. They aim to be of service to all climbers and hill walkers and are concerned with the preservation of mountain and other climbing areas, and their amenities; with problems of access to them; with many safety aspects of climbing – testing equipment, testing of guides, the issuing of warnings to climbers and the general public, and the adequacy of maps; with assisting over the provision of club huts and camping facilities; and with problems of behaviour, litter, etc. The B.M.C. is run by a Committee representing a wide variety of mountaineering interests, including its own Regional Committees; in addition there are a number of other committees dealing with such matters as international relations, equipment and conservation/access. The B.M.C. represents mountaineering with the Sports Council and other public bodies in Britain; and also represents the United Kingdom on the Union Internationale des Associations d'Alpinisme (U.I.A.A.) which is responsible *inter alia* for international agreements on climbing equipment. In 1974 it was decided to move its office from London to Manchester, so as to be closer to the centre of gravity of British mountaineering. The B.M.C.'s magazine *Mountaineering* (see bibliography, 1) was replaced in 1972 by a new magazine, *Mountain Life*, which aims to cover all main mountaineering events and B.M.C. activity, for example in equipment testing. In addition, the B.M.C. publishes an annual handbook with addresses of its officers, committees and member clubs, together with those of the Mountaineering Council of Scotland; and in 1972 it started a new publication, *New Climbs*, giving details of new routes throughout the country. Any inquiries which cannot be answered locally (e.g. at libraries) should be sent to the Secretary of the B.M.C. or the M.C.S., as the case may be, at the addresses in appendix B. Mountain rescue is the concern of the Mountain Rescue Committee (§ 90).

The Continental alpine clubs

The Continental alpine countries have their own national alpine clubs which own huts, publish guide-books and journals, and arrange many other facilities for their members. These facilities usually include preferential treatment in almost all the alpine huts (with a special cheap overnight rate and priority over non-members), cheap rates on the mountain railways and *téléphériques* (cable-cars) in each club's own country and, usually at extra cost, insurance against the often very high cost of a rescue party. Each national club also has local sections whose activities correspond roughly to those of the British clubs, i.e. running meets and administering huts. There is no entrance qualification for the national clubs and their membership usually runs into tens of thousands. Most British climbers visiting the Alps join one or the other (or our own Alpine Club (p. 28) which can now offer broadly similar facilities). It is not only pleasant to be a member, but also, over a fortnight or so, it may save you more than the cost of the subscription through the preferential rates in huts. The amount of saving will, of course, depend on the extent to which you use the facilities, and in bad seasons there may be no saving at all (it is an irony of alpine climbing that the better the season, the less it tends to cost: it is living in the valley in periods of prolonged bad weather that is especially costly). The Swiss (S.A.C.) and French (C.A.F.) Alpine Clubs have been traditionally the most popular with British alpinists – the former has an Association of British Members (A.B.M.S.A.C.) – but many have joined the Austrian Alpine Club (O.A.V.) in recent years. The addresses of these and other Continental organizations are in appendix D.

The Groupe de Haute Montagne (G.H.M.) is a specialist group which requires a very high standard of performance indeed; its membership is mainly French. This group has contributed substantially to the increase in the standard of mountaineering achievement, as well as to the compilation of guide-books to the French Alps. There are high-standard groups also in the other alpine countries, and the United Kingdom has its own, the Alpine Climbing Group (A.C.G.), which has played quite an important part in the post-war renaissance of high-standard British climbing in the Alps.

Safety on mountains

The following list has been prepared by the B.M.C. as giving the most essential points on safety in the mountains.

1. Plan, with maps.

2. Don't try too much too soon. Move gradually to bigger things.

3. Go with others and keep together always. Until experienced don't take charge of others: then take only ten or less.

4. Equip against the worst. Be well shod: have warm clothing and a weatherproof cover, spare clothes and food for all, map, whistle, torch, and compass.

5. Give yourself ample time, and more as a reserve. Move steadily. Don't hurry and don't waste time.

6. Don't throw down or dislodge rocks or stones. Know and observe the Country Code.

7. Eye the weather: it can change completely in a few hours. Don't go on recklessly if it turns bad. Don't be afraid to come down.

8. Don't do rock, snow, or ice climbing without an experienced leader.

9. If lost don't panic or rush down. Keep together and deliberately work out your position and your best way down.

10. Leave word behind you of your route and when you expect to be back. If you arrive where friends don't expect you, phone them or tell the police (to save needless searches).

Part one

Hill walking in Britain

Hill walking is a fine way of getting to know the British hills and of discovering what they can offer. The basic skills needed in good weather can be acquired fairly easily; as experience of the hills and of your colleagues is built up, so the scope for adventure can be widened. Eventually, when you are fully experienced in summer conditions, you should get to know the hills in the much more arduous but sometimes more rewarding conditions of winter and early spring.

Even easy hills can be dangerous for the lone traveller; usually you will need at least one companion (if possible, more than one). Early expeditions should be made with someone more experienced than yourself.

If you hope to progress to climbing proper you should get as much experience of the hills as possible, in all conditions. When you have done a good deal of walking see if you can get an experienced scrambler to introduce you to rock scrambling on ridges such as the Crib Goch ridge on Snowdon or the Aonach Eagach ridge in Glencoe. This is the ideal way of building up the experience and the skills needed for rock climbing and more serious mountaineering later. The borderline between scrambling and rock climbing is sometimes very fine; on most scrambles a length of rope should be taken in case of need, and you should learn beforehand how to use it.

Chapter 1. Hill walking in summer and autumn

When you have obtained a good pair of boots and an anorak and other clothing (§ 4), and have mastered the fundamentals of navigation in low hills or moorland near your home, the way will be open for you to start hill walking proper in one of the areas described in chapter 13. You should start in the late spring, the summer, or the autumn, since in winter the hills are often icy and require a good deal of experience (see next chapter). Find out as much as you can about the area before you go there, by reading books and studying maps. This will help to give you a better understanding of the mountains, which will stand you in good stead when you are finding your way on them.

§ 1. Overall plan of the holiday

You should settle the overall plan of your holiday with your companions before you leave. If you want to get to know an area well, it is best to stay in one centre and walk from there each day; it is useful to have transport of your own to get to other mountains in the same area, but even without it you will probably be able to walk every day for a week on near-by peaks without covering much of the same ground twice. In selecting your base make sure that it is not too far away from the mountains – it is tiresome to have to walk four or five miles along a road at the beginning or end of the day. Staying in one centre has the major advantage that you have a permanent base (a youth hostel perhaps, or a camp – see chapter 4) to return to each evening and do not have to carry heavy loads during the day. The alternative is to plan a tour moving each day from hostel to hostel or, in Scotland, possibly from bothy to bothy. This enables you to see a

3. *Langdale* (*Lake District*). A popular base for walking and climbing. Old Dungeon Ghyll Hotel is on the right, with Middlefell Buttress and Raven Crag (2) behind. Gimmer Crag (38) is top left. The highest point on the skyline is Harrison Stickle.

great deal of the country, but it can be very tiring unless you travel really light (the need for lightness probably rules out camping for all but the toughest), and keep well within your limits. On no account draw up a very ambitious timetable which you feel you must press through at all costs: you will not enjoy it, particularly if the weather gets bad or you get sore feet. In any case allow one or two rest days during the holiday (say one every fourth day) to give yourself a chance to recuperate.

§ 2. The party

Three or four is the best number for a hill-walking party since it is large enough for safety (in the event of an accident one member could stay with the injured person while one or two could go down for help) without being cumbersome.

While it is desirable to have someone with experience in the party, do not worry unduly if this is not possible: there is no reason why you should not go to the hills with two or three friends provided you all recognize your inexperience, take good care, and follow the basic principles of conservation of energy and good route-finding.

An organized party (e.g. from a school or a holiday centre) may be a good deal bigger than this, but it should definitely include one person who is fully experienced as leader, and another who is fairly experienced to bring up the rear to ensure that no one is left behind. On fairly easy walking in good weather two experienced people should be able to cope with about ten novices; but on difficult ground (especially if scrambling is involved), or in bad weather, four or five novices should be the maximum. If there is no one with experience to bring up the rear, these numbers should be about halved. It is as well to find out before you start which members of the party have climbed or walked in mountains before, and how much they can be relied upon to help the others.

The leader. With a small group of friends, well known to each other, there is no need for a formal leader since they will act in harmony and by common agreement. In large parties, however, particularly where most of them are novices or schoolchildren, it is very useful to have a leader. It falls to him to make the decisions when there is doubt, or in emergency, and he saves much time and trouble in settling small details, or when members of the party get tired and cross and want to argue with each other all round. Like most leadership, it is more of a burden than an honour, for although it is part of his duties to divide up the jobs and assign them among the others, it still lies with him to see that they are done properly and up to time; and however tired and wet he is himself he always has to be able to bring out just that extra reserve of strength and good humour which will keep up the tone of the party under depressing conditions.

Leaders of school parties and parties from youth organizations bear an especially heavy responsibility, and it is only fair to them and their charges that they should be capable of sustaining it. The B.M.C. in conjunction with the C.C.P.R. and other responsible organizations recommended in the mid 1960s that a leader of such a party should have basic competence in mountaineering and mountain rescue, broadly of the order required for the Mountain Leadership Certificate (see below). It was emphasized that this is the *minimum* background which a person in charge of young people on the hills should have. It could be multiplied many times over with advantage, but without it he should not venture, and those responsible for training should not allow him to venture. Following two accidents in the Cairngorms and on Snowdon in 1971 and 1972 in which a total of nine young people died, the B.M.C. appealed to Local Education Authorities, voluntary bodies and others concerned with mountain expeditions for the young, to *insist* on their leaders holding the Certificates, as a minimum requirement, within a period of three years (i.e. by early 1975).

Mountain Leadership Certificate. This test of a minimum satisfactory level of competence is administered by the B.M.C. for the Mountain Leadership Training Board (appendix B, 2). To obtain the certificate a candidate must successfully complete a course of training in mountainous country comprising:

1. An introductory course lasting at least one week at a training centre approved by the Board. A series of four week-end courses may be recognized in lieu.
2. A period of at least one year during which the candidate gains practical experience by taking part in expeditions during week-ends and holidays, details of which are to be recorded in his personal log-book.
3. A final week's residential course at which an assessment of the candidate's suitability is made.

Candidates of eighteen years may attend 1, but the minimum

age for the award of a certificate is twenty years. All candidates must be conversant with *Safety on Mountains* and the mountain rescue part of *Mountain Rescue and Cave Rescue* (see bibliography), and must produce a current Certificate in First Aid of the St John Ambulance Brigade or the British Red Cross Society (appendix B, 2). A person already experienced in the leadership of groups of young people in mountainous districts may apply for exemption from 1 but only in exceptional circumstances will a certificate be awarded without attendance at 3.

Responsibilities of individuals. In a large party, the individual members should follow the leader, keeping a rhythmical pace and avoiding crowding each other. They should not go ahead of the leader or break away from the party at any time. Conversely, it is a point of honour never to leave one of your companions behind on the mountain, even when you are almost home. There is safety in numbers, and accidents are more likely to happen to individuals who become separated from the main party, since they may get lost or come to grief on difficult ground. Every member of the party should understand basic navigation so that he can find his own way if he should by chance get separated. In particular, he should:

– know how to set the map so that it conforms to the lie of the land;
– understand contours and other methods of showing relief, so that he can tell the shape and steepness of the main features, and can avoid cliffs;
– recognize the main conventional signs shown on the bottom of the map;
– be able to calculate a bearing from the map, change it into a magnetic bearing, and use the compass to walk along it, allowing for the lie of the land.

These techniques are described in appendix E, and are not difficult to learn. Always take an intelligent interest in the route so that you know where you are on the mountain.

§ 3. Planning the route for the following day

Good route-finding is necessary in any mountaineering: a bad route can lose hours; you may even come down in the wrong valley so that you have a long and laborious trek back to your intended point of return. Study maps and guide-books in advance and try to get the main features of your intended route and of the whole mountain range firmly fixed in your mind. While you have time in the evening, work out the route for the following day, and if it is still light go outside to compare the land against the map.

Choice of route. In the hills, the shortest distance between two points is seldom the quickest or the easiest; in choosing the route it is necessary to balance any saving in distance against the roughness or steepness of the going. The best route usually takes a meandering line, avoiding difficulties and steep sections and keeping to grassy slopes rather than to awkward rock. In most mountain areas there are paths or tracks on the popular routes and these are often marked on the map. These paths have grown up by long usage, and it is safe to assume that they take the best line. In choosing the route, note the position of difficulties, particularly cliffs and stretches of unbridged rivers, so that you can avoid them when on the ground. Remember their general direction so that if you meet them in mist or at night you will know the best way round them. Choose a route that will not cause you to lose height which you will have to regain later; however, if to keep height means crossing very rough ground then it is better to descend slightly. You can always ascend or descend a hillside direct provided it is not craggy or precipitous. For the descent choose a line such that when you get down to the river in the valley you can cross it by a bridge or ford it at a shallow place without a big diversion. Good routes seldom follow streams, because water always tries to find the shortest way to the valley and consequently makes for the steepest places. You can usually find a better route along the spurs enclosing the stream. In Scotland, check before you set out that there is not a newly created artificial loch for a hydro-electric scheme on your proposed route, since it may not be marked on your map and could necessitate a very long detour.

Length of the route. You will need to decide how many hours of daylight are available and grade the length of the route accordingly. Aim to be on easy ground or in the valley well before nightfall unless you are camping or carrying bivouac equipment. Measure the overall length carefully and estimate the amount of uphill going or steep walking involved. You can work out the time needed by Naismith's formula: *allow one hour for every three miles as measured on the map plus an additional hour for every 2,000 ft climbed.* If the party is heavily laden (e.g. with camping gear) more time will be needed (say two and a half miles to the hour, or 1,500 ft to the hour). Rough going, mist, or high winds may also reduce your speed. Allow extra time for halts, mistakes, and emergencies; remember that the larger the party the more time must be allowed for every section of the route and for every halt – however prompt they may be, time melts away unaccountably for any party of more than four. Although the formula is only a rough guide it can prove remarkably accurate when you have become accustomed to using it and have adjusted it to suit your pace; indeed, working back from your time schedule can be the best way of deciding how far you have gone on your route, particularly in featureless country in bad weather.

A pre-calculation will often prevent a youthful and ambitious party being disappointed because it cannot fulfil its plan for the day, or can only do so too tired to enjoy it. Plan never to do as much on the first day as you will be doing later. Hill air and the high spirits of starting a holiday will always encourage you to overdo it at first, and you will probably pay for it in blisters (unless your feet are tough already) and on the second and subsequent days of your holiday. Many mountain accidents occur to parties on the first day of their holiday, possibly because they were trying to do too much too soon, or were not allowing enough for the tiring effects of their journey.

Route card. If the route is complicated, or the party is very large, it may be worth preparing a route card in advance so that no time is lost on the mountain. This quite simply details the length of each leg of the journey, the vertical height to be ascended or descended, and the estimated time. It also gives the grid and magnetic bearings for each leg. It is in any case almost always worth calculating these bearings the night before and jotting them down on a piece of paper, since this is more accurate and there is less chance of making a mistake than when you are in a hurry on a mountain.

§ 4. Equipment and food

It is usually a good deal colder in the hills than in the valleys and even in summer-time wind and rain can buffet and chill you; in Scotland especially it can be very cold, with sleet or snow or freezing rain at almost any time of the year. On the other hand it can also be very hot on a windless summer's day, and it is easy to get overheated if you are wearing too much. To overcome these extremes of conditions you need equipment specially designed for mountaineering and this is described in chapter 3. Note in particular:

- a windproof and showerproof anorak with hood is essential for protection against wind;
- breeches with long stockings, or trousers with socks, are usual; if shorts or skirts are worn, overtrousers should be carried also;
- strong and comfortable, but reasonably light, boots are needed; cleated rubber soles are usual, but remember that they can slip on wet grass, grease, or lichen (or, in winter, on hard snow or ice).

A lightweight rucksack between two persons is useful for carrying odds and ends needed during the day which cannot conveniently be carried in your anorak. The amount taken should be kept to the minimum to avoid burdening yourself.

Unless the route is very short and straightforward, however, it would be prudent to include: a waterproof 'cagoule' (page 380) and spare clothing; food; a map and a compass; large plasters for blisters; torch with spare bulb and mercury batteries (kept separate so that the torch cannot switch on accidentally); whistle; knife; watch; money. A light polythene bag (500 gauge, 8 ft by 4 ft) and/or a Space Blanket (page 325) could prove a lifesaver should you be caught out overnight in bad weather; and a short length of light rope (say fifty feet of $\frac{7}{8}$-in. nylon) may be useful if an emergency occurs while you are scrambling. Extra clothing and equipment is needed in winter (§ 13).

Food for the day. Always have a good breakfast before starting out and keep up your strength during the day by eating regularly. The body has a basic reserve of energy and this must be replaced continuously so that it is never run down. Otherwise exhaustion may result. The risk is greater in cold or wet conditions and more food (including possibly hot drinks or the wherewithal to make them) should be taken then. This is particularly important if for some reason your clothing proves to be inadequate to keep you warm: the energy loss can then be very rapid and must be made up by quickly digested food. Glucose is the best food, and sugar the next best, for quick energy; sandwiches, cake, dried fruit, biscuits, and chocolate are a good basic diet, and oranges are good thirst-quenchers.

Drink. In an average (wet) summer, a water-bottle is not usually necessary, particularly if you take some thin rubber tubing so that you can reach water flowing in such otherwise inaccessible places as between boulders. It is generally safe to drink from *mountain* streams in Britain provided that the water is clear and running, does not smell or taste, and there is not a dead sheep in the water higher up! As a general rule avoid drinking from *valley* streams or rivers, or from any that are below human dwellings, farm buildings, or cattle shelters. Do not drink too much at any one time,

as it may over-cool your stomach. Strong spirits should not
be drunk on the mountain in any quantity because they
upset the body's thermostat and hence cause you to lose
heat rapidly; when the effect wears off you may be a good
deal weaker than before.

§ 5. Conduct of the route

The final check. Before starting, check that you have all the
equipment needed, and that the torch or torches work
properly. Leave a message with a responsible person as to
your intended route and time of return (if by any chance
you alter your plans and do not return to the same place,
take all possible steps to cancel the message so that a search
is not started needlessly). You should all know the where-
abouts of the mountain rescue posts (chapter 13), and the
procedure to be followed in the event of an accident
(chapter 12). In a large party, the leader should check to his
own satisfaction that nothing is left behind and that all are
adequately clothed; it should be known who is carrying the
maps and compasses and other common equipment. He
should also appoint someone to bring up the rear of the
party to round up any stragglers.

Pace and rhythm. Conservation of energy is a prime consideration in moving in the mountains. It is a common
mistake to go too fast at the beginning of the day. The start
should be slow, working comfortably up to an almost
mechanical swing. In this way the party will have plenty of
energy left for any special efforts needed during the day,
and for the long final trudge. Keep the pace steady throughout the day and keep going. After a quarter of an hour or
so, make a brief halt to take off excess clothing: it is very
important when going uphill not to wear too much, since
overheating greatly reduces efficiency. However, don't stop
often; thirty unnoticed minutes lost in dawdling means a
priceless half hour cut off your daylight at the end. Don't
drop out except at the arranged halts; it breaks the rhythm

unconsciously for all the rest and slackens the effort all round. Above all, keep an eye on the ground ahead: your eye should continually be photographing the next four yards or so, so that your feet can automatically adjust to the easiest line. Uphill, aim at an easy swing of the leg. Set the foot down precisely. Do not spring off the toes alone. Wherever possible set the whole of the foot (including the heel) on the ground, horizontally; you can often manage this even on very steep slopes by ascending in zigzags, placing the foot sideways along the line of the hill, or by placing the heel on a stone or a turf. When you wish to increase speed, do so by lengthening the stride, not by hurrying it. Breathe rhythmically as best suits your stride and the angle you are ascending. On steep slopes, ease the effort for lungs and legs by leaning a little forward. If a walker can still whistle or sing to himself while he is walking steadily uphill he is going within his pace. Do not race up the last slopes when you think the summit is in sight.

If the party is heavily laden (for example, if you are carrying camping gear so that you can establish a camp high up), go slowly so that you do not exhaust yourself, and maintain a very steady rhythm. This is particularly important for young people. Avoid scree and scrambling in case the load upsets your balance. Use the waist-strap on your rucksack to ease the strain on your shoulders, to help you to keep your balance, and to prevent the frame of the rucksack riding up and damaging the back of your head should you trip.

Rests. It is a good rule to stop for about ten minutes once an hour, more often if you are heavily laden. The halt should preferably be at a natural stopping-point (e.g. at the top of a steep section), and should if possible be before a level or downhill section so that you can effortlessly regain your rhythm afterwards. It is useful to be able to see the next stage of your route so that you can work out the best line while you are resting. Choose a place sheltered from the wind. Put on spare clothing, and pull up the hood of your anorak. Try to rest completely. Pull up socks and stockings, and if necessary take off your boots to get out small stones or grit, or to ease your feet. Any blisters or hint of soreness should be dealt with immediately *en route* without waiting for a regular halt, since a large plaster put over the rubbed skin in time will prevent a blister developing (but check at each halt that the plaster has not moved). Eat slowly; drink sparingly and in sips. Change round the rucksacks – or some of their contents – so that all do their share of carrying. In a large party, the leader should decide how long the rest should last; do not start off again until all the others have finished eating and packing, though it may be necessary to give the impression that you are doing so to encourage the slower members to move.

Descent. This is potentially a dangerous part of the day because a tired party can easily become over-relaxed and careless. The party may also be rushing to make up time lost earlier in the day. Many accidents have happened in these circumstances, and it is necessary to take special care. Follow the route chosen on the previous night, subject to adjustments needed in the light of your experience on the way up. Be chary of 'short cuts': they may lead into difficult ground and will usually take just as long as the established paths. Watch out carefully for concealed drops – even quite big crags are sometimes not readily visible from above, especially on a convex slope [159]. As noted above, streams always take the shortest route down and consequently often run over cliffs or into steep gullies: keep them in view if it helps with the route-finding, but as a general rule don't get too close to them. In descending, flex the knees and keep the weight well forward. Let your heels dig in if the ground is soft. Shorten your stride on steep ground and let your feet run, with many small steps, turning every few yards to keep your speed down. Do not go so fast that you begin to feel the jar. Lengthen your stride on gentler ground. Stop and tighten your boots if you feel your toes hitting the ends.

§ 6. Route-finding in clear weather

On most standard walks it is best to find the path and stick to it; usually it will be cairned, i.e. marked by man-made piles of stones. Distinguish between the circuitous path which takes the right line for ascent and the direct variations on it which take short cuts down scree or earth slides; these can be time-saving on the descent, but are very laborious in ascent. Useful tracks may be found which are not marked on the map; but remember that sheep also make tracks which do not always lead where humans want to go.

In clear weather direction can be maintained by direct map-reading and landmarks more easily than by compass bearings. As soon as the first clear view over the ground is obtained, and later whenever a good viewpoint is reached, check the route you chose overnight against the actual country. It may be that there is a stretch of boggy ground or of rough going which is not marked on the map and which can be avoided by an easy deviation. Modify your line accordingly. If the whole of the route can be seen from the starting-point, choose the easiest cross-country line and memorize landmarks on it – houses, curiously shaped rocks, streams, sheepfolds, and so on. When you are under way you may no longer be able to see your objective; the inter-mediate marks which have been memorized will then enable the party to keep on the right line. When coming up a hillside from a valley or a flat plain, you may be able to see behind you a road, a river, a railway, the edge of a field or a wood, and you can use this as a guide when both your remote objective ahead and the intermediate landmarks you have noted are blotted out by a fold in the ground, a wood, or a wall. Therefore make a habit of looking back occasion-ally. The ground looks quite different from the opposite direction, and an impression gained of it on the way up may prove invaluable if you later return the same way (even if you don't plan to do so, some unexpected circumstance such as bad weather may force you to).

It is very difficult to estimate your height on a mountain;

from below each shoulder looks like the summit. Given practice, the best method in clear weather is to select a point level with yourself on a near-by mountain, and estimate how much further on that mountain there is to the top. By comparing the height of that mountain with your own, you will be able to estimate your own height from the top.

Direction by the sun. Traditional methods of direction-finding (the way moss grows on boulders, the way trees grow, the way cows face, etc.) are of very little use in the mountains, and parties without a compass will have to rely on the sun should the need arise in featureless country. The sun moves about fifteen degrees every hour, and the time of day will give the approximate direction as in table 1 (in the Northern Hemisphere):

TABLE 1: *Direction by the sun*

G.m.t.	Sun's position
6 a.m.	east
9 a.m.	south-east
Noon	south
3 p.m.	south-west
6 p.m.	west

With the aid of a watch, the direction of north and south can be found more accurately. Lay the watch flat with the hour hand pointing towards the sun. True south will then be midway between the hour hand and twelve o'clock. In winter the sun is not visible in the east or west since it is below the horizon at those times.

Difficulties. When route-finding for any reason begins to grow difficult, the leader should consider suggestions put forward by other members of the party and explain to them why he chooses the line he adopts. After that the party must obey orders, and the leader must not allow any talkative or opinionated member of the party afterwards to unsettle his decision. This may be more difficult in practice than it looks on paper.

§ 7. Types of terrain

Grass. Short grass gives the most pleasant and easiest walking. Grass slopes are usually the easiest way up a hill and may also be descended rapidly and safely – provided that you can see all the way down, and have strong ankles and good boots. Grass may get coated with ice or thin snow in winter and should then be avoided both in ascent and descent; it can give a nasty and long fall. Wet grass can be risky in flexible or worn-down cleated rubber-soled boots; it is extremely dangerous for anyone wearing gym shoes or P.A.s [51A] – a point on which rock climbers have to be extremely careful when they are taking the easy way off the top of a crag (§ 37, 3). Deep grass is laborious and will tire the party needlessly, especially if it contains hard clumps (tussocks) which upset your rhythm.

Bog. Upon most hills there are large stretches of boggy ground. These are rarely dangerous but should always be avoided as they are heavy going.

Bracken. Bracken should be avoided in summer as it is full of heat, damp, and insects. It is treacherous as a handhold since it is brittle and the roots come out easily.

Heather is fairly reliable for climbing as the plant is usually tough and firm. But deep heather or heather-covered slopes of boulders can be a nightmare.

Scree is the name given to steep slopes of loose stones or rocks [4 and 5N]. In ascent it is preferable to avoid scree (unless the stones are large and stable) and to climb grass or heather slopes instead. Scree slopes can provide a rapid means of descent provided that the stones are small (not more than about 2–3 ins. across), there are plenty of them, and there are no minor crags or other drops. Unfortunately, many of

4. *Great Gable and the Napes (Lake District)*. From Kirk Fell. Note the laborious screes on the left. See also 37.

the best scree runs have been worn out by constant use so that now only smooth earth remains. To run down small scree, bend your knees slightly and dig your heels heavily into the scree; the scree should ideally be small enough to start moving down with you, but if not it should at least cushion the shock of your feet, rather like soft snow. Lean backwards rather than forwards, because you must at all costs avoid tripping head first.

Loose stones are often encountered on ledges when scrambling, or in gullies. Take care not to dislodge them, but, if by chance you do, always shout 'Below' to warn anyone who may be in their path. If you see a stone coming for you, try to take cover behind a boulder or below a bulge of rock; but if there is no cover it is best to watch which way it is going and jump to one side at the last moment, covering your head with your arms. To minimize the risk to members of your own party climb or descend on scree or other loose stones as near as you can in arrowhead formation; if you are shut in by steep rocks as in a gully so that you have to

follow in line, keep close together so that any stones dislodged have no time to get up speed and become dangerous
to those below. It goes without saying that you should *never*
throw stones over a cliff or a steep slope. Do not assume
because you can hear or see no one else that there is no one
else near you. Other parties may well be quieter than yours.

Rocks should be avoided by the inexperienced and left for
the scrambler or, if they are difficult, for the rock climber.
Scrambling techniques are described in § 12 below.

Mountain streams and rivers can be dangerous in flood conditions, when it is worth making a considerable detour to
reach a good crossing place (i.e. where the river is not too
deep or fast and there is a safe run-out if you slip) often
found on the approach to a lake. If you have no choice but

5. *The main features of mountains (Tryfan from the north – North Wales).*
A. A plateau, usually wide and featureless (summit of Glyder Fach).
B–A. Head of a cwm, a valley or armchair hollow formed by glacial
action. (Cwm Tryfan.)
c. A pass; a dip or gap in a ridge, usually the lowest point between two
peaks. French: *col*. When the ridge is broad and gentle, the pass may be
called a saddle. (Bwlch Tryfan).
c to A. A steep ridge. French: *arête*. (Bristly Ridge – good scrambling.)
D. A rock peak. (Summit of Tryfan.)
E. A steep crag. (East face of Tryfan, a fine climbing area.)
F. A shoulder; a levelling off on a rising ridge.
G. A buttress; a mass of rock projecting from a mountain-side, upon
which rock-climbing routes are often found. (The Milestone Buttress.)
H. Way off; although easy, a slip could take you over the cliff.
I. A gully; a ravine in the mountain-side, usually with a stream in it,
and flanked by steep walls (§ 45).
J. Slabs; smooth rock at an angle of thirty to sixty degrees (§ 44).
K. A steep, broken face, difficult and laborious to cross or descend (even
for climbers) because it is vegetated, loose, and split by minor crags.
L. A funnel; a wide earth gully, with a stream and scree.
M. A minor spur; a thumb-like extension of highland into lowland.
N. Scree and boulders, a mass of loose stones.
O. Huge boulders, very awkward in the dark.
P. Main road (A5 – Capel Curig to Bethesda), with parked cars.
Q. A lake. (Llyn Ogwen.)

to ford a fast river always tie on to a rope belayed from upstream, preferably with a knotted hand line from bank to bank in addition. Cross on a slanting line with the current. Remember the following points: do not test the force of the water without being secured from the bank; always keep your boots on (though you can remove your stockings); do not make long jumps between boulders (which may move or prove slippery); small or light people can be swept off their feet relatively easily and may need to weight their sacks with stones and remove trousers to reduce drag; packs should be carried high with waist straps undone for quick release; angle the hips at 45° to the current so that it helps you across, but avoid facing downstream since the water can collapse your knees from behind; never try to pull upstream anyone who falls since he is bound to go under; a pole for support may help. Stream-crossing should be practised on training courses where possible.

The Country Code. Do not assume that an arbitrary line plotted beforehand on the map can be followed. You will need to check for example that it is not private land, especially in the shooting season. Landowners and farmers may obstruct passage and you can avoid unpleasantness and delay by keeping to lanes and footpaths. Dry-stone walls are very easily damaged and take a long time to rebuild: gates in the end give the quicker line. If by accident a fence or a wall is damaged see that the damage is repaired before you go on. Farmers are busy men who need our help and not our hindrance. Always close gates after use. Do not walk over growing crops or sowed land. Leave no litter, safe-guard water supplies, and protect wild life, wild plants, and trees. Finally, guard against all risk of fire, especially in wooded country (e.g. Forestry Commission plantations).

§ 8. Weather

The weather in the British hills is notoriously unreliable. May, June, and September often have good weather, and

6. *Llyn Ogwen and Y Garn (North Wales)*. Cwm Idwal is on the left, with the Devil's Kitchen the lowest point on the skyline. Idwal Cottage Youth Hostel is at the far end of the lake. Perhaps the best hill-walking and scrambling day is the Idwal Skyline, which starts up the north ridge of Tryfan (see 5) and finishes on Y Garn.

there is frequently a good winter spell in late February and early March. Generally, August, October, November, and December are the wettest months but you can get soaked in the British hills at any time of the year. In fact part of the fun of hill walking is to be able to travel the hills in all kinds of weather. Some of your finest mountain days will be days of rain or storm. You will have been battered by the elements, but you will also have seen the hills at their most magnificent. There is even a certain moist pleasure in knowing that you cannot get wetter. In bad weather you will need adequate clothing and a good basic knowledge of map and compass work. Provided you are up to scratch on this, do not be afraid of getting wet. But, this said, always take account of the weather in your plans for the day; bad weather, especially wind, will reduce the party's reserve and increase the danger of exposure (§ 99) should anything go wrong.

Rain. Mountains attract rain. The annual rainfall near the top of Snowdon is estimated to average just over 200 ins., reducing to about 160 ins. at Llyn Llydaw, 135 ins. at Pen y Gwryd, and 90 ins. at Capel Curig. At the top of Ben Nevis the average is about 170 ins. At Seathwaite in Borrowdale it is about 130 ins. For lowland England and Wales a typical figure would be 25–30 ins. Much can be done to keep dry by the use of waterproof garments (§ 22), but if you get thoroughly soaked try to stay warm by keeping on the move (unless you are completely exhausted – § 99). It is the chilling effect of wet clothing that does the harm; you will be quite all right if you can stay warm.

Cold and wind. It is invariably a good deal colder on the tops than in the valleys. This is partly because the air temperature drops by about 4°F. in a thousand feet, with some variation according to humidity (this temperature drop is called the 'lapse rate'); but it is mainly because of the chilling effect of wind, which reduces the temperature of any exposed parts of your body considerably (this is known as the 'wind-chill effect'). Wind also makes the going more difficult, and it is usually much easier to go with it than against it. Never skirt the top of a cliff in a wind, no matter how good your balance; mountain eddies swirl fiercely enough to blow the heaviest of us off our footing. Even when it is well above freezing in the valleys, the tops may be freezing, and low cloud or a freezing drizzle can quickly coat a mountain path with very slippery ice (*verglas*) which can be thoroughly dangerous for wearers of vibram-soled boots. Snow and ice conditions proper are dealt with in the next chapter.

Lightning is fortunately not a very common hazard in Britain (it is much more common in the Alps). It is most likely to strike on exposed ridges, especially near summits. Warning signs may be a buzzing sound from metal objects, or a tendency for the hair on the head to rise. If lightning threatens, keep well down from the ridge, or if you are on a plateau, keep away from any large boulders which may attract it. On steep ground, shelter below an overhang if possible, so that you are protected against any rockfall caused by the lightning. However, do not shelter in a crack because the electric charge takes the easiest line from the summit to earth, and would therefore take a crack in preference to solid rock; for the same reason, climbers should not belay their rope in a crack when lightning threatens since the charge may run down the crack and along the rope. On gentle ground avoid sheltering in a hole since the charge may jump the gap from one side of the hole to the other, burning anyone between. Current theory is against taking any special steps to divest yourself of small metal objects, since it is held that these are unlikely to make

7. *Canoeing from the Snowdonia National Recreation Centre, Plas y Brenin.* Most of the mountain centres offer a range of outdoor activities. Snowdon is in the background.

any difference to the likelihood of lightning striking, and may be needed for your safety (but it is probably good for your morale to move them some way away).

Judging the weather. It is worth getting the Meteorological Office's weather forecasts (by looking at the weather maps in the newspapers or listening to broadcasts) if you can, since bad weather moving into near-by areas will also affect the mountains. But the hills of this country, like hills elsewhere, create their own weather, which is almost always worse than the weather in the lowlands near by; quite often while climbing in rain in Glencoe or Snowdonia, for example, you will be able to see glorious weather ten or fifteen miles away down by the sea. You can usually see the weather developing, the clouds getting lower, and rain or sleet beginning to fall some way away. The rain may come your way or pass you by; sometimes you can see rain on all sides but be in a dry pocket yourself. In fact the weather in one valley may be quite different from the weather in another: on a summit ridge you can move from sunshine to cloud in a dozen steps. A west or south wind usually brings moist air, and hence rain, with it; a north or east wind on the other hand is often a good sign. In winter, any strong wind is bad, since it may develop into a blizzard (§ 18).

§ 9. Route-finding in bad weather or at night

Bad weather. In mist, cloud, or heavy rain, visibility will be poor and you will need to use a map and compass as described in appendix E. If possible, make a quick re-study of the ground in relation to the map for as far ahead as you can see before the mist closes down. Small features in mist may look very much bigger than they really are and it may even be impossible to tell whether a slope is level or gently sloping (in snow an extreme form of this is known as 'white out', where it is impossible to distinguish between snow and a drop except by tossing snowballs in front of you to see whether they land or not). If you are on a path, keep to it carefully and watch out for cairns. Watch also for junctions with other tracks (often marked by an extra large cairn) where you could easily take the wrong fork. Be especially careful when descending a ridge in mist: it may be a false ridge, ending at a cliff. Keep to the line of the feature you are following – ridge or stream – since it is easy to lose direction when contouring in mist across a complicated slope.

In featureless country a party of three can keep direction by walking in line ahead at intervals of about ten paces. The direction of the line should be set by compass bearing. The last man carries the compass and directs the party. He should always keep the leader in line with the middle man. Any deviations from this by the leader are corrected by orders from the last man, e.g. 'one pace to the left' or 'two paces to the right'. On ill-defined ridges in mist (e.g. in the Cairngorms) place a man within view on either side to

8. *Basic method of adjusting for detours when marching on a bearing.*

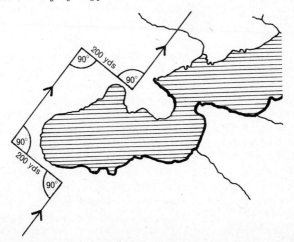

check that the ground is sloping away to right or left as the case may be. Periodically a fresh compass check should be made.

In very bad weather you will need to make a careful estimate of the time required for each leg using Naismith's formula (§ 3). If, for example, the distance is half a mile over flat country, you can reckon on it taking about nine to twelve minutes at walking pace according to the difficulty of the terrain. If you are not at your next check point by then, you should halt and check each direction; this can be done by walking one hundred yards on a bearing, and then reversing it back to the rest of the party. In this way the party should come across the cairn, river, or lake for which it has been aiming. A similar technique can be used for getting back to your original line of march if you have to make a short detour to avoid an obstacle [8]. Such techniques are, however, rarely necessary in Britain in daylight. Most hilly districts have recognizable natural features and practice will make their identification by the map possible, especially if the route has been well studied before setting out.

Night. On a clear night the most convenient check on general direction is given by the Pole Star [9], which stays within $2\frac{1}{2}$ degrees of true north throughout the year. Vary the route if necessary to take full advantage of any moon. If the darkness is dense a compass should be used in the same way as in mist. Here again knowledge gained by study of the route on the map and the ground before dusk closes in is invaluable. Each member of the party will need a torch if travelling far by night. If there is some light (even good starlight) it may be easier to pick out the general topography without a torch, but one is often needed to see a drop just in front (as well as, of course, for map-reading). Do not flash torches at regular intervals in case you give the impression to people in the valley that you are in distress.

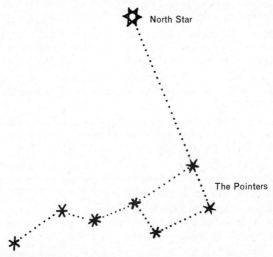

9. *Finding north from the stars*. The Great Bear (Ursa Major) is visible throughout the Northern Hemisphere.

§ 10. Lost on the mountain

If you find yourself lost, do not panic. Carefully study the map and try to assess your position. Do not allow anyone to rush off by himself. If it is impossible to decide your exact position, it is best to retrace your steps until you find a definite position and begin again from there. Most summits are identifiable and can usually be discovered simply by going uphill until you reach the top: but this may be difficult where the summits are very rounded, e.g. in the Cairngorms (§ 101), the Carneddau (§ 106), or the Peak District (§ 105).

If it is difficult to move up or down, it will probably be best to wait until visibility improves, but no hard-and-fast rule can be laid down on this because so much will depend on the circumstances at the time. The weather conditions (rain and cold in particular), the length of the night, the shelter available, the distance to go, and the strength of the party must all be taken into account. If the party can survive the night, or if it is likely that help can be summoned with the International Distress Signal (six blasts on a whistle or six flashes on a torch per minute – § 95) then it will be best to wait. If the party is approaching exhaustion it is almost always better to wait and concentrate on keeping warm than to use up your last remaining resources in trying to keep moving. On the other hand if the party is in an exposed position it will be necessary to move some further distance to get some shelter, despite the risks. With young people in particular the risk of exhaustion is great, and the leaders of the party should keep a very close watch for symptoms (such as stumbling or incoherence); collapse and even death can come very suddenly in bad weather to people who are really exhausted (§ 99). Women tend to have a higher resistance to cold than men, because of their greater subcutaneous fat.

§ 11. Emergency bivouacs in summer and autumn

If you are forced to spend the night out, try to get as low down the mountain as possible, and find some sort of shelter, if only in the lee of a boulder. Ridges are cold and windy and should be avoided. Put on spare clothing next to your skin (i.e. *under* the wet clothing). Your feet should go in your rucksack. Sit on bracken or heather to insulate yourself from the ground. Make sure that none of your clothing is restricting your circulation and try not to keep your knees or your body sharply bent, for the same reason. The polythene bag recommended in § 4 above will prove itself a godsend. Step into it and pull it up around your head, so that only your mouth and nose are exposed [10]. Take your arms out of your anorak sleeves and fold them across your chest inside your anorak, with your hands in your armpits (along with the crutch the warmest part of the body). Huddle together for warmth. Eat emergency rations at intervals (or, of course, make hot drinks if you

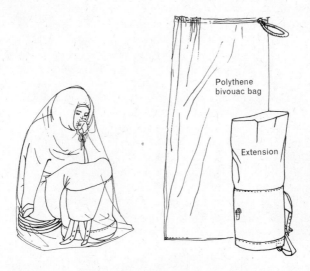

10. *Emergency bivouac bag (§ 4) and extendable rucksack (§ 24) in use.* Note the air-hole for breathing; arms inside anorak for warmth; sitting on equipment; feet and thighs in rucksack.

have the means). If at dawn the weather is still bad or you consider it is still too dangerous to move, sound the International Distress Signal (§ 95) again; this is advisable also if there is any possibility of a rescue party being near by, searching for you. Move off as soon as you can find your way, and telephone your home, or the police, or your place of departure as soon as you reach the valley, to forestall alarm and despondency. Winter bivouacs are dealt with in § 21.

§ 12. Rock scrambling

When you and your companions have gained experience of walking in the hills, you may want to get away from the easy gentle paths and get to grips with rocky ridges, such as the

11. *Striding Edge, Helvellyn (Lake District)*. A good summer scramble.

Crib Goch ridge on Snowdon. Scrambling on these ridges can be extremely good fun, and adds a new dimension to your enjoyment of the hills. See if you can get an experienced scrambler or climber to introduce you to it and get as much practice as possible on small (not big) boulders low down on the hills.

Movement on easy rock. The difference between easy scrambling and rock climbing is one of degree not of kind, and the principles of movement described in chapter 6 apply just as much to easy scrambling as to difficult climbing. Conservation of energy is a basic principle, and this can be achieved by balanced movement and rhythm. Always stand upright, away from the rock. Remember that your safety lies in good footholds, not in hanging on by your hands. Choose each hold carefully and test it before using it. Always have three points of support at any one time. To avoid slipping, or dislodging stones, place each foot neatly and don't shift about on it when your weight comes on it. Think ahead exactly how you will make each movement; and never let yourself get hurried or try to rush it because you begin to think it unsafe. Finally, take account of the conditions: cold, wind, or rain makes scrambling much more difficult.

Easy ground may be dangerous ground. The rock scrambler must appreciate that easy ground may not necessarily be safe ground. The prime consideration must be how far you would fall if you slipped. Although it is not usual to scramble for long directly over a big drop (i.e. in an 'exposed' position) it is often the case that a slip would lead to a long tumble down grass or slabs, possibly steepening into a cliff below.

12. *Cloud boiling up on the Snowdon Horseshoe.* The summit of Snowdon is peeping through on the left; Crib y Ddysgyl is on the right.

In such cases you must take great care and not relax your concentration no matter how easy the going is technically.

Need for the rope. If you cannot be sure that the next move or two will go safely, ask for help rather than attempt to fight your way out. There should be a length of rope in the party for this very purpose and it is no disgrace to use it. The leader should take a secure position above you, belaying if necessary (the proper belay with the main rope is described in § 59; alternatively it may be sufficient simply to run the rope round a convenient spike, as a direct belay [145B]). The leader should tie a figure-of-eight knot loop [167] in the end of the rope before throwing it down so that you can put your arm through the loop, or, if there is time, pass it over your shoulders and adjust it round your waist in the normal way. The leader should take the slack rope in around his waist and keep it fairly taut while you are moving [82] (§ 62, 1). He should check the knots used by any inexperienced members of the party.

Route-finding on rock. On most scrambles the route is well marked by nail scratches (though these are diminishing as rubber-soled footwear is replacing nails) and possibly by cairns. Be careful to keep to the proper route: it is easy to stray into territory which is suitable only for experienced rock climbers, using ropes and other equipment.

13. *The end of a perfect day.* Llyn Idwal with the Idwal Slabs behind (North Wales).

Chapter 2. Hill walking in winter and spring: snow and ice

§ 13. Essential differences between winter and summer hill walking

In winter and spring snow and ice make hill walking a serious proposition. The conditions high up can be arctic. Much greater fitness and endurance may be called for than in summer and the penalties for mistakes can be great; there have unfortunately been many deaths in the British hills in winter. A chill wind will quickly numb you unless your windproofs are really good and you keep moving; and a dull day can soon turn into a blizzard or freezing rain. Scottish blizzards can be extremely serious both because of their ferocity and because of the chilling, damp cold which they bring. The snow itself makes route-finding more difficult because it obscures paths and even cairns. It also makes movement more dangerous; what would be nothing more than a slight slip, easily checked, in summer on long grass or heather, might turn into a long and dangerous fall on snow in winter, unless you know how to stop it at the beginning (§ 16). Finally, winter days are short (as little as eight hours) and the nights are long (as much as sixteen hours), so that it is easier to get caught by nightfall, but all the more important to avoid it. An emergency bivouac in winter on a Scottish peak, even if the party is well equipped, should be avoided at almost any cost: and conditions in England and Wales can sometimes be as bad.

These vital differences between winter and summer conditions are sometimes not obvious. It may, for example, be reasonably warm in the valley (say at 500 ft) on a winter's day when it is freezing hard above 2,500 ft. If the cloud base is low, the snow and ice on the upper parts of the

14. *Braeriach (Cairngorms)*. From across the Lhairig Ghru. As noted in § 101, the Cairngorms are remote and difficult for navigation because they are so featureless. Level plateaux sometimes end abruptly in crags. In good conditions such as these, however, they give excellent hill walking or ski-ing.

mountain are unlikely to be visible from below, and hill walkers or climbers may set out grossly underprepared in equipment and experience for what is in reality a serious expedition. On the Easter week-end of 1951, seven people were killed on Snowdon in such conditions. Easter was in the middle of March that year, and it must be appreciated that when Easter is so early winter conditions should be expected: it should not be treated as the first week-end of the summer season.

On the other hand, winter can afford you some of your finest hill days. The mantle of snow gives the hills a fresh beauty, and paths which are well trodden and popular in summer become remote and exciting. The mountains in a sense are bigger in winter. They are well worth knowing and when you have learned to find your way about the hills in summer, using map and compass, there is no reason why you should not begin to walk on them in winter.

Under snow conditions many of the usual hill walks should be quite satisfactory. Everything will, however, depend on conditions. You should certainly limit your ambitions to the usual hill-walking routes and keep off steep snow – such as the zigzags on the Pyg Track on Snowdon – as far as possible. Routes which give easy scrambling in summer conditions – such as the south and north ridges of Tryfan [5], Striding Edge on Helvellyn [11], or the Aonach Eagach ridge in Glencoe – can be serious mountaineering undertakings in snow conditions requiring a high level of snow and ice climbing ability. They should be left for experienced snow and ice climbers and should not be regarded as reasonable for people whose experience is limited to hill walking and scrambling. Even on the easier routes winter hill walking is much closer to snow and ice climbing than summer hill walking is to rock climbing. You must therefore apply all the lessons already learned, be well equipped, and learn new techniques for safe movement on snow. If possible get an experienced winter hill walker or snow and ice climber to show you these techniques.

Equipment for winter hill walking. In winter and early spring you will need all the equipment suggested for summer conditions (§ 4) plus extra items to enable you to cope with snow and ice conditions. The main points to note are:

– tricouni-nailed boots (with tricouni heel-plates) are very good for British snow and ice (§ 23); they share with other climbing nails the disadvantages that they are colder than rubber soles and also tend to 'ball up' (get clogged with a hard wad of snow), but unlike hobs or clinkers they bite well in ice. If you have only cleated rubber-soled boots you should take crampons (§ 77) with you because they are not safe on the hard snow or ice which can occur on even the easiest routes;

– extra clothing is needed: scarves, gloves (windproof outer and wool inner), a second sweater, and if it is windy, windproof trousers, are the minimum additional items. A *cagoule* is strongly advised, and down clothing is useful (p. 382). At least emergency bivouac gear (plastic bag and Space Blanket – § 4) is needed if there is any chance of being caught out overnight. Shorts, skirts or jeans can be lethal in winter;

- additional food, with a high fat content, is needed to keep out the cold, plus possibly a hot drink in a vacuum flask;
- in bright conditions, sunglasses can relieve eyestrain;
- each man must have an ice-axe (§ 78); for a novice at least it should preferably have a long wrist-sling or other means of attachment. Provided the shaft is strong, any axe will do, since the party should not get involved in excessive step-cutting;
- a deadman (p. 282) if there is a need to belay on steep ground.

The ice-axe can be carried on the rucksack or between the rucksack and your back [30 and 107c] when it is not in use. When walking on the flat, hold the axe by the shaft or the head without the spike touching the ground: though the axe is often used as a walking-stick on roads and level ground, this tends to upset your rhythm and blunts the spike.

A leader's additional responsibilities in winter. It would be unwise to take large parties of inexperienced people, particularly young people, high up on the hills in bad weather in winter. If possible, plan such trips for the summer when the conditions are easier; but if you must go in winter, keep to the lower routes when there is snow and ice on the hills. Anyone in charge of inexperienced people in the hills in winter should be a competent mountaineer, and in particular, in addition to the requirements in § 2 should:

- be able to cut steps in snow or ice (§ 83) in case a short difficult section has to be crossed;
- be able to belay with the ice-axe (§ 17) or deadman (p. 282) as well as on a rock anchor (§§ 58–61);
- know when it is safe to glissade and when it is not; as pointed out in § 19 below, glissading requires both skill and the right snow conditions, and many accidents have been caused by the absence of one or the other.

It is essential that, as in summer, the leader should be able to judge in good time when it is necessary to turn back, on account either of the inability of the weaker members of the party to move safely in the prevailing conditions, or because of technical difficulty (e.g. a patch of steep ice), lateness, or a deterioration in the weather. At the first opportunity the leader should teach each inexperienced member of the party how to use his ice-axe, and in particular how to brake with it if he should slip (§ 16).

Finally, the more arduous the winter expedition in prospect, the more vital it is to plot it out beforehand, with a full study of the weather, the snow conditions, the valley approaches, the time needed for each stage, and the where-abouts of possible emergency shelters (such as bothies or disused cottages) on the mountain. There must be no late start and no racing or minute-losing during the ascent. Only in this way can you be sure of a good reserve of physical energy and mental tone should the final stages of the route prove stormy, dark, or exhausting. In fact all the general rules given in chapter 1 must be followed with much greater care than is necessary in the long and warm days of summer.

§ 14. Snow and ice conditions and order of difficulty

Winter conditions vary considerably. In Scotland, snow is almost always to be found between October and May, and there may be small patches in high corries throughout the year. The snow is usually at its best in February and March, and begins to thaw (and become dangerous on that account) in April. In England and Wales, good snow con-ditions are much less frequent and are usually short-lived, but there is a risk of snow and ice at any time between November and April. The day-to-day weather is very important. The onset of a warm south-west wind for example may bring a quick thaw or rain. Newly fallen snow is simply a hindrance, since it has no substance and does not give firm steps. The process of consolidation involves melting and re-freezing. A series of warm days and cold nights will give powder snow a reliable crust; rain followed by overnight freezing will have the same result. With more melting and freezing the snow will become fully consolidated. If the process continues for long enough it will turn into very hard snow or even ice. Wind will give the same result; and ice and *verglas* may be found high up, even when there is no snow, as a result of damp air freezing and condensing. Above the 3,000-ft level rocks are often thickly encased in masses of frost crystals formed by condensation and by wind action. Lower down, the freezing of streams may produce huge patches of ice where the stream has overflowed repeatedly in the process of freezing up.

15. *Winter wastes*. Frozen lochan in Coire Ardair, below Creag Meagaidh (§ 102). See also 110.

The steepness of a snow slope may be described as follows:

Up to 25 deg.	Gentle
25–35 deg.	Moderately steep
35–50 deg.	Steep
Above 50 deg.	Very steep

To most people, snow looks and feels a good deal steeper than it really is.

The difficulty of a snow slope will depend both on its *condition* and on its *steepness*. The best snow for climbing is snow which has consolidated to some extent but which still gives a very good and secure step simply by kicking your foot in once. A thin crust on top of soft snow can be very tiring, however, especially when it supports your weight for one step but collapses on the next. If the snow gives good steps and is not icy, hill walkers when experienced should be able to cope with short slopes of up to thirty-five degrees, and much longer slopes if the angle is less. The techniques and safety precautions needed for this order of difficulty are dealt with in the remainder of this chapter.

Ice and steep snow. Hill walkers should avoid slopes of ice (or very hard snow) since the ice-axe brake does not work on ice and it may not be possible to check a fall with the rope unless the party is moving one at a time and belaying (§ 17 below). Even where the ice is at a gentle angle, it may be necessary to cut steps. Steep snow is usually found in this country only in gullies, where the slopes are often broken up by protruding rock or by ice pitches. Such steep or very steep snow, like ice, should be left for experienced snow and ice climbers using the techniques described in chapter 11.

§ 15. Movement on gentle and moderately steep snow

The most important single requirement for safe movement on snow, as on rock, is to stand upright. Beginners often think that by leaning in towards the mountain they will be less likely to slip; but in fact the reverse is the case. Rhythm is also extremely important because you may have to kick steps for hundreds of feet at a time.

Making steps. On soft snow, it is not necessary to make steps; simply walk on the snow, and your weight will make its own steps (as noted above, soft snow can be a hindrance if it does not give firm steps). Steps are also unlikely to be needed on firm snow up to an angle of about twenty-five degrees since you can usually walk up on your edge nails, or the edges of your vibrams; do not walk on the flat of your foot because it is likely to skate. Above that angle steps will have to be kicked or cut, unless you are wearing crampons. If the snow is crusted, one or two kicks with the toe of your boot should make an adequate step; but if it is very hard, several blows may be needed; it will probably be easier then to cut steps, using a sideways blow with the adze of your axe [113]. Steps can be made either sideways on (with your heel as well as the sole on the step) or straight in; the former is generally used when traversing or in zigzag ascents or descents, the latter for direct ascents or descents [111]. Be careful not to bruise your toes when step-kicking; if a long bout is necessary, it is best to alternate with the other members of the party so that all can do their share of the work and keep warm into the bargain.

If you are wearing crampons (§ 77), it will not be strictly necessary for you to use steps at all, since they give a good grip on snow and ice up to an angle of about fifty degrees; but in practice, until you are fully experienced, you will probably find it reassuring to do so. Crampon technique is dealt with in § 84: the most important points are (1) that the crampons should fit your boots well, (2) that you should walk with your feet apart so that you don't trip over them, and (3) that with ordinary crampons you should keep the soles of your boots at the same angle as the slope, on hard snow or ice, so that all points of the crampon can bite into it.

Zigzag ascent [16A]. As in summer (§ 5), it is usually best to ascend in steep zigzags to left and right, so that you

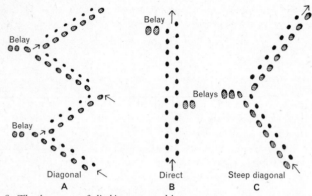

16. *The three ways of climbing snow and ice.*

can rest each side of your body in turn and can get the whole of your foot (including the heel) on to the snow [17 and 111A]. An advantage is that if anyone above you slips, he is much less likely to hit you and knock you out of your steps than if you were climbing up directly below him. In addition any snow dislodged by the leader is likely to fall to one side of you, so you will keep drier and more comfortable. When changing from a left-hand zigzag to a right-hand zigzag, make an extra big step for your left foot at the point of changing (and vice versa when the change is in the opposite direction). Your ice-axe should be in your uphill hand all the time, and it is necessary to change it from hand to hand when you change direction; a wrist-sling can be rather a nuisance when changing direction unless it is so long that you can keep it on one wrist all the time (§ 78). The shaft of the axe should be thrust firmly into the snow at each step, so that it acts as a firm point of support [17A]. It will save effort if you use the hole made by the man in front. If this is inconvenient, hold the axe across your body with the spike in the snow [17B] or the pick in the snow [116A];

the latter has the advantage that your axe is already in the braking position (§ 16) should you slip. The various methods of holding the axe are described in more detail in § 82.

A direct ascent [16B] is shorter than a zigzag ascent, and is therefore preferable when time is of first importance, or when the slope is steep and short. The shaft of the ice-axe should be thrust into the snow above you or alternatively,

17. *Zigzag ascent.* This is the best way of climbing long slopes, since you can get the whole length of each foot on the snow, and can rest either side of your body in turn. The axe is always on the uphill side. The method of holding the axe shown in B is excellent on firm snow for maintaining an upright position, but some climbers prefer to hold it the other way round (as in 116A) since this is more convenient for an emergency brake (20) should a fall occur.

A   B

18. *Direct ascent.* This is the natural way to tackle a gentle slope, as in A, or a short steep section as in B. Always try to get the shaft of the axe into the snow, but if this is not practicable use the pick instead, as in B.

on steeper or harder snow, the pick [18B]. Steps made on a direct ascent are easier to reverse (see below) because, facing inwards, you can use the steps for handholds as well as footholds. A disadvantage of the direct ascent is that if a person falls he may cannon into the others so that a multiple fall results; the risk of this can be minimized by keeping close together (so that he does not gather much momentum) and by taking a stance to one side when anyone is negotiating a difficult section. The arrangement which I personally find most convenient is a very steep zigzag, which combines the advantages of both methods [16C].

Descent [19]. When descending easy snow, try to face towards the valley (or, if necessary, sideways) instead of towards the slope, since this is quicker and easier. But if you are in any doubt about your security, always face inwards and jab your ice-axe securely into the snow (at the back of an existing step, if the snow is very hard); this is most likely to be necessary on steepish, unstable snow. When walking down moderately steep soft snow put your weight well down on your heels, rather like descending small scree (§ 7). Carry your axe by the head, ready to plunge the shaft into the snow should you slip. If the snow is harder and you are not using existing steps, you can kick new steps with your heels (tricouni heel-plates are valuable for this). On steeper snow, kick steps with the sides of your feet, or if you are facing into the mountain, with your toes. Be careful not to kick a new step so close to an existing one that it may collapse into it.

19. *Descent.* Face outwards, as in A, on easy or moderate snow, and sideways, as in B, on more difficult ground. Always face inwards on steep or insecure ground. See also 120.

A　　　　　　　　B

§ 16. Stopping a fall with the ice-axe

If you have thrust your ice-axe firmly into the snow
[17A], all you need do in the event of a slip on moderately
steep snow is to put your weight on to the axe so that it is
instantaneously forced deep into the snow; it should then
give a very firm handhold to stop you slipping further.
Before you stand up again, kick yourself good secure steps
for both feet.

You would be well advised also to learn how to brake
with the ice-axe if this method should fail. Choose a safe
spot where there are no boulders sticking out and where you
will not fall far if the brake does not work. Wear gloves to
save your hands getting scraped. Walk thirty feet or so up
the slope and simulate a fall. As soon as you begin to slide,
roll over on to your chest and get your boots downhill, and
immediately bring the pick of the ice-axe into the snow with

20. *Emergency braking with the ice-axe.* Note that the adze of the axe is held
firmly into the shoulder; the climber is wearing gloves; the spike of the
axe is well clear of the snow; the feet are downhill; boots can help with
braking, as here, but crampons must be lifted off the snow because they
cause somersaulting.

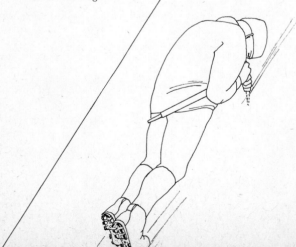

your hands on top of the head and with the weight of your chest and shoulders pressing on it [20]. Do not press the pick too forcibly into the snow at first because the surface may be uneven and might wrench the axe from your grip. The shaft of the axe should be tucked under one armpit and the spike raised well out of the snow so that there is no chance of it hitting a bump and being knocked from your grasp. The friction of your boots on the snow may help to slow you down, but if you are wearing crampons keep them well off the snow since they might make you cartwheel. Always be certain to get your feet downhill, because they can stand up to collisions with boulders and other projections much better than your head (head injuries are the commonest, and most dangerous, of the injuries caused by falls on snow and ice).

This method of braking, if applied properly, should work on snow at an angle of up to about forty degrees, depending on its hardness; it will not work on true ice because the pick of the axe can get no purchase, and its efficiency is greatly reduced in very icy snow. Anyone hill walking in the winter should learn the technique of braking *before* he gets into a position where it could matter, since a slip on easy snow may turn into a long fall if it is not checked at the beginning. He should practise it until his reaction is instantaneous, since a fraction of a second lost in applying the pick to the snow will mean that he is falling that much faster, with a corresponding reduction in his chances of recovering control.

§ 17. Elementary rope technique on snow

When to use the rope. Normally hill walkers should avoid getting into positions where a rope is required; but if the party finds that it has strayed into such a position it should not hesitate to use the rope. The time to do so is when there is any reason to think that the weakest member of the party would not be able to stop an incipient fall by one of the

21. *The ice-axe belay: normal method.* The full-length of the shaft is firmly embedded in the well-consolidated sub-surface at the back of the step. The rope is tied to the shaft with a figure-of-eight knot (167). Ideally, the belay should be well above waist level, so that there is less tendency for the axe to flick out under load. While this system is satisfactory in well-consolidated snow, with a metal-shafted ice-axe, other methods such as burying the axe horizontally (addendum § 4) or those in (22) are preferable in less reliable snow. In all cases, however, the deadman (see addendum) is superior and should be used in preference whenever possible.

methods described above. The rope should also be used where there is a risk of concealed cornices (see next section) particularly in mist or storm conditions. But if the rope is likely to be required for more than a short passage, or if the leader feels that he needs the rope for his own safety, then the mountain must clearly be too much for that day and the party should turn back. A figure-of-eight knot [167] is recommended for tying on (§ 54).

Belaying on snow (see also § 86). When roped up the party should normally be belayed so that a fall by one member will not pull the others off as well. Every member of the party should be belayed while he is not moving. The best belay is a rock belay (§§ 58–61) and this should always be used in preference to any snow belay if possible. Where no rock anchor is available, however, a deadman (addendum) or, less satisfactorily, an ice-axe should be used. For the latter, the belayer should first of all kick good steps for his feet. He then plunges the shaft of his axe vertically into the snow up to its head. If the surface snow is very hard and it is not possible to get the shaft of the axe in adequately, it is best to cut into the top surface until the softer snow beneath is reached; then put the shaft of the axe vertically into the back of the recess thus formed. The belayer then ties a figure-of-eight knot in the main rope and

22. *The ice-axe belay: alternative method.* A has the advantage over (21) that the axe is held in by the belayer's body weight; if the rope is taken in round the waist this effect is accentuated in the event of a fall since the load is transmitted from the waist through the leg to the axe, providing a most valuable counterweight. B is the footbrake, a quick alternative to A and the best way of arresting a fall when moving together. See § 88.

A

B

places the knot over the head of the axe so that it slides
down any part of the shaft which is not embedded in the
snow, and rests at or below snow level [21]. Alternatively he
may pass the rope round the axe and tie it back into his
waist-loop with two or three half hitches as in rock climbing
[80]. The leader holds the second man's rope round his
waist, and keeps it almost taut while he is bringing him up.
If the snow is unconsolidated the belayer should put some
weight on the top of the axe to hold it in under load or
should put one foot or leg on the snow against the axe to
stop it moving [22]. Alternatively, the axe should be buried
in the snow horizontally (addendum, § 4). The normal
ice-axe belay is reliable only in good snow and with a metal-
shafted axe: the deadman is invariably preferable.

Moving together roped up. On very easy ground it is permissible
in the interests of time for the whole party to move together
roped up, instead of taking the standing ice-axe belay
described above. This may, for example, be necessary if the
party is moving across flat snow in bad visibility with a
danger of cornices (see below), or if the leader wants to make
sure that the party keeps together. It must be recognized
that for an inexperienced party the chances of holding a
fall when moving together on moderately steep snow are
not great. The party should, therefore, move together only
where the going is genuinely easy and where there is no
serious drop below. The technique of belaying when
moving together is described in § 88 and the method of
holding the rope is shown in [19A] and [22B].

§ 18. Special hazards on snow

Be very careful to avoid walking over snow-covered streams
or rivers unless the snow is old and reliable, since it may
collapse under your weight and plunge you into the water;
you may even get swept into the tunnel made by the river
under the snow. In late spring retreating snow-beds lying
against steep rocks leave fissures, caverns, and tunnels.

These deep holes, with their thin roofs (like crevasses in the Alps) may be dangerous traps. Open mineshafts, such as those on Miners' Track above Glaslyn on Snowdon, are clear for all to see in summer but may be hidden by snow in winter. Boulders and large scree should also be avoided under snow, since they may cause a nasty tumble.

Cornices. On the sides of ridges, overhanging masses of snow may be formed by wind action. These cornices, as they are called, are usually at their biggest in late winter or spring. They are usually unsupported and very large sections of them can break away. A large alpine cornice is shown in [142]; cornices as big as this are unusual in Britain but can occur in Scotland at the head of a gully, e.g. at the head of the northern corries of the Cairngorms or Ben Nevis. The line of break of a cornice is a long way away from the edge, and it is essential to keep well away from it on safe ground. This can be difficult in mist or when the cornices are very big, and as noted above the rope should be worn at such times.

Avalanches. The main types of avalanche are described in § 129 as:

1. New or unconsolidated dry-snow avalanches;
2. Wet-snow avalanches;
3. Windslab avalanches;
4. Unstable masses of snow or ice, such as cornices.

Although 2 is likely to happen only in thawing conditions, the other types can occur at any time. Avalanches are not usually a serious danger on hill-walking territory, but quite a number have been experienced in the Cairngorms in recent years, and care should be taken at all times, but especially on convex slopes or when unconsolidated snow is resting on an icy sub-surface; soft wet snow lying on grass can also be dangerous. Avalanches may be started by the collapse of a cornice, and it is advisable to avoid slopes overhung by them, particularly in thaw conditions.

Blizzards. Falling snow on the hills must be treated with great caution; it is likely to turn to a blizzard and there is no worse enemy to fight through. If you are caught, stick close together, roping up if necessary, and make for the most accessible valley with a road or footpath down it; the most accessible may not be the nearest – it is easier and far less of a struggle to walk to a more distant valley with a wind behind you than to fight against it to get to a near one.

§ 19. Glissading

Glissading is discussed in most mountaineering textbooks as one of the mountaineering skills. But it is really no more than a controlled slide, and loss of balance can quickly lead to an uncontrolled fall. It has been well said that there are three types of glissade – standing, sitting, and involuntary – and that they usually follow each other in close succession. There have been very many accidents as a result. Unless the party is generally experienced, and conditions are good, there should be no glissading, except on practice slopes.

To learn to glissade, choose somewhere where there are no boulders and where you will not be hurt if you lose control. Wear gloves. A standing glissade is in essence similar to a ski descent and modified ski turns can be used. Stand crouched forward in balance with your feet flat to the slope and pointing downhill. Hold the ice-axe with one hand on the head and the other well down the shaft [24A]. The pick should be pointing away from you. The ice-axe is a rudder and an emergency brake, auxiliary to the action of your feet. Steady yourself with the ice-axe if necessary [24B]. Pace is regulated by driving in the heels to check, or

23. *The Crib Goch ridge in winter (North Wales).* Compare with summer conditions (1 and 12). Routes such as this, which are no more than moderate scrambles in summer, become serious expeditions under snow and ice in winter, suitable for well-equipped and experienced parties only.

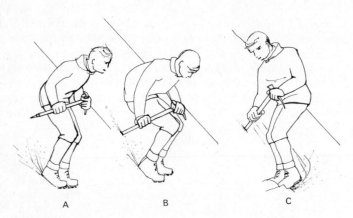

A   B   C

24. *Standing glissade.* A is the ideal position, usually achieved only on good glissading snow at moderate angle. B is normal: the ice-axe is a rudder and helps your stability on uneven snow. C shows the method of turning, essential for a controlled descent. Note that in each case the axe is held in such a way that it is not necessary to change the position of the hands should an emergency brake be necessary (20).

by pointing the toes downwards to accelerate. One foot has a slight lead: the other follows slightly to one side but not straddled out; a wide foot base with the weight on both feet makes only for poor balance and difficulty in withstanding jerks due to varying surfaces or gradients. To change direction, hold the ice-axe on the side to which you want to go, with some weight on it, and turn your feet across the slope, with only the edges in contact with the snow [24C]. Because of the difficulty of changing your axe from one side to the other it is usually best to do a series of small turns in the same direction, rather than to right and left successively as one would on skis. Turning across the slope is also the normal way of slowing down or halting.

The ideal snow for glissading is well-consolidated snow with a soft top surface, as for example where a slope is warmed by the afternoon sun. But this is the exception rather than the rule in this country. Steep or icy snow is dangerous because it makes control very difficult. Even when the snow is not generally icy, sections of ice or icy snow may occur in patches of shadow, and it is advisable to stop and check that there is no ice where patches of shadow occur.

There should be no glissading if the slope cannot be seen to run out gently at the bottom, or if there is any dangerous section – such as boulders or a drop or an icy patch – lower down. A dangerous instance to avoid would be a funnel on an open hillside leading to the top of a gully. This may look like good glissading snow, but the snow in the gully will probably be icy and hence the glissade would become uncontrollable.

A sitting glissade may be feasible where the snow is not quite good enough for standing, as happens in late spring. Control sitting is not so easy as standing. If the snow piles up under you, side roll and get clear. Do not use the pick of the axe as a brake in these circumstances. Grip the shaft near the head and a little lower down with the other hand and press the spike backwards into the snow under your shoulder or to either side as may be necessary to brake or steer. By arching the body upwards between the heels and axe thrust, full brake power is developed. The main disadvantage of a sitting glissade is that it will make you very wet and uncomfortable.

§ 20. Ski-ing

In winter and spring, skis can provide an ideal means of travel for experienced ski-ers. They are particularly useful in big rounded mountains such as the Cairngorms. Ski-ing is outside the scope of this book, but a brief list of useful books can be found in the bibliography, 6.

§ 21. Emergency bivouacs in winter and early spring

As noted in § 13 every possible effort should be made to

avoid an involuntary night out in winter because the nights are so long and can be extremely cold. With strong torches you should almost always be able to get off the mountain. If however you are caught out, make every effort to get as far down the mountain as possible, and search carefully to find some protection against wind and falling snow or rain. If you can get down to the tree line, it should be possible to find a hole in the snow at the base of a tree, but if you are higher on the mountain, the lee of a large boulder or a wall would be a great deal better than nothing. A number of deaths from exposure have in fact occurred close to shelter which the party would have found had it continued searching a little longer. When you find shelter, get inside your polythene bivouac bag, and act as recommended in §11. Huddle together for warmth, but keep still if your clothing is wet, to minimize heat loss to it.

If there is no natural shelter available, do not spend time trying to make igloos unless you have successfully practised this previously and have a snow-saw or deadman for cutting blocks. Instead, try to make one or more snow-holes or caves for the party to shelter in. This should only be undertaken as a last resort – the labour itself would be very numbing and exhausting especially if the party is already wet to the skin. It takes about two hours to dig a hole suitable for two or three people using snow shovels; deadmen (p. 529) are a good substitute but if only ice-axes are available it would take much longer. A bank of snow at an angle of not less than thirty degrees and with a depth of about eight feet is required. This is most likely to be found where the snow has drifted into a stream bed, or where the underside of a cornice contains a natural weakness which can be enlarged – but first make sure that the cornice is absolutely safe. It is hardly ever worth digging into level snow, or a

25. *A snow-hole*. Living comfortably at over 3,000 feet in the Cairngorms. The exit is as low as possible to conserve heat.

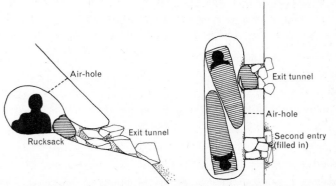

SECTIONS OF SNOW-HOLE SHOWN IN PHOTOGRAPH ABOVE

main slope, since it is most unlikely to have the required depth, and will probably be icy beneath.

Use a deadman or your feet, preferably with crampons, for scraping the snow out. It is quicker and warmer to dig in at two points about five feet apart. When far enough in, work towards each other until you meet. One of the entrances should then be completely filled in. If possible make the other entrance lower than the chamber as warm air will then be trapped inside. Block this hole with snow and rucksacks overnight. Make a small hole (using an ice-axe) in the roof for ventilation, and clear it periodically (and the entrance if there is drifting).

Other points to remember are:

- if you are not already soaked, take off as much clothing under your windproofs/*cagoule* as possible while digging (a very wet process) so as to preserve dry clothing for the night;
- sometimes a combined hole/igloo (i.e. using blocks to make a part wall to fill the hole) is quickest;
- roofs and walls should be at least two feet thick for strength and insulation;
- maintain extra ventilation while cooking to prevent possible carbon monoxide poisoning or oxygen starvation; also to reduce humidity and hence damp;
- mark the top with a stick or axe to avoid anyone walking on it and to assist any search party;
- sleep as close as possible to the roof where the air is warmest; and put clothing, ropes etc. below you for insulation;
- keep two axes or deadmen inside with you to dig out with if part of the roof collapses.

Should it not be possible to make a proper snow-hole, any combination of trench and wall which protects against the wind would be better than nothing.

Chapter 3. Equipment for hill walking

The equipment needed for hill walking in summer and winter is summarized in § 4 and § 13 respectively. This chapter gives a detailed description of the main items – clothing, footwear, rucksacks, and maps and compasses – leaving camping equipment to the next chapter and crampons and ice-axes to chapter 10. Since the equipment is used by climbers as much as by hill walkers, it is described from their point of view as well.

§ 22. Clothing

The essential requirements are:

– protection against wind, cold, and rain;
– adjustability to meet the extremely wide variety of conditions which may be encountered in a single day;
– lightness combined with durability.

Air is a good insulator and it is a good basic principle to use clothing that will trap air. One or two items (socks or a hat) should be brightly coloured (e.g. red or blue) so that you can be seen from a distance: this is particularly useful in case of accident. Clothing should be kept in good repair and should never be put away damp.

Windproof anorak. Wind is the worst enemy on the hills: without protection on a cold and windy day your vitality would quickly be reduced to danger level. An anorak has a hood and good long sleeves; it should be large enough to wear with a lot of clothing underneath, and it should be long enough to sit on. A zipped front gives adjustability at the expense of being slightly less windproof; a half-zip from neck to waist is a satisfactory compromise. The openings at the bottom, sleeves, and neck, and the hood itself, should be adjustable so that they can be closed up tight to keep out wind or opened in warm weather to allow heat to escape. The waist should have a draw-cord. A large zipped map pocket is desirable. The material should be windproof and should be as water-resistant as possible while avoiding condensation on the inside (Ventile, Gannex, and Wyncol are among the materials designed for this purpose). A double thickness in the shoulders (and at the elbows) is advisable; if the extra thickness in the shoulders is completely waterproof, so much the better, since they take most of the rain. A lining or quilting is not recommended because it adds weight without being as warm or as adjustable as a sweater; it also takes a long time to dry. Various types of anoraks can be seen in, for example, [19] and [29].

Waterproofs. All sorts of combinations of clothing have been tried to keep out the persistent rain so common in the British hills, but none has been completely successful until recently, mainly because fully waterproof materials tend to produce condensation on the inside as a result of over-heating. The lightweight materials now available however are much less prone to overheating, and it is well worth while taking a second lightweight anorak made of water-proof nylon (polyurethane) or terylene to put on if it rains heavily. This need not weigh more than $\frac{1}{2}$ lb. at the most, and can be conveniently kept in your pocket when not in use. A long, waterproof, lightweight anorak (a *cagoule* – § 124) is particularly useful because it protects your thighs as well as your body; it can also be used for a bivouac, in conjunction with an extension on your rucksack which reaches to the top of your thighs when your feet are inside. A plastic macintosh is a good alternative (though it un-fortunately lacks a hood) but cycling capes etc. are not satisfactory because they billow out in a wind, obscuring footholds and possibly upsetting your balance. Even though a waterproof smock may make you damp through condensation, you will stay drier than without it, and will keep very much warmer and more comfortable. Waterproof trousers are however not recommended because they make the wearer too hot.

Underwear, shirt, sweaters, and scarf. A long string-vest traps air and gives the smallest contact with the body; hence it keeps you warm when wet. A disadvantage is that it may chafe your skin when you are carrying a heavy rucksack. A woollen vest, or a lightweight sweater worn next to the skin, is very good in cold or wet weather. Cotton or nylon vests will not absorb sweat sufficiently and are cold when wet. A woollen shirt with long sleeves is good; it should be long in the body to prevent chills in the bottom of your back and should be capable of being fastened at the neck to keep out draughts. A combination of one lightweight sweater with a medium-weight one is warmer and more flexible than one heavy one. The sleeves should be long enough to come well down over your wrists. A scarf can be a great boon, both for warmth and for preventing rain from getting down your neck. Down jackets (§ 124) are mainly used in the Alps, but could be useful for snow and ice climbing in Britain.

Trousers and breeches. Flannels or woollen trousers are adequate for summer hill walking. In windy or winter conditions, windproof overtrousers can be worn in addition. Among climbers, breeches worn with long stockings are popular because they give greater freedom of movement than trousers and are less likely to obscure footholds or catch in nailed boots or crampons; cut-down trousers tucked into knee-length stockings are a cheap alternative. Breeches should fasten just below the knee with a buckle or a button [48]. They should not be too long nor too baggy. Zips or covers over the pockets are useful and one or more cash pockets for compass, watch, or camera filters are needed. Climbers often have a rule pocket in the thigh for a piton hammer (§ 69). An extra patch on the seat is advisable. A waterproof patch between this and the seat is a help for keeping out damp when sitting on wet hillsides. The material should be robust and wind-resistant. Corduroy is heavy when wet and does not dry quickly. Moleskin, special woollen material, or Bedford cord are better. In hot weather, stockings can be rolled down and the knee buckles undone to give better air circulation. The choice between belts and braces is one for the individual: braces have some advantage when clothing is wet and heavy because they give the necessary support without undue constriction of the stomach.

Shorts and skirts are not recommended, except in settled summer conditions. Even then it is advisable to carry a pair of lightweight overtrousers in case the weather turns bad. Shorts can however be very pleasant in really hot weather, for walking up to alpine huts (§ 133) or for sea-cliff climbing.

Stockings and socks. Most British mountaineers wear a pair of oiled wool stockings (Harris and Norwegian wools are the most popular) and a pair of wool socks. Continental mountaineers prefer simply a pair of stockings. Two thicknesses cushion the feet better than one, but one thickness is quite adequate if your boots fit you well. One thickness is more sensitive for rock climbing, and is not necessarily colder since your blood circulation will probably be better. Spare socks are useful for a change in the middle of the day (and dry socks are invaluable if you get caught out overnight). Thin cotton or pure nylon stockings are not very satisfactory, but thick nylon/wool mixture stockings can be very good, especially since snow does not stick and melt on them.

Gaiters. Elastic or proofed cloth gaiters [111] are useful for keeping snow out of your boots, and for keeping your feet warm by restricting the air circulation. They keep stones out of your boots also, but a pair of socks folded over the top of your boots does this almost equally well. Knee-length gaiters have recently become popular for alpine climbing.

Gloves or mitts are required for hill walking in cold weather and for climbing. For hill walking, a pair of woollen inner gloves with canvas windproof outer gloves is the best combination. Leather is unsatisfactory because it is cold when wet and it takes a long time to dry. For climbing, a combination of woollen mitts [111] and woollen fingerless gloves [53c] is probably best; but leather gloves are by far the best for holding the rope (a rope can cause very bad burns to the hands and wrists of a second who has to hold a falling leader (§ 62), unless he is wearing good, long gloves). All gloves and mitts should cover the wrists. The lower arm, wrists, and hands are particularly vulnerable to cold and the temperature of the whole of your body can quickly be lowered because the blood circulates close to the surface there, especially at the pulse in the wrists. Cold hands and wrists are very much weaker than warm ones, and this is an important consideration when climbing or scrambling in cold weather: there have been cases where a leader has fallen because he has lost all feeling and strength in his hands without appreciating that he was doing so. For climbing in bad weather or for snow and ice climbing, it is useful to wear long stocking tops on your arms and wrists: combined with a scarf they are almost as good as an extra sweater, and are a good deal lighter and less cumbersome.

Headgear. Some sort of hat is desirable in bad weather in addition to the hood of your anorak, in order to conserve body heat. A hat with a brim will protect you from rain and snow. The woollen balaclava is popular in British conditions and has the advantage that it can be pulled down over your ears and chin. For climbers, protective helmets (§ 123) are strongly recommended as protection both against stonefall and in the event of a head-first fall; they also give warmth for winter climbing.

§ 23. Boots

Boots are needed for hill walking or climbing. Admittedly, stout nailed shoes are worn by gamekeepers or deerstalkers, but they are not very satisfactory on rocky going because they give too little support to the ankles. Gym shoes or basketball boots are unsuitable because they cannot protect the soles of your feet adequately on rough going, and are slippery on wet rock or grass. There are many different types and qualities of mountaineering boots, and rather different requirements for hill walking as against rock climbing. It is most important to select a pair which suit you well, because badly fitting or inadequate boots can completely ruin a mountaineering day, and may possibly be dangerous.

Hill-walking boots [26] need neither be very expensive nor very heavy. The main requirements are:

- they should give a good grip: moulded rubber soles are usual, but nails have some advantages in wet, greasy conditions (see below); whichever type of soling you use, it should be kept in good condition;
- they should be fairly broad for their size, and the uppers should not be too heavy or rigid (a high, rigid-sided, or tightly tied boot may hurt the ankles and Achilles tendon);
- they should have a solid, but slightly flexible, curved sole and a wide heel;

26. *Mountaineering footwear.*

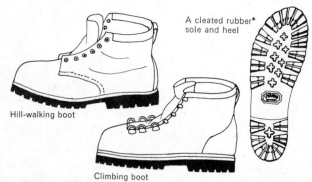

A cleated rubber*
sole and heel

Hill-walking boot

Climbing boot

* Vibram is the registered trade name for soles of this description produced by Vibram S.p.A. of Milan.

- they should be watertight; the welt and other joins (as few as possible) should be well stitched, and the tongue should be sewn in up to the top of the boot.

Climbing boots [26] need:

- rigidity for support on small holds. In the case of rubber-soled boots the soles may be strengthened with metal or fibre-glass plates, to achieve rigidity without increasing weight. Nailed boots are not much used for rock climbing nowadays (see below); for rigidity they need soles of 15 mm., but 13 mm. or even 11 mm. soles can be used by ladies, and 17 mm. soles may be preferred by people of above average weight. The soles should be straight, not curved, and should be continuous for the whole length of the boot (with no break at the heel);
- very narrow welts so that there is no avoidable leverage;
- as close a fitting (particularly over the instep) as is consistent with comfort, so that there is no unfilled gap inside the boot;
- a narrow, not a square, toe, so that it can be jammed in narrow cracks (§ 45).

Lightweight footwear for rock climbing (P.A.s, etc.) is illustrated in [51].

Composition rubber soles and heels. Only soles and heels specially designed for mountaineering should be used (e.g. those made by Vibram, Richard Pontvert or Itshide); these are moulded to resemble a combination of clinker and mugger nails [26]. Do not use general-purpose industrial protective soles, since these are not moulded in the required way and are usually too flexible to give the required edge-grip on sloping ground. These cleated rubber soles (sometimes also known as lug soles) give an excellent grip on dry rock and will grip on wet rock provided there is no grease, lichen, or mud to act as a lubricant. On soft snow they are very good because the snow does not ball up on them as it does with nails and because they give good insulation against the cold. Because of these advantages, and their general durability, comfort, and lightness, cleated rubber soles are the standard wear for hill walking 'and climbing. Always remember, however, that they can be dangerous on hard snow or ice, and on greasy rock, since they are liable to skate unexpectedly. In winter, take crampons (§ 77) in case you come across hard snow or ice (or alternatively wear nailed boots). On greasy rock much depends on the skill with which the rubber soles are used; they can be reliable on spike holds or on holds which have been cleaned by nails, or where the rock is so rough that tiny rugosities penetrate the grease and grip the sole (§ 40). The condition of the soles is also important: new ones bite much more effectively than old, rounded ones. Some climbers prefer a combination of rubber and nails, since the nails will bite on greasy holds, but this has the disadvantage of reducing the all-round versatility of the rubber sole on dry rock, so that you may get the worst of both worlds.

Climbing nails [27] were in common use in this country up to the end of the 1930s but have been generally superseded

27. *Some mountaineering nails.*

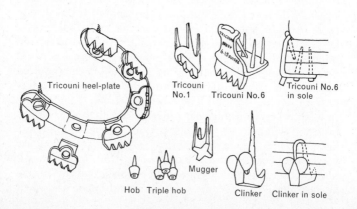

Tricouni heel-plate

Tricouni No.1   Tricouni No.6   Tricouni No.6 in sole

Hob   Triple hob   Mugger   Clinker   Clinker in sole

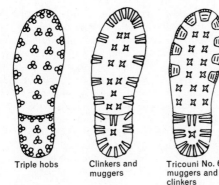

| Triple hobs | Clinkers and muggers | Tricouni No. 6, muggers and clinkers | Tricouni Nos. 6 and 1, with heel-plate |

28. *Selected nailing patterns.*

nowadays by the cleated rubber sole. They do however have certain advantages over the rubber sole on greasy rock or on hard snow or ice, and their value should not be overlooked, particularly for Scottish conditions. There are two main types of nail: (1) soft iron nails which grip as a result of the rock biting into them (muggers and clinkers), and (2) hard steel nails (tricounis) which bite into the rock. Triple hobs fall in between, since they are made of cast iron, which is hard, but are not sharp like tricounis. Suitable nailing patterns are shown in [28]. Note that:

– *Triple hobs* are adequate for hill walking, and are cooler than vibrams for road walking. They are unsuitable for rock climbing. The nails should be well spread over the sole and the arch (essential for boulder-hopping) but should be close together on toe and heel.

– *Clinkers* are edge nails, used in conjunction with *muggers* in the middle of the sole. They are sometimes used for rock climbing, but require rather a muscular technique. They are good for scrambling and general purpose use, but are not good on snow and ice. A disadvantage is that if a clinker works loose and comes out it is likely to take part of the sole with it because the shaft is bent round after it has passed through the sole.

- *Tricounis*. The most popular tricouni is the No. 6, an edge nail with a sharp serrated edge made of very hard steel. It bites very well on small incut rock-holds and on ice because the biting edge is set at a slight angle from the vertical so that the more weight is put on the nail, the more it is held in towards the hold (see [27] and [50]). The tricouni No. 1 is not as good as the mugger for the sole of the boot, because it wears smooth too quickly and also tends to come out. Tricouni heel-plates are useful for descending snow and ice. Unfortunately, all tricounis wear smooth in time, and must then be replaced because they are likely to skate.

Rubber soles or nails? Anyone starting hill walking or climbing now would do best to use moulded rubber soles. For hill walking and scrambling in summer and autumn these will be perfectly adequate, provided greasy rock is treated with care. For winter, however, either crampons (§ 77) or tricouni-nailed boots are necessary; if he intends to go on ultimately to alpine climbing then crampons would be the better buy, but if not then tricounis would be of more all-round use. The same considerations apply to the embryo rock climber's choice of footwear: but there is a special advantage for him in having tricounis as a second pair of boots because they undoubtedly teach a very neat and reliable use of footholds. This is not to say that all your early rock climbing should be in nails, far from it: the undue use of nails is steadily wearing away many of the most popular of our easier classics, and nails have been forbidden by common agreement on very soft rock such as the sandstone of Harrison Rocks or Helsby Crag (perhaps this prohibition should be extended now to some of the easier Wales and Lake District classics). Moreover, the use of nails, if continued too long, encourages you to climb slowly and in rather a rigid way, because you have to be so careful in placing your feet. But any beginner would benefit in steadiness and the correct use of footholds from using nails occasionally, and learning to climb well in them in all weathers. They are certainly desirable for some Scottish climbing.

Fit of mountaineering boots. There may be some conflict between the need for a tightly fitting boot for rock climbing, and the need in more general mountaineering to avoid restricting your toes, which can lead to great discomfort and possibly even frostbite (§ 98) in extremely cold conditions. If the correct boot is chosen, however, there is no reason why it should not be satisfactory for all forms of mountaineering including rock climbing. As noted above, most British climbers wear a pair of socks as well as a pair of stockings, whereas Continental mountaineers tend to wear only a pair of stockings. A good compromise for a rock climber is to wear only one pair for walking up to the crag, and then to put on the second pair to ensure a tight fit for climbing. Boots will usually stretch about half a size with wear (possibly less if the soles are specially stiffened). An extra pair of socks will take up any slack but alternatively it is pleasant to wear a thin pair of plastic insoles; the latter will keep your feet warm and your socks cleaner (because they do not get rubbed into any mud and grit which gets on to the inside sole of your boots). Always make sure that your toes do not touch the end of the boot when you buy them. If the boot is on the small side at first, insert a piece of sponge rubber between the tongue and the foot so as to avoid hitting your toes when coming downhill; your toe-nails should be cut very short in these circumstances. It is difficult to relate British sizes to Continental sizes since the boots are usually shaped differently, and there may be variations in the lasts from year to year, but table 2 gives a rough indication:

TABLE 2. *The conversion of boot sizes*

British	4/4½	5/5½	6/6½	7/7½	8/8½	9/9½	10/10½	11/12
Continental	37	38–9	39–40	41	42	43–4	44–5	46–7

Design of uppers. As noted above, the tongue should if possible be sewn in up to the ankle to keep water out. The less outside stitching on the uppers of the boot the better, because it can be damaged by scree and rock friction or may give way simply through rotting (unless it is nylon, the best stitching for mountaineering boots). The Continental design of climbing boot [26 and 50] is very good in this respect. It also has other advantages: the lacing goes right down to the toes, which makes it much easier to get the boots on, especially when they are frozen or very wet; the lacing can also be adjusted more accurately; and the toe is high, giving a welcome freedom to your toes without sacrificing a narrow fitting. Double leather in the uppers is good insulation and protection, but extensive use of sponge rubber is not recommended because it gets very heavy when wet and also takes a long time to dry. Hooks are generally preferred for lacing, because of their speed and ease; they should however not be placed near the toe on climbing boots because they tend to get damaged when foot-jamming in cracks [58A] and also tend to catch in *étriers* during artificial climbing [100]. When lace holes are used remember that square lacing gives more support to the ankles than diagonal lacing. Nylon football-boot laces are conveniently long, and do not rot.

Care of boots. Boots require care and attention if they are to last satisfactorily. The treatment depends upon the type of leather and it is best to treat it in the way that the manufacturer recommends. Dubbing or mars oil can usually be used for softening and waterproofing a new pair of boots, but the treatment should not be continued for long because it may rot the stitching. Silicone polish well rubbed in is the best general treatment. Boots should never be put away wet; they should be dried carefully – not in the direct heat of a fire – and polished. To dry out the insides of the boots stuff them with paper and leave them in a dry, draughty place; replace the paper frequently. Shoe trees will help to preserve the proper shape of the boots. When replacing nails (not a difficult operation, except for clinkers), plug the old holes with plastic wood so that they do not leak.

§ 24. Rucksacks and packframes

As a general principle, a rucksack should be long rather than wide, and the centre of gravity should be high rather than low. It is much less tiring to have the weight *pressing down* on the spine and shoulders rather than to have it *pulling back* from below. The material should be robust and waterproof, but should not be heavier than necessary for the purpose in view (heavier material would be needed for rock climbing than, say, for mountain walking, because the wear is greater). The main flap and any pocket flaps should be big so that they keep out the rain, and the main flap strap should be very long so that it can go over high loads (e.g. a tent, or, in the Alps, loaves of bread) carried on top of the sack. The shoulder-straps should be broad and comfortable. A waist-strap is advisable to prevent the sack swinging to one side if you trip. A long waterproof extension to the sack [10] is useful both for protecting loads carried on the top,

29. *Rucksacks and a packframe.* A. Lightweight knapsack. B. Large framed sack. C. Packframe. The packframe is an experimental one, with separate sack for fuel and stoves, and many other good design features.

and also for use in an emergency bivouac (§§ 11 and 21). The main types of sack are as follows:

Lightweight knapsack [29A]. This usually has two or three outside pockets, and is small and cheap. The design is not very important since it is used mainly for light loads, such as for a day's hill walking or climbing. Instead of a knapsack, some ski-ers and walkers prefer a waist-bag.

Large rucksack with outside pockets [29B]. This is suitable for carrying heavy loads, as for camping, though it is not as good as a packframe (see below) for very heavy loads. Usually these sacks have a frame to keep the load off the back, for comfort and to enable the air to circulate between your back and the sack. The frame must be long enough to allow the cross-strap to rest on the hips and not on the waist (which is relatively weak). Frames are usually 15 ins. (for women) and 17 ins. (for men). Lightweight versions (e.g. the Bergen) can be used for a day in the hills, but the heavy versions are too cumbersome and heavy to be satisfactory for this. It may be noted in passing that the ex-W.D. 'Commando' sack, and its various imitations, is badly designed in that it forces the wearer to bend forward. Framed rucksacks are generally unsuitable for climbing, since the frame can catch on the rock and also keeps the centre of gravity of the sack too far away from your body. In some cases, however, the frame is detachable. Be careful when placing a framed rucksack on the ground, because it is easy to damage the corners of the frame.

Packframe [29C]. This is an excellent way of carrying very heavy or awkwardly shaped loads, since it spreads the weight evenly over the back (i.e. it does not press unduly on any one point) and allows heavy items to be carried very high on the shoulders, the ideal position. In addition – a sobering thought – the frame can be used for supporting the back of an injured man in the event of having to evacuate him by rope stretcher (§ 91). It is too cumbersome and heavy to be used simply for a day on the hills

30. *Climbing rucksacks*. A. 'Don Whillans' by Karrimor. B. Experimental sack in terylene. C. Millet sack. B shows the extra capacity which a bivouac extension gives.

unless the sack can be detached and used separately from the frame. It is possible to make a simple packframe at home, using four pieces of wood for the sides, top, and bottom of the frame, and 2-in. webbing for the cross-straps and shoulder-straps; a kit-bag can be used as the sack.

Climbing sack [30]. This is really essential only for Scottish and alpine climbing, but provided it is large enough to carry bulky loads it is the best buy for the British climber who wants a rucksack suitable for all purposes. It must be long upwards and also narrow. The shoulder-straps should have quick-release buckles at the bottom to allow the sack to be taken off without disturbing a rope coiled over the shoulders. The sack should have straps on the back for attaching the ice-axe, shaft uppermost, when it is not in use, and also a waist-strap to prevent the sack swinging. A D-ring strongly secured to the top of the sack is useful for sack hauling and also so that a karabiner (§ 56) can be inserted into it for clipping the rucksack to the belay when it is taken off on a ledge. There should be no outside pockets, because they tend to catch on rock when hauling or climbing. A waterproof, reinforced bottom is desirable, and a waterproof extension sleeve is an advantage in case of a bivouac.

Packing a rucksack. Make sure that the load is well balanced and that items you will need first (e.g. the tent) are near the top. When using a frameless sack the part nearest your back should be well padded with clothes and should be free from tins, cooking utensils, and other uncomfortable objects. Plastic bags are useful for packing small items, or for keeping sleeping bags and clothing completely dry.

Care of rucksacks. It pays to look after rucksacks carefully. The stitching and straps and, if there is one, the frame should be examined frequently; any holes in the canvas should be repaired immediately in case vital items are lost.

§ 25. Maps for use in Britain

The 2½-in. (about 1 : 25,000) Ordnance Survey map is excellent for very detailed use, for example in locating minor cliffs on complicated hillsides; but for most purposes the 1-in. (1 : 63,360) map is preferable since it gives the detail you need in a concise and logical form. The Ordnance Survey is now publishing a 1 : 50,000 series based on the 1-in. series (which is being withdrawn in some areas); but this cannot be unreservedly recommended if only because the footpaths are sometimes shown in a confusing way (being similar to boundaries, which however pass over cliffs). Scales of less than 1-in. do not give enough detail, though the ½-in. Bartholomew's map is useful for *planning* a tour (S1). There are special Tourist Editions of the 1-in. maps for the Cairngorms, Lorn and Lochaber (Glencoe and Ben Nevis), Loch Lomond and the Trossachs, the Lake District, the North York Moors, the Peak District, and the Wye Valley. The relevant 1-in. maps are listed in chapter 13 and their use is explained in appendix E. In the mountains it is advisable to keep the map in a transparent plastic bag to protect it from wet and wear; in gusty weather, tie the bag to your anorak so that it cannot blow away.

§ 26. Compass

In addition to the map, there should always be at least one
compass in a hill-walking party since this is the only means
of finding direction in mist on featureless ground. An error
of one degree in a compass gives an error of thirty yards in
a mile, so it is necessary to have a compass which is accurate
in use to within a few degrees. Very cheap compasses are
not really good enough. The Army prismatic compass is
very accurate indeed, but it is too heavy and cumbersome
to be used really effectively in mountains, where speed and
simplicity are essential. For mountaineering, one of the
lightweight liquid-filled compasses, such as the Silva or the
Recta, is best. Get the type which has a protractor and
ruler in the base (e.g. Silva 2) since this is very simple and
accurate in use, and eliminates the need for a separate
protractor. Methods of taking bearings with a compass are
described in appendix E; the use of a compass on the hills
is covered in § 9.

31. *The Silva 2 compass.* One of several compasses with a transparent
base-plate.

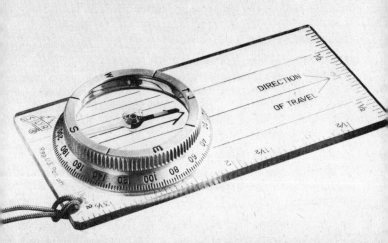

Chapter 4. Living in the British mountains

For a mountain holiday or week-end you will almost always need a firm base near or in the hills. There is an endless variety to choose from, ranging from hotels to sleeping under boulders and camping. The choice between them will depend very much on your mountaineering plans and the time of the year. If you want to visit remote areas far from hotels or huts, then you will probably need to use a bothy or other natural shelter, or to camp or bivouac. Usually, however, in England and Wales the distances involved are small enough to enable you to spend the night under a roof if you wish. The weather is a very important consideration: only the very hardy camp in the late autumn and winter; even at the height of summer rain or gales may make camping unattractive. It is best to be flexible; the mountaineer should acquire camping equipment so that he can camp if he wishes, but should also join the Y.H.A. or a club so that he can get accommodation when he wants to.

§ 27. Accommodation

Hotels. Most mountain districts have inns or hotels, some of which have a time-honoured place in the traditions of mountaineering. Among the most famous are Sligachan (Skye), King's House (Glencoe), Old Dungeon Ghyll and Wastwater (Lake District), and Pen-y-Gwryd (North Wales).

Residential centres. Many on their first visit to the hills will be attending courses at the permanent schools, which provide their own accommodation. These are listed in appendix B.

32. *Idwal Cottage Youth Hostel*. Many climbing hostels, huts, and hotels are also mountain rescue posts (§ 90) and bear the sign shown here.

Youth hostels. The Youth Hostels Association (Y.H.A.) and the Scottish Youth Hostels Association (S.Y.H.A.) have many excellent hostels in mountain areas; Glen Brittle (Skye), Glenmore (Cairngorms), Black Sail (Lake District), and Idwal Cottage [32] and Snowdon Ranger (North Wales) are particularly well sited for mountaineering. Youth hostels are open to all simply by joining one of the associations; the addresses are in appendix B, 1. Most hostels in England and Wales provide inexpensive cooked meals and also the facilities to cook your own; in Scotland, however, they usually provide only the latter. The use of your own motorized transport is not permitted at hostels in England and Wales, though hitch-hiking is not objected to. It is usually best to book in advance.

Mountaineering huts. Many of the mountaineering clubs have huts for the use of their members, details of which are given in their handbooks. Some clubs permit the use of their huts to members of any club which is a B.M.C. member, and a list of these huts is available from the latter (appendix B, 1). They are often very comfortable cottages, with electricity and baths, and are an ideal form of accommodation for mountaineers because there are no restrictions as to the time when you may leave in the morning or return in the evening (a great advantage on a short winter – or a long summer – day). It is necessary to cook your own food. The huts in this country are run by voluntary wardens and it is important for all occupants to do their full share of hut chores and to leave the huts clean for subsequent parties. At busy periods it is often advisable to book in advance, and in some cases this is compulsory at all times.

Many hotels, schools, hostels, and huts are also mountain rescue posts. These are marked on recent O.S. maps as such and usually bear the sign shown in [32].

§ 28. Bothies and natural shelters

In Scotland, particularly in the Cairngorms, there are many bothies in the remote areas. These range from well-built shelters to old shacks. Recently, a number of emergency shelters have been built for ski-ers and climbers. There are no blankets or cooking utensils provided, though it is customary to leave spare tinned food (unopened) behind so that parties in need can at least keep body and soul together. Caves or recesses under large boulders also provide natural shelters; the most famous of the latter is the Shelter Stone at Loch Avon in the Cairngorms, which unfortunately, however, is often wet. Bothies or natural shelters are a great help to the hill-walking or climbing party which wants to travel long distances without being burdened by the weight of a tent. Their position is usually marked on the 1-in. O.S. maps, but it may be hard to find them without local knowledge. It is advisable also to check that a bothy is still usable before starting out. In depopulated areas, disused cottages can be useful.

§ 29. Camping

This section is written on the assumption that you already have some general camping experience. If not, the general technique is given in the books listed in the bibliography, 6.

Nowadays many mountaineers camp habitually on their week-ends or holidays in the hills, either because there is no suitable accommodation available, or to save money, or simply for the pleasure and freedom of movement it gives. The amount of equipment needed will depend very much on whether the camp is a standing camp in a valley (near to the road and transport), a standing camp high up in the hills to serve as a base for sorties, or a moving camp or bivouac. In the latter cases weight is a very important consideration, and the camper will be unable to take more than is absolutely essential; indeed some campers do not even take a tent, relying on a polythene bag or other simple cover instead. Solitary camping high up in the hills is not recommended; a party of four is ideal so that someone can raise

33. *Close to nature and the mountains.* A 'Good Companion' tent near the Pyg Track on Snowdon. Note the boulders on the tent pegs.

the alarm if an accident should occur in a remote place while walking or climbing from the camp. Be careful at all times of the risk of fire: candles, stoves, and fuel containers can easily cause mishaps.

Restrictions on camping. In the hills, there is generally no restriction of camping, though there may be occasional exceptions as, for example, during the grouse season or on Forestry Commission land. In some mountain valleys, however, the local authorities have found it necessary to confine camping to approved sites where usually they aim to provide drinking water, toilets, parking and litter-disposal facilities. In those valleys where camping is freely allowed, it is courteous to secure the farmer's permission before pitching your tent, and to offer to pay him for the privilege. Be most careful not to pollute the water supply or to leave rubbish after you have left. If possible, take your rubbish with you, but if not, then bury it. Obvious though it may seem, it is perhaps worth mentioning that it is no good burying rubbish in the snow in winter, since the snow does not last for ever, and eventually an unsightly pile of rubbish comes into view.

Bad weather. The main difficulty in mountain camping is the British weather (§ 8); wind and rain are common and incredibly hard conditions can result. Very few tents are able to withstand driving rain completely unless a fly-sheet is used. A spare change of clothing should always be taken and kept in the tent in wet weather (inside a rucksack or polythene bag to keep it dry). The temptation to put on your spare change on the second wet or doubtful day, instead of the clothes wetted the day before, should be resisted. Damp clothes can be put on again without ill-effect provided you move off straight away and keep warm. Much can be done to dry clothes, with lavish expenditure of fuel and some sacrifice of comfort, by hanging wet clothes up in the tent and keeping the stove going. But no matter how hardy or ingenious you are, it will not usually be possible to continue walking or climbing from a camp for more than about three or four days in bad weather. A lightly equipped bivouac is even more vulnerable. In really bad weather, especially on sites remote from shelter, don't be pig-headed about maintaining the camp. If the evacuation route is over difficult ground it is more sensible to beat a retreat in time rather than get washed out in the middle of the night. In compensation for the hardships which high mountain camping involves, however, you will have the benefit of being much closer to your hill walks or climbs, and will enjoy a new freedom and closeness to the mountains which is one of the most rewarding aspects of camping.

Winter camping. In winter, conditions are often arctic (§ 13), and special equipment and a good deal of experience and toughness are required. It will be only in very exceptional circumstances that a long camp will be undertaken in winter conditions; if the snow is well consolidated a snow-hole (§ 21) may prove a good deal more comfortable than a tent because it is not affected by wind and keeps reasonably warm when occupied, but tents are generally preferable because snow-holes take two hours or so to make and you will get wet in the process.

The camp site. In choosing and preparing the site you must guard against the worst imaginable conditions – sooner or later they will arrive. In general it is not sound to pitch a tent at a good viewpoint, since this rarely gives the wind shelter which you will need in a gale. Try to find somewhere protected by boulders or a small rise. The entrance to a cwm will often provide good sites with large boulders and hillocks for protection, and with a stream or a lake near by for water and possibly bathing. There is often a calm area high up on the mountain, on the lee side just below the summit, but usually the higher you are the colder and more windy it is. The site must be free from objective dangers, such as rockfalls or, in winter, avalanches (§ 18). It should be dry and not liable to flooding. Hollows and ground very

close to watercourses should be avoided, as mountain streams can rise very rapidly in bad weather and overflow. Do not camp close to the edge of a lake since a strong wind may whip water off the lake and soak the tent. For a few days' camping it is worth while building a wall of boulders on the windward side of the tent. In winter, a wall of snow blocks can be very useful instead, but a wall should not be used if new snow is falling or if snow is drifting since it would result in snow piling on top of the tent. Level sites are rare, but only a very uncomfortable camp can be pitched on a steep hillside, and if you have no choice it is usually worth while building a level platform of rocks and turf as a foundation for the floor of the tent. In snow, it is relatively easy to dig out a level patch. In wet weather it may be necessary also to dig drainage channels uphill from the tent to divert water seeping down the hillside. Pitch the tent with the entrance away from the wind. Put boulders on the valance to hold the tent down, and also on top of the pegs [33].

§ 30. Camping equipment: the tent

The tent is vastly important. A mountaineer's whole enjoyment may be spoiled by anxiety as to the stability of his tent during the day when he is away, or at night when he should be asleep. It must be robust and weatherproof, but not so heavy that it cannot be carried to where he wants to use it. Twelve pounds is about the average weight for a mountain tent with poles and sewn-in groundsheet. The tent should give the maximum protection and room to cook

34. *A Commando winter camp in Coire Cas (Cairngorms)*. The slope at the head of a coire is often more sheltered than the level lower parts. It may make a good camp site if platforms can be dug out of the slope, as in this case. Make sure that the slope is not likely to avalanche before weakening it by digging. Keep each hole as small as possible to minimize the risk of wind-blown snow drifting over the tents. Note the ice-axes holding down the main guys. The tent in the foreground is an Arctic Guinea with A-poles.

and sit up in relative to its weight. An extension at one end is useful for stowing gear.

Design of the tent. A two-man tent is usual. Generally, the less complicated and easier to erect it is the better. The best shape is the **A** shape, with at least one and preferably two **A**-poles. Framed **A**-tents have been used very successfully in the Himalayas (by the 1963 U.S. Everest Expedition, among others) but the only framed tents in common use in this country at the moment are rather large. Pneumatic tents have been used successfully, but suffer from the disadvantage that the air-tubing may get damaged. **A**-tents with a double roof (the two thicknesses of canvas being an inch or two apart) are warm and dry, but are expensive and rather difficult to obtain; a fly-sheet (see below) is the usual alternative. The ridge of an **A**-tent should be very strong, and can usefully be roped or made in double or triple canvas to ensure rigidity. The tent should have side walls about ten inches high, preferably with eaves, so that the rain does not run down the lower walls on to the groundsheet. Pockets along the inside of the lower walls are extremely useful for putting odd things out of hand, but unfortunately do not seem to have found favour with British tent manufacturers. There should be an outside valance or sod cloth at least six inches wide on which to put rocks, turf, or snow to prevent the wind getting under the tent. Good ventilation is necessary to reduce condensation and also to avoid the possibility of carbon monoxide poisoning when cooking by paraffin or petrol stove inside the tent. A sleeve entrance keeps out the wind best, and also helps to keep out midges in summer. Another advantage is that if two tents with sleeve entrances are pitched facing each other, the entrances can be linked to form a communicating tunnel. For winter camping there should ideally be a sleeve entrance at each end of the tent, so that clean snow can be brought in from one end for cooking and so on and refuse can be deposited temporarily at the other; this would, however, add to the cost of the tent. There should be plenty of guys and all guy points (and other points of stress) on the tent should be taped. Nylon or terylene guys are best since they give a little under strain, but do not rot or shrink when wet. Usually, metal runners are fitted so that the guys can be adjusted, but these are not required with nylon or terylene guys as the Tarbuck knot [168] is ideal for this purpose. It is best to attach the single end of the guy to the tent so that the adjustable bight can be placed round boulders when the ground is too hard for pegs. Remember to take plenty of spare guy line and pegs. The groundsheet should be sewn in and ought to come about three to six inches up the walls and across the entrance; this prevents water flowing in over the valance. About one quarter of the groundsheet should be attached to the bottom of the tent by press-studs so that it can be folded back for the putting on and taking off of boots, and for cooking.

The materials used in a tent must be strong and durable, and should so far as possible be waterproof and windproof, while allowing the tent to breathe so that condensation is kept to a minimum. Closely woven fabrics are best. Ordinary cotton is the cheapest material, and provided it is well water-proofed is quite satisfactory (it is perhaps worth mentioning that some tent manufacturers do not automatically water-proof their tents, since they may be used in the Himalayas or other very high mountains where not rain but snow is usual; it is most important to check that any tent you buy is proofed). Pure nylon and terylene are not recommended for tent (as distinct from fly-sheet) materials as they cannot be waterproofed without stopping them breathing; they are also rather difficult to stitch, so that guys tend to pull off under strain. A possible way of reconciling the various requirements using standard inexpensive materials and construction is to use rubberized fabric (or waterproofed nylon or terylene) for the upper sloping surfaces of the tent, but to make the walls and door out of cotton or other material which breathes well. Russian tents are made like this, and are watertight and windproof, yet not particularly prone to condensation. The groundsheet should be of heavy-duty plastic or other fully waterproof material and should be replaced when worn.

A fly-sheet will keep out the rain and hence make it unnecessary to avoid touching the inner walls of the tent in bad weather. It also helps to keep the tent cool in very hot, windless weather. However, it adds weight, tends to be costly, and may prove troublesome in a strong wind. It is best made of completely waterproof lightweight material such as polyurethane or waterproofed terylene, and should come down to the ground at the sides so that the wind cannot easily get under it.

Tent poles. As noted above, exterior A-poles are recommended. These give stability and avoid taking up valuable space inside the tent. The joints and grummet must be mechanically sound. A-poles need to be stronger than single (vertical) poles, particularly if they are fitted into sleeves in the tent, since the wind on the tent can cause a high sideways force to be applied to the poles with a risk of bending or breaking. Duralumin poles are very strong. The individual sections should not be longer than fifteen inches; special rubber or spring connectors can save much time in fitting them together. The bottom ends of the poles should slot into the tent valance. If lightness is at a premium, one A-pole and one single pole will do; for moving camps in winter poles can, if necessary, be replaced by ice-axes (tied together to give the necessary length, or combined with one section of a pole), skis, or ski sticks.

Tent pegs. Steel bulldog pegs are best for ordinary use. On very stony ground where it is not possible to insert pegs, the guys can be tied round heavy boulders instead. In snow, wide pegs at least fifteen inches long are required; but, for moving camps, crampons, ice pitons, or ice hammers can be buried in the snow instead.

Choosing a tent. Don't be impetuous in buying a tent: they are expensive and you will need to be able to use yours for a long time. It would, for example, be wasteful to buy a tent suitable only for valley camping if you later found that you wanted a tent which could be used for high mountain camping or for winter camping. Look at tents when they are in use in the mountains, and if possible discuss their merits and disadvantages with their owners. For high camping or winter camping the best British tents available at the time of writing are probably the Meade (Benjamin Edgington Ltd), the Arctic Guinea [34] and the Mountain (Thos. Black Ltd). The Good Companion (Thos. Black Ltd – [33]) with sewn-in groundsheet and exterior A-pole, the Itisa (Camtors Ltd), and the Mummery (Benjamin Edgington Ltd) are suitable for lower camps. Very light-weight tents such as the Tinker (Thos. Black Ltd) or the Solite are good for temporary, lightweight camps in summer, but are too light for prolonged bad weather. Most of the tents referred to here have been in production for a very long time and can thus be regarded as well proven, though not necessarily of the most modern design. Some French tents are very good also. Ex-Army bivouac tents are cheap and can be modified fairly easily at home (with extra guys for storm-setting and for extra space) to make them suitable for mountain use. They are however rather heavy and too low for comfort.

Lightweight bivouac sacks are dealt with in § 124.

§ 31. Camping equipment: sleeping gear

A good-quality sleeping bag is a sound investment. To combine compactness and lightness with warmth, the best bags are filled with down (not feathers or kapok). Although terylene filling is not as warm as down, weight for weight, or as compact, it is the second-best filling because of the ease with which it can be dried out or cleaned. The bag should be roomy and for cold conditions should cover the head.

Box-join   Heat loss
                           Ordinary join

35. *Why a box-pleated sleeping bag is warmer than an ordinary one.*

The top should be secured with a draw tape, with a toggle for easy adjustment. Ideally the stitching of the compartments containing the down should not join the inner and outer walls of the covering together, since heat would be lost through the stitching [35]. Instead, an inner partition about one inch high should be placed at each joint so that the two containing walls are not brought into contact with each other; these are called 'boxed joints' [35]. In cold weather, two sleeping bags may be necessary; but a more flexible alternative is to use a down (*duvet*) jacket and short sleeping bag (§ 124) inside the main bag, since the *duvet* jacket can be used for winter climbing or alpine climbing as well as for sleeping in. The cheapest alternative, however, is to use a flannelette or wool inner bag, made from a blanket. It is important to insulate yourself from ground cold, particularly when using a down bag, because the down is easily compressed (and thereby made less efficient) where your body lies on it; sweaters, newspapers, and air or foam mattresses (see below) are good insulation. It is difficult to keep a sleeping bag clean when camping and a cotton outer cover and inner lining can be used to protect it. On the mountain, a sleeping bag should be kept in a waterproof bag when not in use. But it should be unrolled when being stored at home so that the down can expand. Always air a sleeping bag after dry-cleaning since it may retain poisonous fumes.

An inflatable air mattress is comfortable and also a good insulator, and helps to keep you off the floor when there is water on the groundsheet. It need not be full length: from shoulder to hip is all that is really necessary. Take repair equipment and a spare stopper.

A foam rubber pad is a good alternative, especially for insulation. It should be about three feet by two feet (two pads taped together can be used if desired). A thickness of one inch is comfortable but a quarter of an inch (as used for carpet underlay) is sufficient for insulation. It should preferably be covered with plastic sheeting as otherwise the foam absorbs moisture like a sponge. Such a pad can also be very comfortable if placed next to your back when carrying a heavy load in a frameless rucksack.

If no form of mattress is used, dig a small hole for the hip.

§ 32. Camping equipment: stoves, fuel, and cooking utensils

Your stove must be reliable and should preferably be broad based so as not to upset easily. A paraffin one-pint or half-pint stove is the most reliable and safest, and gives a very hot flame; a disadvantage is that it needs methylated spirits or meta fuel for priming. Petrol stoves work effectively, but some types have been known to catch fire or explode. A good deal of care must be taken to protect them from damage. When they are in use they should not be allowed to build up excessive pressure or to overheat; any release valve on the stove must be kept closed until the stove is completely extinguished because of the risk that highly inflammable hot petrol vapour might be ignited by the flame. Lightweight petrol stoves do not have a pump and take rather longer than paraffin ones to reach full pressure. Gas stoves are becoming increasingly popular; the uncertainty of obtaining replacement canisters in remote places and the relative dearness of the fuel must however be offset against the advantages of cleanliness and speed. In cold weather, a gas stove can conveniently be switched on for a few moments in the night to warm the tent; but it is essential to use propane and not butane because the latter will not light below about $-1\,°C$. Possible dangers with a gas stove are that it might be turned on unwittingly, the valve might jam open (as, for example, if sand gets into it), or the canister might get damaged, with the result that gas escapes in the tent and explodes when a match is struck. Whichever type of stove you use, always ensure adequate ventilation, especially if cooking in a van, to avoid carbon monoxide poisoning or oxygen starvation. Carry spares such as a jet, washers and prickers, and matches in a waterproof container. See § 124 for lightweight bivouac stoves.

Fuel. Paraffin (kerosene) or petrol should be kept in a rigid polythene or, preferably, nylon bottle with a secure top. It is best carried in an outside pocket of the rucksack, away from food and clothing. It should be kept outside the tent and out of the sun, particularly if it contains petrol. Tractor Vaporizing Oil (T.V.O.) is a satisfactory alternative to paraffin, and may be available on remote farms when paraffin is not. On no account use petrol in a paraffin stove. Petrol stoves usually run better on commercial-grade petrol than on higher octane petrols because lead in the latter may block the jet.

Pots, pans, and utensils. Many of the standard nesting sets of billies are too small and too complicated for mountain use. A two- or three-pint pot will save much time in making stews and tea, and space in your rucksack need not be wasted because fragile items such as eggs can be packed inside it. If a frying-pan is taken it should preferably be of *cast*, not rolled, aluminium since this is porous and absorbs fat, with the result that it does not stick so easily. A universal grip (e.g. Bulldog type) is invaluable. Plates will probably be unnecessary since lids of billies will serve. Mugs should preferably be one-pint plastic as they retain heat longer and have a wide base. Where the party is large, each member's cutlery and mugs should be marked and used only by him: it is difficult to wash them really clean in camp conditions and if used communally they can serve to pass germs among the party, causing stomach upsets. Don't forget a tin opener: the Nippy Baby Can Opener is lightest and best; it also opens tins neatly so that they can be used as additional receptacles. A lightweight water bucket is useful. The handles can be clipped to a tent guy to stop it overturning. A lightweight vacuum flask is a boon in really bad conditions for a welcome hot drink in the middle of the night.

§ 33. Food

The food required for a day's hill walking or climbing has been dealt with in § 4. The choice of food for a camping holiday or a week-end in a climbing hut or in a Scottish youth hostel, where usually no meals are provided, depends very much on personal taste. The main requirements are that food should:

- be light and easy to carry and store. For this, dried and dehydrated foods are best (e.g. potato powder instead of potatoes and biscuits in place of bread). Screwtop tins (used drug tins, often obtainable in a variety of sizes from chemists, are excellent) and plastic bags should be used as containers;
- be easy to cook, to save time and fuel. Pre-cooked foods are particularly useful. Boiling and frying make up camp cooking, but in some of the better equipped huts you can roast, grill, and bake as well;
- contain plenty of carbohydrate and protein, especially in cold weather. The absence of fresh fruit does not matter for a few days, but for longer spells you should ensure that your diet is reasonably balanced, since otherwise you will start losing strength. Vitamin C tablets are useful when fruit is scarce.

You will be having only two main meals a day, so make sure that they give the bulk and warmth you need. Porridge is very good for breakfast: it can be cooked with condensed milk, etc., or alternatively can be eaten uncooked, simply with the addition of hot milk; the latter method has the advantage that it leaves the pan clean, and saves fuel.

Sausages, bacon, and eggs are fine but large quantities are needed if they are to keep you going throughout the day. In the evening, a stew is the usual meal. It should be based on dried soups and meat, with a little onion or carrot, perhaps, or meat extract or bouillon cubes thrown in to flavour it. Pemmican is useful in extreme cold or when very long carries are involved but is not normally necessary or desirable. Great progress has been made in recent years with the processing of dried vegetables, with the result that they can now be eaten with very little pre-soaking, but if you are using the older types, remember to soak them over-night. Jam is useful for the sweet course. Drink plenty of well-sweetened tea or other beverages. When camping as a group, it is pleasant to put the tents face to face so that each pair can cook one of the courses of the main meals.

Part two

Climbing in Britain

The British hills offer a wide variety of climbing, much of it reasonably accessible for week-ends from our big cities. This part aims to give an up-to-date summary of the climbing techniques and equipment currently in use, in summer and in winter. It also describes the main climbing areas and mountain rescue procedures.

The personal element is tremendously important in climbing. The climber must temper boldness with prudence, so that while he exploits his potentialities to the full, he recognizes the narrow margin between safety and danger and adjusts his plans accordingly. The necessary judgement can only be developed by experience.

It is assumed that the would-be climber has already mastered the elements of mountain craft by hill walking in summer and winter and by scrambling on easy ridges. Such an apprenticeship is desirable on aesthetic as well as technical grounds because it is the best way to that deeper appreciation of the hills which gives strength and permanence to what might otherwise be no more than a temporary or passing attraction to the excitements of climbing.

Chapter 5. Climbing in Britain

Most climbing, particularly on the easier climbs, is not as dramatic as it might appear. From a distance, a cliff may look quite blank, particularly if the sun is shining on it so that the features are not thrown into relief. But on closer acquaintance it will be found that the cliff is split into buttresses and that there are many ledges. It is an understandable failing of mountain photographers to avoid showing these ledges in photographs, which as a result frequently give an exaggerated impression of the effective drop below the climber. Between the ledges there are sections of rock ('pitches'), but these are often split by chimneys and cracks, and in any case the rock is almost always rough to the touch, with holds on it for hands and feet.

There is a great variety of climbable rock within fairly easy reach of our big cities, so that with modern means of transport it is possible for enthusiasts to climb regularly at week-ends throughout the year, and in some cases on outcrops on summer mid-week evenings as well. This is perhaps the main reason why the standard of achievement on British rock is very high. Another factor is our concentration on pure technique, made possible by the relatively small scale of our cliffs, most of which are in the range 100–500 ft; because of this smallness of scale certain alpine time-saving techniques (e.g. pitons – § 68) have not become popular here. The British custom of climbing in bad weather as well as good (reducing the standard of the climb

36. *The Isle of Skye: a mountaineer's paradise (on the Bhasteir Tooth, part of the Cuillin Ridge).* Competence in rock climbing, even at a moderate standard, opens up a whole new world of mountaineering which is closed to the hill walker.

attempted to suit the conditions) doubtless also helps to improve the all-round level of competence.

In winter, the scope for rock climbing is much more limited, because even the lower rocks are cold and greasy, and snow and ice and *verglas* are common. On the other hand, there are often good opportunities for snow and ice climbing, particularly in Scotland where excellent climbing can be found throughout the winter.

§ 34. The development of climbing in Britain

The techniques now used in British climbing are the result of three quarters of a century of development, during which more and more has been learned about technique, and new practices have been adopted only to be discarded in favour of newer ones.

I. ROCK CLIMBING

The early days and the gully era. In the early days of climbing the obvious ridges were ascended and the easier ribs and buttresses were attempted. This was in line with developments in the Alps and indeed most climbers then were principally interested in alpine climbing. Attention subsequently turned to the great rifts and gullies, and rock climbing entered the 'gully era'. Gullies are usually dark, greasy places, frequently with water running down them. But they usually have large ledges at frequent intervals and the enclosing walls give a sense of security. As a result, a very high standard indeed was reached in this type of climbing. The Great Gully on Craig yr Ysfa, Walker's Gully on Pillar Rock, and the Water Pipe Gully in Skye were all products of this era, being first climbed around the turn of the century.

Balance climbing on slabs and walls. As men gained confidence and equipment improved, so the centre of interest moved

37. *Where it all began.* The Napes Needle, first climbed by W. P. Haskett-Smith in 1886, and now nail-worn and smooth. Needle Ridge, a Difficult, is the skyline ridge behind the Needle. See also 4.

from gullies to slabs (rock at an angle of 30–60 degrees – see [60]), and the art of balance climbing was developed, i.e. the ability to move up on small footholds rather than by pulling up and taking the weight on hands and arms. Steeper and steeper slabs were climbed and eventually even sheer walls. Climbers by now were learning not to be afraid of 'exposure' over a considerable drop, which tries the nerves and so reduces a climber's ability to climb well and easily. We now know that a climber can get accustomed to exposure at any height, so that he can climb near to the limit of his ability no matter how exposed the pitch. Exceptional achievements in this period included the first ascents of Botterill's Slab (1903) and Central Buttress (1914) on Scafell. Between the two World Wars the technique of slab climbing, with long run-outs, great exposure, and the hazards of grass and bad rock making it thoroughly serious mountaineering, reached a very high level of development. At the same time more and more difficult cracks were climbed though not with any substantial advance in technique. Outstanding achievements at this time included the exploration of the West and East Buttresses of Clogwyn du'r Arddu ('Cloggy') and of the East Buttress of Scafell, all of which required climbing skill and determination of the highest order. C. F. Kirkus, M. Linnell, and J. M. Edwards took the major part in this.

The 1940s. During the War there was little civilian climbing but the mountains were used for training troops, and some notable exploration was done by the instructors, many of whom had been civilian climbers before the War. In Wales, for example, instructors did the first ascents of Suicide Wall in Cwm Idwal and Sheaf Climb on Clogwyn du'r Arddu. When peace returned, the number of people going to the hills increased, but it took some time for standards to start

38. *Asterisk.* A short Very Severe (§ 35) on Gimmer Crag, Langdale (Lake District).

39. *Clogwyn du'r Arddu (North Wales)*. One of the most impressive crags in Britain, with some of our hardest climbs and no easy ones. The East Buttress and the Pinnacle (on the left) give crack and wall climbing, while the West Buttress (on the right) is famous for its very exposed slabs.

rising again, partly no doubt because of the difficulty of week-end climbing with petrol and food rationing. New equipment such as nylon rope and the rubber-soled ('Commando') boot helped confidence to increase, and there were tremendous improvements in rope technique with the thoroughgoing application of the running belay (§ 63), and with the introduction of the sliding friction arrest, mainly by K. Tarbuck (§ 62). Climbers like A. R. Dolphin, P. R. J. Harding, and A. J. J. Moulam led the way and did much new exploration, generally on steeper cliffs than had been in vogue before the War.

The 1950s and early 1960s. In the 1950s, the standard of rock climbing took another great surge forward, based on the new techniques and attitudes of Joe Brown, Don Whillans, and their colleagues. These improved techniques have been evident in all forms of climbing, but perhaps the most significant were the improved methods of crack climbing by

40. *On Clogwyn du'r Arddu.* Joe Brown on the Steep Band.

jamming which enabled extremely steep and hitherto hopeless cracks to be ascended. In the early 1960s the number of climbers capable of achieving the hardest routes in the country has increased considerably, as part of an overall improvement in the standard of achievement, and the standard of the first ascents has also continued to rise. Unfortunately there has been some tendency for pitons to be used for assistance on climbs which had previously been led without them (§ 61). Since the War the main developments have been on Clogwyn du'r Arddu, filling in some of the gaps left in the 1930s, but new cliffs have also been developed, ranging from the Three Cliffs of Llanberis to Castle Rock, Thirlmere, and many more besides. The postwar period has also seen the intensive development of other important climbing areas, such as Ben Nevis and Glencoe, and the beginnings of high-standard exploration in Ireland. At the same time, cliffs outside the main mountain areas – on gritstone, the Avon Gorge, and in Cornwall – have continued to yield many new routes and to contribute to the further development of climbing techniques.

2. ARTIFICIAL* CLIMBING ('PEGGING')

As British climbers have come to appreciate the importance of piton climbing for major alpine climbs, so new practice grounds have been opened up, in quarries and on limestone. In the Peak District (§ 105) there is gritstone pegging at Lawrencefield Quarry and Millstone Edge (near Hathersage), and limestone pegging in, for example, Dovedale, Miller's Dale and at Matlock High Tor. In the Pennines (§ 105) there is extremely impressive climbing at Gordale Scar, Kilnsey Crag, and Malham Cove; these provide hard

---

* Climbing is 'artificial' if artificial aids such as pitons or wedges are used for direct aid (by contrast with 'free' climbing). The term 'artificial' is also used in an entirely different sense to describe a climb from which it is easy to escape by traversing off, or where difficulties can be avoided.

41. *A typical post-war discovery: Craig Bwlch y Moch, Tremadoc (North Wales).* This cliff gives steep hard climbs, close to the road. As it is low down and away from the main mountain mass it often has good weather when it is raining on the traditional cliffs.

and possibly dangerous climbing, reputed to be as serious as any likely to be encountered in the Alps. There are further possibilities at Swanage and Avon Gorge (§ 108), and numerous quarries. An interesting – and welcome – recent development is that quite a number of free climbs have been found on these crags, sometimes on lines previously climbed with pitons. The equipment and techniques needed for piton climbing are quite separate from the techniques traditionally used in British rock climbing (except that pitons are sometimes used on traditional routes for belays – § 61) and are dealt with separately in chapter 9.

3. SNOW AND ICE CLIMBING

Most of the standard gullies and ridges were climbed early on. Modern snow and ice climbing on major Scottish routes began in the 1930s; but in the post-war period there has been much new exploration involving very advanced techniques, both in the steepest and longest gullies, and on exposed faces which give hard climbing even in summer. The standard has risen even further in recent years with the fuller exploitation of new equipment such as the Terrodactyl ice-axe which gives much greater security on very steep terrain [119]. Inevitably, locally based climbers have taken the lead, J. Cunningham, H. MacInnes, W. March, J. Marshall and the late T. W. Patey and R. Smith being among the most prominent.

The titles of the main books relating to the development of British climbing are in the bibliography, 2 and 3.

§ 35. Guide-books and standards

Guide-books. The state of exploration is recorded in the climbing guide-books, which have been written by experts and published by the climbing clubs. They are listed in chapter 13. A guide-book gives a wealth of information about an area, in summer and winter, and about the cliffs and the climbs. It describes each cliff in general and tells you how to get there. There are photographs or drawings showing the climbing routes and the ways down. If the illustrations are good you will be able to tell from them which routes take an attractive line, before checking from the text as to what they involve. The text gives the length of the climb, together with descriptions of the individual pitches on it. It almost always tells you where the most difficult section (the 'crux') is, and often gives an indication of the nature of the difficulty. Perhaps most important of all, it tells you the approximate standard of the climb.

Standards. Since the early days of climbing, the climbs in this country have been graded so that any experienced climber coming new to the district could assess the difficulty of the climbs. The grading has to take account of all the relevant factors: technical difficulty, exposure, the security and frequency of belays, length of run-outs, and the quality of the rock. It always assumes perfect conditions for the climb, i.e. dry rock and a reasonably warm and windless day. Although the standards given are on the whole accurate, particularly on the easier routes, one should never regard them as more than an approximate indication of the difficulty of the climb. Any worsening of the conditions, for example, as by wind or rain, may increase the standard disproportionately, in exceptional cases by as much as two standards, but normally by at least one standard. Moreover, different men (e.g. tall men and short men) and different classification systems may lead to considerable variations in standards. This is particularly the case as between areas: the guide-book writer will be fully at home on the local rock and will have adjusted his technique to it so that he may find it rather easier than would someone coming new to the area. You must evaluate the gradings in the guide-book in relation to your own assessment of the difficulties when you use it for the first time, to see whether it grades climbs easier or harder than you would expect. Do not assume that because you can do climbs of a particular standard in one area you can necessarily do climbs which are given the same standard in all other areas.

The classification generally used today stems from that introduced into the Lake District by Owen Glynne-Jones around the turn of the century. It is, in increasing order of difficulty:

Easy	(E.)
Moderate	(Mod.)
Difficult	(D. or Diff.)
Very Difficult	(V.D. or V. Diff.)
Severe	(S.)
Very Severe	(V.S.)

Often further qualifications are used to denote gradations

42. *The Gribin Facet* (*Ogwen, North Wales*). This short cliff has *inter alia* several Difficult and Very Difficult chimney climbs which are not much affected by bad weather.

within a category; for example, the Severe grade may be split into Easy (or 'Mild') Severe, Severe, and Hard Severe.

This system works well enough for climbs up to Hard Severe standard; above that it becomes increasingly difficult to classify a climb because differences of technique, build, and strength between climbers mean that what one finds hard, another may find relatively easy. In any case the range of difficulty of climbs of Very Severe and above is probably as great as of all the lower standards put together and becomes greater each year as the standard of achievement among the very best climbers is raised. To allow for this other categories above Very Severe have sometimes been used. For example, some of the Climbers' Club's guide-books have used Extremely Severe and Exceptionally Severe, the latter being reserved for the most serious climbs of the day. The difficulty about this is that the supply of superlatives required to describe newer standards is too limited. Another system, used by the Fell and Rock Climbing Club, is to draw up a classified list of all routes in ascending order of difficulty: however, a margin of error of between five and ten places in the scale must be assumed, to allow for individual variations. The system employed by the Guide Vallot for the French Alps (§ 116, 1) has not found favour in this country but is in many ways the most logical, flexible, and expressive. This is to grade the technical standard of any one pitch by numbers (for which, in the nature of things, there is no limit – a big advantage) but to describe the overall difficulty of the climb in words. This is, however, a field where opinions flourish, and as a climber you will have many an interesting hour discussing the merits and demerits of the various guide-books and their writers!

Artificial climbs (chapter 9) are usually graded on the French system (A1, A2, etc – see § 116, 1).

Because of the great variety of conditions in winter, snow and ice climbs are not usually graded in the same way as rock climbs, though the guide-books sometimes give a rough indication of the range of difficulty. There is an interesting departure in the case of the New Series S.M.C. guides to the Cairngorms and to Ben Nevis, which grade snow and ice climbs by numbers.

§ 36. The personal element

The personal element is tremendously important in climbing. It is one of the freest of sports in that it is entirely up to you and your colleagues on the rope to make your own decisions in the light of your judgement of the situation at the time. To take responsibility in this way when the rewards and the penalties are both high is one of the most satisfying of the attractions of climbing. At the same time the fact that things can so easily go badly wrong means that you must prepare yourself thoroughly in experience, in techniques, and physically, and that you must exercise a good deal of judgement and self-discipline when you are on the mountain, so that you always keep within your safety margin.

Experience. As noted earlier, it is advisable to get to know the hills by hill walking and scrambling before taking up climbing proper. When you do start, recognize your own inexperience and make every effort to get an experienced climber to introduce you to the sport, going on a course if necessary. Begin with the simplest climbs (see § 37 below) and move on to harder ones only when your experience and skill have built up.

Mental approach. Almost anyone can make a climber provided he or she has the will to climb, the necessary temperament, and average strength and agility. The will to climb is the most important: climbing is often uncomfortable and tiring and there is always a certain element of risk; you have to be genuinely keen to take it up and you must be willing to put up with the hardships and difficulties as well as to enjoy the pleasures. Some of the greatest climbers have been nervous and excitable, but most people would find an equable temperament a considerable asset because undue outpourings of nervous energy can lead to exhaustion just as quickly as physical exertion can.

Physique and fitness. The easier rock climbing or snow and ice work does not require any special physique. Much more important than brute strength is balance and agility, which together enable you to move with the maximum economy of effort. Most of the very best rock climbers, however, have a very good power–weight ratio, with considerable strength in the hands and arms; they also have the ability to recover their strength rapidly so that they can safely undertake a long series of strenuous moves with only short rests in between. Always try to keep reasonably fit by

43. *A climbing corner.* It is not necessary to be on a cliff to practise climbing. (For further information see *Artificial Climbing Walls* by Kim Meldrum and Brian Royle, Pelham Books, 1970, £1·25.)

walking as much as possible. City-dwellers can benefit by making a habit of using stairs instead of lifts. Outcrop climbing is probably the best training for climbing proper, but much can be done at home, for example by pull-ups on door lintels, or by press-ups. Finger exercises with a finger strengthener or with a tennis ball can also be useful. It should be noted that the effect of fitness and strength is cumulative; because you feel confident in your strength, you do not hesitate so much in working out a move or a series of moves, with the result that you do not use so much energy and therefore remain well within your safety margin. Each individual needs a certain level of strength and should try to develop it if he does not possess it initially.

A climber's generation. It is an interesting debating point as to how far a climber is the product of his own generation. There can be little doubt that men like Owen Glynne-Jones, Herford, Edwards, Kirkus, and Linnell, each of whom was among the very finest performers of his generation, would also achieve the top rank were they starting afresh today;

yet today's climbs are much harder than theirs. In practice, it seems that each climber starts with the preconceived attitudes of his own generation, and that the average competent climber finds it most difficult to switch his approach to that of the next generation, no matter how hard he tries. Some very brilliant climbers who started in the 1940s have succeeded in this, and are achieving climbs of the highest standards of the present day, but they are few and far between. It is therefore important for any serious would-be climber to start off with a knowledge of what is new and best in climbing, without restricting himself to the techniques and attitudes of earlier generations where they have been changed for the better since. At the same time, the basic principles have not changed, and this book endeavours to bring out the best of both present and past.

§ 37. Rock-climbing equipment and methods

Equipment. A climber usually needs all the equipment listed in § 4, since most rock climbing in the mountains also involves hill walking. On a cold day, additional clothing will be needed because climbing tends to be a slow process. Leather gloves are required for tending the rope. A safety helmet (§ 123) is strongly recommended to help protect you both from falling stones (nowadays a serious hazard, particularly on some easy routes, as a result of the increasing traffic) and in the event of a head-first fall. Well-fitting, well-designed footwear is essential [§ 23]. Cleated rubber-soled boots or lightweight boots or rubbers [51] are now the standard footwear for British, as for alpine, rock. A 120-ft $1\frac{3}{8}$-in. nylon rope (or preferably two 120-ft $1\frac{1}{4}$-in. ones) is recommended for the leader (§ 51) and the party should have slings and karabiners for belaying and running belays (between three and eight for the leader are needed, according to the difficulty of the climb: § 55). Pitons (§ 68) and a piton hammer (§ 69) may sometimes be needed for making main belays where no natural anchor exists (§ 61);

it is probably best to carry one or two pitons at all times on long or infrequently climbed Scottish routes, though this would rarely be necessary on popular climbs in England and Wales.

Size of party. Never climb alone. For experienced climbers two is the best number since this is quick and allows them to 'lead through' (see below). On serious climbs or remote cliffs, however, a three or two pairs is safer than a single pair. It may be doubted whether a novice, a young schoolboy, or, with some notable exceptions, a woman would be capable of holding a leader on a long fall, and it is generally advisable for them not to second on a serious climb (but see [94c] for a special belaying method).

Choice of climb. For your early climbs it is best to choose cliffs in areas where you have previously walked, since this will increase your confidence. A crag which is sunny and not too steep is preferable. In bad weather, choose a low cliff. Try to find a climb which is on good clean rock, with good belays, and with fairly short pitches. If it is one of the 'trade routes' so much the better, because the rock is likely to be scratched, so that you will have no difficulty with the route-finding, and because most of the loose holds and vegetation will already have disappeared. It goes without saying that the party should be competent for the climb chosen. It is best to start with the very easiest climbs and gradually work your standard up. If you are seconding Very Difficult climbs well, then you ought to be able to lead Moderately Difficult or Difficult climbs. The weather conditions are of course a major factor: in cold, wet, or windy weather choose climbs which are protected (on low cliffs or where most of the climbing is in chimneys or gullies) and reckon that the climb is probably not less than one standard harder – maybe more – than in perfect conditions. In winter, ice or *verglas* can make even the easiest face climbs hard and serious, and the beginner should not attempt them in such conditions.

METHOD OF TACKLING THE CLIMB

1. *The climbing sequence* [44]. When the leader is satisfied that he has found the start of the climb (it is often marked, by a cairn for example) the party should tie on to the rope (§ 54). There should always be at least sixty feet of rope between each two climbers, and the leader will need much more on most routes (the guide-book usually says how much rope is needed). If there is steep ground below, the second should belay, i.e. secure himself by tying himself to a spike or other anchor, using the main rope, or a sling. The leader then leads the first pitch, perhaps protecting himself by putting on one or more running belays [88]. When he reaches the ledge ('the stance') at the top of the pitch, he belays and takes in all the spare rope between himself and the second. He then passes the rope round his waist or over his shoulder in order to bring up the second, who has the moral encouragement of the rope from above but no direct assistance (unless he slips or asks for help). When the second reaches the ledge, he also belays, and takes the leader's end of the rope around his waist. He then puts on gloves so that the rope will not burn his hands in the unlikely event of the leader falling on the next pitch; this is in the interests of the leader as much as the second, since the latter will be able to arrest a fall much more effectively if he is wearing gloves. The leader then takes off his belay and goes on to tackle the next pitch, putting on running belays from time to time. When he reaches the top of this pitch the same process is repeated. Where both members are experienced and competent, it is normal to 'lead through' (i.e., for

44. *The climbing sequence.* The second and third pitches of Crackstone Rib, a Severe on Carreg Wastad, Llanberis Pass (North Wales).

A. The leader climbs, protecting himself with a running belay (§ 63).

B. He has belayed (tied himself to the cliff so that he cannot be pulled off) and is bringing up his second.

C. The second has belayed and is paying out the leader's rope around his waist (§ 62, 1).

A

number one to lead the first pitch and for number two to lead the second pitch) since this saves time in changing over belays. Rope management is described in detail in chapter 8.

2. *Climbing technique.* The two essential principles are:

– planning ahead, so that you can anticipate the difficulties and work out the best way of solving them;
– conservation of energy, so that you can deploy your full strength when it is necessary to do so. It is best to stand upright, well away from the rock, and to take most of your weight on your feet, and not your hands (§ 39).

In tackling each pitch:

– work out the general line, and note where it is possible to rest. When you reach each resting place calculate exactly how to do the next bit. Get the right sequence of holds – often a move will seem difficult because you are using your right foot where your left foot should be and vice versa (as second man, watch the way the leader does the pitch);
– try not to get held up for too long on any one move; but do not press on until you are sure you can do it. Slowness in working out the right combination of holds may be a sign that you are off form – recognize this;
– take care in finishing off the pitch; do it quickly but neatly and remember the footholds as you go over the top in case it is necessary for some reason to reverse it;
– if you decide to retreat, climb down with determination so that you reach safety before your strength gives out; wavering and lack of determination can lead to delay and exhaustion.

Rock technique is described in detail in chapter 6.

3. *The descent.* There are standard routes off the top of most of our cliffs, and it pays to identify these from the guide-book before you start, and to memorize them for future use. Take great care in the descent. It is very easy to relax when a difficult climb has been completed, and many accidents have occurred on the way down as a result of carelessness on easy but potentially dangerous ground. British climbers

tend to neglect the art of climbing down because it is relatively simple to find an easy way down by the side of a cliff. There are, however, strong advantages in being able to descend almost anything that you can climb up, since this :

– greatly improves your all-round technique and understanding of holds;
– enables you to reverse difficult moves with safety should it not be possible to complete a pitch;
– is essential training for alpine or Scottish routes where much climbing down is necessary. A high proportion of the involuntary bivouacs which British climbers undergo in the Alps is probably due to slowness in descent.

On outcrops make it a rule to climb down at least half as many routes as you go up. When descending a full-scale climb, the best climber should be last; but an experienced climber should if possible go first to find the route. Descending is also a very good way of training an embryo leader, since he can get valuable experience of route-finding and rope management (selecting belays and so on) with the security of a rope from above. (See §§ 50 and 65.)

Leading. Leading is usually much more fun than seconding. The leader has the interest of working out the route, and has to rely on his own skill and judgement to get him up safely. He must always hold a good deal in reserve, since he needs to be able to retreat to safety if he finds that a pitch will not go. He must treat bad rock with special care, both so that a hold does not give way under him, and so that he does not send rocks down on his (defenceless) second. He should not give up a pitch unnecessarily: it often takes some time to find the crucial hold which solves the problem. On the other hand he must never push a pitch so hard that he risks a fall: it is a basic principle of all climbing that *the leader never falls*, and everything else must be subordinated to this. Some would argue that this needs qualification in that the ambitious leader may contemplate a fall in

situations where he can be certain that the rope will hold him. But this is arguable and can be ruled out for all but the most expert climbers on the most advanced routes. If the leader should fall there is always some chance that he will hurt himself, and if he is unlucky there may be serious or even fatal results. The only safe rule is never to trust in the rope when you are leading. The beginner should start leading as soon as he is competent at seconding the easier routes. Even when he is climbing with an experienced leader he can benefit by leading the easier sections, as well as by going down first on rock descents.

Sea cliffs can give first-rate climbing with the advantage of relatively mild weather not only in areas remote from the mountains (e.g. Cornwall or Swanage – § 108) but also close to them (e.g. Craig Gogarth – § 107). Only a small proportion of the coastline has sound rock however and this, combined with the difficulty of identifying the correct way down from above, makes it essential to follow the guidebook carefully. The sea with its big variations in tide and roughness can impose special difficulties of access and retreat – and danger of drowning even for strong swimmers – which require the following considerations to be taken especially into account:

– ascertain the times of high and low tide either locally from H.M. Coastguards or from tidetables in almanacks or the R.A.C. or A.A. handbooks. The guidebook or these handbooks will usually give the constants for each area from which you can work out the tide in relation to High Water at London Bridge (given daily in e.g. *The Times*). For example: Aberdeen (subtract 0.20), Anglesey (subtract 3.32), Pembrokeshire (add 5.36), Cornwall (add 3.00) and Swanage (subtract 3.23);
– there is a 12½ hour difference between high tides, so half to low tide normally starts after about three hours and lasts for six; the

45. *Pillar Rock (Lake District)*. The excellence of the climbing more than repays the long walk to reach it.

tide can flood quickly thereafter with a strong swell and risk of cutting off the retreat;
- before crossing sea-swept ledges first observe at least ten waves (usually enough to show the limits of the cycle); but still maintain a close watch for the occasional huge wave caused by ships, or tides clashing, far out;
- always rope up on easy traverses or elsewhere if there is the least chance of slipping into, or being snatched by, the sea, as it is impossible to swim far against the tide in climbing gear.

Given due care sea cliffs can offer marvellous climbing in especially pleasant surroundings, easily combined with family holidays.

The 'V. Diff. man'. For every top-grade climber there are probably a hundred more moderate ones, who may get just as much satisfaction from the sport. A climber, to satisfy himself, needs to climb at the standard to which he is best suited by nerve and technique. Some find that only Very Severe climbs provide the necessary test, others that anything above Difficult or Very Difficult is too much for them. There is no special merit in concentrating on the harder climbs; but a high level of skill opens up a much wider range of climbs, and also takes you into more interesting positions of greater exposure, longer run-outs, greater steepness and isolation. The ideal is to develop a high standard of technique but to use it for all standards of climbing, so that you can choose your climb according to the mood of the day. It is a big mistake to equate quality with technical difficulty. There are some low-standard climbs which are of high quality, e.g. the Cioch West climb on Sron na Ciche in Skye; Agag's Groove on the Rannoch Wall of Buachaille Etive Mor; Woodhouse's Route on Dow Crag; the Flying Buttress on Dinas y Gromlech; the Great Slab of Cwm Silyn; and the lower part of Commando Ridge at Bosigran, Cornwall. Equally, some very hard climbs have little merit other than the sheer difficulty of getting up, though success in this is admittedly its own reward.

§ 38. Snow and ice climbing in Britain

Experience. Before starting snow and ice climbing proper, you should already have gained some experience of winter conditions and of the elementary snow and ice techniques described in chapter 2. In particular you should:

– know about the different conditions of snow and ice, and be able to recognize obviously unconsolidated or dangerous snow;
– have practised braking and belaying with the ice-axe, and be able to move up and down moderate snow slopes (up to thirty-five degrees) safely and easily.

In addition, experience of rock climbing up to at least Difficult (preferably Very Difficult) standard is advisable since most snow and ice climbs involve some rock climbing as well. It is desirable if possible to do your first few snow and ice climbs with an expert climber who knows the area and its conditions. A party of three, or two ropes of two, is safer than a single rope of two.

46. *Lochnagar in winter (Cairngorms).*

Equipment. The basic equipment for the easier snow and ice work is summarized in § 13. The party will need all this, together with some of the additional items described in chapter 10, according to the length or difficulty of the climb. In short, the party will need:

- cleated rubber-soled boots with well-fitting crampons (§ 77) or alternatively tricouni-nailed boots;
- a good ice-axe each (preferably, for beginners at least, with a sling). The leader's axe should be short, for one-handed step-cutting, while the second's should be of standard length (§ 78);
- possibly some very short axes of Terrodactyl design [108] for use on steep ice, either as handholds (when picked into the ice – [119]) or for cutting holds in very confined spaces;
- a nylon rope; for pure snow and ice climbing a 1¼-in. rope (⅞-in. doubled) is permissible, but 1⅜-in. rope is advisable if any serious rock climbing is involved (§ 51);
- slings and karabiners (§ 56), though fewer than for rock; rock pitons (essential) (§ 68), a hammer, and a deadman/ice screws (§ 81) for belaying (§ 61 and 87);
- head torches, or at least one for the leader so that he can keep his hands free for step-cutting. The batteries should be kept separately in the rucksack until they are needed so that there is no risk of the torch switching on accidentally during the day;
- plenty of clothing (especially windproof clothing, headgear, gloves, and gaiters) and food, to keep out the cold. A safety helmet (§ 123) gives valuable protection and warmth.

Scale and seriousness of British snow and ice climbing. Although the mountains in Britain are much smaller than in the Alps, winter climbing in Britain can be just as serious a proposition as summer alpine climbing. This is partly because some of our snow and ice climbs (e.g. on Ben Nevis) are 1,500–2,000 ft long and are thus comparable in length with the difficulties on major alpine routes. In addition, the angle of snow and ice can be abnormally high for hundreds of feet: the exits of gullies in particular are usually steep and often corniced. Moreover, the British winter brings weather varying from intense severity (wind, cold, and rain) to unseasonal mildness, with the additional hazards of limited hours of daylight. Finally, snow and ice conditions are not usually as good as alpine conditions: the ice is more brittle and therefore less reliable for belaying, and the snow is often temporary, damp, and unconsolidated, particularly in England and Wales.

Main dangers on British snow and ice (see also § 18) are:

- *Avalanches.* All the types of avalanche described in § 129 can occur, though the risk is smaller than in the Alps. Gullies are always liable to avalanche in thawing or unconsolidated conditions. Ridges and open faces are not so liable to avalanche, since they do not usually hold as much snow.
- *Storms.* Storms can bring snow and rain very quickly. Summit winds can blow a climber off balance when he is making an exit from the shelter of a face or gully.
- *Underestimation of technical difficulty.* Ice sections may be much steeper than they look, and snow and ice and *verglas* may make rock harder than is realized.
- *Fatigue.* By the end of a long day all members of the party may be very tired, particularly if there has been much step cutting and waiting on stances in cold and unpleasant conditions. Fitness is of paramount importance for any serious winter climbing.
- *Benightment.* On long and serious climbs it is easy to get caught by nightfall. A bivouac is to be avoided if at all possible, especially in bad weather, because it is likely to be very punishing even when the party is well clothed and well fed. An early start should be made (possibly before dawn) so that there is a good reserve of time in hand. Keep a close eye on your watch so that if necessary a retreat can be made in good time. The party must be able to find its way off the top in darkness and if necessary a reconnaissance of the descent should be made before the climb is attempted, to ensure this.

Always remember too, that the safety margin on snow and ice may well be less than on rock, and that it is almost as important for the second not to slip as it is for the leader.

Because of the seriousness of winter climbing in our mountains, the British snow and ice climber leading the more difficult snow and ice climbs must be experienced,

47. *Tower Ridge and the Ben Nevis summit plateau in spring.* Note the two climbers in the middle of the picture, on the final section of the Ridge. The Tower Gap and the Tower itself are out of sight below. The final vertical section is avoided by a steep snow slope on the other side.

thoroughly fit, careful in his judgement, and reliable in his technique, and the other members of the party must be competent as well. Given this, British snow and ice climbing can be one of the most interesting and rewarding branches of mountaineering, and the British hills can give much enjoyment to its devotees.

The choice of climb must be governed largely by the conditions at the time and the experience of the party. The guide-book will give an indication of the problems likely to be encountered, but cannot grade the climb as accurately as a rock climb because the standard of the climb varies from week to week, or even day to day, according to the snow and ice conditions. Generally, it is more difficult to climb ice than snow since it is necessary to cut steps (unless you are wearing crampons) even on moderately angled slopes, and because ice belays are not very safe (§ 87). Snow and ice climbs in this country fall into the following three broad categories:

1. *Gullies*. The quality of a gully when filled with snow and ice may bear no relation at all to its quality in summer. Indeed, some gullies which in summer are either positively dangerous because of bad rock, or too easy to be interesting, provide first-class snow and ice climbs in winter (e.g. No. 2 Gully on Ben Nevis). Most gullies start with a long, easy approach which provides a rapid means of ascent up the first part of the face. The steep part of the gully may consist either of a continuous slope at up to about fifty degrees, or it may be divided by a series of steep ice pitches, overlaying what are in summer steep rock pitches or chockstones. Most gullies culminate with a steeper section, probably with a cornice. Gullies are usually at their easiest in a very snowy season, because the heavy accumulation of snow shortens the ice pitches. Some gullies (e.g. Zero Gully on Ben Nevis) are formidably difficult, but there are many easy gullies which give a good introduction to snow and ice climbing, with the benefit of fairly good belays. As noted above, gullies are prone to avalanches and should not be climbed in thawing conditions. The risk is usually greater when there is a cornice at the top. Treat cornices with respect even in cold conditions: always tackle them at the easiest possible place, and not in the middle; be certain that the cornice is safe if you decide to tunnel through it. Some gullies, e.g. South Castle Gully on Ben Nevis, are liable to be swept by snow avalanches from the walls, because these are formed of downward-shelving rocks which hold snow temporarily without giving it any real support (rather like a tiled roof).

2. *Ridges*. Ridges may be either long and fairly level summit ridges (e.g. the Aonach Eagach ridge in Glencoe, or the Snowdon Horseshoe [23]), or steeper ridges running up main faces (e.g. Tower Ridge on Ben Nevis – [47]). Ridges are usually at their easiest in a dry season because it is possible to use the rock, and rock belays. In a snowy season, they can be a much more serious proposition, with much possibly unstable snow and probably with cornices along

the sides of the ridge (see § 18) : belays tend to be insecure in these conditions. In Scotland at least there is almost always a very heavy accumulation of snow above the 3,000-ft level, and the final sections of ridges may need much time and effort. Ridges provide some of our finest and longest winter climbs, and are an ideal training for the Alps (though they may be technically a good deal more difficult than most alpine ridges). In easy conditions the easier ones may be suitable for inexperienced parties, but because of their length, and the difficulty of retreating, the more serious ridges should be left for thoroughly competent parties.

3. *Faces.* As noted above (§ 34, 3), an important development in post-war Scottish climbing has been the exploration of steep faces and buttresses, which provide mixed rock and ice climbing, sometimes of a very high order of difficulty and seriousness. Many of the harder rock climbs have now been done in winter conditions. This is however a very specialized form of mountaineering requiring great technical skill and experience, and it is best left to parties which are thoroughly proficient and experienced in Scottish winter mountaineering.

The techniques of movement and rope management on moderately steep snow have been described in chapter 2, and the advanced techniques needed for the steep and very steep snow and ice encountered in winter climbing proper are described in chapter 11.

Chapter 6. Rock technique

Rock climbing has been described in general terms in chapter 5. This chapter concentrates on one aspect alone, the art of movement on rock. As noted in § 37, 2, the two essential principles are:

- planning ahead, so that you can anticipate the difficulties on a pitch and work out the best way of solving them;
- conservation of energy, so that you can deploy your full strength when it is necessary to do so.

§ 39. A good climbing style

Usually there are quite a few different ways of climbing any particular section, and the best climbers will do it in the least strenuous way. The more flexible and agile you are the easier it is to do this. In rock climbing:

- *the fundamental rule is to stand upright.* Beginners often make the mistake of clinging close to the rock. This not only makes it very difficult for them to move as the result of the friction of their clothing on the rock, but also prevents them seeing the holds properly and increases the risk of their feet slipping off. By standing well clear you can move much more easily and notice all the available holds and the best order and method of using them [48];
- *balance and rhythm are vital.* On most rock you should try to use your hands only for balancing grips (rather as you would use them in climbing a ladder) and move from foothold to foothold in a controlled and rhythmic way, with the minimum of effort;
- *preserve strength* by keeping your hands below shoulder level so that the supply of blood to your arms and hands is not reduced; and rest them frequently. In cold or wet weather, wear fingerless mitts [53c];

- *use the small intermediate holds* as much as possible; but it is not worth delay in searching for small holds if you can quickly and easily solve the problem by making a high step;
- *keep three points of contact* with the rock; this enables you to move on smaller holds and also leaves you with two points of support should one of your holds give way (but check all holds carefully before using them);
- *adjust your position* if your feet start shaking on holds; the best way is to put the side of your foot or your heel on the hold for a moment.

Rushing, scrabbling, or muscling up on holds is merely dangerous. Neatness, coolness, settling beforehand just what holds to use and how, and then making the movement deliberately and smoothly with a reserve of strength, is the hall-mark of good climbing. But given this, it is better to move fast where possible since less effort is needed than in hanging about on small holds.

§ 40. Use of holds in general

The usefulness of a hold depends on:

- *its shape and size*; some holds, e.g. incuts, give a mechanical grip, while others, e.g. sloping or jamming holds, are mainly friction;
- *its direction*; a direct pull or push is very satisfactory but side-holds and undercut holds are valuable for maintaining balance or for moving 'in opposition', e.g. laybacking [66] or bridging [69]. On some cliffs, e.g. Lliwedd, side-holds predominate and climbers with a clumsy technique find the climbs there relatively difficult;
- *its roughness*; rough rock, e.g. Cornish granite, Skye gabbro, gritstone, or sandstone, gives very good friction and sometimes it is possible to grip simply by placing hands or feet flat on the rock; smooth rock, e.g. slate or basalt, gives very little friction.

---

48. *A good climbing style.* The climber's body is well clear of the rock so that he can see all the holds and move easily. Most of his weight is on his feet.

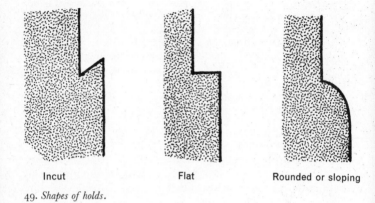

Incut   Flat   Rounded or sloping

49. *Shapes of holds*.

Even on rough rock, individual holds may be slippery because
they are nail-worn, wet, or greasy;
– *its soundness* (§ 47).

Whatever the type of hold, the two basic principles in using
it are (1) not to use more energy than necessary, and (2) to
apply the force as nearly as possible at right angles to the
hold, so as to push or pull *into it*.

Footwork is tremendously important in climbing. If you are
climbing in boots (particularly in nails) keep your heels
low so that your toe is forced into the rock [48 and 50];
in flexible footwear on the other hand the main requirement
is to get as large an area of sole on the rock as possible, and
it is often necessary to place your foot on sideways [51B].
Make sure that your foot fits on to the hold precisely, and
do not move it or shake your heel once you have put
it there. When the rock is wet or slippery, the holds are
much less reliable than when it is dry and warm, and
they must be used with great care. As noted earlier (§ 23)
rubber-soled boots tend to skate on greasy rock and it
is advisable to select spiky or very rough holds where

50. *The use of footholds.* The holds though small are positive, except for the very sloping hold for the left foot in B. The climber's heels are lower than, or level with, his toes. Note the rigidity of the soles of the boots. A is a typical mountaineering and rock-climbing boot (Lawrie), B is a lightweight rock-climbing boot (Terray-Saussois), while C is an Army boot with an extra through sole. (See also § 23.)

possible. If it is necessary to use really smooth greasy holds the leader should climb in socks [51F]. Nailed boots are hardly affected by grease or wet and are often better than cleated rubber soles in such conditions, provided you have the skill to use them properly (they tend to slip on very smooth or rounded holds).

§ 41. Use of incut, flat, and sloping holds

Incut holds. A large incut hold (a 'jug-handle') in good rock is the most secure of all holds since your fingers can curl over it like the rungs of a ladder, and your whole weight could if necessary be taken on it for a straight hoist [52].

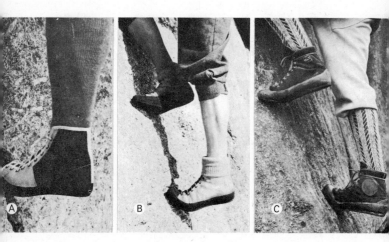

51. *The use of lightweight footwear for rock climbing.*

Although cleated rubber-soled climbing boots (§ 23) are suitable for
most rock climbing, many climbers prefer lightweight footwear because
of the greater freedom of movement it gives, and because of its better
grip on indefinite holds or in very thin cracks. All lightweight footwear
demands special care on grass and mud, particularly on the easy way
down when the climb is finished. Gym shoes (or, in bad weather, socks)
were used for most of the hardest rock climbs of the 1930s, but went out
when the moulded rubber sole and the P.A. came in. There is probably
little that they can do that the cleated sole cannot do better – indeed
they are inferior on small positive holds – but they have the merit of
cheapness and are thus useful for someone trying out rock climbing for
the first time who does not have climbing boots, or for practising on
sandstone or other soft rock where boots are forbidden. Cheap, thin,
black-soled gym shoes are best: crêpe soles slip too easily on damp rock,
while basketball boots or thick-soled tennis shoes tend to squelch on
small holds. Nowadays, the footwear shown above is generally used in
place of gym shoes.

P.A.s (A) take their name from the French climber Pierre Allain who
first designed and produced them. For several years they were undisputed
leaders of the field, but other manufacturers have now produced similar
models, such as the Masters boot (B), the Brigham Mk III (C), and the
Lawrie Rock-Climber. The R.D. boot is similar but has a slightly thicker
sole. All have thin canvas or suède uppers reaching over the ankle, and
pointed toes which fit into small cracks. Some have stiffened soles to

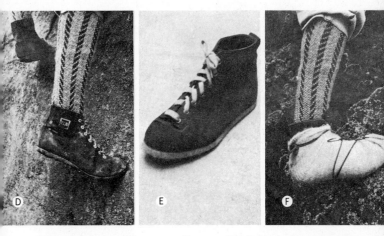

reduce twisting and hence to allow smaller holds to be used; this stiffening is usually across the sole, not along it, to give sideways rigidity without destroying the lengthways flexibility so important for friction holds. Most of them employ a special rubber with high frictional properties. They will grip almost anywhere on dry rock and many people consider that they improve their climbing by as much as half a standard.

Kletterschuhe (D) usually have special thin moulded soles and heels. They must be stiffened to give support on small holds, and should preferably have pointed toes. The uppers are usually of suède or leather, and should be strengthened inside to prevent them going out of shape. Perhaps their main advantage is that unlike the P.A. or the gym shoe they can be used for walking to and from the cliffs in good weather. They do however suffer from the disadvantage that they have neither the flexibility of the P.A. nor the rigidity of the boot; few climbers find them completely satisfactory.

Felt-soled kletterschuhe (E) and *socks* (F) are useful in place of rubber-soled footwear on wet or greasy rock. Socks can be worn either over P.A.s or – at the expense of discomfort – on bare feet. Carry a spare lace so that as the toe wears out the sock or stocking can be drawn back and secured on the top of your foot: in this way its whole length can be used. Any old woollen socks will do but cotton and nylon ones tend to slip. Socks grip better wet than dry, but take care to keep them out of mud which acts as a lubricant.

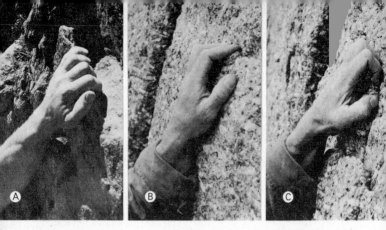

52. *Handholds.* A is a 'jug handle', B is normal, while C is the best way of using a very small hold.

Incuts are equally good as footholds but when these holds are small, boots may give much better support than gym shoes or P.A.s whose flexibility can be a disadvantage.

Flat holds. When holds are flat rather more care is needed in using them, particularly in wet conditions. They can be

53. *More handholds.* A is a downward pressure or 'push' hold, most useful in slab or chimney climbing. B is an under-hold. C is a side-hold, often useful for individual layback type moves and for balancing. The fingerless mitts are recommended for climbing in rain or cold weather (§ 22).

54. *A mantelshelf.*

surprisingly awkward in the final stages of a pull-up since your fingers cannot curl over them and consequently you must rely on friction alone. In the extreme case of a large flat hold with no other holds within reach above or below it may be necessary to 'mantelshelf' on to it [54]. Depending on your agility, this may involve difficult problems of balance. Mantelshelves are however generally easier than they appear and once you have worked out the move it is usually best to make it without undue delay since it may become more – not less – intimidating with contemplation.

Sloping or rounded holds can give a perfectly satisfactory grip for the good climber, but require a delicate sense of balance and care in use. Whereas with incut or flat holds it would often be possible to hold on in the event of one point of support giving way, this will almost certainly not be possible in the case of sloping holds, particularly in wet weather. They are most useful as pressure holds [53A]. It is often necessary to get a large area of foot on to the hold if it is to stay on by friction alone; rubber-soled footwear is better than nails for this [51]. Unfortunately, the passage of countless thousands of nailed boots on the easier classic routes in Wales and the Lake District has transformed many holds

55. *Grip-holds.* These are usually most effective when they are to one side, when it is possible to get some side pull as well as down pull.

which used to be good square holds into polished round holds, and the difficulty of the climbs has been increased considerably (some gradings in the older guide-books, which were written before this happened, are now too low, but this is being put right as the guide-books are revised).

§ 42. Use of jamming and wedging holds

Much of the recent development of British climbing has been due to improvements in the techniques of jamming in

56. *Finger and hand jamming.* Note that in A the hand is upside-down, which often gives a better jam than the straightforward method shown in B. In C the thumb has been brought into the palm so that the whole hand is thickened, and hence securely jammed.

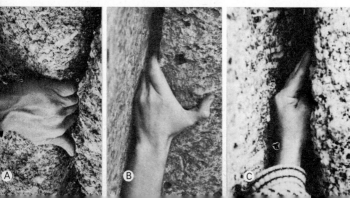

cracks. Gritstone (see § 105) is recognized as the ideal rock for perfecting jamming techniques and most of the best British crack climbers have trained on it. To avoid damaging their hands, many climbers use very thin gloves with the fingers cut out. The main reason for preferring boots with narrow toes for rock climbing (§ 23) is that they can be jammed in narrow as well as wide cracks.

Finger jams. In very narrow cracks the fingers can be inserted and twisted as shown in [56A and B]. Such holds can be used for vertical pulls, but are especially useful as side holds. Sometimes a better jam can be obtained by jamming the hand upside-down; this applies to all vertical finger, hand, and arm jamming.

Jammed hand- and fist-holds. In slightly wider cracks it may be possible to jam the whole hand. The essential point here is that the thumb is moved into the palm of the hand inside the crack so that the thickness of the hand is increased; the hand then cannot easily be pulled out of the crack [56C]. Alternatively, press with the fingers on one wall (catching against any hold in the crack) and with the back of the hand on the other; this is rather more strenuous and less reliable. In wider cracks it may be necessary to insert the fist and

57. *Fist and arm jamming.* A and B are pure jamming, but C is a combination of a finger-hold with an elbow jam.

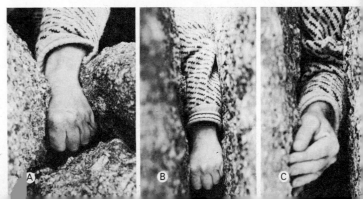

then clench it so that the sides of the hand are pressed firmly against the side of the crack. This also is a satisfactory hold and can be relied on quite confidently provided the crack is a suitable one [57A and B].

Arm and elbow jamming. If the crack is too wide for fist jamming it will often be possible to jam the whole arm, with the shoulder or upper arm and elbow pressing on one side and the flat of the hand on the other [67A and B]. Or it may be possible to use one of the hand jams at the back of the crack and gain additional support from a jammed elbow [67C].

Jammed foot- and knee-holds. In most cracks the feet can be jammed by inserting them at an angle and twisting them in the crack. It is necessary to twist them in this way because the boot can then be untwisted by the reverse process: if you put your foot straight in without twisting, it may be difficult to remove it. Some cracks are so thin that you can only jam a gym shoe or the tip of a P.A. [51A]; in slightly wider cracks, on the other hand, the sides of a boot

58. *Foot jamming.* A is typical toe jamming: note the twisting of the boots. B is foot and knee jamming with the right leg only. C is the foot and knee action in backing up in a chimney (68).

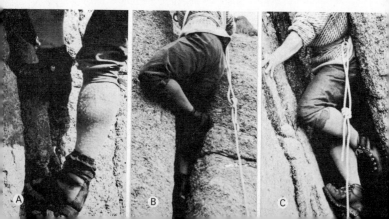

will jam comfortably while in yet wider cracks or chimneys a boot will only jam by putting the toe on one side and the heel on the other [64B]. It may be necessary to press the foot on one side and the knee on the other [58C].

§ 43. Main cliff features and formations

The variety of cliff features and formations is tremendous, but basically they may be divided into the following four broad categories:

1. *Face features*, defined according to their steepness – *glacis* (up to thirty degrees), slabs (thirty to sixty degrees), walls (sixty to ninety degrees), and overhangs (over ninety degrees).
2. '*Fissures*' (for want of a better term), defined according to their width – cracks (too narrow to get inside), chimneys (wide enough to get inside), and gullies (ravines, wide enough to walk around inside).
3. '*Open book*' *formations*, formed by the junction of two rock faces. They are defined approximately according to the angle between the containing walls and their width, and include open or V-chimneys, corners, and grooves. The French use the term '*dièdre*' for all these formations, but there is unfortunately no omnibus English equivalent in general use.
4. *Ridges and arêtes* [5], *and ribs, etc*. These do not, however, require any separate techniques.

The first three of these categories are used below to describe the various formations and the methods of climbing them; although they are convenient for this purpose, the distinctions are to some extent theoretical, and are often blurred in practice, e.g. a slab or wall may contain cracks, and a gully may contain slabs, walls, and chimneys.

§ 44. Face features

A *glacis* (a face at an angle of up to thirty degrees) usually provides an easy means of ascent or descent; no special techniques are required, but care must be taken, since a slip could be difficult to check.

60. *A steep slab.* Flannel Avenue, Chair Ladder (Cornwall). The holds are good.

Slabs range from thirty degrees to about sixty degrees. They usually involve delicate climbing on small holds, which is very good for learning correct use of the feet and a good climbing position. It is usually possible to rest at frequent intervals. Slabs are often very exposed and the run-outs may be long. As well as slabs providing Moderate or Difficult climbing (e.g. Idwal Slabs) there are some slabs providing very hard and serious climbing (e.g. West Buttress of Clogwyn du'r Arddu, and the Trilleachan Slabs in Glen Etive).

Walls are between sixty and ninety degrees. In practice, anything over about seventy-five degrees feels extremely steep, even vertical. Good holds are needed because some of your weight has to be taken on hands and arms. The steeper the wall, the more important it is to climb it

59. *The central buttress of Clogwyn y Grochan, Llanberis Pass (North Wales).* A training ground for tigers.

61. *A wall*. The footholds are good, but the handholds are inconveniently spaced. Note the use of the under-hold in C to permit a high reach with left hand.

62. *A steep wall*. No place to linger.

properly, because otherwise you will tire quickly and become unsafe. You must plot your moves ahead on any very hard section so that you can maintain rhythm and balance while moving. You may, however, need to feel the situation before you can see the right solution; if so, go up some way and come back down for a rest before making a serious attempt. Generally, it does not pay to hang about on walls: they must be climbed with determination and reasonable speed.

Overhangs are over ninety degrees. On the easier routes, overhangs are short and usually have good holds. Longer and more pronounced overhangs are often split by cracks. Even in climbing an overhang direct, it is possible to take a good deal of weight off your hands by keeping your feet well up [63]. On overhangs in corners, it is usually possible to bridge across the corner so that the worst of the overhang can be avoided. On all strenuous overhangs, it pays to wait until you have worked out the correct sequence, since you must not check once you have started.

63. *A short overhang.*

64. *Climbing a chimney/crack by wedging and outside holds.*

§ 45. Fissures

Cracks are fissures which are too narrow to get the whole of
your body inside. They are usually strenuous – skilled
climbers can often rest in cracks, but this requires a good
deal of technique. As with walls and overhangs, it is best to
work out how to climb the crack before you start. Once
embarked on a steep crack, climb it resolutely so that you
complete it before your strength runs out. There are three
main methods of climbing cracks, as follows, though they
are often used in combination:

   1. *Using holds in the crack* (usually jamming or wedging
holds) *in combination with holds on the face* [64]. This is the
commonest method.

   2. *By jamming or wedging alone.* This is exceptional since
there are usually outside holds of some sort. It is not
especially difficult on rough rock at slab angle [65], but it
is hard when the rock is steep or smooth.

   3. *By a layback.* Where the crack is in a corner and with a
sharp edge, grip the near edge, set your feet against the rock
face opposite, and lift against your foot pressure; if the
opposite wall is smooth, your feet must be close to your
hands to prevent your feet slipping [66]. A pure layback

65. *Climbing a crack by jamming alone.*

66. *A layback.* Note that in c the climber is using positive holds for both feet, and is thus able to relieve the strain on his arms by adopting a more upright position.

calls for power because your arms are carrying a good deal of your weight; it is essential to move quickly before your finger strength gives out. However, the strain may often be reduced by using footholds on the walls [66B and c], or by jamming your inside foot in the crack; in this case you can keep your feet a good deal lower than with a pure layback. On the easier routes, it is usually possible to find footholds so that only one or two genuine layback moves are necessary. Even on the harder routes, it will often be possible to combine jamming with laybacking, and many of the best climbers nowadays jam where laybacking was formerly thought to be essential.

Chimneys are fissures which are wide enough for a climber to get most of his body inside. Chimneys can provide a way up what might otherwise be a very hard cliff. Lockwood's Chimney in the Nantgwynant, for example, gives a Difficult route up a steep cliff where all the other routes are much harder. Chimneys are not much affected by bad weather because the enclosing walls protect you from wind, and the technique is usually imprecise, so that wet holds do not matter. In deciding which way to face in a chimney, the main considerations are:

- face the wall which has most holds so that you can use them easily;
- put your back on the smoother wall, since this provides less friction against movement;
- avoid putting your back on an overhanging wall, where possible.

Chimneys usually vary in width in different parts and it is best to vary your line to take the easiest and least strenuous route; this may involve turning round in the chimney so that you can make the best use of the holds. The three main ways of climbing chimneys (according to the width of the chimney) are shown in [68] and described as follows:

1. *Wriggling.* In very narrow chimneys or chimney cracks it may be necessary to squeeze into the chimney and climb

67. *Arm and shoulder jamming in a chimney*. Note that in A and B the climber is pushing downwards on his forearm wedged across the crack. In C a hand jam enables him to move farther out, to a less strenuous position.

it by wriggling and hand pressures on the walls. It is vital to get as much push from the feet as possible, since otherwise the process can be extremely tiring. Although wriggling is strenuous, it has the advantage that you can rest whenever you wish simply by breathing in and jamming your chest. Conversely, to move upwards, it is usually necessary to breathe out. If the chimney is wide enough, you can turn towards the opposite wall to move, and turn sideways to wedge. Arm pulls are of limited value because it is exhausting to pull against the friction of your clothing on the chimney walls. Some chimneys are so narrow that large people cannot enter them, and those of medium chest size may have to take off excess clothing (e.g. the Monolith Crack on the Gribin Facet in Cwm Idwal). Sometimes, where the chimney is holdless and narrows further in, it is best to climb it with the body in a near-horizontal position so that your feet can be jammed securely inside, while your

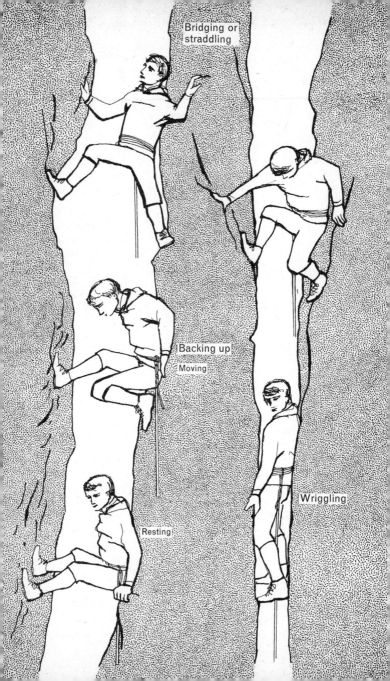

chest and arms (which are nearer the outside) can have some freedom of movement. Generally, wriggling is such a strenuous way of climbing that it is better if possible to take to a wider part of the chimney so that you can back up or bridge instead. You may even need to climb the chimney at its outside edge and use holds outside for one hand or foot (as in the chimney/crack in [64]).

2. *Backing up.* If the chimney is about two feet wide, set your feet or knees against one wall and your back against the other. You will find that you are then jammed. To move up, push downwards with one foot against the back wall, keeping the other pressed against the opposite wall; press with your hands as well. Your shoulders will then come clear of the rock, and it will be possible to move upwards to a higher position where you can jam again.

3. *Bridging.* This is the most effortless way of climbing chimneys, but it requires satisfactory holds on each wall. Face along the line of the chimney, and set one foot and one hand on either wall, or possibly take handholds in the back of the chimney or on chockstones in it. Most of your weight is on your feet.

Gullies are wider than chimneys, and are usually a main feature on a cliff face dividing one buttress from another. They are usually a drainage line and are therefore often damp and greasy. Most gullies contain banks of loose stones on the level or gently sloping sections between pitches, and it is very important to avoid disturbing these with your feet or the rope, particularly if there is another party below: as far as possible climb on the rock on the sides of the gully, just off the loose stones. Loose holds are also common, and it is necessary to treat them with great care (§ 47). Some gullies are well worth climbing for the extremely impressive rock scenery and the interest of certain pitches. The Great

68. *The various ways of climbing a chimney.*

Gully on Craig yr Ysfa, the Clachaig Gully and the Chasm in Glencoe, and the Waterpipe Gully in Skye are among the best gully climbs in Britain.

§ 46. 'Open-book' formations ('dièdres')

This category covers a wide variety of formations, formed by the junction of two rock faces; they are defined approximately according to the angle between the two containing faces and the width of the faces. The main ones are:

- open or V-chimneys (up to sixty degrees between the faces, which are usually not more than about five feet wide);
- corners (sixty to 120 degrees between the faces, which may be very wide);
- grooves (over about 120 degrees between the faces, which are usually not more than about five feet wide and may be as little as twelve inches).

The main advantage of these formations is that it is often possible to bridge across the two walls (as in [69]) – or even to back and foot in the case of V-chimneys – with the result that you can save a great deal of energy; indeed you can often be in a completely relaxed position even when the surrounding rock is extremely steep or overhanging. More-

69. *Climbing a corner by wide bridging.*

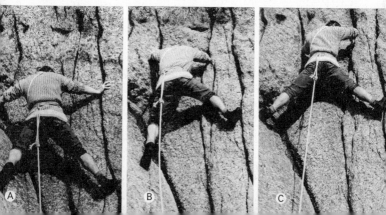

over, there is usually a crack at the back, so that running belays can be arranged on existing or inserted chockstones or jammed nuts (§ 63). In the Alps, corners and grooves often afford a route through otherwise unclimbable rock, and most of the major alpine rock climbs include a long *dièdre* or two.

§ 47. Loose and brittle rock

Even the very best climbing cliffs have patches of loose rock, or contain loose chockstones or scree, and you must know how to deal with them. Most loose rock can be climbed safely if the holds are used carefully and in one particular direction (usually downwards). The best way to test whether a hold is firm is to bang it gently with your fist or foot; a hollow sound usually indicates that it is not part of the mountain. You must then examine it carefully to see whether it is safe for a downward pull or push: it is almost always dangerous to pull outwards or upwards on loose rock. The same considerations apply to brittle rock such as sandstone, limestone, or quartz, though unfortunately unsound holds are much more difficult to detect, because they are in fact part of the mountain, and it is usually the weakness of their composition which makes them give. It is particularly important when climbing on loose, brittle, or friable rock to distribute your weight carefully between three holds so that you are never depending on a single, possibly frail one (see also § 7 and § 45 (gullies) for loose stones).

§ 48. Grass and heather

On the more difficult or more remote climbs you may find it necessary to deal with grass and heather. It is important to examine all vegetation to see whether it is likely to have a ledge underneath it, or whether it is simply lying on smooth rock. In either event treat it with care. Quite often you will find holds for the hands and feet made in it by previous climbers. In a wet summer grass may grow a good deal more strongly than in a dry summer; in extremely dry conditions it can roll off a cliff like a carpet. If you are climbing in rubber-soled footwear and come across grass or heather, be careful to wipe the soles subsequently since they will probably have picked up mud and grease; vibram soles demand particular care because mud may be retained in the clefts. Grass will almost always be encountered at the top of a cliff or on the approach. This can be dangerous especially if it is wet.

§ 49. Traversing

It is often necessary to traverse horizontally on a cliff to reach a new line of ascent or descent. Some climbs, known as girdle traverses, traverse right across a crag. In traversing it is possible to use less satisfactory holds than in ascent, because you do not have to *raise* – but only *support* – the weight of your body. Moreover, you can stretch much further than you think, so that long moves are often easier than they look. Sometimes it is convenient to use the same hold for both feet in succession; you can change feet on it by making a small jump, provided your handholds are good, but if the holds are small, it is better to step through to the next hold with your rear foot. Where there is only one line of holds, it will usually be easier to use them either for the feet or for the hands, and it is necessary to decide which level is best: it is surprisingly easy to take the wrong line. Occasionally, there will be good holds for the hands, but no holds for the feet; it will then be necessary to 'hand traverse' [70].

70. *A hand traverse*. These are rarely needed, and if one arises unexpectedly first make sure that you are not off route. Your hands take most of your weight, so you must move quickly. To reduce the strain, keep your knees and feet high. It is extremely unusual for a hand traverse to last for more than three or four moves.

§ 50. Descending

Chimneys give the easiest line of descent; overhangs, steep walls, and mantelshelves are usually difficult. As a general rule aim to keep your hands low and use holds as press-holds. This will enable you to keep well away from the rock and see the best line. In descent as in traversing it is usually possible to use smaller holds than in ascent because the body weight has merely to be supported and not raised on them. The three main ways of climbing down on faces (as shown in [71]) are as follows:

1. *Facing outwards*. On easy ground face outwards as much as possible. Your legs should be flexed and slightly apart; your hands should be low down and should take a good deal of your weight. This method enables you to see the best line of descent as well as the holds immediately ahead.

71. *Descending*. Outwards, sideways, and inwards.

2. *Facing sideways*. When the ground becomes too steep or too difficult to face outwards, face sideways. Keep well away from the rock. This position also enables you to see the line of holds, but not as easily.

3. *Facing inwards*. To be used only when the rock is too difficult or too steep to face sideways. Keep as far away from the cliff as possible with your legs apart so that you can see the holds beneath.

On very steep or difficult ground it is better to slide down the doubled rope (abseiling – § 66) than to attempt to climb down.

Above all, in descent, be careful not to relax your concentration. As noted in § 37, 3, it is only too easy to relax when a climb has been completed, and as a result many accidents to good climbers have occurred when descending easy ground.

Chapter 7. Rope for mountaineering

Rope is a most important part of a mountaineer's equipment, being in effect his insurance policy (the world being an imperfect place, however, family men should have a real insurance policy as well – § 120). Until the Second World War Italian hemp and manila were in general use, but these natural fibre ropes have since been superseded (except for waist-bands – see § 54, 2) by ropes made of nylon (or perlon or grilon as it is sometimes called in other countries). Other artificial fibres such as terylene have been tried, but these have been proved to be inferior to nylon for general use.

§ 51. Types of rope in current use

Only ropes of the highest quality, specially designed for mountaineering, should be used. All mountaineering rope is essentially a compromise between two conflicting needs:

- strength and robustness, so that the rope can absorb the energy created in a fall without breaking either at the knot or over an edge of rock; a rope's strength depends mainly on its extensibility, because it is the stretch of the rope that absorbs energy progressively, rather like the brakes on a motor-car;
- lightness and ease of handling.

It is a matter of judgement as to how far strength should be sacrificed for lightness in any particular case. Where a great strain is possible, as for example in a fall when leading on rock, the maximum manageable strength is vital and only heavy ropes should be used; where on the other hand very big loads are unlikely, as for example in abseiling (§ 66), a lighter rope may be used. The two main methods of moun-

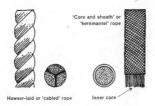

72. *The two main methods of rope construction.*

taineering rope construction (as shown in [72]) are as follows :

- *hawser-laid (or 'cabled') ropes*, in which a number of fibres or filaments are twisted together to make strands, and three strands are twisted together to make a rope. This construction, which is traditional in Britain, has many merits including a high extensibility (not less than forty per cent when nylon is used), flexibility, and stability;
- *'kernmantel' ropes*, in which a large number of filaments running more or less straight down the length of the rope are contained in a braided sheath (hence sometimes called 'core-and-sheath' ropes). This construction, which has been used for a long time on the Continent, gives a high tensile strength, some protection of the load-bearing filaments against abrasion, and comparative freedom from twisting. Recent developments have given these ropes a much greater extensibility than hitherto and a much higher energy absorption. The best kernmantel ropes are now superior in these respects to the best hawser-laid ropes. On the other hand, knots tend to work loose if the rope is very springy. Rope which is braided throughout, i.e., without a core, is very much inferior and should not be used.

These two types of construction are discussed in more detail below. In table 3 I have also attempted a rough assessment of the merits of the various ropes for the different mountaineering uses. The suggestion that only 1⅜-in. nylon rope (or 1¼-in. doubled) should be used for leading on rock, and that ⅝-in. nylon should not as a general rule be used for

TABLE 3. A short guide to ropes for mountaineering

	TYPES OF ROPE (§ 51)					LEADING		
Description	Construction	Circumference in inches	Weight per 100 ft (lb.)	Strength when new (lb.)	Extension when new (%)	Rock, single (§ 37, ch. 8 and § 122)	Rock, double	Artificial, double (ch. 9 and § 122)
B.S. 3104 No. 4 nylon	H.[1]	1⅜	5·5	4,200 [2]	40 [2]	A [4]	B	B
B.S. 3104 No. 3 nylon	H.[1]	1¼	4·25	3,500 [2]	40 [2]	C	A	A
B.S. 3104 No. 2 nylon	H.[1]	⅞	2·5	2,000 [2]	40 [2]	X	C [5]	B–C [6]
B.S. 3104 No. 1 nylon	H.[1]	⅝	1·25	1,000 [2]	40 [2]	X	X	X
12 mm. diameter perlon [3]	K.[1]	1½	5	Above 5,000	About 45	A	B	B
9 mm. diameter perlon [3]	K.[1]	1	3	About 3,350	About 45	X	A	A
¾-in. hemp [3]	H.[1]	¾	2·3	About 700	About 10	X	X	X
0·19-in. diameter steel wire [3]	H.[1]	⅗	10	About 3,700	Very small	X	X	X

1. H=hawser-laid. K=kernmantel.
2. Minimum specification figure.
3. These ropes are available in several other sizes.
4. The following classification gives a very approximate and subjective indication of the value of the different ropes for the various uses, assuming that the rope is new in each case.
   A. Ideal.
   B. Safe, but inconvenient.
   C. Can be used safely only in ideal circumstances, taking special precautions.
   X. Lethal.

Snow, single (§§ 17, 38, 85–88, 122)	OTHER USES			SLINGS (§ 55)			
	Top rope, single (page 24)	Abseiling, double (§§ 66 and 122)	Crevasse rescue (§§ 122, 135 & ch. 18)	Main belay (§§ 57–61)	Abseil anchor (§§ 66, 122 and 138)	Runners (§ 63)	25-ft Waist-band (§ 54)
A	B	B	A	A	B	A	B–C [8]
A	A	B	A	C	B	A–C	B–C [8]
C	B–C [6]	A	B–C [6]	C	A	C	C [8]
X	X	C	X [6]	X	C	C–X	X [8]
A	B	B	A	A	B	A	C [8]
C	A	A	C [7]	C	A	C	C [8]
X	X	C	X	X	A	X	A
X	X	X	C	B	B	B	

5. A double $\frac{7}{8}$-in. nylon rope is often used for rock climbing, but a combination of a $1\frac{1}{4}$-in. and a $\frac{7}{8}$-in. rope gives a more reliable safety margin.
6. Hard to hold and stretches easily.
7. Sheath may slip.
8. Melting risk.

slings, is based on B.M.C. recommendations; but the whole table is inevitably arbitrary because so much depends on the circumstances, and the way in which the rope is used.

Nylon, and the closely allied perlon and grilon, has the following main *virtues* as a material:

- it is light and supple;
- ropes can be made with continuous threads throughout their whole length, with a consequent increase in tensile strength;
- it has very high extensibility and hence very high capacity to absorb shock;
- it absorbs very little water, and hence remains light and flexible even when it is wet or frozen;
- it is not affected by ordinary rot or mildew, though some chemicals (e.g. the acid from car batteries) can damage it.

It does, however, suffer from three major *limitations*:

- it starts deteriorating at approaching 400°F. and melts at about 480°F. These temperatures can easily be reached on the standing rope if the active rope runs across it under load. You can test this for yourself by using a piece of rope to 'cross-saw' through a nylon sling; a $\frac{5}{8}$-in. sling will melt through in about ten seconds and a $\frac{7}{8}$-in. sling will not last much longer. Special precautions must be taken in rope management to avoid situations where this might happen;
- it is fairly soft and can be cut rather easily over sharp edges;
- it deteriorates with use. In 1970 Austrian opinion was that the safe life might be only 19 to 37 days' use, but B.M.C. tests in 1971 showed that at least 100 days' use could be expected before a *rope* became unsafe; nylon *slings*, however, would by then have lost about 25–30 per cent of their strength and should be discarded earlier.

For these reasons it is invariably safer to climb on two $1\frac{1}{4}$-in. (or 9 mm.) ropes rather than a single, heavier, one.

Disadvantages of Italian hemp and manila. These materials are still available but they are not recommended for general use because:

– they have neither the strength nor the extensibility of nylon;
– they rot easily if left damp for any length of time (consequently they must always be dried carefully after use). Sometimes this rotting is not readily visible as it is inside the lay;
– because of the risk of deterioration these ropes need to be discarded more frequently than nylon ones (hemp waist-bands should be used for only about six months for this reason);
– they become stiff and unmanageable when wet or frozen.

These materials are recommended only for waist-bands (§ 54, 2), where their freedom from the risk of melting gives them a marked advantage over nylon, and they can also be used for abseil belay loops (§ 66). Make sure that any you buy are of high quality and rot-proofed (there is a British Standard: B.S. 2052), and that you discard them after about six months.

Hawser-laid ('*cabled*') *nylon rope* is in general use in Britain. The whole question of the design, strength, and durability of nylon ropes has been exhaustively examined by an expert group on which the B.M.C. was represented and a British Standard (B.S. 3104) for these mountaineering ropes was introduced in 1959. Further work is in hand to ensure that the Standard is kept up to date and improved. It is advisable to make sure that any cabled rope which you buy or use conforms to the Standard. The minimum strengths specified in the Standard are given in the first four groups of table 3; as noted above, No. 4 ($1\frac{3}{8}$-in.) is the only rope recommended for leading on rock when a single rope is used. This rope is thick enough to withstand most laceration and has a very high minimum breaking load. Its chief drawbacks are its cost and weight, but these are more than offset by the considerable increase in safety which this rope gives. It is even safer to use two $1\frac{1}{4}$-in. ropes because their combined strength is greater and they give a second chance in the event of one of them breaking over a sharp spike, or an edge. No. 2 ($\frac{7}{8}$-in.) rope should be used only for snow and ice climbing or artificial climbing (in each case doubled), for belay slings (§ 55) and for abseil ropes in the Alps (§ 122); it is too thin to be used safely for leading on any rock where there is a risk of a fall by the leader (it is not always appreciated that a five-foot fall can in some circumstances break a rope as easily as a fifty-foot one). No. 1 ($\frac{5}{8}$-in.) slings are sometimes used for running belays where the anchor is too small for $\frac{7}{8}$-in. or thicker rope, but these slings must be used with great caution because $\frac{5}{8}$-in. rope is relatively weak and is particularly liable to cutting on sharp edges (as noted in § 55, webbing or wire slings are useful for small belays). The $\frac{5}{8}$-in. rope is not robust enough to be used regularly as an abseil rope.

Kernmantel rope is commonly used on the Continent, and it is now widely available in this country as well. Its main advantages are its high strength, and its general ease of handling, including relative freedom from twisting. It is particularly recommended for tension climbing (chapter 9) where its freedom from stretching, particularly on relatively small loads of up to say 200 lb. is a distinct asset, since the energy applied by the second is transmitted to the leader and not absorbed by the stretch in the rope. Further research is however needed to establish how well kern-mantel ropes resist laceration (including the extent to which the outer sheath protects the load-bearing inner core from damage) and the B.M.C. hopes to publish results in due course in its magazine *Mountain Life*. Some 'springy' types of kernmantel rope suffer from the very serious dis-advantage that knots tend to work themselves loose with movement; the figure-of-eight and overhand knots are least prone to this and are recommended in preference to others for this reason (appendix F).

Polypropylene fibre-film rope is now widely used for many industrial purposes and is relatively cheap. It is, however, much weaker than rope of mountaineering specification and the B.M.C. advises against using it, even for top roping.

Length of rope. For most climbs in this country, 120 ft of rope is sufficient for two climbers. On the easier ('trade') routes this length may do for a party of three, but there are exceptions such as the routes on the Idwal Slabs in North Wales where many pitches involve run-outs of eighty feet or more. If a doubled rope is used it is better to use two separate ropes rather than tying into the middle of one long one because either member of the party can then detach himself from either rope if he needs to (e.g. if one rope jams). The guide-book usually mentions the amount of rope required for each climb. In the Alps, large quantities of rope are sometimes needed (§ 122). It is always better to have too much rope rather than too little. Ink marks made on the rope at the half-way point and possibly also at the quarters are useful for indicating how much rope there is left when the leader is climbing.

§ 52. Care of rope

In use. When climbing, be careful not to stand on the rope – especially with boots or crampons. Nylon rope deteriorates steadily with use (it also becomes furry) and you should consider discarding it when it has had about 100 days' use; slings should certainly be discarded by then, regardless of their apparent condition. Serious damage (cuts, abrasions, and overstretching) may be caused to a rope by a falling leader, or by a falling second if he swings a long way. A rope should never be used for any purposes other than climbing: it should certainly not under any circumstances be used for towing cars! Nor is it safe to use someone else's rope or slings unless you can be sure that they have not been mishandled in the past.

At home. A wet rope should not be left coiled, as this will delay drying and encourage deterioration. The rope should be hung up in a relaxed coil, out of direct sunlight, but where air can circulate freely; it should never be dried in direct heat. Chemicals and old car batteries should be kept well away. Dirt or grit should be washed off the rope with cold water if possible, followed by drying. When travelling, the rope should preferably be kept in a bag so that it is protected from grease and dirt, but it should be taken out when you arrive at your destination.

Regular examination. A rope should be examined frequently to make sure that it is in good condition. This should be done before each climb, and also during the climb, if, for example, the rope has been badly jammed, or there is a possibility that a falling stone may have damaged it. Watch for cuts, unevenness, or excessive wear in the rope, and in the case of natural fibre waist-bands open the lay every foot or so to see that there are no brown stains (which indicate rotting) or mildew: the lay should not be very loose, since this also indicates weakness.

Dyeing the rope. Where a doubled nylon rope is used it is desirable to dye part of it so that the two halves can easily be distinguished; this is particularly important for artificial climbing (§ 67). Nylon rope can be dyed at home using nylon dye. Some types of dye do not need boiling, but nylon can in fact be boiled safely provided that it is kept off the bottom of the pan where very high temperatures may be reached (e.g. by putting pieces of wood or sacking there).

§ 53. Coiling and uncoiling the rope

The two main methods of coiling the rope are shown in [73] and [74]. Most climbers coil the rope in a clockwise direction, in the hands or over knee and foot. This unfortunately puts a twist in the rope with every turn, with the result that it tends to kink. One way to avoid this risk is to coil the rope figure-of-eight fashion, with a half turn to the left and a half turn to the right each time round; the twists can be shaken out for carrying (if the rope is supple), and will in any case cancel each other out as the rope is withdrawn in use.

A long rope can if necessary be coiled in two separate halves, using either of the two methods illustrated. If you

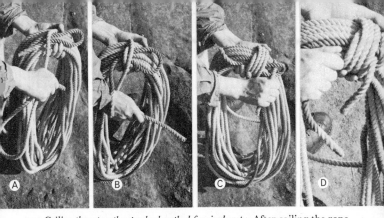

73. *Coiling the rope: the standard method for single rope.* After coiling the rope singly, tie a simple whipping with the ends; the whipping should be of not less than three turns (because it could work free), nor more than six (in case the rope is wanted urgently in an emergency). Carry the rope over your shoulder, or like a rucksack with the coil divided into two loops to form the shoulder-straps.

74. *Coiling the doubled rope.* This is preferable with a long rope (more than 120 ft), or for carrying the rope when scrambling.

are likely to need the rope again shortly, it can be coiled temporarily over your shoulder, provided the end is secured [77A].

When uncoiling a rope, always take care to untie it in the exact reverse of the order in which it was coiled, since starting at the wrong end is likely to cause a tangle ('knitting'). It is advisable to uncoil the rope completely before the leader starts on the first pitch of a climb, since this is the only way to be certain that it will run freely below.

§ 54. Tying on to the rope

Although there is no reason why the beginner should not use the direct tie for seconding, it is recommended that he should go on the waist-band system, or preferably the chest-tie, when he has gained experience and starts leading, since these provide much better cushioning to the body in the event of a fall. When using direct ties or waist-bands, make sure that the rope fits snugly round you, so that it is less likely to pull over your hips should you fall upside-down. The party should rope at the bottom of the first pitch of the climb, or earlier if there is dangerous ground *en route*. Stay roped until the climb is completed and everyone is on safe ground: accidents have been caused by unroping too close to the top of the crag.

1. *Direct waist-tie*. The recommended knot, for both the end men and any middlemen, is now the figure-of-eight knot, which is markedly superior to the bowline, which is liable to distortion under sideways loading, and cannot be tied in some 'springy' types of kernmantel rope (appendix F). When tied in single rope, it should be secured with a full hitch or two half hitches to prevent it working loose during the climb. When using double ropes it is better for the end men to tie on separately with each rope, so that one can be untied if the rope jams. If one continuous rope is used doubled, it is better for the leader to tie on with the two ends for these reasons,

75. *Tying on using karabiners*. A is a waist-band of Italian hemp with a strong screw-gate karabiner (ASMU **D**). B is a webbing waist-band. Never clip a karabiner into a waist-sling (or *baudrier*) in the way shown in c since this puts a three-way loading on the karabiner, which will fail far below its design strength.

and for the second tie to tie on with a figure-of-eight knot at the other (doubled) end.

2. *Waist-band and karabiner system*. Instead of tying the main climbing rope direct to the waist as in 1, many climbers prefer to use a waist-band and karabiner [75]. There are two main types of waist-band:

1. About twenty-five feet of $\frac{3}{4}$-in. *hemp or manila* (not nylon) is wrapped round the waist (at least seven times) and secured half-way and at the ends by fisherman's knots or reef knots. The ends are tucked neatly into the lay of the rope. The hemp must be of good quality and must be replaced every six months or so;
2. A waist-band of very strong 2–3-in. nylon web with a special buckle.

In both cases the karabiner to which the main climbing rope is tied must be of the same order of strength as the rope and must have a screw sleeve on the gate so that it cannot be opened accidentally (see § 56). A waist-band and karabiner has the following main *advantages* over a direct waist-tie:

– it spreads the load of a fall more evenly over the body and consequently reduces the risk of internal injury;

- the possibility of nylon running across nylon is avoided; this exists in the direct waist-tie when a belayed climber is holding a falling climber with a waist belay, unless he pulls his anorak or other clothing over his waist-loop to protect it (§ 62);
- it is easier to exchange rope ends on restricted stances (§ 62);
- the hemp line may be used for abseil anchor slings (§ 66) in an emergency.

The waist-band system was originally popularized by K. Tarbuck to enable his energy-absorbing sliding knot to be used [168]. This is, however, much less important now that double ropes and heavy nylon ropes are common. Moreover, the knot cannot be tied properly in most kernmantel, or even modern hawser-laid, rope. The waist-band system also permits the use of eye-splices for attaching the main rope. In theory, these are a good deal stronger than knots, but further testing is needed before they can be recommended unreservedly.

On the other hand, a waist-band system is potentially vulnerable to the following *weaknesses*:

- using $\frac{5}{8}$-in. nylon instead of hemp; this nylon is particularly vulnerable to melting and ought not to be used in a waist-band;
- using insufficient rope in the waist-band, which is consequently weak and fails to spread the load over your waist;
- using a karabiner without a sleeve, with the result that the rope may jump out unexpectedly;
- using a karabiner which for one reason or another (design, materials, etc.) is not strong enough (§ 56).

A waist-band with any of these weaknesses is worse than useless and it is far better to tie direct on to the rope than to try to use it. The possibility of a weak karabiner is a matter of considerable concern since, unfortunately, not many karabiners of the required quality are available at present; the failure of some so-called 'strong' karabiners at relatively low loads has discouraged climbers from relying on one karabiner alone, except where it is known to be of the strength required. At the time of writing some of the best climbers employed the following variations on the waist-band and karabiner system described above:

- use of two karabiners for attaching the main rope (this has been recommended by the B.M.C.);
- tying the main rope on to the waist-band direct, without using any karabiners at all: this combines the simplicity and security of the direct tie with the cushioning effect of the waist-band;
- when a doubled rope is used, tying one on direct, and the other with the waist-band system.

The possibility of a weakness in one of the parts of the waist-band system, combined with the fact that it is rather cumbersome and takes some time to tie, has led many climbers to prefer the direct waist-tie, especially where two heavy ropes are used. Nevertheless, if used properly the waist-band system can be very satisfactory.

3. *Chest-ties.* On the Continent (particularly among German and Austrian climbers) it is common practice to tie the main climbing rope or ropes round the upper chest (underneath the armpits) instead of round the waist, on the grounds that this is likely to avoid internal injuries or a head-first fall. A figure-of-eight knot is usually tied five feet from the end of the main rope and a shoulder-loop made with the spare end. Alternatively, a sling can be used for the shoulder-loop. With a doubled rope the bowline on the bight can be used [165]. A development of this idea is the *baudrier*, a thick length of hemp or of nylon webbing with a loop at each end, which can be taken once round the lower chest and fastened with one or two karabiners; a web strap goes over one shoulder, and there may also be thigh-loops or straps to take the load off your waist in a fall (see below). With a *baudrier* it is essential to clip into the main climbing rope with an additional karabiner since use of the karabiner which links the *baudrier* together would create a three-way loading, with a high risk of failure [75c]. Most chest-ties have the disadvantages that it is difficult to move the rope round to your back or from side to side, that they tend to constrict

76. *Thigh harnesses* are preferable to simple waist- or chest-ties since the thigh loops provide support if a fall takes you clear of the cliff, or into a crevasse. The harness in A is the Whillans thigh and waist harness; while B shows it with the addition of a separate chest and shoulder sling. An improvised alternative is shown in C. See also 93 and 165.

your breathing, and that in a fall it is possible for the knot to catch under your chin. Nevertheless, the reduced risk of internal injury and of turning upside down in a fall makes them the most promising hope for the future, especially in conjunction with thigh-loops.

Merits of shoulder- and thigh-loops. The risks of internal injury and of falling out of the waist-band can be minimized by using a thigh-loop and shoulder-loop system as in [76]. The improvised method in [76C] does not impede the movement of the rope around your waist because the waist-loop can move within the karabiner. The thigh-loop must be adjusted fairly tightly so that it does not slip out of position when you are climbing, but this need not be awkward. These loops, or one or other of them, may prove helpful in the following cases:

– when climbing on very steep rock, where a fall might leave you suspended from the rope; the human body cannot withstand being suspended in this way for more than about ten minutes because the pressure of the rope cuts off the blood circulation through the diaphragm. A thigh-loop avoids this (prusik-loops [152A] may also be desirable);

- when crossing crevassed areas, for the same reasons (§ 135);
- in abseiling (§ 66), when the thigh-loop provides a cradle;
- in artificial climbing, when the thigh-loop relieves strain on your waist and the shoulder-loop takes the strain off your back when leaning backwards from a piton on tension (§ 67).

Joining two ropes. Sometimes, with a large party or where the pitches are long, it may be necessary to join two ropes. It is best to tie them both to the second man, or the third man, as the case may be. It is possible for the two ropes to be under opposing loads, as for example where the leader falls on the first rope while the second's belay is made in the second rope. Consequently, the second should never tie the two ropes independently round his waist, since his stomach could be damaged by the opposing strains (and he might also be unable to release himself from the rope system). Instead, he should tie the second rope into his main karabiner, or into his waist-loop (but not if a bowline is used for the main knot in the waist-loop, since the second rope under load might put sufficient sideways loading on the bowline to turn it into a slip knot). Where it is essential to join two ropes other than at the middleman – for example, for abseiling – use a double fisherman's knot, or if the ropes are of very unequal thickness, a double sheetbend [170C and D]. Check the knot frequently (there have been many accidents from knots working loose). It must be recognized that any knot in the rope will weaken it, and a knot should never be tied in the leader's rope, which may have to take a big load (it would also tend to jam in running belays). Splices are stronger than knots, but they are inevitably weaker than the rope, and a climbing rope which has been cut should never be spliced as a permanent measure.

Shortening the rope. In snow and ice climbing (§§ 85 and 88) or alpine climbing (§§ 135–7, I), it is often necessary to climb on less than the full length of the rope. If it will not be necessary to lengthen the rope again during the climb, it is convenient to carry the spare rope in the rucksack.

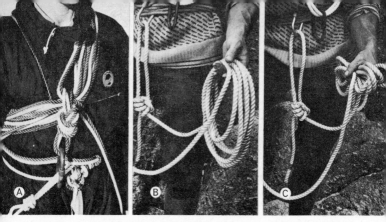

77. *Shortening the rope.* Note that in A the shortened rope is tied back into the waist karabiner so that any load comes on this and not on the coils which could tighten up and possibly strangle the climber. B is the normal method of carrying hand coils, with the active rope coming off the top of the coil. C avoids the risk in B of the rope tightening on your fingers, but for this reason is a less certain way of holding a fall.

Usually, however, you will need to be able to adjust the rope (e.g. to let it out so that the leader can run out the whole length on a difficult rock pitch) and the best way is to carry short coils over your shoulder. The rope must be re-tied into your waist-loop since otherwise any strain would come on to the coils, which could tighten and strangle you. The best knot is a figure-of-eight knot clipped into the main karabiner. It is usually best also to take a hitch round the coils to prevent them swinging around on your chest [77A].

§ 55. Slings and nuts

Most British climbers carry nylon slings (3-ft–6-ft closed loops of rope or webbing tape, often with metal nuts) for belaying (§§ 58–61) and for running belays (§ 63); slings can also be useful for abseiling (§ 66) and for prusik-loops on very steep rock or on glaciers (§ 140, 2). The use of slings has been very highly developed by British mountaineers; mainly, no doubt because natural running belays have come to be used much more here than elsewhere.

Four to ten slings and karabiners are useful for rock climbing, depending on the difficulty; up to three or four slings are needed for artificial climbing, and for snow and ice climbing where rock belays occur. The B.M.C. recommends that running belay slings should withstand 4,400 lb.; it is as well to take mostly heavy rope ($1\frac{3}{8}$-in. and $1\frac{1}{4}$-in.) slings but take some lighter ones, preferably webbing or wire (see next page), as well, for small anchors.

Nylon rope slings. Note in particular that:

- well-made splices are stronger than knots, but spliced slings have the disadvantage that they are not adjustable and tend to twist (twisting is particularly likely if the rope has not been fully relaxed before being spliced);
- knotted slings should be secured with a fisherman's knot, or a double fisherman's knot [169], and the ends should be whipped, or secured with insulating tape or Elastoplast, to prevent them coming undone. The nylon fibres at the end of the sling should be melted with a flame for the same reason. It is useful to taper one end so that it can be threaded more easily;
- always use the thickest sling possible for the size of the anchor, preferably $1\frac{3}{8}$-in. (or 11 mm.) slings. Some thin slings have held remarkable falls without breaking, but on the other hand others have broken at only about one-fifth of their advertised strength. The $\frac{5}{8}$-in. nylon slings are weak and should be used only where it is quite impossible to use a thicker sling and you do not have a wire sling (see below);
- it is desirable to put a sheath of thin leather or plastic on your slings, and certainly on any $\frac{7}{8}$-in. or $\frac{5}{8}$-in. slings, to protect them from cutting on sharp edges of rock. Sheaths also enable a sling to stretch where it is pressing on the belay and hence to develop its full strength. Two sheaths, about six inches long, are needed for each sling. It can be argued that if the anchor is large enough to take a sheathed sling, a thicker sling could be used instead, but often you will find that you have used all your thick slings as runners lower down on the pitch and only a thin sling is available. If the anchor is sharp and the sling is without a sheath, you can protect it with a handkerchief;
- use doubled slings wherever possible. It is better to use two separate slings of, say, three feet in circumference (but *exactly* the same length) than one of six feet or eight feet doubled, since one sling may hold even if the other is broken.

Nylon webbing tape. This material, developed in America, is now widely used for slings (especially on small anchors where its thinness is a great advantage), and for *étriers* (§ 70). The latest position is discussed in the addendum on p. 535. Note particularly that the material slips easily and it is desirable for the sling to be stitched in a special way [176]; alternatively a special knot [167] may be used, with generous loose ends stitched down. Normal knots are highly dangerous.

Risk of melting nylon. Special care must be taken to avoid using nylon slings where heat may be generated through rope friction. It is universal practice to attach the sling to the main climbing rope with a karabiner in making a running belay (§ 63). If nylon is used as an anchor sling for an abseil take special care not to move the abseil rope in the sling when it is under load since this could generate heat.

Old slings are dangerous. It is risky to rely on slings found in place on a mountain because they may be rotted or damaged; any natural fibre slings will almost certainly be rotted. Nylon slings are less subject to rotting, but they may have been damaged by sunlight, by laceration or by melting if, for example, one has been used for an abseil and a long abseil rope has been pulled through it quickly. It should be noted that old cotton slings may look just like nylon, but will probably be very weak indeed. In the Alps it is often tempting to use abseil slings left behind by previous parties (§ 138), but this is a major cause of accidents; instead, enough $\frac{7}{8}$-in. nylon or $\frac{3}{4}$-in. hemp should be taken for all your needs. Slings should always be discarded before about 100 days' use as they will have lost 25–30 per cent of their strength by then, or earlier if necessary.

Wire slings. Thickness for thickness high-tensile-steel wire rope is much stronger than nylon rope, and it is also less liable to cutting. As a rough guide, wire rope of the same circumference as No. 1 nylon ($\frac{5}{8}$-in., 1,000 lb.) is rather stronger than No. 3 nylon ($1\frac{1}{4}$-in., 3,200 lb.). However, it has little extensibility and consequently may not be capable of absorbing heavy *shock loading*. Swaged joints (made by inserting the two ropes into a short metal sheath which is squeezed on to the ropes with a special tool) are far stronger than spliced ones. Correctly made and used, it appears that wire slings of over $\frac{3}{16}$-in. diameter can increase the security of belays on small anchors which can take only No. 1 nylon at the expense of some inconvenience on account of their stiffness and weight. Wire is, however, markedly superior with nuts (see below) because it is easier to manœuvre the nut. Always ascertain the guaranteed strength before using a wire sling since some have proved dangerously weak.

Nuts. It is now universal practice among good British climbers to thread nuts of various sizes onto slings for use as jammed-nut belays (§ 61), probably the greatest single new contribution to rock-climbing safety in recent years. A wide variety of specially designed nuts is now available for all widths of the thinner cracks, and it is advisable to carry a good assortment so as to use all opportunities of anchoring. Most nuts take nylon rope or tape, but probably the most useful of all, at least in the smaller sizes, are those on short swaged wire slings since the rigidity of the wire enables them to be inserted and withdrawn relatively easily.

Sling threader. Because of the difficulty of threading nylon slings in narrow or awkward cracks, some climbers carry a piece of malleable wire to help them. Heavy-gauge fence wire is suitable; a hook (for pulling) is needed at one end and a small cup at the other (for pushing).

§ 56. Karabiners ('*krabs*')

A karabiner (= snaplink; Fr. *mousqueton*) is a metal link used for joining two ropes. It has a gate or keeper on one side which can be opened inwards to allow the rope to be inserted; the gate is spring-loaded and clips home to prevent the rope jumping out. A wide opening at the gate (preferably 18 mm. and certainly not less than 15 mm.) is desirable so that thick ropes can be clipped in without difficulty, and the spring should not be over-powerful because this may be awkward to operate and use up finger

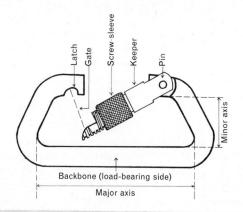

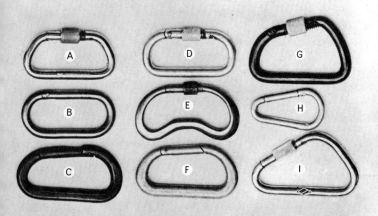

78. *Karabiners*. A. ASMU D. B. Simond 10 mm. oval. C. Cassin 1,800 kg. D. D. Hiatt D. E. Marwa kidney. F. Allain D. G. Stubai large D. H. Cassin: for rucksacks and *étriers*. I. Russian karabiner: note the large gate opening. As noted opposite, most current karabiners have secured U.I.A.A. approval.

strength unnecessarily. The gate has a pin at one end and usually has a latch (or a pin and slot) at the other. These should be free from sharp edges likely to damage a climbing rope or injure the user. Many types of karabiner have a screw-sleeve on the gate to prevent it opening accidentally.

The U.I.A.A. (see p. 29) has recommended a standard for karabiners on the *major* axis of 2,640 lb. (1,200 kg.) with the keeper *open* and 4,820 lb. (2,200 kg.) with the keeper *closed* (the keeper open criterion is used to ensure uniformity of testing – not because the karabiner should ever be used in a way in which it might open under load). The Standard also provides for a load on the *minor* axis of 1,320 lb. (600 kg.) and for minimum impact resistance (e.g. if dropped). For various reasons only certain of the karabiners made by only two firms (Stubai and Bonatti-Cassin) had secured U.I.A.A. approval by 1973; and in the case of certain Stubai light alloy karabiners the B.M.C. in 1973 warned British climbers that British tests have shown them not to meet all the U.I.A.A. requirements. In general, karabiners may still not be completely reliable and great care should be taken to buy only those of good design and strength. Karabiners without a brand name should be avoided as some have failed at very low loads, as little as 300 lb.

The strength of karabiner depends on the following factors:

1. *Materials.* There is a wide variation in the strengths of the materials used. Most karabiners are made of steel; the best are of hardened and tempered alloy or carbon steel, preferably with a rustproof finish. Chrome-vanadium steel, as used in the ASMU, is exceptionally strong and also resists corrosion. Aluminium alloys, as used in some of the Bonatti-Cassin, Chouinard and Stubai karabiners are light and can be very strong if correctly processed; they may, however, be subject to corrosion in wet acid, alkaline or saline conditions – hence they should be washed after use on sea-cliffs. The amount of metal used seems to be less important than its quality: some of the heaviest karabiners

are also the weakest, while some very light ones are among the strongest.

2. *Outline shape*. This can be oval, pear, kidney, or D-shaped. Tests have shown that the D shape is best because this ensures that most of the load is taken on the continuous side of the karabiner (i.e. the one without the gate); there is, however, one type of D karabiner which has the gate in the load-bearing side, and this is dangerous. The load-bearing side is usually thicker than the other, but this differentiation should not be carried too far because it is important to retain strength in the side containing the gate in case this gets some sideways loading in the initial stage of a fall (before the karabiner turns to take the load along its main axis).

3. *The cross-section*. This should ideally be trapezoidal; a rectangular cross-section is stronger than a round one. The ends of the karabiner which are in contact with the rope under load should have a radius of at least 5 mm. since a narrower cross-section would turn the rope through too sharp an angle.

4. *The gate*. As noted above, the gate must be strong so that it can take an initial sideways load. In the Allain karabiner there is no latch and the gate therefore adds nothing to the strength of the karabiner. In most other cases, however, the gate plays an important part under load. Results suggest that the most common cause of failure at the gate is shearing of the pin; a screw-sleeve thus adds little to the gate's strength but performs the very important function of ensuring that it remains closed.

Tests carried out by John Seevers and John Horn in the U.S.A. in 1969 showed that of a specimen range of eighteen karabiners (which did not however include the Hiatt, Stubai or Allain karabiners) :

- only seven exceeded 4,800 lb. with the keeper *closed*, including the ASMU chrome-vanadium (7,500 lb.), the Cassin Large (7,050 lb.), the Bonatti (6,900 lb.), the new Chouinard (5,800

lb.), the Salewa (5,500 lb.) and the Cassin Locking (5,600 lb.);
– of these seven, only five exceeded 2,600 lb. with the keeper *open*,
namely the ASMU (4,500 lb.), the Salewa (4,125 lb.), the
Bonatti (2,725 lb.), the Cassin Large (2,675 lb.) and the
Chouinard (2,650 lb.).

It has also been shown in the past (B.M.C. tests of 1963–4)
that many karabiners were weak under sideways loading,
with one otherwise good karabiner in particular failing at
only 300 lb. The U.I.A.A. is carrying out further tests and
is arranging to approve particular designs manufactured to
agreed specifications. Details will be issued from time to
time in *Mountain Life* (bibliography, 1). In the meantime,
mountaineers would do well to treat karabiners with a good
deal of circumspection and use only those certified as having
U.I.A.A. approval.

Uses of karabiners. It is vital to ensure that a karabiner does
not introduce a weak element into a rope system, and this
requires some appreciation of the loads likely to be placed
on karabiners in the different uses.

– *A main belay or a waist-tie* needs a karabiner of the same order of
strength as the main rope, and it should have a screw-sleeve. A
strength of 4,800 lb. with keeper closed is suggested. If in doubt,
use two karabiners (see also § 54).
– *Running belays* (§ 63). A karabiner taking up to 4,800 lb. load
is also needed for running belays. It need not have a sleeve on
the gate. As noted above the gate should not have a sharp hook
since this is likely to damage the rope in the event of the karabiner opening out under heavy load. Weight is an advantage,
since this helps to keep the running belay on a spike.
– *Abseiling* (§ 66). For the karabiner method of abseiling a karabiner with a sleeve is desirable.
– *Artificial climbing* (chapter 9). Alloy karabiners are best because
of their lightness; but make sure that they are not weak under
sideways loading which is likely to occur in peg climbing. The
gate should close securely to minimize the risk of opening under
sideways loading, but the connection should be rounded (i.e.

not a sharp hook) since this saves much time, temper, and damage to the fingers. The Bonatti-Cassin and Chouinard alloy karabiners are very good.

- *Minor uses.* Some light, weak karabiners [78H] are made for special purposes such as for attaching *étriers* (§ 70) to pitons, or for hauling rucksacks; it is most important that these should not be used where a bigger load is possible. The safest course is not to use them at all: use strong alloy karabiners instead.

Dangerous uses. The following are among the most likely causes of accidents in using karabiners:

- attaching a belay to the waist-band by a karabiner gate upper-most: the moving rope can open the gate and enter the kara-biner under load and the main belay sling can jump out at the same time [84B]. The waist-band karabiner should always have the gate downwards when belaying to avoid this (§§ 58–61) and the gate should also be screwed tight;
- linking three karabiners together in a belay system. The twisting action set up can open one of the karabiners (unless it is closed with a screw-gate) so that it becomes disconnected;
- accidentally disconnecting a waist-band karabiner from the main rope while climbing. Always have the sleeve screwed firmly home so that the karabiner cannot be opened accidentally;
- putting a three-way or sideways loading on a karabiner [75C];
- leaving a karabiner face towards the rock on a running belay [84C]; pressure from the rock may open it under load;
- clipping a karabiner into a piton with the gate next to it; the gate can be twisted open with the result that the karabiner is released [101C].

Never use a karabiner which has been dropped down a cliff, as even a short drop on to a hard surface may set up invisible fractures, particularly if the metal is brittle.

Chapter 8. Rope technique on British rock

The general principles of rock climbing and of rope technique (the rope sequence, etc.) on British rock have been covered in chapter 6, and are not repeated in detail here. It can fairly be said that only good rope technique makes rock climbing as we know it justifiable or indeed possible. Although the basic principles are simple, a good deal of expertise is needed to apply them safely in every situation. Incorrect use of the rope may possibly lead to quite unnecessary accidents: at best it may result in a failure to protect the moving climber adequately so that a fall is not arrested as quickly as it might have been; at worst, it may cause a general failure of belays with fatal results for the whole party. If the rope is to be effective in safeguarding the party on a rock climb in the event of a fall by the leader (the most difficult case) all the four parts of the rope system must play their proper part:

1. *The waist- or chest-ties*, by which the party is attached to the main rope or ropes. Although chest-ties (§ 54, 3) are potentially safer, most British climbers still use waist-ties (§ 54, 1 and 2). The figure-of-eight knot is recommended for tying on in preference to the bowline (appendix F).
2. *The rock or artificial belays*, by which each non-moving member is attached to the mountain so that he cannot be pulled off his ledge (§§ 58–61 below).
3. *The body belay* (waist or, exceptionally, shoulder), which the anchored man uses to arrest a fall by the moving member of the party (§ 62 below).
4. *The running belays*, placed by the leader to safeguard himself or the second man (§ 63 below).

As explained in chapter 7, it is essential for the leader to use a $1\frac{3}{8}$-in. nylon rope or preferably two $1\frac{1}{4}$-in. nylon ropes, and to use safe karabiners and slings. No matter how much care you take with your rope technique or with your equipment, however, *by far the best safeguard is for the leader not to fall*, since there is always a risk of a failure in the rope system because of the enormous shock load imposed upon all parts of it. He must climb well within his limits at all times, especially in bad weather, and should never willingly risk a fall on the assumption that the rope can be guaranteed to save him.

§ 57. Main possible sources of danger in arresting a fall

Rope technique has been continuously evolving in the light of new equipment and of experience of climbing accidents in which the rope system, or a part of it, has failed. The B.M.C. among others has analysed the causes of certain accidents where the rope system has been at fault, and has made recommendations to avoid these failures recurring in the future (e.g. the recommendation against the use of war-surplus karabiners – § 56). Every climber needs to have some appreciation of the possible causes of failure so that he can guard against them when belaying on a cliff. The experience of the last ten years or so suggests that the following are possible hazards, and the methods recommended in the remainder of this chapter take them into account as far as possible:

– the anchor itself giving way because it is not truly a part of the mountain. Even large flakes and boulders can move: the Matchstick, a huge spike of rock on the West Buttress of Lliwedd, heeled over in 1958, when a party was belayed to it, fortunately without fatal results. The anchor must always be examined carefully, particularly on a route which is climbed only infrequently;
– the rope slipping off the anchor, either because the rock is too rounded, or because the pull comes from an unexpected direction. This is particularly likely to happen if the leader falls on to a running belay, because the pull on the second is likely to come upwards instead of downwards. Thread belays (§ 60) or belays in opposition (§ 59) can minimize this risk;

- the active rope, or the belay rope or sling, breaking. This is most likely to happen when a thin rope is used;
- the active rope when under load running across a nylon waist-loop or belay rope and melting it;
- a karabiner breaking, or opening accidentally and becoming unclipped; strong karabiners must be used, with a screw-gate in the case of a waist-band karabiner, and you must avoid putting a three-way or sideways loading upon them;
- the second being pulled off his stance, or turned upside-down, because the belay is not in the correct position or is not adjusted properly;
- the second being unable to grip the rope properly when holding a fall because the rope friction is burning his hands or wrists – long leather gloves are needed;
- the second being unable to release himself from his belay to go to the help of a fallen leader who is suspended from the end of the rope. On steep rock at least the second should belay in such a way that he can release himself without disturbing the belay by which the victim is supported.

§ 58. Belaying in general

Needless to say, the test of a belay is that in the event of a fall it will protect those members of the party who are secured by it. Great care is needed to ensure this: it is very easy to put on a belay which superficially appears to be a good one but which fails to hold in case of need. The main methods of belaying are described in §§ 59–61. It is important if possible to use an anchor above the waist-level of the belayer, since this will reduce the chances of the rope being pulled off. If there is no high anchor the belayer should sit on the ledge in order to get below it. The belay ropes should be tight, to help hold the belayer in position and prevent him being pulled over the edge of the ledge. In a party of three it is best for the second to belay with the rope between him and the third man so that the leader has the whole length of his rope for the next pitch.

Sometimes it may be tempting to use an anchor which is fairly unlikely to be satisfactory if a fall occurs. This is

inadvisable. It gives a 'psychological belay' and an illusion of security which in turn may give sufficient confidence to enable the leader to complete a difficult pitch safely; but if he falls off, the rest of the party may be pulled off with him. The second should first check very carefully that he has not overlooked the correct belay. If there is no satisfactory existing anchor it would be wise to use a piton. Anyone who has difficulty in deciding whether a belay is 'psychological' should ask himself whether he would be prepared to rope down from it (§ 66) without a safety rope: if he would not, it is 'psychological'. Many climbers do not appreciate the huge forces involved when a leader falls, and are casual in their rope management as a result. There is therefore much to be said for novices gaining experience in holding a fall on practice cliffs. This can be arranged by making a very secure belay and getting someone to tie a sack of earth or turf (or, say, a 56 lb. weight) on to the rope and to drop it from ten feet or so above you and slightly to one side. Wear gloves and do not use a rope which may subsequently be needed for climbing. This could with advantage be a feature of any course of instruction.

Belays fall into the following three broad categories:

1. *Spike or flake belays*, where the rope or a sling is looped over a spike or flake, or round a secure bollard (§ 59 below).
2. *Thread belays*, where a sling (preferably) or the rope is threaded through a hole or behind a secure chockstone (§ 60). These are preferable to 1 because they can take a strain from any direction, including upwards.

79. *Basic rope management.* On Flannel Avenue, Chair Ladder (Cornwall). The second is tending the leader's rope ($1\frac{3}{8}$-in. nylon) carefully, to prevent it snagging on the rock. He is belayed to the big spike on his left, using the proper belay with the main rope 80. He has passed the active rope round his waist (waist belay, § 62, 1) with his back to the rock so that the leader cannot fall behind him, snatching the rope from round his waist and out of his hands. He is wearing gloves for protection from rope burns should the leader fall, unlikely though this is.

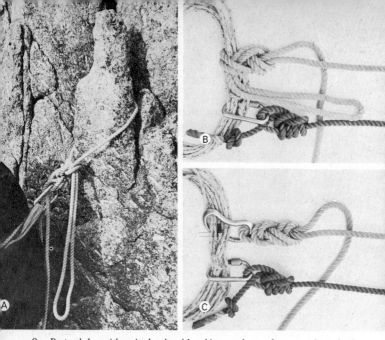

81. *Proper belay with waist-band and karabiner.* A shows the normal method of tying back to the waist-band, with two or three half hitches round the two belay ropes as in 80. In B and C the figure-of-eight knot is used for tying back direct to the waist-band, and to a separate karabiner, respectively.

parts of the rope between the belayed man and the belay; there is no need to pass it round the third rope (the rope from the belay to the moving climber) as is sometimes recommended, because this adds nothing to the strength of the belay, and indeed may weaken it since a load on the third rope might pull sideways on the knot and open it.

When a waist-band and karabiner is used [81A] the proper belay can still be completed with three half hitches. If the karabiner is full strength and has a screw-gate, it is probably easiest to tie back into it, but if this is not the case it would be safer to tie back into the waist-loop. The only disadvantages of the latter are (1) that it is slightly more difficult to turn round in the belay and (2) that it may be difficult to escape from the belay where the fallen climber is hanging from the end of the rope. It is often argued that

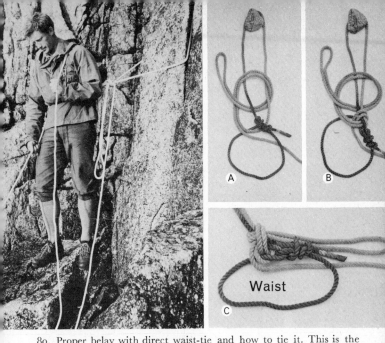

A

B

Waist

C

80. Proper belay with direct waist-tie and how to tie it. This is the basic rock belay, tied back with two or, preferably, three half hitches round both belay ropes. The waist-loop itself is tied with a bowline which is secured with an overhand knot ('full hitch' or 'thumb knot') (§ 54, 1). The rope has been dyed simply to make the knots show up more clearly. The climber is holding the rope with a shoulder belay (§ 62, 2).

3. *Artificial belays* (on pitons, jammed nuts, inserted chockstones, etc. – § 61).

Running belays (§ 63) use any of these anchors, though it is considered unsporting to use pitons where others have climbed the pitch without them.

§ 59. Spike or flake belays

The proper belay with the main climbing rope, as its name implies, is the basic rock belay. It can be used wherever there is a sound spike or flake of rock. There are many climbs where no other type of belay is required. As [80] shows, the main rope is passed round the projection and brought back through the waist-loop, where it is secured by tying two or, preferably, three half hitches round the two

220 CLIMBING IN BRITAIN

there is a risk of the main climbing rope running across the nylon belay rope when it is tied direct to the waist-band, but this is unlikely to happen in practice because the load on the second will pull the knot on the waist-band two or three inches away from his back. Two other ways of tying back into the waist-band are shown in [81B and C]; these can also be used with the direct waist-tie, but this is rare. Note that when a Tarbuck knot is used, it should be tightened back to the karabiner so that it cannot move under strain and thus upset the second's holding position. The main karabiner should be secured firmly with a screw, and the gate must be turned to face downwards so that there is no possibility of the moving rope unscrewing the gate, entering the karabiner, and unhooking it from the belay rope [84B].

The figure-of-eight knot belay [82]. This consists of a loop tied in the main rope with a figure-of-eight knot [167] and placed over the flake or spike. The overhand knot [167] can be used instead but it jams much harder when under load than the figure-of-eight knot. This belay is particularly useful in a case where the anchor spike is not directly above the stance, since if the second is pulled off the stance and swings below the anchor, the small belay loop should not roll off. Ideally a second belay should be used in opposition to the main belay (see below) to prevent the second swinging in this way. This belay is quick, and usually more economical of rope than the proper belay, but is mechanically weaker, since the rope between the belayer and the anchor is only single. (This weakness can be avoided by the use of a sling [83A]).

Spike belays with slings. It is often convenient to use a sling instead of the main climbing rope for belaying. For example,

82. *Figure-of-eight knot belay with the main climbing rope.* This is sometimes preferable to the proper belay, but it is weaker and stretches more. The climber is holding the rope by the waist belay (§ 62, 1).

the full length of the rope may have been used in climbing
the pitch so that there is none left to belay with, or alternatively the use of a sling may facilitate changing places when
the second man arrives (this is particularly so on narrow or
restricted stances or where the belay is very difficult to
arrange). The use of slings also reduces wear on the ends of
the climbing rope. The main ways of tying belay slings into
the main rope or waist-loop are shown in [83]. Never
belay with a single sling which is thinner than the main

83. *Spike belays with slings.* Normally, the main climbing rope is clipped
into the sling with a karabiner and then tied back to the waist by one of
the methods shown in 80 and 81. When a sling is clipped direct to the
waist-band, use one of the methods shown in B or C, since these avoid
the risk of opposing loadings on the stomach if you have to hold a fall,
but it is safe only when both karabiners are securely locked so that they
cannot twist each other open.

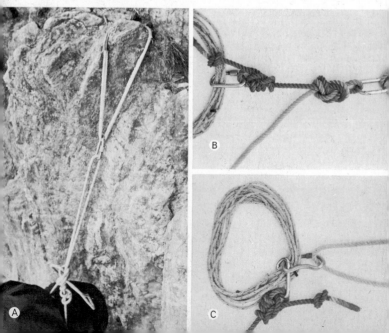

rope (i.e., $1\frac{3}{8}$ in.) unless the anchor is so small that this cannot be avoided. Where they are used doubled, $1\frac{1}{4}$-in. or $\frac{7}{8}$-in. slings can be as strong as, or stronger than, a $1\frac{3}{8}$-in. sling but as a general rule $\frac{5}{8}$-in. slings are too easily cut to be used for main belays even when trebled. Where the anchor will take two thicknesses, it is better to use two short slings of *exactly the same length* rather than one long one doubled, since one sling may hold even if the other is cut through. Where a doubled sling is used on a flake belay, twist it as shown in [83A] so that if one thickness rides off the belay the sling cannot unthread itself from the karabiner. Clip the karabiner into the sling in the ways shown in [83] rather than in the way shown in [85] wherever possible since the latter (which is really only necessary when thread belays are used) can put a three-way strain on the karabiner (particularly when the sling is rather short). Always make sure that the sling is long enough to develop its full strength – a short sling will break relatively easily under sideways loading [84A].

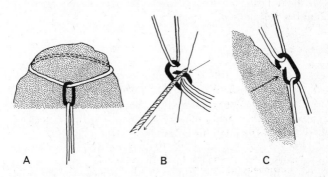

A   B   C

84. *Some incorrect uses of slings and karabiners.* In A the sling is too short and hence exposed to excessive cross-loading. In B the waist karabiner is the wrong way up: the main rope under load can enter the gate and depress the karabiner so that it detaches itself from the belay sling. In C the gate of the karabiner should face outwards so that it cannot be opened by pressure from the rock.

Double belays and belays in opposition. Where there is more than one anchor on a stance, many climbers make a habit of using two belays. The supplementary belay can be made with the main climbing rope (if the leader will not require all the rope on the next pitch) but a sling is usually easier and quicker. The method used for tying it into the main belay system depends very much on its position, but usually it is convenient to clip it into the waist-band with a karabiner, or to link the two belay slings together. Two belays in opposition to each other are essential when the main belay is safe only for a pull from one direction: acting together they can give an excellent belay for most directions of pull. Double main belays are also desirable (though unfortunately not always available) when the leader is using running belays, because the first pull on the second will probably come upwards: if the second does not have a second belay below him [88B] to hold him down, he is likely to be pulled above his belay, which will slip off, and the whole party would then depend on the running belays. Jammed nuts (see § 61 below) are particularly useful for making supplementary belays.

§ 60. Thread belays

As noted above, this is the safest type of belay because it should take a load from any direction. It is made by threading a sling or, exceptionally, the main climbing rope, through a hole, and then tying it back into the waist-loop [85]. Thread belays can be made in various places:

– through a hole formed naturally in the solid rock;
– where two masses of rock join (e.g. at the back of a ledge where the main structure rests on the ledge, or where a huge chockstone is jammed in a gully, or where a crack has a bottleneck in it so that the rope can be passed behind it but cannot come out);
– round a chockstone jammed soundly in a crack. The crack should be narrower at the edge than inside so that the chockstone cannot be pulled out.

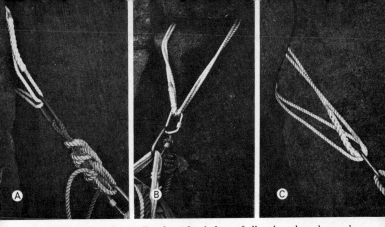

85. *Thread belays*. Generally, the safest belays of all. A is a thread round a chockstone. B and C use holes formed by the junction of two rock faces. Note that the sling must be long so that it does not put a three-way loading on the karabiner. Any of the methods shown earlier can also be used for tying back to the waist-band.

Thread belays with slings. Because a thread belay with the main climbing rope is usually very awkward and complicated (see below) slings are normally used. Often the aperture is in any case too small to take the main rope. Even where the hole is very small it is not usually necessary to thread a single thickness of sling since in most cases a thinner sling can be used doubled: but it is worth carrying one or two $\frac{7}{8}$-in. knotted slings so that if necessary one can be undone and threaded singly (a tapered serving at one end will help it to pass through more easily). It should be re-tied with a double fisherman's knot [169C and D]. If the aperture is big, the easiest way is to drop the karabiner down the back of the chockstone so that its weight carries the sling down. In all cases, it is best to keep the splice or the knot outside the hole since an attempt to pull it through may jam it. If the aperture is very small or in an awkward position it will save time and effort to use a piece of bent wire to push or pull the sling through (§ 55). The karabiner on a threaded sling is tied back into the rope system in the same ways as for spike belays [83].

Thread belay with the main climbing rope. When the main rope has to be used (e.g. where the thread is too long for a sling or where no thick sling is available), the belayer threads a bight of the main rope through the hole and then pulls both parts of the bight back to his waist-loop and completes it as for the proper belay [82]. Alternatively the bight on the main belay may be secured with a knot (e.g. two or three half hitches) tied back on to itself where it enters the hole. Sometimes it may be necessary to untie and thread the rope singly, but this is not recommended if the stance is in an exposed position. A thread belay with the main rope is undoubtedly very safe – but it is also very cumbersome, it uses a lot of rope, and it may be very difficult for the leader and second to change places unless they are using waist-bands and can thus exchange rope ends (§ 62). When belaying on a tree it is usually necessary to tie on as for a thread belay. But if the tree is also the main part of a stance, it is advisable to belay on a rock anchor instead of, or in addition to, a tree. Tree belays are commonly used on many low crags, e.g. Castle Rock (Thirlmere), Tremadoc, the Llanberis Pass and Harrison's Rocks, Sussex. On many very popular climbs, however, they have been mutilated or even destroyed by the passage of many climbers.

§ 61. Artificial anchors and belays

On the easier climbs in this country, the stances almost always have adequate natural belays, but very occasionally this is not the case, e.g. at the top of the fourth pitch of the Tennis Shoe climb on the Idwal Slabs, or at the top of the seventh pitch of the Troutdale Pinnacle climb on the Black Crag in Borrowdale. On some of the harder climbs, natural belays are not infrequently poor. Continental practice in cases where there is difficult climbing above an unprotected stance would be to use a piton (peg) to protect the party, but traditionally in this country there has been some prejudice against this, founded no doubt partly on the belief that if pitons are used as belays on stances they may tend to be used as running belays or direct aid on pitches which have been done without them. Consequently British climbers have gone to great pains to manufacture belays by other methods, e.g. inserted chockstones, jammed knots, or jammed nuts (see below). The extent to which these are different in kind from natural belays on the one hand and pitons on the other is a matter for argument. The trend at the time of writing seems to be against jammed knots and inserted chockstones, and in favour of jammed nuts and pitons. It can certainly be argued that the use of one or more pitons *on a stance* where natural belays are inadequate is in an entirely different category from using pitons for direct progress or as runners on rock climbable without them, and there does not seem to be any reason why this should be frowned upon when the alternative is the risk of an accident that could have been avoided. This is, however, not to condone the unfortunate modern tendency for pitons to proliferate on *pitches* which have been climbed clean in the past: if a party cannot do such a pitch safely without putting in pitons, then it is in the best interests of the sport as it is known in Britain for them to retreat, and come back another day when they are on better form. Otherwise more and more climbers will tend to piton their way up climbs which are beyond them, with the result that the standard and quality of these climbs will be reduced.

Piton (peg) belays. The extent to which pitons (§ 68) are required depends very much on the type of rock; on limestone, for example, natural belays are rare and pitons are generally used, whereas the rock in Wales and the Lake District usually gives adequate natural belays. On some Scottish cliffs (e.g. the Rannoch Wall on Buachaille Etive Mor) peg belays are common. Generally, if a piton has to be used on a recognized climb as a belay, it will already be in place. In such a case it is extremely important to test the security of the piton before using it since it may possibly not have been inserted correctly or may have rusted through. If the existing piton is doubtful or there is no piton in place you

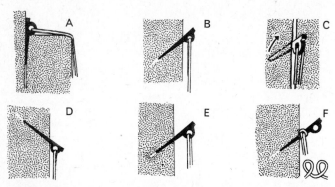

86. *Use of pitons for main belays.* A and B are ideal. C is only moderate where the piton is held in by friction alone; note also that a piton with the eye at an angle to the blade is safer than the type shown because it twists against the sides of the crack under load. D may be safe for a hold, but is useless for a belay. The dangerous leverage in E can be avoided by using a clove hitch as in F.

will need to insert one of your own. Many leaders carry a small selection (say, three or four) of the types described in § 68 for this purpose; they should all be well-designed, high-tensile alloy-steel pitons, and there should be at least one thick and one thin one. A hammer (§ 69) is also needed.

The insertion of pitons is dealt with in § 72. Note that:

- the piton should be put into a crack at right angles to the line of pull (i.e., in the case of a wall, a horizontal or slanting crack). Even an alloy steel peg may hold no more than about 800 lb. in a vertical crack, while a malleable steel one can give at only 200 lb., even when it appears secure;
- the piton size should normally allow half to three-quarters of the blade to be inserted before hammering. If the peg will not go in for its whole length, tie the rope to it at the rock face, instead of creating unnecessary leverage by using the eye [86E and F];
- it should be tested by sideways blows as it goes in; but it must not be over-driven when finally in place since this will prevent satisfactory removal.

If you insert a piton, it is a point of honour to remove it afterwards, but do not remove ones which are already in

87. *A piton main belay and a jammed-nut running belay.* The crack narrows below the nut so that it jams securely. It is best to remove the thread from inside the nut because it may cause unnecessary wear on the sling (§ 55).

place if it is generally recognized that they are necessary there since other parties may need them. Moreover, successive pegging and de-pegging may damage the crack to the point where it no longer provides a secure anchor.

Jammed-nut belays. A convenient and very effective belay developed mainly in the 1960s uses metal nuts (p. 207) jammed in a suitable crack or slot and linked to the main rope by a nylon or wire sling and a karabiner in the usual way [87B and C]. As small cracks and crevices are commonly found, this technique provides a large number of anchorages for belays. Make sure that the crack narrows lower down (and preferably on the outside also) so that the nut cannot be pulled out. This technique has greatly increased security on long leads where spikes for running belays (§ 63) are scarce or insecure; and has also to some extent reduced the use of the wider pitons in artificial climbing. On stances, too, it has improved safety because like the chockstone belay (§ 60) it can withstand a pull from more than one direction – hence particularly valuable for belays in opposition. Altogether a most important development.

Inserted chockstone belay. On quite a number of hard climbs, before the advent of the nut, inserted chockstones of hard (i.e. non-friable) stone were used in the same way as nuts, to provide anchors where none existed previously. A thread belay is made in the usual way to tie into the main rope system (§ 60). This technique requires skill and care because it is difficult to judge whether an inserted stone (which unlike a nut is probably not an ideal shape) would stay in under load. Correctly used, however, it could provide a makeshift alternative to the nut and the piton, either for protection, or in some cases even for direct aid (the Left Wall of the Cenotaph Corner on Dinas y Gromlech was first climbed in this way).

Jammed-knot belay. This is a very specialized anchor of limited utility, which usually comes within the category of 'psychological' belays referred to above (§ 58). A simple overhand or figure-of-eight knot is tied in the inactive rope (or in a sling) either single or double according to the circumstances, and the knot jammed in a crack of suitable width and pulled down until it jams firmly. As with inserted chockstone belays, this belay has been generally superseded by the jammed-nut belay (above) which is vastly preferable.

§ 62. Holding the rope: the two body belays

Body belays. When the leader or second is securely belayed on a stance using one of the belays described above, he is then free to attend to the rope of the climber who is about to move. First of all he must roll down his sleeves and put on long leather gloves so as to prevent his arms and hands being burned in the event of a fall. This is essential where the leader is climbing, and desirable when bringing up the second if rope of less than $1\frac{3}{8}$-in. circumference is being used, or if the belayed climber is not directly above his second. He then takes in all the rope and passes it round his body (always with his back at least partly to the rock so that the rope cannot be snatched from round him – see [79]) in one of the following two ways:

1. *Waist belay* [82]. The rope passes round the second's back above the waist-loop. The active rope should always

be paid out or taken in with the hand closest to the moving climber (the 'directing hand') and a twist of the rope is taken round the other arm (the 'controlling arm'). This is the best body belay for all uses since it puts the least strain on the body and can be combined with the friction arrest (see below) in holding a leader's fall. Where the waist belay is used with a direct waist-tie (§ 54, 1), clothing should be pulled over the waist-loop so that there is no chance of the main climbing rope running over the nylon waist-loop (with the risk of melting it).

2. *Shoulder belay* [80]. The rope from the moving climber passes under one armpit (the one nearest to him) and over the opposite shoulder. The shoulder belay is not recommended for belaying a leader, since it may turn the belayed climber upside-down. However, it is useful for giving a tight rope or a pull to the second, since the whole back and shoulder can be employed.

Bringing up the second man. If the second is ascending directly below the leader's stance, he can fall only until the rope becomes tight between them – a foot or two at the most if the leader is taking in his rope correctly. The leader should always be paying attention and feeding the rope through his hands so that the rope between himself and his second is just taut. He should never take both hands off the rope at once: instead he should grip both ropes with alternate hands and take in the slack with the free one. A falling body gathers speed very quickly and even a second could quickly get out of control if the rope is not tended carefully. This is particularly likely to happen if thin rope is being used, for example on practice rocks. The belayed man should continue to protect the second man until he has reached the stance and belayed. It is best to play the spare rope on to the ledge, since there is always a risk that it may get caught on a downward-pointing spike if you let it drop down the cliff. Always be most careful to prevent it falling into a deep chimney, especially if it has any kinks in it, since it may get jammed among chockstones.

Paying out the leader's rope. As noted above, the second should use the waist belay and should be wearing gloves. It is of the utmost importance that he pays close attention to the leader's progress and makes sure that his rope does not snag. The directing hand (which pays out the rope to the leader) should always be on the side on which the leader is climbing (if the leader moves across above the second, the latter should ask the leader to halt in a safe place, preferably with a temporary belay, while he rearranges the rope). The controlling arm (which has a twist of the rope round it) should be braced against the thigh with the elbow against the body to ensure rigidity, and the hand should point towards the spare rope. This should be relaxed on the ledge, lying in irregular loops rather than in neat coils; the leader's end should be at the top and there should be no kinks in the rope as this would prevent it running smoothly. The leader should be allowed enough slack in the rope to enable him to make a few swift moves, but this should never be more than a few feet. The life of the leader may depend on the action of the second; no more need be said to remind him of his responsibilities. In fact some climbers are much better seconds than they are leaders; and a good second can give tremendous confidence to a leader by encouragement or silence as appropriate and by giving him all the security possible through good rope technique.

Holding a falling leader: the sliding friction arrest. As noted earlier, it is a basic principle of climbing that the leader does not fall. If, however, a fall is likely, he should warn the second so that he can be ready to hold him. The type of fall depends very much on its cause: if your hands give way, but not your feet, you are likely to fall backwards, probably upside-down (which is very dangerous on account of the risk of head injuries); if your feet come off, then the fall will probably be in the much safer upright position. If a fall, despite all precautions, is inevitable, it is much better to jump for a ledge, even though it is some way below you, than to let events take their course. A great deal of energy is created by a falling leader and it is vitally important that this energy is absorbed gradually, since this minimizes the strain on all parts of the rope system. Ideally, the rope should be allowed to run under friction for approximately one fifth of the overall height of the fall before the arrest is completed. If the leader has placed running belays, the second must expect an upward pull: he should allow the rope to run through the runners, because this will make him less likely to be pulled upwards and because it will avoid producing a very high load at the top running belay with the risk that either the runner or the rope may break. If the leader falls off on the first pitch of the climb, and is using running belays, the second may be able to stop him hitting the ground by jumping ten feet or so downhill: this is particularly relevant for outcrop climbing. Should a leader fall, all the safety precautions recommended above – the $1\frac{3}{8}$-in. nylon rope (or doubled $1\frac{1}{4}$-in. rope) with its strength and elasticity, the wide waist-band which cushions the fall, the Tarbuck knot which absorbs energy, and the gloves worn by the second – will be very much appreciated by all concerned.

Changing over belays. As noted in § 37, 1, it is convenient for two climbers of equal ability to lead through, since the same belay can be used both for bringing up the lower man and for protecting him when he leads the next pitch. When belays have to be changed the second should put on his belay before the leader takes his off, so that there is no chance of one of them accidentally falling off the ledge (e.g. if he is hit by a falling stone) in the process of changing over. Where, however, the party is belayed through a sling and a karabiner some way away from the ledge by the method shown in [83A], it may not be possible to arrange this, and it is simplest for the leader to pull all the rope through the karabiner until it becomes tight on the second, who can then belay in the normal way. Where both members are using a waist-band and karabiner method of attachment (§ 54, 2), it may be easier on a constricted stance for them to exchange rope ends. The arriving climber should clip his karabiner into the leader's belay; he is then secured and the leader (preferably still held by the belay) can unclip from the main rope to exchange ends.

Before the leader starts the next pitch, it will be necessary to rearrange the rope on the ledge so that his end comes off the top of, instead of from underneath, any coils on the ledge; if this is not done, a bad tangle may result. He should also check his knots.

§ 63. Running belays ('runners')

A running belay is normally made by placing a nylon sling over a flake (or threading it) and clipping the main climbing rope into the karabiner (which is turned so that its gate is away from the rock). The karabiner acts as a pulley in the event of a fall. Placing runners is an art in itself and a good leader can find anchors in the most unlikely places. Any of the anchors described in §§ 58–61 can be used as running belays, though it is bad form to use pitons for running belays where others have passed without them (except perhaps – on a very hard climb – when it comes on to rain). Flakes and spikes are not as good as threads for running belays, because a sling tends to lift off them with the movement of the rope (two karabiners will, however, help to weigh it down). When a running belay is placed below a bulge make sure that the sling is long enough to let the rope run freely without catching on the bulge [102]. After placing a running belay the leader should move the climbing rope round to his front so that he would not risk being turned upside-down by the rope in a fall.

Positioning of running belays. A leader who is not using running belays would fall twice the distance between himself and the second man before the latter could begin to check his fall. A running belay correctly used can reduce this to twice

88. *When the leader is placing running belays (as in* A*), the second should if possible belay himself to take an upwards pull (as in* B*).*

the distance between the leader and the runner, a very considerable increase in safety. Even the most competent leader may fall as the result of a hold unexpectedly breaking or a stone hitting him from above, and it is therefore good climbing to place running belays at frequent intervals, say every twenty feet or so. There is no reason why the first running belay should not be placed close to the second man, particularly if his belay is not above suspicion. Sometimes the use of a running belay may substantially reinforce the confidence of the second without helping the leader much; in these cases the good leader would use it. Such a case is· a pitch consisting of two sections, a steep hard vertical section, followed by an easier horizontal traverse. The running belay fixed to the top of the vertical section would safeguard the second against a bad swing [89A]. On the other hand, a runner may help the leader at the expense

A

89. *Protecting the second when using running belays.* In A, the second will be directly protected on the hard section by the running belay, which avoids the risk of a bad swing. In B, on the other hand, the leader's rope x would not give the second direct protection on the initial hard traverse. The leader has accordingly thrown down the spare end y, and is protecting him with it. Do not fix running belays on doubtfully secure blocks, since under load they may be pulled on to the second or the fallen leader with serious results.

of the second; for example, a running belay at the far end of a traverse may help the leader's confidence if a hard vertical section follows, but the second cannot be assisted or completely safeguarded on the traverse. In such circumstances, it is best for the leader to use a doubled rope (if the pitch is not more than fifty feet or so the normal climbing rope can be doubled); he can then clip one half

B

of the rope through the runners to protect himself, and use the other half to protect the second directly [89B]. Ideally, the leader should arrange his runners so that the second does not have to deviate from the easiest route to recover them. But there can be no hard-and-fast rule on this because so much depends on the nature of the pitch and the climbing ability of the second.

§ 64. Climbing calls and signals

A regular climbing pair will understand each other so well that there will be little need for calls between them. But sometimes the use of standard calls can save a good deal of time and confusion. It does not matter what the calls consist of so long as each member of the party knows their exact meaning and they are regularly adhered to. The following are possible calls; those in capitals are the most useful:

'Runner on'	By the leader, indicating that he has put on a running belay and hence the second must expect any pull to come from the direction of the runner.
'I'M THERE'	By the leader to indicate that he has reached the end of the pitch (the second takes off his gloves, but generally should not dismantle his belay until the leader has taken in all the rope).
'Taking in'	By the belayed leader to indicate that he is taking in the rope between himself and the second man.
'That's me'	By the second to inform the leader that the rope between them is tight (and not caught anywhere on the rock).
'COME ON'	By the leader to indicate that he is ready in every respect to bring up the second man.
'CLIMBING'	By the second to indicate that he has taken off his belay and is about to start climbing.
'O.K.' or 'AYE AYE'	By the leader, indicating that he realizes that the second is about to move, and is fully prepared.
'SLACK'	By the moving climber when he wants more rope to be paid out (e.g. if he wants to descend for a few moves).
'TAKE IN'	By the moving climber when he requires spare rope to be taken in. It is important not to confuse this with 'SLACK' since the rope might be let out when it should be taken in: nor should the two calls be combined – 'Take in the slack' – since the leader may hear only the last part and let the rope out.
'TIGHT ROPE' or 'PULL'	By a climber who wants assistance from the rope.
'HOLD!'	By a climber who thinks that he is about to fall. The belayer should immediately be

ready to arrest the fall. If it is the second who is in difficulty, the leader should continue to take in the rope, holding it very tightly and pulling as hard as possible since the second may succeed in climbing over the hard section and will want the rope to be kept tight until he can relax again.

'Twenty (or ten, etc.) feet'   By the second when the leader has only twenty feet of rope left.

When shouted calls cannot be heard, the party should use a system of gentle tugs on the rope, e.g. three tugs by the leader to indicate that he is ready for the second man to move. If the leader when climbing cannot establish contact with his second to find out how much rope is left, he can draw it all in momentarily, and then release it again (so that the second does not mistakenly think that he has completed the pitch and start to come on).

§ 65. Rope management in descent

Rope management in descent (§§ 37, 3, and 50) is different from that in ascent in the following respects:

- the best climber comes down last (since the last man is not protected by the rope from above);
- the first man down (i.e., the weaker climber) has responsibility for detailed route-finding and belays;
- the first man should put on running belays to protect the last man.

If there is serious difficulty, the last man can put on a running belay (§ 63) above himself, and after descending flick it off or, if this is not possible, untie and pull the rope through. Before detaching himself from the end of the rope he should if possible tie in to the middle of the rope so that he is not unsecured. This manœuvre is useful where an abseil (see below) is not convenient.

§ 66. Roping down (abseiling or rappelling)

If it is not practicable to reverse a pitch safely (e.g. because it has come on to rain), the party will need to abseil. This involves:

1. doubling the rope and attaching it to a secure anchor (see below);
2. throwing the two ends of the rope down the desired line of descent so that they both reach the ledge and are untwisted;
3. standing astride the rope and passing it round or attaching it to your body by one of three methods (see 1–3 below);
4. moving over the edge of the ledge – being very careful not to disturb the anchor – and 'walking down' the cliff at a steady pace with the rope sliding round your body and taking your weight. Your speed is controlled by bringing your lower hand in towards your body so that it increases the friction of the rope (see 1 below);
5. when you reach the ledge checking that the rope can be pulled round the anchor without jamming and that it is not twisted;
6. number two descending to the ledge in the same way;
7. pulling the rope round the anchor and down (the '*rappel*' from which the manœuvre takes its name).

If at all possible a second rope should be used for the abseil so that the party can be protected in the normal way by the main rope (i.e., only the last man down does not have a rope from above). If there is no second rope, a safety rope can be arranged for all but the last man in the way shown in [95].

The anchor for the abseil rope must:

– be absolutely secure (i.e., it must be firm and there must be no chance of the rope rolling off it) since the whole weight of the descending climber will probably be taken on it;
– permit the rope to be pulled down when the operation is completed (i.e. the rope must not jam behind it or jam in the sling if one is used).

Any good natural anchor or a piton in a horizontal crack (preferably not a vertical crack) will do. Note in particular that:

- a high belay is better than a low one since it enables you to start the descent from a more comfortable position;
- it is necessary to use a sling on most anchors because the rope will jam if it is used on the anchor direct; this is particularly important where the abseil ropes pass through a big angle (e.g. over the edge of the ledge) below the anchor since the friction of this will make recovery of the rope difficult [90]. The sling should be of good quality $\frac{7}{8}$-in. nylon, Italian hemp, or manila and should be tied with a double fisherman's knot or a double sheetbend [169C, D and 170C, D]. A piece of new $\frac{3}{4}$-in. hemp waist-line can be used if necessary. If there is no good sling of any kind available, cut a piece off the main climbing rope. In Britain at least (and as a general rule, in the Alps also – see § 138) old slings found in place in the mountain should not be used, because they are likely to be rotted: be on the lookout for old white cotton slings (which look much like nylon but are very dangerous), or nylon slings which may be partially melted as a result of abseil ropes having been pulled through them by previous parties;
- if the anchor is sharp, protect the rope or the sling with a handkerchief or a wad of paper so that it does not fray;
- if the abseil rope is knotted at the centre, put the knot below the sling on the inside. In any case, always pull down the *inside* rope first (the white rope in [90C]) because that creates a good deal less friction at the sling than pulling the outside rope.

90. *Abseil anchors.* A sling is necessary wherever the rope would tend to jam when being pulled down, as in A and C.

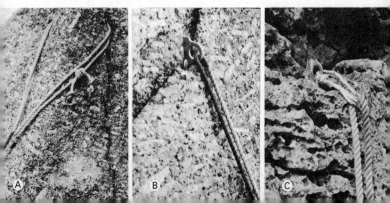

Safety
rope

Abseil
rope

A

B

91. *The classic abseil.* The safety rope tied to the climber's waist is recommended as a standard precaution.

1. *The classic method* [91]. The doubled rope is taken in the left hand and the climber stands astride it facing the anchor so that the rope passes between his legs from front to back. The rope is then taken behind the right thigh, up across the front of the body and over the left shoulder – front to back (turn your collar up so that the rope does not rub your neck). The hanging rope is held in the right hand. For the left-handed, of course, the opposite hands may be used throughout. On vertical ground the climber walks backwards down the cliff keeping his body and his legs fairly straight, and his feet about eighteen inches apart horizontally. On less steep ground, however, turn sideways to the face so that you can see where you are going more easily. The speed of descent is controlled by the position of the ropes held in the right hand. If there is a long length of rope hanging below, or if the rope is wet, it will not slide easily over the shoulder in any case and it will be necessary to ease the rope round by lifting it with the right hand. If it is found, on the other hand, that there is a tendency to go

too fast, the hanging ropes can be brought round to the front of the body, still in the right hand: the increased friction produced by the longer length of rope in contact with the body will provide more than enough braking capacity. The following points should be noted in particular:

- go over the edge carefully to avoid any possibility of the rope rolling off the belay, slipping off your shoulder, or slipping from the upper thigh to behind your knees;
- lean well out from the cliff so that you can see where you are going, and take the strain with your lower (controlling) hand and not with your upper (steadying) hand;
- do not go down too fast or in leaps and bounds since this puts an unnecessary strain on the belay; descend at a steady walking pace, smoothly and rhythmically;

92. *Abseiling by the snaplink and* descendeur *methods*. These are more comfortable than the classic method, but they are also more complicated and there is more to go wrong.

A   B

– watch out for overhangs. It is best to take a little jump backwards and descend rapidly for a few feet so that by the time you swing back into the cliff your head and shoulders are below the overhang and you do not hit them on the rock.

The classic method is simple and safe. It can, however, be painful if your trousers are not thick enough to prevent the rope cutting into you.

2. *The snaplink method* [92A]. A good-quality short sling should be twisted so that it represents an eight. Place your legs through each of the holes in the eight and then pull the sling to the top of your thighs. A snaplink (with sleeve) is then attached to the middle of the sling, which is pulled forward between your legs and is linked also into your waist-loop for extra comfort and security [93]. Alternatively, a single loop on one thigh may be used [76]. The doubled abseil rope (anchored as described above) is clipped through the snaplink from front to back (so that it runs

93. *A cradle for abseiling (see also 76)*. Note that in B the abseil karabiner is clipped through both the cradle and the safety rope: this is a good deal safer than clipping into the cradle alone and is also more comfortable. The upper karabiner in C may prove justified if you have to abseil without a safety rope: a knot is tied at the bottom of the abseil rope so that the karabiner would prevent you falling off the end if you lost control (which might happen if, for example, you were hit by a falling stone).

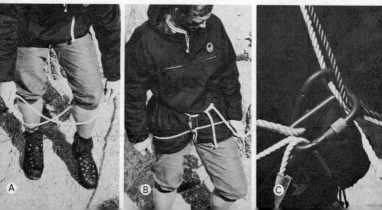

A   B   C

easily) and over the left shoulder. The hanging ropes are held in the right hand as before and the ropes from the anchor in the left. Note that:

– the screw on the karabiner should be tightened home;
– if there is no screw, it is best to turn the hinged end of the karabiner uppermost so that there is no chance of the rope slipping out inadvertently; or use two karabiners turned opposite ways;
– the sling should be fairly tight since this keeps the karabiner low and hence gives greater stability. It also avoids the rope pulling your anorak into the karabiner: this can be a considerable hazard because it may jam the rope so firmly that you cannot move at all; it will in any case damage your anorak;
– a knot can be placed at the end of the rope, so that if the descending climber is knocked unconscious (e.g. by a falling stone) he cannot run off the end of the rope. It is useful but not essential to use a separate karabiner as in [93c] in this case. The knot should be untied before the rope is pulled down;
– a steady and continuous descent is desirable to avoid getting the karabiner hot or keeping it in contact with a section of rope long enough to risk melting it.

3. *The descendeur method* [92B]. This is mentioned here only for completeness as it is really more relevant to alpine descents, where many abseils are involved, than to this country. Three of the main types of *descendeur* are shown in [94]. The *descendeur* is clipped into a harness made of a linked thigh- and waist-loop, and the rope is twisted round it in the way shown in the illustrations. The twisting of the rope gives almost all the friction required to control the descent, and only light hand pressure is needed in addition. The rope is not taken over your shoulder as in the two other methods, and this saves a good deal of wear and tear on your clothing, and strain on yourself. On very steep ground, with inadequate ledges, you can take a hitch round the *descendeur* if need be so that you can have both hands free to put in a peg for the next anchor, but only if the *descendeur* is not hot enough to risk melting the rope. If it

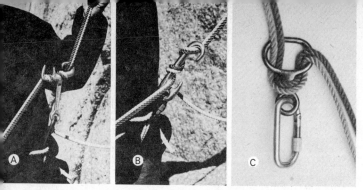

94. *Descendeurs*. A is the Pierre Allain. B is the Peck. C is a smaller and possibly more foolproof one made by Fisher of Keswick, which can also be used in a belay system for controlling the active rope; this is recommended in cases where it might not be possible to arrest a leader's fall with the waist belay (§ 62, 1), for example, in artificial climbing (§ 73) or where the second is a woman or an adolescent. See also 92.

is hot it is necessary (as with 2) to descend at a steady rate and without stopping. A *descendeur* can also be used to good effect on rescue operations (§ 94). The main disadvantages of a *descendeur* are:

– it is an extra piece of equipment to carry;
– most *descendeurs* tend to twist the rope so that quite bad tangles can result.

The use of a safety rope has saved many abseiling accidents and it is recommended wherever possible. The belayed climber should find a separate anchor for the safety rope. If there is only one rope available, a safety rope can be arranged for all but the last man by the method shown in [95].

All the methods of abseiling described above should be practised in a safe place before being used on a crag.

95. *Arranging a safety rope for all but the last man when there is only one rope in the party*. 1. Thread the rope through the anchor sling in the normal way. 2. Tie a figure-of-eight knot in the rope and clip this into the anchor sling with a karabiner (as in the lower piton in the illustration). 3. The last man then belays with half the rope and uses it to protect the other members as they abseil on the other half as a single rope. 4. The last man undoes the knot and removes the karabiner (leaving the rope still threaded through the abseil sling) and then descends on the double abseil rope in the normal way (but without a safety rope).

Safety rope

Abseil rope

Chapter 9. Artificial climbing ('pegging')

This chapter describes the extra equipment and special techniques needed for artificial climbing. As noted in § 34, 2, this form of climbing has been developed in this country on limestone crags and gritstone quarries outside the main mountain areas. Its main value is as training for the great alpine rock climbs where familiarity with the technique pays dividends; it is often practised in winter when many of the free climbs in our mountains are out of condition. Most British climbers prefer free climbing, but pegging has its own devotees who enjoy it for what it is: an arduous, technical form of climbing, which can give continuous steepness rarely encountered in free climbing.

§ 67. The party and its equipment

The same considerations apply as to a rock-climbing party (§ 37). Two is the best number on a climb, but as artificial climbing is rather a slow process it is pleasant in Britain to have a 'ground party' of two or more so that they can take turns at holding the rope. This is particularly useful in winter when seconding can be a cold business. In addition to normal clothing and equipment, the party will need:

- a double rope, preferably each half a different colour so that they can be easily distinguished; 1¼-in. nylon is probably best, but ⅞-in. is adequate if there are no long free sections. Kern-mantel rope is preferable to cabled rope because it does not stretch or twist as much (§ 51);
- possibly a third rope for sack hauling and maintaining com-munications with the ground;
- a supply of assorted pitons, and possibly wedges or bolts (see § 68). Try to find out what is needed before starting the climb.

Where the guide-book says that fifty pegs are needed, it means that there are fifty places where a peg is used (whether or not they are already in place) and not that you have to take fifty with you;
- about twenty or thirty karabiners, of which two or three should be full strength and the remainder alloy (§ 56);
- a hammer per man (§ 69);
- two or more *étriers* per man (§ 70). For most pegging two are sufficient and avoid unnecessary complications; but on loose pegs or steeply overhanging ground three or even four *étriers* per man may be needed;
- about three nylon slings per man, which could be used for prusiking if you swing clear of the rock [152].

The waist-band and karabiner system of attachment (§ 54, 2) cannot be unreservedly recommended for artificial climbing because:

- the rope arrangements are sometimes extremely complicated, and there is a risk of opening the waist-band karabiner by mistake and accidentally becoming detached from the main rope; and
- the waist-band karabiner prevents your waist being pulled tight against the karabiner in the piton.

If a hemp waist-band is used, it is best to tie into it direct without using karabiners. The leader at least should tie into both ropes separately so that he can release himself from one of them should it jam. It is useful to have a thigh- and shoulder-harness [76] to relieve the strain on your waist. In addition, a nylon sling can be made into a 'cow's tail', a short loop from your waist or chest which can be clipped on to a karabiner to take your weight off the double rope; it is sometimes convenient to make this adjustable by using a Tarbuck knot. The hammer is usually carried in a rule pocket or in your belt when not in use; special hammer holsters are also available. One sling (or the shoulder-loop) can serve as a bandolier for all your kara-biners and pitons (the latter clipped into two large D karabiners or a piton carrier). The *étriers* are best carried over one shoulder, or in your pockets. It is worth using different colours for your hammer and fifi lines, and for each of your *étriers*, so that they can be distinguished readily.

§ 68. Pitons (pegs), wedges, and bolts

Rock pitons are available in a very wide range of shapes and sizes [96]. There are four basic types:

1. *leaf*. These have a thin blade for narrow cracks;
2. *channel*. These have a U cross-section, and are excellent for wider cracks. Narrow channels are being increasingly used for thin cracks in place of leaf pitons, since any one peg can be used in a wider variety of cracks, and because they grip very well;
3. *universal*, with a V cross-section.
4. *thick aluminium alloy*. Made commercially only in America.

On the Continent, pitons have traditionally been made of malleable steel or iron, but tests in 1967 by Dr Griffin of the National Engineering Laboratory confirmed earlier

96. *Rock pitons*. High-tensile alloy-steel pitons (F and G) have been proved much stronger than traditional soft steel types (A–E). A–C are blade pitons, D and E are channels; the channelled sleeve (D) is for use in conjunction with Peck pitons where they would otherwise be slightly too narrow for the crack. F is a universal American piton and G an improved American channel piton, both made of hard steel. The well-designed cross-section of G is shown also in 97B.

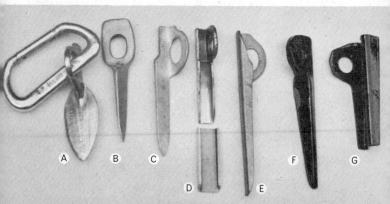

suspicions that well-designed, high tensile alloy steel pitons (originated by Chouinard in California) have much greater holding power: in horizontal cracks 1,950–5,000 lbs. (according to the shape of the crack and the nature of the rock) as against only 410–4,200 lbs. for soft steel, and in vertical cracks 800–4,600 lbs. as against 200–3,200 lbs. They can also be inserted and extracted more easily. Although they cost more than the traditional types, they are strongly recommended in preference to most of them.

Some pitons are well designed, others not. Points to bear in mind are:

- a piton must be robust enough to withstand a great deal of hammering and rough treatment, particularly when it is being taken out of a crack after use. Channel pegs are rather vulnerable to damage in de-pegging. Examine pegs frequently to check that there are no incipient cracks, especially if there is a sharp angle where the eye joins the blade;
- movable rings on pitons have proved very unreliable because of the difficulty of welding them; the B.M.C. has recommended that they should be avoided. A fixed eye is very much stronger;
- the eye should be in a plane at an angle to the plane of the blade so that the pull tends to twist the piton in the crack, thus holding it more securely. It is also useful when a piton has to be inserted in a crack in a corner (as is very often the case) since it will always be possible to insert the karabiner in the eye (if the eye and the blade are in the same plane, on the other hand, the eye may be blocked by one of the walls). On the other hand, the twisting under load can tend to tear the piton at the junction of eye and blade; pitons with the eye offset *at a full right angle* to the blade are most susceptible to this form of failure. More research is needed on this aspect. The distinction sometimes drawn between pitons for vertical cracks (eye in the same plane as the blade), and horizontal cracks (eye at an angle to blade) is of little significance.
- the eye of the piton should only be large enough to allow a little clearance around a single karabiner, and should be round, not oval;
- the shoulder (where the eye meets the blade of the piton) should allow only slight bending of the piton before the eye comes into

contact with the rock, to avoid any tendency to withdraw the
peg under load;
- short pitons well in are safer than long ones only half in. But use
  a piton with the longest possible blade consistent with its complete entry into the crack;
- the blade of a piton should taper only gradually; most cracks
  maintain the same width, and a sharply tapered piton will be in
  contact with the rock for only a very short distance and hence
  be likely to swivel under load;
- on limestone, soft steel pegs may be preferable to hard alloy ones
  because they damage the rock less; in such cases allow for the
  lower strength of these pegs.

Always remember that pitons already in place may have
suffered internal corrosion or damage, particularly to
welded rings which, as noted above, are not recommended.
Pitons should be kept dry when not in use; alloy steel rusts
particularly rapidly. Ice pegs are described in § 81.

Wedges. Where the cracks are too wide for channel pitons,
wedges may be used instead [97]. Wooden ones must be of
a good enough quality to withstand hammering without
splitting. Recently, hard steel hollow wedges ('bongs') have
become available from America; these are more robust
than wooden wedges, and are becoming generally used.

97. *Wedges.* The American hard steel wedge (c) is lighter and probably
better than the normal wooden wedge (A).

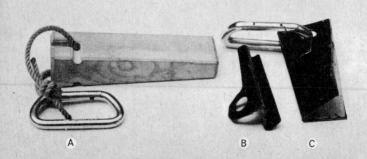

A   B   C

Wooden wedges vary in width to up to four inches or so at the wide end, and usually narrow by about one and a half inches over their length. Sometimes they have a slight twist so that they jam more securely. A hole is drilled in the wide end and a short length of nylon or (better) wire is threaded through it and tied into a loop. Two quarter-inch grooves are made from the hole to the edges on each side so that the loop is not damaged when the wedge is inserted. Wedges are not safe as main belays because they have no torque and hence tend to come out rather easily; a piton should be used in conjunction with a wedge instead [103B]. Sometimes it is better to use the wedge as a chockstone and loop a sling round it rather than create a turning moment by using the loop. Wedges which are already in place are likely to be rotted and must be treated with caution.

Expansion bolts and ring screws have been used a good deal in British pegging on rock where no natural cracks exist. They are commonly used in the U.S.A., in the Dolomites, and at Chamonix. It is usually necessary to drill a hole in the rock, and they are unlikely to appeal generally because of the labour involved in this. To many they are objectionable on aesthetic grounds as well: pitons do at least use an existing crack and hence do not permanently damage the rock, whereas the holes made by expansion bolts or ring screws do.

§ 69. Piton hammer

For full-scale artificial climbing a heavy hammer-head is desirable since this greatly reduces the amount of effort involved in putting in pegs, but for occasional British use a light hammer is satisfactory. The Stubai shown in [98A] is a good general-purpose hammer. The head should be wide rather than narrow since this enables you to hit the pitons more easily, and the other half of the head should be a wedge or a spike so that it can be used for 'gardening' (i.e., clearing out loose stones, earth, and vegetation) and for knocking out pitons in awkward positions (e.g. in narrow

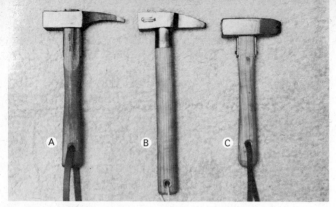

98. *Piton hammers*. A is a Stubai, B is a Charlet-Moser, C is a Simond. Note the metal on the top of the shaft to protect the wood and prevent the head working loose.

corners). The spike should be strong enough to be used for chipping sharp edges off flakes, so that they can be used safely for abseil anchors. The shaft of the peg hammer should have two metal strips or a metal sheath where the head is attached, to protect the wood from damage and to prevent the head working loose. The best way of securing a hammer in use is to thread a long length of nylon rope (preferably $\frac{7}{8}$-in. as $\frac{5}{8}$-in. is too easily tangled) through a hole in the end of the shaft, and knot it at one end to form a shoulder-loop, and possibly at the other also to form a wrist-loop. A coat hook screwed into the shaft can also be useful because it enables you to hook the hammer into your waist-loop easily yet leaves the hammer ready for instant use. Some people use a rule pocket or a hammer holster. Ice hammers are described in § 80.

§ 70. *Étriers* (stirrups)

These are short rope ladders, with two or three, or even four small steps [99]. Plaited terylene or nylon, or hemp or manila, are better than cabled nylon, which is too elastic; plaited terylene or nylon with a wire core is extremely good. The steps should be made of aluminium alloy and should be broad so that you can work your feet on to them when they are lying against a rock face, and so that they do not restrict your blood circulation if you have to sit on them for any length of time. There should be no knots above the steps because it is often necessary to slide a step up, particularly in very steep situations, so that you can push your knee between the two sides of the *étrier* to gain a more comfortable position. There should be a loop below the bottom step so that another *étrier* can be clipped into it; this is necessary to enable you to climb down linked *étriers* to knock the lower pitons out (§ 74). The number of steps and the distance between them is a matter of personal preference, though it is best to have the top step as high as is comfortable so that you can reach the next piton more conveniently; most British climbers prefer three steps about eighteen inches apart.

A very simple *étrier* made of one-inch wide nylon webbing has been developed on the very advanced piton climbs in the Yosemite Valley, California. The main advantages of this type over the metal-step *étrier* are claimed to be that:

– it is more comfortable and secure for the feet, and for sitting in;
– the slings are strong enough to be used as runners on flakes, trees, etc.;
– they can be carried more easily, and do not jam when hanging down below the climber;
– they make no noise.

It is however easier to get your feet into a metal-step *étrier*. It is useful to tie a loop of this webbing into the top of each of your *étriers* so that when you are standing on the top step you can put the other foot into the webbing loop and 'sit back' on it (as in [100B and C], though there the climber is using two separate *étriers*).

Temporary *étriers* can be made out of knotted slings; make sure that one side is longer than the other so that it is easy to get your feet into the loops.

Traditionally, a karabiner is used for clipping the *étrier* into the karabiners attached to the piton [100]. A fifi-hook may be used instead; there are several types of these, but by far the most convenient is the *griff fifi* which incorporates a handhold [100C]. Usually, the fifi-hook is attached to the climber's waist by a length of nylon line (not too thin and preferably each one differently coloured), so that the hook can be retrieved when the climber is two or three feet above it; but the lines can be very inconvenient, especially where any free climbing is involved, since they can get wrapped round your legs or caught on projections, and consequently many climbers prefer fifi-hooks without lines. As a general rule, *étriers* with karabiners are adequate for sections of artificial climbing of one hundred feet or so, but fifi-hooks save time on long artificial routes, especially where the pegs are regularly spaced.

Étriers are useful also for artificial climbing on ice in crossing bergschrunds (§ 135) and for crevasse rescue (§ 140, 1).

99. *Orthodox procedure on pegs and* étriers.
A. The leader is standing in an *étrier* clipped into the first peg and the second is holding him in position by pulling lightly on the white rope, which goes through the lower karabiner on the second peg to the leader's waist. The second man is using his body weight rather than his arm strength.
B. The leader, standing in the *étrier* on the second peg and with some tension on the white rope, reaches as high as he can and places the third peg in a suitable part of the crack.
C. When the third peg has been hammered well home, two linked karabiners are clipped into it and the top one is turned upside-down so that it cannot be opened accidentally by pressure from the peg (see also 101).
D. The leader has clipped the red rope into the lower karabiner on the third peg with the part going to the second man on the inside and the end to him on the outside (this is so that the rope will run smoothly through the karabiner when he is above it). The second is giving some tension on the red rope as the leader reaches down to retrieve the lower *étrier* (this movement is unnecessary if using fifi-hooks).
E. The leader clips the *étrier* into the higher karabiner attached to the third peg so that it hangs down between the rope and the rock (alternatively it can be clipped direct to the peg).
F and G. The leader pulls partly on the inside red rope (on which the second may also pull) and partly on the *étrier*, and moves up on to the *étrier*.
When the leader is standing in the top rung of the *étrier* the process B to G is repeated with the fourth peg and using the white rope.

§ 71. Procedure for the leader

It is vital to develop an automatic system so as to minimize delays and complications. On most routes quite a few of the pitons will already be in place (in the Alps they are almost always in place), but it is as well to practise also on routes which have no pegs in place so that you can perfect your technique (the insertion of pegs is covered in § 72). A suggested sequence of movement from peg to peg is shown in [99] and methods of standing in *étriers* and of clipping in karabiners are shown in [100] and [101]. Each climber will however develop his own preferences and these can be no more than a rough guide (thus, some climbers use only one rope where the pegs are all in the same crack on the score that this is simpler and quicker). Note in particular:

– the leader takes most of his weight on the *étriers* and by pulling on the inside rope. If necessary he could clip a short sling (a 'cow's tail') into the karabiner on the piton, while he is stretching up to hammer in the next peg, or alternatively he could use a second *étrier* or foot-loop to 'sit back' as in [100]. Gone are the days when the second man used to pull the leader bodily up to the piton and hold him there – a very strenuous process;

– the importance of being able to distinguish easily between the two ropes, since a pull on the wrong rope would have the opposite effect to that intended. Different-coloured ropes are extremely useful for this reason;

– the desirability of using two karabiners on each peg (except, possibly, where *griff fifis* are used) since the upper karabiner can be used as a handhold. Try to avoid holding on to the karabiner containing the rope because the rope is likely to damage your hands when it is under tension. (The linked karabiners also help to minimize rope friction when you are above the peg [102A]);

– never hang on to a peg without putting a karabiner in first, because this is very tiring, and it may be impossible, or at least extremely painful, to clip the karabiner in subsequently;

– where the pitons are insecure, never put all your weight on one alone. If possible put two pegs in next to each other and use two or three *étriers* to stand on while putting in the next peg. Sometimes it is worth while to link the pitons with a sling so that the weight is taken on both of them evenly;

100. *Use of* étriers. A shows the standard method used in 99: note that two karabiners are used for connecting the rope to the piton (so that you can use one as a hold without the rope cutting your hand) and a third for the *étrier*. B and C show the much higher position achievable where a second *étrier* is used for 'sitting back' – and without any tension from the second man. To avoid the loss of time involved in clipping in a second *étrier* – and the risk that it may open the gate of a karabiner accidentally – it is recommended that those using this method habitually should tie a sling (preferably nylon tape or webbing) permanently to the top of their *étriers* and use this for sitting back on.

- on very steep ground you can relieve strain by sitting in the *étriers*, with the rungs under your thighs.

Rope friction is a serious problem, and it is normally necessary to limit pitches to eighty or one hundred feet. Friction can be minimized by:

- putting the ropes through the karabiners correctly [101], so that the rope runs through them cleanly, without jamming;
- using two karabiners on pitons so that the rope swings free of the rock more easily. Wherever there is a bulge above a piton it is advisable to use a sling between the piton and the karabiner so that the rope is not forced into contact with the lip of the bulge [102];
- running the two ropes in parallel as far as possible, avoiding criss-crossing;
- leaving karabiners only on alternate pitons or on occasional really secure pitons. This also uses fewer karabiners, but it requires a good deal of judgement to be able to do it safely.

101. *Clipping into pitons*. A is correct: the karabiner has been turned upside-down after clipping in so that the gate is away from the piton and any load would come on the backbone of the karabiner. The rope runs freely. In B the rope has been inserted the wrong way round with the result that the karabiner is pulled up: considerable rope friction results and a load might come on the weak side of the karabiner. C may occur where the gate and not the backbone is next to the karabiner.

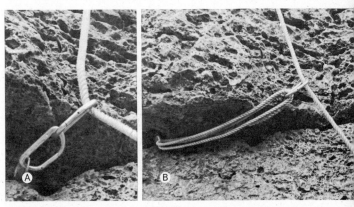

102. *Avoiding rope friction on bulges*. Make sure when using linked kara-biners as in A that they cannot twist each other open. With B, it is preferable to clip the sling into the peg with a karabiner if time is important.

On the other hand, a limited amount of friction is desirable since in the event of a fall by the leader this helps to spread the shock load over several pitons.

§ 72. Placing of pitons

As noted earlier, on many climbs the pegs are already in place and it is only necessary to check that they are secure – i.e., that they have been inserted correctly, have not worked loose, and have not rusted. The insertion of pitons requires a good deal of care and skill. It must be borne in mind that a peg may be needed for quite different purposes:

1. *As a main belay, an abseil anchor, or as an occasional sound peg on an artificial pitch for protection.* Pitons for these purposes must be secure and it is worth taking all the time and trouble needed to see that they are. Use more than one if in doubt.
2. *For progress.* These do not have to be nearly as secure as 1, since they need do no more than bear the weight of the man who is climbing on them. Indeed one should aim to avoid spending too much time and effort on inserting these pegs because this would slow the party down unnecessarily. The scaling down of your safety margin to enable you to peg and de-peg quickly should however be delayed until you have a good deal of experience.

The security of a piton depends on the following factors.

1. *The design, strength, and frictional properties of the piton itself.* As noted in § 68, well-designed, high-tensile alloy-steel pitons are much better than traditional soft steel types, and welded rings are particularly dangerous.

2. *The roughness and the soundness of the rock.* A hollow noise when you are hammering in the peg means that the rock is unsound. Be careful to avoid prising off a flake of rock.

3. *The shape and depth of the crack.* A deep continuous crack is much better than a shallow or interrupted one, and parallel sides give a much better grip along the whole length of the piton than sharply converging ones. Ideally place the piton between two constrictions so that it is prevented from moving, or swivelling on its axis, within the crack. Contrary to popular belief, the sound produced by a piton as it is hammered home is no guide to its holding power; in particular, a rising 'singing' note does not in itself mean that it is secure (the best guide is the resistance

103. *Use of wedges.* A is orthodox. B and C are preferable where the original sling has rotted.

to downward blows of the peg as it goes home). If a whining note results, the end of the piton has met an obstacle in the crack and cannot go further. It is better in such a case to use a shorter piton, but if none is available attach a sling to the piton with a clove hitch [86F] at the point where it emerges from the rock (to avoid increasing the leverage by using the eye of the piton). Alternatively, in the case of a piton for progress, bend it over by hammering so that the leverage is reduced (this is very useful with pegs which are upside-down).

4. *The direction and angle of the crack.* A horizontal or slanting crack gives a much better grip than a vertical one, and a horizontal crack which is downward-sloping inside is better than one which is upward-sloping. As noted in § 61 a piton used for a main belay should not be placed in a vertical crack if the pull is likely to come downwards, since even a piton which seems secure may give under as little as 200–400 lb. load; a crack as nearly as possible at right angles to the direction of pull should be used instead. For progress, however, pegs can be placed in any type of crack, even upside-down in cracks running under overhangs or between the main face and a leaf of rock attached to it; clearly there is less scope for clumsy use in such a case, because only friction will prevent the peg from withdrawing.

To take a piton out, knock it backwards and forwards along the line of the crack. If it is loose, but will not come out, attach a sling to it and pull, or prise it with the pick of the hammer. It is advisable to tie the peg to you because otherwise it may drop down the cliff.

§ 73. Stances and belaying

It is usually possible to arrange a stance and belay in the normal way (see previous chapter). In exceptional cases however there may be no stance and it will then be necessary to arrange one, sitting or standing in *étriers*. In such circumstances, it is far safer to insert a good piton for a belay than to rely only on the climbing pegs; the extra piton will protect the party in the event of a fall at the crucial moment of changing over, when the rope is passing through only two or three pitons. It is advisable also to pass the two climbing ropes through the first couple of climbing pitons on the next pitch. This is not only safer, but also ensures that all is ready for the leader to move on with the least complication when the second arrives. A direct belay [145] should be used when belaying from *étriers*, since a waist or shoulder belay (§ 62) would tend to turn you upside-down. In the Alps, the sacks can be hauled up between stances on the third rope, though this is tiring and time-consuming, and should be avoided where possible.

§ 74. Procedure for the second man

Artificial climbing is, if anything, more strenuous for the second man than for the leader. While the leader is climbing, the second may have to help him by pulling on the rope (though this is much less common now with the use of *étriers*, 'sit slings', and 'cows' tails'). So far as possible, try to avoid using valuable arm strength for this: one method is to pass the ropes under your buttocks, and when a pull is required to bend your knees so that your whole weight comes on to the rope [99A]. It is the second's job to remove the karabiners from the pitons, and where necessary to take the pitons out also (it is usual to remove a piton if your leader has put it in, but pitons which are already in place on artificial pitches or as essential belays are usually left in place, especially in the Alps – § 137). A leader can give very little direct help to his second, owing to the friction of the rope and the stretch in it, and he is essentially dependent on his own devices. When first reaching a karabiner through which (say) the white rope is passing, the second should ask for slack so that he can pull that rope down from above the karabiner and help to hold himself into the karabiner by pulling down on this part of the white rope. This is much less of a strain than trying to hang on to the karabiner itself. The second may also find it useful on hard sections which require de-pegging to climb up twenty feet, unclipping the karabiners as he passes them; he can then clip two or three *étriers* into each other, attach the top one to a peg, and use these as a ladder to climb back down to extract the pitons. The second may save himself much effort by using prusik-loops on a standing rope to overcome a hard pitch (§ 140, 2).

Even for very practised climbers, artificial climbing is a slow and complicated process. A party of two is therefore much better than one of three. If, however, three cannot be avoided, then the second should leave the pitons in place with the third man's rope threaded through karabiners here and there to prevent him swinging into space. As noted above, however, it is often pleasant in British artificial climbing to have a 'ground party' to keep the second company and to take turns with holding the rope while the leader is equipping the first part of the climb.

§ 75. Traverses

Sometimes a line of cracks will peter out into a blank wall and it will be impossible to go further. If there is a transverse crack then it is simply a matter of traversing to a new line of ascending cracks, if necessary using pitons and *étriers*, in the same way as in ascending. If possible put one of the ropes into a high piton as this will give the leader and the second protection from above. If there is no suitable transverse crack it will be necessary to do a pendulum or a horizontal rappel. The former involves abseiling (§ 66) from a piton and swinging over to the desired new position. The latter also necessitates abseiling, but the climber takes advantage of any excrescences or side holds on the rock to move in the desired direction; pitons may also be used if necessary. Both of these manœuvres are a good deal easier for the second man since he can be pulled into his destination by the first man.

§ 76. Descents

In artificial climbing it is only very rarely necessary to descend by any means other than the standard abseil (§ 66). Where, however, the pitch is steeply overhanging, and the rope ends in space some way further out than the ledge, it is best for the first man down to clip the safety rope into pegs so that he, and the next man, can maintain contact with the cliff. It is also worth while to have some prusik-loops handy in case the abseil cannot be completed and it is necessary to climb back up the rope (§140, 2). If an artificial passage has to be reversed other than by an abseil the technique is similar to ascent.

Chapter 10. Snow and ice climbing equipment

The clothing and equipment needed for winter mountaineering in Britain has been listed in §§ 13 and 38, and the clothing has been described in detail in chapter 3. This chapter covers crampons and the various types of ice-axes, hammers, and pitons.

§ 77. Crampons

Crampons are sets of spikes which can be strapped underneath boots [104]. They grip on hard snow and ice and enable steep slopes to be climbed without step-cutting (§ 84). They are generally used in the Alps, but have only recently come into favour in this country in preference to tricouni-nailed boots (which are however perfectly adequate for most British snow and ice climbing, and are still used a good deal, especially on routes where iced rock predominates).

Crampons or nails? It is unsafe to use rubber-soled boots without crampons on slopes of hard snow or ice, and the climber who only has these will have to decide whether to invest in tricouni-nailed boots or crampons. The advantages which cleated rubber-soled climbing boots with crampons have over tricounis are:

– they enable the party to move much more quickly and effortlessly;
– they are much more secure on slopes which are near the limit for climbing in nails without steps;
– they are warmer.

On the other hand, they are rather more cumbersome than nails on rock, and they are an extra item of equipment to

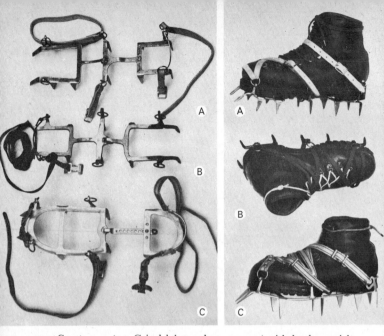

104. *Crampons*. A is a Grivel lobster-claw crampon with leather quick-release straps, one of the very best crampons made. B is a Stubai ordinary crampon with a single long nylon strap. C is a Simond adjustable lobster-claw crampon; it is perhaps less satisfactory than A since the vertical spikes on the sole of the boot are too far away from the toe to be in contact with the ice when using the front points alone on steep ice (see 115B and C).

carry. Most British climbers prefer them to nails because of the time they save on long and serious snow and ice routes, especially where there is a long, steep approach on hard snow which would require step-cutting in nails; the time saved here can greatly increase the party's security since, as noted in § 38, benightment is one of the main dangers in British winter mountaineering. There can be no possible objection to their use by thoroughly competent parties, but they can be dangerous for the inexperienced (see below), and beginners should get accustomed to them on practice slopes or frozen waterfalls before using them on a proper climb. In deciding whether to go for nails or crampons, much depends on whether or not you intend to climb in the

Alps later. If you do, then you will need crampons anyway, and experience gained with them in the meantime will be useful. If on the other hand you do not, and if you will not be doing much British snow and ice mountaineering, you will probably get better all-round value from a pair of tricouni-nailed boots, since these are not only good on snow and ice but are also useful on the very greasy rock which is common on British cliffs in the autumn and winter. The ideal solution, however, is to have both nails and crampons, because you can then suit your footwear to the character of the climb.

Possible hazards with crampons are:

- it is easy to trip over them, by catching them on stockings or trousers, or on the climbing rope;
- damp snow tends to 'ball up' on them (as very cold snow does on nailed boots) with the result that they are prevented from biting into the slope (§ 84);
- they can cause serious injuries if they come into contact with your body in a fall;
- they tend to make a falling climber somersault so that it is more difficult to apply the ice-axe brake (§ 16).

Types of crampon. Get a good pair made by a reputable manufacturer: Cassin, Charlet, Grivel, Simond, and Stubai are among the best makes. They should be reasonably lightweight (ex-Army crampons, incidentally, are too heavy by modern standards). There are two main types in current use:

1. *Ordinary crampons*, with ten or possibly eight points [104B]; these are still used a good deal, but are gradually being displaced, at least for the harder snow and ice work, by
2. *Lobster-claw crampons*, either twelve point or ten point [104A and C]. These are very effective on steep snow or ice because the front spikes can be kicked direct into the slope; this enables very steep ice to be climbed without step-cutting and without excessive flexing of the ankles as is necessary with 1. They are particularly good where snow is lying on ice because they bite

through the back of the step (as distinct from the bottom) with the result that most of your weight is taken on the ice instead of the snow. Their main disadvantages are that they are rather more cumbersome on iced rock and easier to trip over. Grivel and Stubai make good crampons of this type.

Whichever type of crampons you use, the points should for general use be not less than about $1\frac{1}{4}$ ins. long, as they will need to bite through loose snow or ice chippings lying on ice steps; for Scottish conditions, however, where there is a great deal of iced rock, shorter points are preferable. Crampons with less than eight points do not give enough contact with the snow or ice to be reliable. Most crampons are made in two parts, sole and heel. The two halves are linked together by an arm, which should allow them to be folded completely over when not in use.

Bindings. It is essential to be able to put on and take off crampons quickly: any delay can cause irritation in a party which is cold in the early morning, or which is in a hurry; and on a long, mixed climb involving many changes, there can be a serious loss of time. Because of the importance of speed, quick-release bindings are normally used; two types are shown in [104A and C]. They can be made either of leather or of webbing (preferably nylon); webbing straps should have metal end-pieces to prevent them fraying. There is a definite sequence for fastening straps: note that all the buckles should be on the outer side of the foot, since this reduces the risk of tripping over them. The alternative to these straps is the single strap, usually about five feet long; this need not be slower than quick-release straps if it can be clipped under hooks on the crampon, but it is a good deal slower if it has to be threaded through rings. Any rings must be hanging outside the crampon before the boot is placed in it.

Fitting crampons. Crampons are made in the same sizes as boots, but it is usually necessary to adjust them so that they fit perfectly. This is best done under heat by a blacksmith who can retemper the metal afterwards. Cold hammering of crampons should be avoided if possible (though it is often done). There should be no gap between the front points of the crampon and the front of the boot, and the rest of the crampon must fit securely. The test of a correct fit is that the boot can be picked up and lightly shaken without the (unstrapped) crampon dropping off. *It is most important to achieve this perfection since any movement of the crampon on the boot will reduce your confidence.* A good fit also means that the straps do not need to be tied tightly, thus minimizing the risk of frostbite (§ 98). It is dangerous to use borrowed crampons without getting them adjusted to your boots.

Carrying crampons. Do not carry crampons swinging from the back of your rucksack since they may work loose and fall off, or they may injure someone walking behind you. Instead, carry them strapped tightly on the outside *with the points towards the sack* or, alternatively, under the flap or inside the rucksack. To protect the sack and its contents, use rubber tubing on the spikes or even place the crampons between pieces of balsa or other very light wood.

Care of crampons. The points should be sharpened from time to time, particularly after they have been used on rock, and the rings and straps should be checked for damage and replaced as necessary.

§ 78. Ice-axes

An ice-axe [105] is essential for all snow and ice work – for cutting steps, as a third leg, for belaying (though the deadman – see addendum – is far better) and, in the Alps, for probing crevasses. The choice of axe is very much a personal one depending on your size and the types of climb you will be doing. For difficult snow and ice work a well-balanced axe is necessary; it should balance about a quarter or a third of the way from the head to the spike.

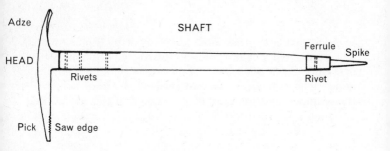

105. *The parts of an ice-axe*. Nowadays the pick will normally be more curved, as the next photograph shows.

Ice-axes are made with a five-centimetre (about two inches) difference between sizes.

In the older textbooks, long ice-axes (over 32 ins.) were usually recommended, but the modern trend is towards shorter axes, because these are far more convenient both in use and when the axe is being carried on rock sections. The three main types of axe are:

1. *General-purpose axes*, which must be long enough for step-cutting downhill, for belaying, and for probing crevasses. The overall length usually varies from 27 to 30 ins. for men between say 5 ft 8 ins. and 6 ft. The spike of the axe should be about one inch off the ground when you are standing upright in climbing boots, holding the head of the axe by your side in the resting position. This is a little too short to use the axe as a walking-stick on *level* ground (roads, etc.), but this is in any case not recommended because it tends to blunt the spike, to use energy unnecessarily, and to upset your rhythm.

2. *Very short axes for very steep ice*. On very steep ice, or in confined spaces such as are encountered in Scottish gullies, axes of about 18–20 ins. are better than 1. It is not too much to say that the whole of modern Scottish snow and ice technique is based on the use of these axes. These axes (or

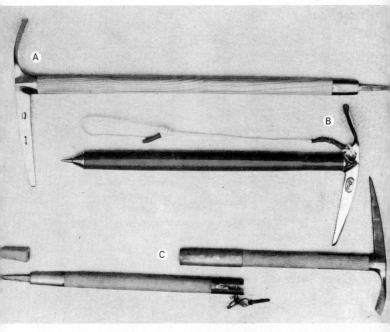

106. *Ice-axes*. A is a Grivel, thirty inches long, B is a MacInnes hiduminium-shafted axe, and C a Simond demountable axe. The rubber stopper on the left is for the spike of an axe when travelling.

hammer axes – see § 79) are also used on the Continent for hard mixed routes, and for sections of snow and ice on rock climbs. Recently, the Terrodactyl axe, with its inclined pick [108], has come into common use on high standard climbs.

3. *Demountable axes* [106c] are made by Simond and M.S.R. to cover both 1 and 2. They are full-length axes which can be broken in two so that the head can be used for very steep cutting or so that the axe can be stowed in a sack when not in use (especially in alpine rock climbing or ski touring).

They are, however, not well-balanced, and are rather heavy and expensive.

On steep Scottish snow and ice, it is now common practice to use two very short axes, or one and an ice hammer (§ 80). The second axe or the hammer, which should preferably be of Terrodactyl design [108], can be used:

- as a supplementary handhold when you are cramponing. This gives much greater security, and also enables you to climb steeper ice without step-cutting. A specially made implement, the climbing dagger, is available for this purpose; but the embedded pick of a Terrodactyl short axe or hammer is better because the inclined pick gives much better holding power, the greater weight gives better penetration, and the shaft acts as a prop so that it is more stable [118 and 119];
- as a handhold when cutting one-handed with the other axe;
- as a foothold or handhold on very steep snow, hammered in horizontally (axe only).

In such cases it is useful to have a general-purpose axe in the party as well, in case it is necessary to cut steps downhill or for the second to belay on snow.

Shaft. The cross-section of the shaft should be oval so that it can be held without effort and guided accurately when step-cutting. The shaft must be strong, because it is likely to bear the main load in the event of a fall when it is being used as a belay (§§ 17 and 86). Metal shafts are preferable for this reason (being at least twice as strong as wood), but these – see e.g. [106B] – are relatively expensive and do not have quite the same handling qualities. Accordingly, many climbers prefer a combination of wood-shafted axe (for step-cutting) and a deadman (for belaying – see addendum) as the best all-round solution. Laminated shafts are considerably stronger than natural wood but are rather brittle and fairly dear. The best of the natural woods is hickory meeting B.S. 3823 (i.e. straight grained, about 5–16 annual rings per inch, no knots), which is stronger than the relatively light lower quality ash frequently used in Continental manufacture. A wood shaft should be replaced by the maker every four years or so, since it tends to weaken with age, and should never be intentionally strained by testing since this can cause permanent invisible damage.

The head of an axe is made of a single piece of forged steel securely attached to the shaft. The *pick* has two main functions: (1) to cut into ice or hard snow to make holds or steps; and (2) to hold securely when partially or wholly embedded for self-arrest [20], or for a handhold [18B] or belay [121], though this last is not recommended. Note in particular that:

– *a correctly curved pick* [106] gives the least shock when step-cutting since its radius of arc should conform to the radius of your arm swing (about 26″ is normal); it also holds securely for (2) above;
– *an inclined pick* such as the Terrodactyl [108], which is set at about 55° to the shaft, gives the maximum possible holding power for (2) above; and also facilitates the cutting of inward-pointing handholds;
– *the cross-section* should be thin and well tapered for maximum cutting efficiency; but this gives less holding power on hard snow for self-arrest; and
– *notches* are needed just underneath the tip to enable it to grip securely, though they make it difficult to extract the pick when cutting in glutinous ice.

The *adze* is also very important for step-cutting on hard snow since it takes out a much greater volume with each blow. A heavy head is desirable for prolonged step-cutting but remember that you will have to carry the axe with you at other times when lightness is an advantage.

Ferrule and spike. These should be made and fitted separately. They should be streamlined for sensitivity in probing crevasses and the spike should be sharpened frequently and renewed when the shaft is replaced. A rubber stopper for the spike is useful for travelling.

Wrist-slings. There are various opinions about the merits of wrist-slings. A sling is awkward in that it restricts the ease

107. *Slings for ice-axes.* A shows two sliding wrist-slings and a fixed-line sling with an adjustable wrist-loop. B is perhaps the best method since the axe can readily be changed from hand to hand, and can be secured over the shoulder as in C, when not in use.

of transferring the axe from one hand to the other, and it may also lead to serious wrist injuries and body cuts if the axe gets entangled with your body in a fall (the theory that you must hang on to your axe at all costs in a fall is generally sound, but it is helpful to be able to get rid of it if it is damaging you). Most alpine guides do not use a sling, except when the axe is very wet or icy, when they may improvise one. Their ice-axe, however, is so far a part of them that it is most unlikely that they would drop it. Whether amateurs can in all circumstances hold on to their axe is more open to question; quite a few of the best British climbers have been known to drop their axes and been seriously inconvenienced (as well as embarrassed) as a result. Because the loss of an axe can be so serious, some form of sling is recommended, at least for the inexperienced. The solution which I personally favour is to tie one end of a five-foot length of No. 1 nylon to the head of the axe, and the other into the waist-loop [107B]. This safeguard can be particularly useful when the axe has been pushed between the rucksack and your back [107C], since it is all too easy to forget about the axe when taking off the rucksack. If a sliding ring is used, put a rubber retaining band on the shaft, since a metal band or a screw may weaken the shaft slightly [107A].

Carrying the ice-axe when not in use. Never carry the axe with the spike upwards to your rear; carry it with the head under your arm, and the spike pointing forwards and downwards where it can harm no one. The axe can be carried on your sack in the following ways:

– on the straps at the back; this is useful when you are walking up to huts, or at other times when the axe is not likely to be needed quickly [30c];
– inside the rucksack spike upwards; this is useful for *descending* rock climbs in the Alps, since it is least likely to catch on the rock;
– between your back and the sack, spike downwards, tucked through one of the shoulder straps or a karabiner on the D ring. This is preferable where the axe is likely to be needed at short notice, or for *climbing up* on alpine rock [30B and 107C]. If the axe is a short one, however, this is the best way for all-round use.

A very short axe can conveniently be tucked into your belt or waist-loop.

108. *Hammer axes and an ice hammer.* A is a Horeschowsky, B is a Simond, and c a MacInnes hiduminium-shafted hammer axe. D is a Grivel ice hammer. See [119] for a Terrodactyl hammer axe and short axe, used for 'traction' in steep ice-climbing.

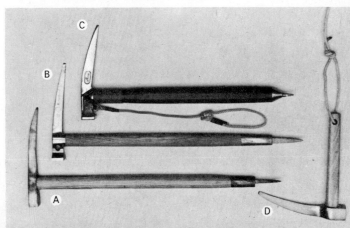

§ 79. Hammer axe

This is a very short axe, about 18–22 ins. long, but with a hammer in place of the adze [108]. The lower end of the shaft is sometimes thickened so that it is easier to hold. It is intended for use on steep mixed climbs where pitoning as well as ice climbing is involved, and is sometimes known as a North Wall axe. Its usefulness for British snow and ice is limited by the absence of the adze, which makes it much less effective for step-cutting on hard snow, and particularly for cutting handholds [111c and d].

§ 80. Ice hammer

As [108D] shows, this is the same as a piton hammer (§ 69) except that it has a much longer pick. It can be very useful, not only for inserting and extracting pitons, but also for cutting holds on very steep ice (where the long pick

109. *Ice pegs and screws, and a climbing dagger.* A is a Charlet, B a Stubai, and C a Simond. D is a Russian peg which can be extracted by un-screwing (it has a hexagonal head which fits into a hexagonal hole in the head of a Russian-made ice-axe). This and F – a tubular peg by Peck – are robust and well designed. The ice screws (Stubai) are made in varying lengths to suit the hardness of the ice. The climbing dagger (K) is a Charlet (A) with Elastoplast round the head.

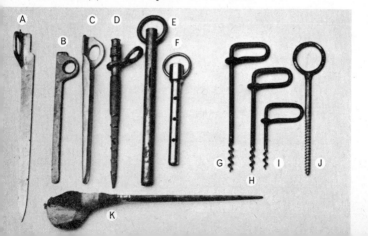

enables you to make full-size steps), or iced rock, or in very restricted spaces such as chimneys. With its pick firmly embedded in the ice, it is also useful as a handhold for cramponing or one-handed step-cutting [118]. As with ice-axes, a hiduminium-shafted version is available (the MacInnes 'gully hammer'). A slater's pick is much cheaper than a purpose-made ice hammer, and is good for step-cutting because the pick is long; it may not be so satisfactory for pegging, however, if the head is narrow.

§ 81. Ice pitons, ice screws etc. and the 'deadman'

Ice pitons or ice screws are necessary for belaying on difficult alpine ice, and are reasonably reliable there though not as secure as rock belays (the preferred method of belaying on snow and ice, § 85). In Britain, the ice is much more brittle and ice pitons or ice screws are not usually reliable as main belays (§ 87); fortunately it is often possible to use rock belays instead. Pegs and screws are, however, very useful as running belays and for resting on very steep ice (by putting a peg in above you temporarily so that you can take the weight off your arms).

Ice pitons [109] are made of harder steel than most rock pitons, since they do not have to bend to follow the line of an existing crack. There are three main types:

- *blade.* These are the most secure as they are least inclined to set up fracture lines in the ice when they are hammered in; but some blade pitons are too thin to take the loads which might possibly be placed on them. A blade piton can also be useful as a climbing dagger [109K], for a supplementary handhold when cramponing (provided it is well bandaged so that it does not damage your gloves), but a very short axe or ice hammer is better (see above);
- *channel*;
- *tubular.*

Unlike rock pitons (§ 68) the line of pull on an ice piton

should be central: the torque under strain, which is so important in a rock piton, would only tend to split the ice. The line of pull must also be at right angles to the widest section of the piton to give the maximum purchase with the least chance of the piton cutting through the ice. Ice pitons should not be less than nine inches in length, though shorter ones may possibly be satisfactory in very glutinous ice for artificial climbing. As with rock pitons, the loose rings have sometimes proved to be very weak, and pegs with rings are not recommended as a general rule.

Ice screws [109] have recently come into favour in preference to ice pitons. They can be inserted and extracted with very little hammering, and save a great deal of time and effort – and damage to the metal – in consequence. They are also much lighter than ice pitons. Apart from these important advantages they have the major advantage that they split the ice less. There is no doubt that they greatly increase the effectiveness of ice belays, but even so the brittleness of much of the ice encountered in the British mountains will limit their reliability to some extent.

Snow stakes are made from alloy tube or angle, 18–24 ins. long. They provide a satisfactory belay in hard snow (in which they can be hammered home) and are especially useful for abseil anchors (p. 303) where the alternative might be to sacrifice an ice-axe. If however you are able to drive an axe into the snow more than about a foot with a single thrust, the snow is too soft to support a heavy load on a stake.

The deadman was developed in the late 1960s as a means of belaying on snow far superior to the standard ice-axe. It is described in detail on p. 529, and its use is recommended wherever possible.

Chapter 11. Snow and ice climbing techniques

British snow and ice climbing has been described in general terms in chapter 5, and the techniques of movement and rope management on moderately steep snow (up to about forty degrees) have been covered in chapter 2. In snow and ice climbing proper, it is necessary to deal with steep (forty to fifty degrees) and very steep (over fifty degrees) snow and ice in a very wide variety of conditions; although the basic principles of economy of effort, balance, and rhythm still apply, more sophisticated techniques are required, and these are described in this chapter.

§ 82. Holding the ice-axe

As noted in § 15, it is usually possible on gentle or moderately steep snow:

1. to force the shaft of the axe vertically into the snow (or, more accurately, at an angle of about 120 degrees to the downward slope) on your uphill side, preferably in the hole made by the man in front [18A];
2. to hold the axe horizontally with the spike in the snow and your weight pressing downwards on it (good for traversing and zigzags [17B]); or
3. as for 2, but with the pick in the snow [116A]. This has the advantage that your axe is already in position for braking should you slip.

Sometimes, however, especially on steep or very steep snow or ice, it is necessary to use the following methods instead:

4. embedding the pick in the snow, with the shaft of the axe lying on the snow [18B]. An excellent handhold for steep and very steep snow; and now the basis of very advanced ice-climbing techniques using a Terrodactyl axe [108] in each hand [119];

5. on ice, as for 4, but with the pick only fractionally in the ice, and the lower hand well down the shaft. Useful for steep ice when cramponing, but cannot be relied on for much more than a balance grip [116B–F].

§ 83. Step-cutting

Steps should be kicked (§ 15) in preference to being cut, where possible, because this is quicker and the steps are firmer; on long slopes of hard snow, however, it may be easier to cut steps with a blow of the adze since this saves strain on your feet. Crampons greatly reduce the need for step-cutting, but even with them steps are necessary on slopes above about forty to fifty degrees, according to your experience. On soft snow lying on ice, it is safer to cut through to the ice beneath rather than to rely on snow which might slide off, laborious though this can be; lobster-claw crampons can save step-cutting in these conditions because they enable you to grip on the ice by kicking inwards through the back of a step. Step-cutting is an art in itself, and a great deal of practice is needed before you can become really proficient: take every opportunity of practising. The main points are:

- speed is vital. A step is a means to an end and not an end in itself. Attack the slope with determination, and do not be afraid to use some energy, though avoid wasting it;
- cut two-handed where possible;
- make the weight of the axe head do most of the work;
- make steps secure, and large enough to stand in without discomfort; but where possible economize in time and effort by

---

110. *A moderate snow and ice gully (Raeburn's Gully on Creag Meagaidh – § 102).* Gullies are safe only in freezing conditions and provided the cornice at the top is not in a dangerous state (§ 38, 1). The icicles on the left might avalanche in thaw conditions. Usually there is more snow than this in March: see 15 which was taken a fortnight later when the lake was frozen.

alternating a good step for one foot with a toe scrape for the
other;
- choose the easiest line of ascent, and place the steps in the most
convenient positions;
- always cut at least two steps ahead, more on very steep ground.

These points apply equally to all step-cutting (uphill,
downhill, and across) and are dealt with in detail below.

Hold the axe as near the spike as possible. The oval or
flat shape of the shaft will enable you to guide it accurately
without gripping it tightly until the moment of impact. It
will usually be possible to cut two-handed, and this has the
advantage of speed, but practise cutting one-handed until
you are proficient with either hand (step-cutting on very
steep ground is usually one-handed, and a very short axe or
ice hammer [108] is best for this). Most of the work should
be done by the falling axe guided by the lower arms and
wrists. Swinging the shoulders wastes effort and also tends
to upset your balance. Some of the main methods of step-
cutting are shown in [113]; of these [113A] is particularly
useful on slopes of up to about forty-five degrees, since the
weight of the axe is taken from directly above, with the
result that there is no sideways strain on your wrists and
arms and the adze hits the snow in a horizontal plane, producing a good long even step.

There are two main types of steps:
- *inward-pointing steps* [111B] which usually take only the toe
or sole of your foot, though on very steep ground it is advisable
to get your heel as well on to, say, alternate steps, to relieve the
strain. These are best on direct ascents;
- *long, horizontal steps* [111A] which take the whole length (but
not necessarily the whole width) of your foot, sideways to the
slope; these are best for traverses or zigzags, or when steps have
to be cut in descent;

Handholds [111D] are normally cut with the adze, though
in very hard ice the pick may have to be used to start the
hold. They must be sharply inward-sloping, so that gloved

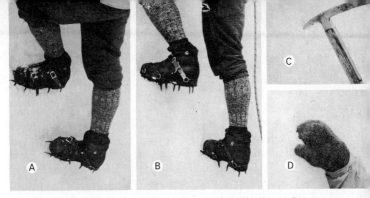

111. *Types of step.* The horizontal steps in A are best for diagonal ascents and the inward-pointing steps in B for direct ascents or descents. The adze of the axe is particularly useful for cutting handholds.

hands can get a good grip. On direct ascents footholds cut well ahead can usually be used first as handholds [114], and the need for special handholds can also be reduced by using the embedded ice hammer as a hold or, on very steep ground, taking your weight on an ice peg or screw planted temporarily above you.

Speed is of the essence. Only one or two blows of the axe should be needed for a step in snow or brittle ice (if the axe

112. *Always cut towards the hole made by your previous blows, so that you break the ice into it.*

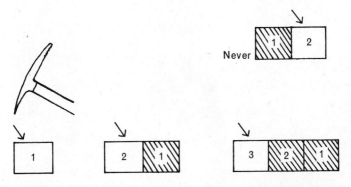

head is heavy and very sharp) and more than three blows should only be needed on hard or glutinous ice, or in very awkward positions. Use the adze as much as possible since this is much more effective than the pick (except for deep steps when the extra length of the pick may be needed); a sharp adze can be used even in ice. The bottom of the step should slope slightly inwards, though this is less important with crampons than with nails. Do not weaken the snow or ice below the base, which you will be standing on; hack out the top of the step with a downward blow only *after* you have cut the base of the step with a horizontal blow or blows, so that the top of the step is separated from the base, and the force of the downward blow can therefore not be transmitted to it. When cutting horizontal steps, the first adze blow should be at the near end of the step, and

113. *Step-cutting*. In ascending moderate slopes of hard snow it is often easiest to cut one-handed with the axe inside, held from above as in A. Note that in B (traversing) and C (descent) the climber is in balance with most of his weight on the lower step.

114. *Sequence of movement on steep ice.* The use of a very short axe permits a much more natural and relaxed cutting position than a long one. To 'pick' the axe into the ice as in B requires confidence; most climbers would hold on to it, preferably with a sling. On very steep ice an ice screw placed above the climber will increase his security and reduce the need for handholds.

any others should be progressively further away; in this way you will benefit on the second and third blows from the hole made by the first [112]. Listen to the sound of the blows when step-cutting on ice; a hollow thud means that the ice is fracturing behind or below the step and you will have to re-cut it in a different place.

Positioning of steps. Snow and ice climbing is easier than rock climbing in one important way – you have the choice of where to put your holds. Take full advantage of this. Cutting a step uses energy and for this reason it is best to place steps far apart so that fewer are needed. This must be balanced however against the increased difficulty of moving from step to step (particularly for the shorter members of the party) and the need for reasonably close steps in the event of having to retreat back down them later. Try to get an even spacing, since this improves rhythm, and place steps so that you can brace your legs widely, since this gives greater stability. The positioning of the steps varies according to the line you are taking on the slope ([16] and § 15):

– *on steeply inclined diagonals (zigzags)*, place the steps for each foot on parallel lines about nine inches apart, with the lower steps bigger than the upper ones (indeed, in good snow or ice the upper steps need be no more than scrapes to take your weight momentarily). Make an extra large ('bucket') step when the direction is changed. In ascent, move the inside foot up and the outside foot across to the same level; in descent, conversely, move the inside foot across and the outside foot down;

– *on horizontal traverses* [113B], move in the same way as on zigzags, with your weight on your lower foot;

– *on direct ascents*, the steeper the angle of the slope, the further ahead the steps must be cut; on very steep snow, cut them at shoulder height, or even above your head [114]. On really steep slopes careful planning is needed to take advantage of any lessening of the angle (e.g. where there is an opportunity to bridge across two walls, or where a more circuitous route will enable you to avoid the steepest parts). It may be necessary to come down to the stance for a rest, in which case make sure that you leave yourself sufficient strength to climb down safely. It is not usually possible to climb ice above sixty-five degrees for more than about twenty feet unless ice pitons or screws are used for resting;

– *direct descents* [113C]. When descending steep snow and ice, it is easiest to cut directly downwards, facing sideways to the mountain. The steps above can then be used as handholds. On very steep snow or ice, however, it may be safer to abseil than to climb down, if a secure abseil anchor (§ 89) can be arranged.

§ 84. Crampon technique

With crampons (§ 77), it is possible to climb steep and very steep snow and ice without cutting steps. The angle which can be climbed before steps become necessary depends on:

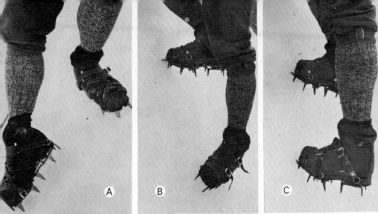

115. *Cramponing.* A is the orthodox technique with standard crampons. Note that all the points are in contact with the ice. The flexing of the ankles is reduced by pointing the lower foot downwards, but even so the strain is considerable. B and C show the more natural position achieved with lobster-claw (twelve-point) crampons. Note the similarity between C and the use of the feet in rock climbing (50). Stiff-soled boots are advantageous with twelve-point crampons to reduce the strain on the feet, and to give better control of the front points.

- the hardness of the snow or ice. Well consolidated snow is easiest because you can grip with the whole length of the crampon points, and can also get extra purchase from the pick of your ice-axe and ice hammer. If the snow is not hard, it is best to kick steps with your crampons because otherwise the points may slide down the surface of the snow. On ice, cramponing is more delicate because the points bite only on the surface and you may not be able to get any significant purchase with your axe;
- the type of crampon; lobster-claw crampons enable steeper ice to be climbed than ordinary crampons; the sharpness of the points is also an important factor;
- whether you rely solely on the ice-axe for hand support; an ice hammer or dagger in the other hand is safer, and allows steeper ice to be climbed. It also improves rhythm;
- the experience of the party. Competent snow and ice climbers should be able to move on slopes of up to about fifty degrees without cutting steps; thirty-five to forty degrees should be possible for most people.

Confidence will enable you to do wonders in crampons, but always remember that there is a limit to what is possible.

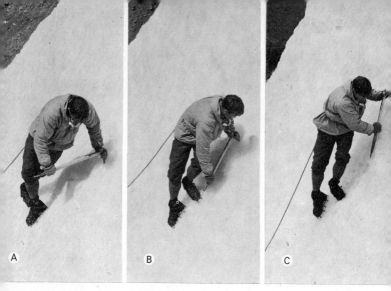

116. *Changing the position of the ice-axe as the angle of the slope increases (see § 82).* On moderately steep ice, the axe is held across the body as in A, or as in 17B. On steeper ice, B is better. On very steep ice (C–F), with ordinary crampons, the axe is forced hard into the ice, high up; but it gives little more than a balance hold and consequently the manœuvre is rather precarious. For this reason, lobster-claw crampons and two axes are preferable (118 and 119).

If the slope is steepening progressively, you can avoid stepcutting for a while by making small cuts in the ice into which several points can go, but you *must* cut the first proper step before the slope becomes too steep. Otherwise a delicate and dangerous situation may result in which you are unable to move up or down, or take your axe off the slope to cut a step. Take short steps and keep your feet well apart to avoid catching the crampons in your clothing (baggy trousers should be avoided because of the risk of tripping) and watch the ground carefully so that you do not trip over the rope or a bump. The techniques vary according to the type of crampon as follows:

1. *Ordinary crampons* [115A]. The basic principle with ordinary crampons is to flex your ankles so that all the points of the crampon are biting in the snow or ice. This requires a great deal of strength and flexibility in the ankles and knees.

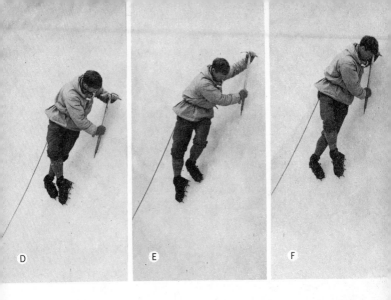

D   E   F

The axe is held in one of the positions in § 82, according to the angle of the slope. The techniques are shown in [116] and [117]. Note in particular that:

- all crampon points are in contact with the snow or ice;
- the toes are pointing either horizontally or even slightly downwards. On steep ice, one foot should be pointing sharply downwards to preserve balance;
- it is easiest to move on an upward-sloping, diagonal line, changing direction when your ankles get tired;
- in descent facing outwards, it is easier to get all the points into the ice but balance may be very delicate [120A].

2. *Lobster-claw crampons* [115B and C]. The technique is broadly similar to 1, except that it is possible to stand on the front four points alone; this greatly facilitates movement on steep ground because it is not necessary to strain ankles and knees to get all the other points into contact with the ice. Moreover, the body position is more natural in that you can face the slope, as in rock climbing. It is better to climb straight up than to bother with the wider zigzags as in 1. In this way it is easy to work up a steady, secure rhythm, particularly if you use an ice hammer or climbing dagger as a handhold in addition to the pick of the axe [118].

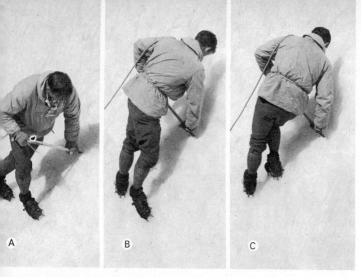

117. *Turning on a diagonal ascent.* There is a definite sequence for changing direction. When changing from right to left, as here, it is: (1) take the weight on your right foot; (2) change grip on the axe; (3) place the left foot in the new direction; (4) take the weight on the left foot and move on. The ice in these photographs is soft glacier ice; on harder ice the climber would have to flex his ankles more in C to get all the crampon points into it.

These crampons are also better than ordinary crampons when climbing on steep snow with ice beneath, since the front claws bite more easily into the ice at the back of the step. They are, however, more cumbersome than ordinary crampons on rock (see below).

Soft snow: 'balling up'. On soft or wet snow, crampons are likely to 'ball up', i.e., heavy masses of packed snow ('*sabots de neige*') form on them. Balled-up crampons are dangerous because the snow and not the crampon is in contact with the slope. The solution is to bang the side of your boot with the metal ferrule of your axe as you move it, to dislodge the *sabot*. After a little practice this will become second nature.

Putting crampons on early. It is usually best to put crampons on as early as possible and keep them on until the snow becomes so soft that it is balling up seriously. This is because you are more likely to be able to hold a fall with crampons than without them. It is particularly important when moving across easy frozen snow which runs out over a long drop.

Crampons on rock. It is often necessary to climb short sections of rock in crampons. The technique is basically similar to nail technique, and involves placing the crampon points very carefully on small, flat, or incut holds, in preference to large sloping holds. Care is needed because a crampon badly placed may give without warning. With practice you should be able to climb to within about two standards of your normal performance. The strain on the crampon is considerable, but well-made crampons will withstand it unless they have been damaged. Even so, treat them gently.

118. *Double-axe technique.* On steep snow or ice this is preferable to the single-axe technique shown in 116 and 117. You always have one axe in the snow for a handhold and this not only enables you to climb steeper ice with greater security but also gives a better rhythm so that it is quicker and less tiring. Lobster-claw crampons are far better than standard crampons for this. A heavy-headed hammer axe, hammer, or short axe (108) is preferable to a climbing dagger (109) for the supplementary handhold since it requires less effort to hold and use.

119. *Double axe technique – maximum angle.* Use of lobster-claw crampons and Terrodactyls on extremely steep ice. Note the relaxed and well-balanced position as in steep rock-climbing (compare with [48]). Photo: John Cleare (Bill March climbing).

120. *Descent.* Outwards, sideways, and inwards. Note that when facing inwards as in c the climber is in a good position to check a slip. See also 19B which shows the normal method of sideways descent on moderately steep ice.

A   B   C

and in descent avoid even trivial jumps, since they might damage the points.

§ 85. Rope handling and the selection of stances

Tying on. The methods of tying on to the rope are as in § 54. The best rope interval is forty to sixty feet, and more should be used only if the infrequency of stances or belays necessitates it. The spare rope should be carried as in [77]. It is best for the leader's rope to pass to the second man over his shoulder, since this keeps it out of the snow and also reduces the risk of tripping over it in crampons.

Stances. It must be recognized that the belays which can be made in British snow and ice (§§ 17, 86, and 87) are rarely very reliable, and it is vitally important to belay wherever possible *on rock*, with one of the rock or artificial belays described in §§ 58–61; rock piton belays are commonly used in British snow and ice climbing because of the difficulty of excavating rock belays from their covering of snow and ice. It is best to make the stance in a place where such belays are likely to be available, as for example near the wall in a gully. The stance itself should preferably be on rock also, since a snow stance will give a little under a big strain and most of the load will be transmitted to the belay. Other considerations in selecting stances are:

– where the party has to rely on snow or ice belays it is particularly important that the stance should be close to the difficulties so that any fall by the leader is brought under control as quickly as possible: a long fall could be very hard to stop and could conceivably take the whole party down. This is one reason why it is dangerous for the leader to attempt a cornice without first bringing up the second man;
– the stance should be to one side of the line of possible fall, so that there is no chance of the leader hitting the second man from some way above and dislodging him from his stance;
– the second should be able to shelter from any snow and ice chippings sent down by the leader;

– so far as possible choose a comfortable place, out of the wind, because the second may have to stay there for a long time if the next pitch is hard.

On steep zigzag ascents, the best place for a stance is two or three feet outside the turning point [16c]; this enables the second to lead through without complications. On direct ascents or descents, a stance five or six feet to right or left should be used [16B]. Cut extra big bucket steps for the stance so that the belayer can stand there in comfort and have room to move his feet.

§ 86. More about belaying on snow

As noted above, belay on rock wherever possible, since this is the safest of all belays.

The normal methods of belaying with the ice-axe on snow have been described in § 17, but all of these are subject to the risks that under load:

1. the axe may be pulled out of the snow (either because the snow is soft, or because the axe is put in at the wrong angle); and
2. the shaft of the axe may break, particularly if it is a wooden one which is past its prime.

These are important weaknesses which seriously reduce the effectiveness of the ice-axe belay for holding a falling leader. For these reasons a deadman (see addendum) is preferable, but if none is available use two or more ice-axes interlinked like the pegs in [122c] or bury the axe horizontally in the snow to give the maximum load bearing surface (addendum, § 4). If there is room on the stance, it is also helpful for other members of the party to secure the second man from above, or to stand on the ice-axe belay to keep it in place under load.

The pick belay [121]. On extremely hard snow where it is not possible to get the shaft of the axe in far enough to make the normal ice-axe belay, the pick belay used to be used for

121. *Not recommended – the pick belay.* The normal ice-axe belays (21 and 22) or ice screws (122) should be used in preference to this, since it pulls out too easily. It may, however, prove adequate for bringing up the second man on gentle ground, provided that the snow is firm and the full length of the pick goes in. Obviously, the longer the pick, the more secure it is. Note that the rope runs along the snow and that the shaft is held in place with the knee.

bringing up the second man. It is however very weak (certainly useless for holding a falling leader) and fortunately nowadays the deadman is available instead. As an alternative cut the snow out until you get to slightly softer snow below, and then make the ice-axe belay at the back of the step in the normal way, or if there is ice beneath, use an ice screw or peg at the back of the step [122].

§ 87. Belaying on ice

On ice it is very difficult to belay adequately. If you can safely continue, go on until you reach a good rock (or snow) belay, if possible putting on running belays (§ 63) in the meantime. If, however, you have no choice but to belay at once, use ice screws or ice pitons (§ 81). Unfortunately British ice tends to be brittle and it would usually be unwise to rely on one piton alone; put in two or more and link them individually into the belay system [122]. An ice piton should go in at an angle of about 120 degrees to the slope at not less than shoulder level (the higher the better). If the surface ice is unreliable cut out a step and put the piton in at the back. The hammer should make a steady singing noise; a hollow noise means that the piton is cracking the ice, and it will be necessary to try another place. If an ice piton is well frozen in (which does not take long on a cold day) it can often be loosened by giving it an extra tap *inwards* with the hammer. Otherwise it will be necessary to cut it out. Although this may be laborious, it can also be comforting to know that the peg was, after all, well and

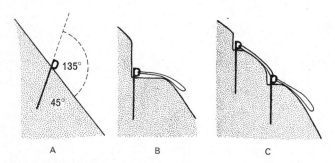

122. *Use of ice pitons or screws.* A is sound ice, B is ice under a layer of unreliable snow. C shows linked ice pitons, useful for main belays especially where a single piton or screw is doubtful.

truly in the ice. As a general rule ice screws are preferable to ice pitons because they are easier to insert, do not crack the ice as much, and can be extracted simply by unscrewing. Tie into the piton or screw in the same way as for a rock piton (§ 61). Ice pitons or ice screws can also be used for running belays; they will probably not be very secure on British ice, but may hold and would in any case reduce the speed of the fall, thus helping the second man to arrest it. Sometimes it may be possible to belay on the ice-axe jammed in a crack in the ice, but the pick belay [121] should not be used.

§ 88. Rope handling and belaying when moving together

If the snow or ice is not very steep, it is usual and preferable for the whole party to move together, since this saves time and keeps everyone warm. It is also good training for alpine mountaineering where the party moves together most of the time. When moving together, the party should usually be about ten feet apart, and certainly not more than about twenty feet. If the party is too spread out, a falling climber may gather too much momentum for the others to be able to hold him. Each man should carry a few hand coils [77], so that he can let out or take in the rope according to the relative speeds of the individual members of the party. The second has the general responsibility of securing the leader and seeing that the rope does not catch (the leader can help by hitching the rope over his shoulder).

Belaying when moving together: the footbrake. All members of the party should be ready to check a slip on the part of any other member instantaneously. On a traverse the ice-axe should be held by the head in the uphill hand (i.e., in the left hand on a rightward traverse, and vice versa) while the point of the axe is automatically thrust into the snow alongside the uphill foot at each step. The coils should be held in the downhill hand, and the rope played round the axe just below the head at all times (passing through the fingers as in [19A]). At the instant that the axe is plunged into the snow to belay, the rope is released from the fingers and falls to boot level round the axe to give the footbrake [22B]. Note that this method, like the dynamic belay on rock (§ 62, 1), relies on frictional braking, in this case in the S-bend created by the boot against the axe. The gradual application of the brake (by bringing the rope round towards the heel of the boot) is very important since this minimizes the load on the axe, and hence the risk of it breaking or jumping out. It is however also essential to pay out the rope as low down the shaft as possible (to minimize leverage) and to press down on the head, especially where the snow is soft or (at the other extreme) so hard that the axe is hardly in. An alternative method in emergency is to let the rope fall to the snow round the axe and stamp your foot over it as in [22A], so that at least you force the axe in and prevent the rope jumping up. The risk of damaging the rope even wearing crampons is small since it will quickly bite into the snow as it moves under load. One of the advantages of holding the rope in two hands in this way is that it greatly facilitates normal rope management – the taking in and letting out of coils. This is all very much a matter of taste and opinion; but I have proved this two-handed system practically on a number of occasions.

On a ridge it may not be possible to belay adequately in a hurry, and the only way of holding a fall may be to go over the opposite side of the ridge, to act as a counterweight. In practice this need not be nearly as dramatic as it sounds. Make sure that you can tell which side the leader is falling and do not go further over the side than you need to. Five or ten feet should be quite enough. When moving together on ridges, you must always be prepared to do this, and should be looking at the terrain all the time from this point of view. This concentration can be tedious but it may save yourself and the whole party one day.

§ 89. Abseiling on British snow and ice

If possible, a rock belay (natural or piton) should be used as an abseil anchor, as in [90]. If, exceptionally, this is

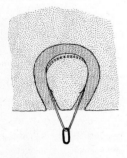
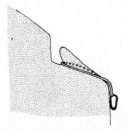

123. *An ice bollard.*

impossible, and an abseil is imperative, one of the following anchors may have to be used:

On ice, either

1. put in at least two ice screws or ice pitons and link them with a sling [122c]. If a single peg or screw has to be used, put it in at an internal angle of $40°$–$50°$ to the line of pull because ice melts under pressure and they can tend to angle downwards during an abseil; or
2. make an ice bollard. Cut a channel three to four inches deep for the rope in a semi circle about eighteen inches in diameter, making sure that the channel has an overhanging lip at the back so that there is no chance of the rope riding up [123]. Check that the ice is sound (i.e., that no fracture lines were set up in cutting the channel) before using it.

In the Alps, some climbers have perfected a technique of abseiling down ice slopes by using a brace-and-bit to drill the ice, and inserting a strong bamboo cane or alloy pole into the hole as an anchor.

On snow, either

1. sacrifice a snow stake (p. 282) or an ice-axe as an anchor; or
2. make a snow bollard. Cut it a good deal larger than an ice bollard (see above) and make the channel deeper. If there is any chance of the rope cutting through the snow, sink one or two objects (e.g. ice pitons) down the back to prevent it. If it is freezing it may be worth while to wet the channel at the back of the bollard so that ice can be formed there. Never use a snow bollard left by a previous party because, in being pulled down, the abseil rope will probably have cut through the snow, like a wire through cheese, while appearing to leave the structure undisturbed.

When one of these snow and ice anchors is used, abseil very carefully, putting as little load as possible on the anchor.

Chapter 12. Accidents in the British hills

As noted in the introduction, the number of accidents in the British hills in the past decade has been high, partly no doubt because of the great increase in the popularity of the hills for recreation. Most accidents are the result of slips on snow or ice or rock, or of getting lost, and are usually due to inexperience, lack of the right equipment and clothing, or underestimation of the task attempted in the prevailing conditions. Unfortunately, everyone is capable of making mistakes, not only the beginner but the expert as well. The table below shows the proportions of accidents involving physical injury in the main groups. The figures are based on accidents reported to the Mountain Rescue Committee (§ 90), and are necessarily approximate.

TABLE 4. *Mountain accidents in the United Kingdom (annual average 1967–1968)*

	Total accidents	Walking and scrambling	Climbing	Caving
Scotland	50 (8)*	31 (4)	19 (4)	—
Lake District	63 (8)	44 (6)	18 (2)	1
Wales	44 (6)	27 (5)	17 (1)	—
Pennines	24 (6)	11 (1)	6	7 (5)
Sea cliffs	10 (4)	2 (1)	8 (3)	—
TOTALS	191 (32)	115 (17)	68 (10)	8 (5)

*The number of fatal accidents is shown in brackets in each case.

Of the total, about two fifths were to persons aged twenty-one or under. Reports suggest that this is due not only to the relatively large numbers of people of this age visiting the hills, but also to the following special factors:

- young people often go in groups to the mountains inadequately equipped and without knowing the risks;
- leaders of school and other parties may be inexperienced (see § 2);
- young climbers with slight experience may try climbs which prove too difficult.

Sooner or later nearly everyone who walks or climbs in the British hills will be confronted with an accident, just as nearly everyone who uses the roads will be so confronted. In the latter case, however, professional help can usually be obtained quickly, whereas in the mountains the difficulties of movement may cause a delay of many hours between the time of the accident and the arrival of the victim in hospital. This delay is often a most serious factor and it is every mountaineer's duty to know how to minimize it and its effects.

§ 90. The rescue service

The Mountain Rescue Committee (M.R.C.) is responsible for the organization of mountain rescue facilities in this country.*
It maintains rescue posts and equipment and assists in and encourages the formation of mountain rescue teams. It is composed of representatives of the mountaineering clubs and others with interests in mountain country. The cost of the basic equipment for recommended posts is met by the

---

* This chapter is largely based on the M.R.C.'s handbook *Mountain Rescue and Cave Rescue*, which provides an up-to-date summary of the best practice, together with details of mountain rescue posts and several maps. It can be obtained from the Honorary Secretary, M.R.C. (see appendix B, 1). The M.R.C. has also produced an instructional film (bibliography, 7).

National Health Service, but the Committee relies on voluntary subscriptions for its other expenditure.

The posts. The principal first-aid posts are listed in the next chapter. They are identified outside in most cases by the sign which is shown in [32]. They are marked on recent issues of the Ordnance Survey maps. It must be emphasized that *the position of a post is sometimes changed* when circumstances alter. Inquiry should be made locally when visiting a district.

The supervisors of the posts accept no payment for their own service to mountain rescue, and their co-operation is the foundation of the whole service. It is important that mountaineers and walkers should do all they can to minimize the upset and disturbance to the supervisor's home and livelihood. Many of the supervisors themselves organize and lead rescue parties, and they have a distinguished record of gallantry and self-sacrifice in the saving of life.

Rescue teams. In some districts local mountaineers have joined together to form teams ready to turn out at any time to give help. The main teams for each area are listed in the next chapter. They are composed of experienced men and expert climbers, competent to deal with mountain problems in any conditions of weather, and are equipped with whatever special means their local knowledge has shown to be of value in bringing safe and speedy rescue. Except in cases of minor injury, they should always be summoned immediately an accident happens in their district.

The Royal Air Force maintains mountain rescue teams, composed of volunteers, to cover the areas of particular hazard to aircraft. Their help is not restricted to aircraft accidents, but of course Service requirements come first, and they are available only subject to these. To be able to call on the efficient aid of these R.A.F. teams in the case of real need has brought a most considerable reinforcement to the mountain rescue service. Here again, it should be remembered that changes in organization occur. Requests for their assistance must be made through the police.

H.M. Coastguards should be alerted for sea-cliff rescues where help is needed.

The police will always give efficient assistance and know what arrangements to make. In a few districts special police teams have been formed for mountain rescues. In some cases the local police station is the mountain rescue post. In general, however, the police themselves are not trained and equipped to deal with mountain accidents, and particularly where an accident can be efficiently dealt with by the people on the spot it will usually save time and trouble to go direct to the nearest mountain rescue post.

The St John Ambulance Brigade, the St Andrew's Ambulance Association, and the British Red Cross Society (appendix B, 1) have built up over many years an extensive service of first aid to the injured. The special problems of mountain country are outside their province, but in some cases they have placed first-aid boxes where they could be very valuable in a mountain accident. They also arrange evening classes in first aid and have published handbooks (see bibliography, 6).

§ 91. Rescue equipment

Each of the main mountain rescue posts holds the standard rescue equipment. This consists of a stretcher and two rucksacks containing medical supplies, cooking gear, and sleeping bags, and other clothing for the injured. Take both rucksacks. Before leaving the base, stimulants, food, sugar, and hot drinks must be added. Take plenty of rope; check lights.

The Thomas Stretcher [124] is standard equipment in the M.R.C.'s rescue posts. Particular features are:

1. Long extending handles which allow the carriers at either end to see where they are placing their feet. The handles slide inside

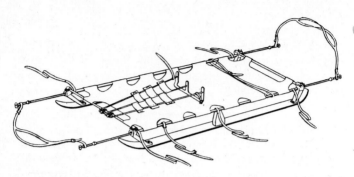

124. *The Thomas Stretcher.*

the frame when not in use and are released by catches on the frame underneath each handle.

2. Yoke straps. Put the head through the yoke straps, which distribute the weight. If it is desired to keep the stretcher horizontal on a steep slope they also permit the carriers to turn sideways without being constricted.

3. Wooden runners to allow it to be lowered down rock, grass, heather, scree, or snow. It will stand ordinary hard usage, but it has been designed as a lightweight stretcher for carrying; to be dragged roughly over rocky ground would wreck it.

4. A double Thomas splint to keep the victim steady on the stretcher, especially when he is being lowered. Essential for leg fractures.

Duff Stretcher. Details of this design are:

1. Four-and-a-half-inch wide runners are tilted to give wide bearing in snow.

2. Detachable wheel undercarriage (9 lb.) for paths.

3. The stretcher bed can be detached from the runners, and the frame folds into two separate sections (14 lb. each) to be strapped to the back by means of the slings.

4. Double Thomas splint (see 4 above).

5. Raised footpiece and the corselet give support in vertical position.

This stretcher was developed by Mr D. G. Duff, F.R.C.S., for rescues in the relatively big distances of the Scottish Highlands, with their few roads and sparse villages.

Other types of stretcher. Experiments are continuously being made to improve the design of rescue equipment, and several lightweight stretchers and a casualty-evacuation bag were under trial at the time of writing.

Pigott Rope Stretcher [125]. This improvised stretcher can be made quickly from a 100 or 120 ft length of rope. It can be very useful where no other stretcher is available, but it is tiring to carry and uncomfortable to lie on. *It must not be used if there is a possibility of spinal injury.* To make it, leave six yards of rope free and then make a series of eight

125. *The Pigott Rope Stretcher.*

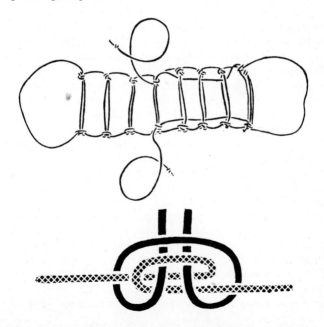

loops a hand span's length apart. The loops should all be of the same length, say three feet, or the distance from chin to outstretched finger tip, and are made with a simple overhand knot [167]. Leave enough rope to pass over the shoulder of the end bearer, and then fasten the end of each loop to it in turn, with the knot shown in [125], spacing them evenly. Make another shoulder-loop at the other end, and if the rope is long enough, thread the ends back to the middle to make slings to help the carriers at the side. The bed of the stretcher should be well padded and the frames of one or two packframes [29c] can be used to give increased stability.

Other improvised aids to carrying. Carrying by hand is practicable only for short distances. The patient can sit on the crossed hands of two people, with a third to take the weight of the legs. Or he may be carried by one person pick-a-back, or by the fireman's lift (the carrier brings the patient's left arm over his right shoulder from behind, passes his left arm between the patient's legs and hoists him up on his shoulder). A coil of rope can be helpful when carrying pick-a-back. Separate the coils into two and put your arms through the loops, as if wearing a rucksack; the patient is then lifted up and his legs passed through them. A frame rucksack can be turned into an effective carrier by cutting slits in the bag for the patient's legs. Quite a useful stretcher can be made from one or two pairs of skis with the aid of two or three wooden battens and screws carried ready for the purpose, and ingenuity can make do at a pinch with one pair, across which have been lashed pieces of ski stick broken to a suitable length.

All these and other improvised means of carrying an injured man have to be used with discretion. It is always easier to carry a patient on a rigid stretcher, and some injuries demand it. Remember that warmth and freedom from pain are more important than speed. But only the man on the spot can decide how best to help the victim of an accident, considering his injuries, the weather, position, time of day, distance from help, and so on, and while laying emphasis on the importance to the patient of using equipment designed for the job, it is nevertheless clear that there will be many situations which call for prompt energy and enterprise in using whatever means are at hand.

§ 92. Immediate action for dealing with an accident

The first thing to be done is to make the victim as warm and comfortable as possible. His body should be insulated from the cold mountain by heather, bracken, and any spare clothing from other members of the party. Be careful, however, not to warm him *quickly* if he is very cold and suffering seriously from exposure, as this may precipitate a flow of core blood to the surface, possibly with fatal results (§ 99). First aid should be given (§ 98). Attention is particularly directed here to the danger of moving the patient in any case of suspected fracture, particularly of the spine, and to the very great care with which he must be handled. In remote areas, or if exposure is likely to be long or serious, every effort should be made to get him to shelter to await the rescue party. In cases of exhaustion or minor accident the rope stretcher (see previous section) can be used, but if the injuries are too serious for him to be moved without a rigid stretcher, a windshield should be built round him and everything possible done to keep him comfortable. Tie him to a rock if there is any chance of him falling further.

Where an accident has happened in a party of inexperienced people, the leader should get the remainder on to safe ground, to a position where they can all return easily and safely to the valley on their own. If access to the scene of the accident is difficult, a fixed rope should be left to assist the rescuers, but not at the expense of the safety of the rest of the party. Caution is particularly necessary immediately after an accident because the natural desire to hurry to render assistance can lead to risks being taken, and so cause more accidents.

§ 93. Help from the valley

When the injuries are not apparently very serious you may be in doubt whether to send for help or to try to get the victim to walk down without delay. All that can be said is that the effect of shock and exhaustion is easily under-estimated, and that help should be sent for in good time whenever there is a possibility that it will be needed. No one should call out a rescue party, with all that it entails in demands on other people's time and effort, unless there are reasonable grounds, but if you always wait until you are certain that help is needed, you may find that you have waited too long.

Fetching help. Help should be summoned from a rescue post if one is near, by telephone if that is quicker. The supervisor will generally be able to assist in collecting helpers, advising on the route of evacuation, summoning an ambulance and medical assistance. If help is sought in more than one valley, take care that requests for doctor and ambulance are not duplicated. Although early warning should be given to the ambulance service, the ambulance should not be asked to arrive at the road much before the victim since unnecessary waiting by the ambulance must be avoided. The messenger sent for help should travel as quickly as safety, his first consideration, allows. He should carry, preferably in writing, a message giving the exact place of the accident, the time it took place, and a description of the injuries. Money may be needed if a telephone has to be used.

Special precautions if leaving the victim alone. If there are more than two in the party, one should remain with the victim if he can be spared from the duty of safeguarding the messenger. If the patient has to be left, he should in any case be tied to the rock so that he cannot fall further: this is essential if he is unconscious as he may try to get up on returning to semi-consciousness. *It is very important to mark the position as conspicuously as possible* so that the rescuers can easily find it, remembering that it may be dark or misty when they arrive.

A brightly coloured garment or an extended rope may help. A set of compass bearings taken from the spot to prominent features, and one of the route away from it, should be written down and taken by the messenger whenever there is a possibility that the rescue party may have difficulty.

Organizing the rescue party. In the valley, a leader should be appointed to direct the rescue and to organize relief measures at the base. The mountain rescue teams are the obvious source of help in their own mountain areas, and they can be relied upon to organize and lead the rescue. No time should be lost in summoning them. It must be remembered that a comparatively small injury can become a serious one through unskilful handling or exposure, and *it is always better*, even at the cost of a little delay, *for the rescue and evacuation to be carried out by men who have experience of the task* and who in some cases will bring special equipment that they have developed to deal with local conditions. Other sources of help are the police, mountaineering club huts, youth hostels, farms, and cottages. To carry a stretcher over rough country, taking care not to jolt the patient, is very tiring. At least four men are needed, six are better, and extra reliefs are needed for a long journey. Up to fifteen or twenty men can be used where much lowering of the rope is involved. Where local people are asked to help, they should be compensated for their services (§ 97).

§ 94. Transport of the injured

Place eiderdown bag and/or blankets on the waterproof cover opened out on the stretcher. The double thigh splint is placed on top of the eiderdown, and care should be taken to see that it is securely fastened to the cross-bar by its leather hinge. After giving the necessary first aid and immobilizing fractured limbs (§ 98) adjust the patient in this splint. Make him as comfortable as possible. Wrap the waterproof cover overall. Secure with four straps provided (Thomas Stretcher) or canvas body belt attached to the frame (Duff Stretcher). If the single iron leg splint is used, the bottom must be tied or strapped to the cross-bar. It is, however, less generally useful than the large double thigh splint. The central 'bicycle saddle' of the double splint must be well padded. Make a sling for an uninjured leg and fasten it to the top cross-bar to take part of the weight (in the case of semi-conscious or unconscious males care must be taken to arrange the sling to one side of the testicles). Support will also be needed at the armpits if the stretcher is to be lowered vertically; this can be given with another sling attached to the top cross-bar of the stretcher. Make sure the patient is comfortable and that there is no weight on injured limbs. A pillow can be improvised with a ruck-sack. If the patient is unconscious, remove any false teeth, and carry on side or face down (but not if turning him over will risk bending his spine). Protect his head from possible falling stones (a modification to the Thomas Stretcher is being made for this purpose).

It is very rarely feasible to *raise* a stretcher on a cliff and it is general practice to *lower* the stretcher even though this may be much further. An exception is in sea-cliff rescues, but special stretchers (Neil Robertson) or casualty-evacuation bags are available at H.M. Coastguard posts for these. When the stretcher has to be lowered down a steep rock-face or slope, make sure that the patient is firmly secured to it, and test for comfort before beginning to lower. Strap down all loose ends of straps and the yoke straps so that they do not catch, and lock the handles into their recesses so that the stretcher can land on its runners. The weight of the laden stretcher is considerable. Two ropes should be used, if possible; they should be tied to the top

126. *Lowering a Thomas Stretcher*. Note the method of strapping the victim to the stretcher. On steeper ground it would be advisable for the victim and the escorts to wear protective helmets as a precaution against falling stones, and for the escorts to be attached to the main belays by separate ropes instead of being attached to the stretcher.

cross-bar of the stretcher and also round the main supports. At least four men are needed on the stance from which the stretcher is being lowered:

- one for each of the ropes on the stretcher;
- one for lowering the man who accompanies the stretcher (4, below);
- one to give instructions and pass messages to the lowering party; he must be able to see over the edge.

Note in particular that:

1. The stretcher lowerers should be well belayed (§§ 58–61) and should control the rope with the waist belay (§ 62). They must be experienced and must wear gloves.
2. It is sometimes useful to use direct belays [145] for lowering, because a half hitch can be taken on the karabiner to increase friction. This is, however, not recommended in general because it may put too much strain on the available anchors, and because it may twist the rope so that a tangle results.
3. The only good belay may be fifty feet or so above the ledge, so one rope may be needed solely for making the belay.
4. It is generally desirable for an experienced helper to descend alongside the stretcher to keep it clear of snags. He should be on a separate rope (i.e., not tied on to the stretcher) since he must have freedom to move separately. He needs a cradle to sit in, preferably a triple bowline [166] and possibly also a chest loop attached to the main rope with a prusik knot [153] so that he can easily adjust his position. A safety helmet (§ 123) is desirable in case of falling stones.
5. To avoid confusion, the names of the lowerers must be agreed with the guide, or alternatively standard descriptions must be used (e.g. East and West). Some of the standard calls and signals in § 64 and § 95 may also prove useful.
6. If there are sufficient rescuers, several of them should go on ahead to reconnoitre the descent and to prepare the next lower by fixing belays and abseil ropes. They should, however, be on the ledge when the stretcher and guide arrive.

On snow and ice, the same general rules apply, except that it is even more important to move quickly. A half turn of the rope round an ice-axe in firm snow gives a good direct belay, but rock belays are preferable (see §§ 86–7). Ice pegs or screws are also useful. Ice-axes can be used to hold the stretcher in position on a slope, but do not let the stretcher slide down on to a firmly embedded axe as it may break the shaft.

The stretchers can be dragged as sledges on easy ground for greater speed and ease of transport, provided the patient is comfortable. In cases of spinal and serious head injuries it is advisable to keep the stretcher as level as possible, carried with its long axis parallel to the contour of the slope, and to take great pains to avoid jolts. In difficult country send a man ahead to reconnoitre the best route.

§ 95. Signals

To attract attention in an emergency, use a whistle, a torch, or flashes of the sun on a mirror; alternatively shout, or wave bright clothing. The following signals are used:

Message	Flare	Light, Sound, or Semaphore
1. Help wanted here	Red	Alpine: six long flashes/notes in quick succession repeated after a minute's interval S.O.S. – three short, three long, three short – repeated
2. Message understood	White (from party on hill)	Alpine: a series of three long flashes/notes repeated at one minute intervals
3. Position of base	White (or yellow)	Steady white or yellow light, or car headlights pointed upwards
4. Recall to to base	Green (used only at base)	Succession of notes (e.g. whistle), or of white or yellow lights, or of thunder flashes

A white flare is used to attract attention or to give illumination.

The code for raising or lowering on a rope is:

One whistle or flash   = Stop
Two whistles or flashes   = Pull up
Three whistles or flashes = Slack off or lower

§ 96. Search parties

One of the most difficult decisions is when to get together a party to go out and look for someone overdue. It would be a lot easier to make if everyone, before setting out in the morning, left word where he was going and when he intended to return, and even more important, could be relied on to send a message if he changed his plans (§ 5). To turn out again when you are looking forward to a welcome bed, to slog through all the weary hours of a wet and bitter night – this is one of the least pleasurable parts of mountaineering; to find then that the people you had been called out to save had spent a comfortable night in the next valley is undoubtedly the most exasperating. Where local men, shepherds and quarrymen, have to give up a night's rest after a hard day's work, the offence is unpardonable.

Parties are however delayed without there being a reproach of selfishness, stupidity, or thoughtlessness, and if they are seriously overdue, say more than three hours, the possibility that they need help must be faced. With rock climbers it is fairly simple if it is known on which cliff they have been climbing, since in rock-climbing centres there will usually be a number of people who are competent to go up in the dark to find out what has happened. If the party is walking or is climbing, but has not said where, the difficulty is much greater. If there is a bright moon a search party can set out at once, but only if it is composed of experienced men with good local knowledge (a large party of inexperienced people is useless and may result in further accidents). In other cases it is usually better to make arrangements so that the search can start on the hills at the crack of dawn. Any delay beyond that is inexcusable. The party must move off at first light from the nearest track or road to the area to be searched. A search generally demands a high degree of organization and the acceptance by all of a strict discipline under an experienced leader. The help of a shepherd and his dogs can be most valuable.

§ 97. After the rescue

Expenses. Costs incurred on a rescue are the responsibility of the patient, his friends, or failing them, his club or association. Sometimes it is necessary to pay for special transport to bring helpers, for the cost of meals for rescuers and for the services of local shepherds, quarrymen, or labourers, to whom the loss of a day's earnings may be serious. The continuance of just and friendly relations with the local people is so important that the M.R.C. will when necessary advance the money to pay suitable recompense, although it expects that any payment made will be refunded. Payment should bear some relation to the work done and be made on the recommendation of the supervisor or some other responsible person.

Checking the kit. It is very important that the equipment is cleaned and reconditioned promptly. The suffering of another may be prolonged, or even a life lost, if the kit is not in good order and ready for the next call. Deficiencies or damage should be reported to the supervisor, or to the Hon. Secretary of the M.R.C. (appendix B, 1).

Reports on accidents. After an accident:

1. a suspected fatality *must* be reported to the police;
2. details of the accident, including the patient's name, address, and Club, and how it happened, should be sent to the Hon. Secretary of the M.R.C. (appendix B, 1) since this helps the Committee in its search for better methods of relief and knowledge to help reduce the number of accidents in the future. *It is essential that such a report be made when morphia has been used* since every ampoule must be accounted for.

The press. Relatives of the injured should be informed of the accident, and it is better to give reporters a considered factual account of what has happened than let them gather information from casual sources, which may result in the publication of a distorted version, causing unnecessary pain and distress.

§ 98. First aid

To give medical assistance requires both knowledge and practical training. An outline is given here of the principles to be observed by an unskilled person in the absence of a doctor. The instructions have been kept deliberately very simple and brief and do not necessarily state the best method to be adopted by someone of greater skill and experience (see bibliography, 6, for useful books which treat the subject more fully). The first-aid kits contain rather more medical and surgical supplies than an unskilled person would be called upon to use.

The principles are:

1. Before touching the patient, inquire and look to decide if his spine may be injured. Pain in the back, with or without inability to use his legs, is suggestive of a fractured spine.
2. Stop bleeding and apply dressing to open wounds. Uncover wounds in the cold as little as possible.
3. Immobilize broken limbs so that the slightest pain is not caused by movement.
4. Keep warm and relieve pain. Warmth and freedom from pain are far more important than speed.
5. Handle and transport with care
6. In general, attempt little else. What can be postponed is better left to the skilled attention and aseptic conditions of a hospital.

Unconscious patients. In unconscious patients, difficulty in breathing, and a blueness of the face, may be due to the air passage being obstructed by the tongue, false teeth, mucus, etc. Remove any dentures; the jaw may need to be pulled forward as well. Carry the patient strapped to the stretcher on his side or face downwards, keeping watch to ensure that the mouth and nostrils are never blocked.

Shock. You must expect the victim and possibly the other members of the party to be suffering from shock. Keep the patient warm with all available clothing, an eiderdown bag, and blankets. If the patient is conscious, give hot drinks and glucose frequently, unless internal injury is suspected. Be careful, however, not to warm him quickly if he is very cold and suffering from exposure, because this will precipitate a sudden flow of core blood to the surface, possibly with fatal results (§ 99).

Morphia. Give morphia readily when there is pain, EXCEPT (1) in cases of severe head injuries; (2) where the patient is unconscious.

Inject one ampoule. If pain is present an hour later, inject another. On a long carry, if the patient is warm and pain is still present, inject a third ampoule three to four hours after the second. Children under twelve must be given only one injection of one half-ampoule. Inject in the outer surface

---

127. *How to inject morphia.* A. Tear off metal cap. B. Take out ampoule-syringe. C. Push down pin (to pierce container). D. Remove pin and gently expel air. E. Pinch up loose skin, insert needle, avoiding veins, and inject solution.

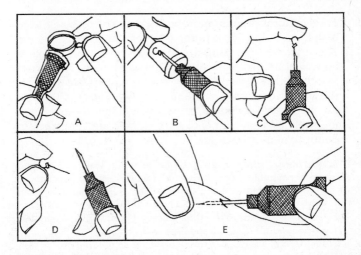

of the arm [127]. The exact place does not matter. The skin should be first cleaned with antiseptic available.

The leader should see that the doctor and ambulance men are informed about the amount of morphia which has been given, and the time. This is essential to avoid a possibly dangerous additional dose being given later. The best way is to mark 'M' on the patient's forehead, with a ball-point pen, and to write the information also on a piece of paper pinned to him.

Wounds. Dust or spray wounds with antiseptic solution or powder. Apply factory or shell dressing, or gauze and Elastoplast, or cotton wool and bandage. Do not plug non-bleeding wounds. Do not stitch wounds.

Bleeding. Bandage firmly, applying direct pressure over a pad of wool or gauze, or use shell or factory dressings which are supplied in the mountain rescue kits. Morphia reduces bleeding and is helpful. No stimulants should be given where it is necessary to control bleeding.

Fractures. Broken limbs must be immobilized by being fixed to splints, to the body, to the other leg, or to the stretcher. If transport causes pain, it must be stopped and the splints improved until movement does not cause pain. It is better to immobilize a broken limb at the outset than to try to straighten it, causing pain and possibly damage. Fractures can be easily overlooked, particularly when the patient is unconscious. Compare both sides of the body, and when in doubt treat as a fracture.

1. *Arm fracture.* Place angular splint on inside bend of arm and straight splint or pieces of wood all round. Place jersey, cloth, or cotton wool between the skin and the splints. Bandage from wrist to shoulder and fix the whole tightly to the chest.
2. *Collar-bone fracture.* Place hand near opposite collar-bone and bind the whole shoulder and limb to the chest.
3. *Leg fracture.* Insert boot through the circle of the Thomas iron leg splint (short iron on the inside). Pass the ring up until the

patient is apparently sitting on the ring. Fasten firmly by the attached gaiter, or rope loops, to the boot; then pass climbing rope through the gaiter strap or rope loops, and pull on the boot to make the leg immobile within the iron splint by fastening the rope to the bottom end of the splint under tension; it will slacken later. Then pass a bandage of puttees, scarves, or rope round the leg and splint from the foot to the groin so that the whole is one solid piece and can be moved roughly without causing pain.

4. *Ankle fracture.* Unlace boot, but leave it on the leg. Immobilize the limb as above.

5. *Fractured spine.* This injury demands the greatest care of all. Any movement is dangerous. Unfortunately it is one of the most difficult for the layman to diagnose. If the patient is conscious he can tell you of any pain in the back or numbness of the legs. In other cases look carefully, before you attempt to touch him, for any sign, such as damaged clothing or unnatural posture, or the way in which he fell, that may indicate that the back has been injured. In every case where there is the slightest suspicion that the spine is fractured, you must proceed on the assumption that it is. If it is found later that it is not, you will have lost nothing but your own extra care. No attempt should be made to move him from where he lies without a proper stretcher and plenty of help. With infinite gentleness lift him slowly on to the stretcher, doing your utmost to avoid disturbing the position of his back. Make him comfortable with cushioning. Rope him securely to the stretcher so that he cannot move. Carry the stretcher with the utmost care. *It is particularly dangerous to allow the spine to bend.*

Head injuries. Scalp wounds. Bleeding can be readily stopped by pressure dressings, i.e. shell or factory dressings. Do not give morphia if injuries are severe.

Frostbite. Be watchful where this may be present (in extreme cold, or cold winds, or in snow and ice when your boots are too tight). Warm immediately by putting the affected part against the warm body of another person or by immersing it in warm water. Do not on any account rub with snow – or anything else.

Suffocation. A victim of drowning or avalanche should be given *urgent and immediate* artificial respiration (after clearing his mouth and nose) by the mouth-to-mouth or mouth-to-nose methods. This should be continued until a doctor tells you to stop.

§ 99. Exposure and its treatment

Even when there is no accident exposure is a serious and often unrecognized danger in bad weather, especially among young people. The essential feature of exposure is severe chilling of the body surface, with a reduction in the heat content of the body. This becomes very serious when the deep body temperature begins to fall below its normal 98·4°F. (37°C.). It leads to mental deterioration, loss of muscular co-ordination, and eventually to unconsciousness, heart and respiratory failure, and death. The body itself acts to maintain core temperature by restricting the flow of blood to the skin so that core blood is not cooled at the surface. Contrary to popular opinion, *it is wrong to warm the patient suddenly*, since this only upsets the body thermostat and causes a rush of core blood to the surface, which is cooled and then returned to the heart. Unexpected deaths of raft survivors are often due to this. It is equally important to avoid exertion, since this may use up the man's last remaining energy.

Symptoms. It is not always easy to recognize exposure in its early stages, but it may be vital to do so. Watch out for:

– unexpected and apparently unreasonable behaviour, often accompanied by complaints of coldness or tiredness;
– physical and mental lethargy, including slowness to respond to or understand questions;
– failure of, or abnormality in vision (a usual symptom);
– some slurring of speech;
– sudden shivering fits;
– violent outbursts of unexpected energy, possible physical resistance to succour, violent language;
– falling.

Anyone taking drugs for psychiatric depression is particularly liable to exposure since these can upset the body's thermostat with consequent dangerous heat losses.

Treatment on the mountain. As noted above it is wrong to warm a man quickly (e.g. with hot-water bottles, rubbing or alcohol). The essential and immediate treatment is *to prevent further heat loss by insulating the body.* If possible put him into a sleeping bag or a Space Blanket (an ultra-lightweight heat-conserving cover available commercially since 1966), with insulation from the ground, and protection from wind and rain (e.g. with a tent, bivouac bag, or wind-break). Place a fit companion alongside him, to give body warmth, if necessary for 24 hours. Give sugar in easily digested form, e.g. glucose or condensed milk. If breathing ceases, give artificial respiration by mouth-to-mouth method. It is extremely difficult to diagnose death from exposure since the patient may appear dead when in fact he is only in a deeply chilled condition and will recover if treated properly. It is essential for this reason to continue mouth-to-mouth respiration until the patient recovers or a doctor allows you to stop, and for rescue teams to ensure that there is nothing impeding possible breathing (e.g. the stretcher cover) while the patient is being carried down. Do not carry him head up; and be careful to avoid impeding his circulation, particularly if, exceptionally, you have to carry him some way between two other climbers, with his arms over their shoulders, when he could easily get frostbite in his hands. Even if he appears to recover, he should be treated as a stretcher case and evacuated accordingly.

Treatment at base. Do not heat too rapidly. A warm (115°F.) bath, or soaking his hands in hot water, is usual.

It is far better to avoid exposure than to have to treat it: protection against wind and wet (a *cagoule* is invaluable), warm clothing, regular food, the avoidance of very heavy loads (say more than a third of one's own weight), and a steady pace with adequate rests, are the best safeguards.

Chapter 13. Where to walk and climb in Britain

It would take a whole book to cover this subject fully. This chapter briefly describes the main walking and climbing areas, and lists the relevant maps and guide-books so that you can find out more about them. It also includes details of mountain rescue facilities: the addresses sometimes change, and as noted in § 90 should be verified by local inquiry.

Most of the centres mentioned have good accommodation in the form of hotels, youth hostels, club huts, farms, cottages, or camping grounds (see also chapter 4).

Where to Climb in the British Isles by E. C. Pyatt and *Rock Climbing in Britain* by J. E. B. Wright are useful gazetteers to British climbing areas as a whole. *Rock for Climbing* by C. D. Milner and *Hard Rock* by Ken Wilson have pictures of most British areas. Many of the other books in the bibliography are useful for background.

Guide-books and other books which are directly relevant to particular areas are listed in this chapter; I have included out-of-print ones (without prices) since they may be available second-hand or from libraries. Apart from these, the Youth Hostels Association and the Ramblers' Association (appendix B, 1) publish handbooks to most of the areas, and there are innumerable short guide-books published locally describing hill walks. Where no address is given for the source of guide-books write, in case of difficulty, to the Hon. Secretary of the club concerned at the address in *Mountaineering* (see bibliography, 1).

The references after individual mountain areas in this chapter relate to the sketch maps. All the Ordnance Survey map references are to the Seventh Series 1-inch maps unless otherwise indicated, though the 2½-inch or 1:25,000 maps are preferable where available.

§ 100. The Northern Highlands and Skye

Extremely remote, the Northern Highlands give marvellous hill walking and climbing, especially in Wester Ross. A great deal of exploration remains. Like most other areas in Scotland, the distances are great and the days can in consequence be long. The Isle of Skye is a mountaineer's paradise, and all climbers should aim to visit it. There is potential sea-cliff climbing in the Hebrides and on the west and north coasts, including the Old Man of Hoy in Orkney.

Sutherland and *Easter Ross*:[1] Foinaven; Quinag; Ben More Assynt; Suilven; Stack Polly. (O.S. 13.)

The Dundonnel–Fionn Loch group:[2] An Teallach (accessible from Dundonnel); Beinn Dearg Mhor (accessible from Strath na Sheallag); Slioch (accessible from Kinlochewe). Carnmore Crag is one of the finest in Britain. (O.S. 20.)

The Torridon group:[3] Beinn Eighe; Beinn Alligin; Beinn Dearg; Liathach. (O.S. 19 and 26.)

The Black Cuillin of Skye[4] give excellent climbing and scrambling, on very rough gabbro which is mainly good. They are our closest approach to alpine climbing and are especially good for the medium-grade climber. The scope for the hill walker is rather limited. The traverse of the Cuillin ridge is probably the best expedition in Britain, but much of it is for rock climbers only. Some of the best rock climbing is on Sron na Ciche in Coire Lagan (all standards) and on the Coruisk face of Sgurr Mhic Coinnich (Severe and Very Severe only). Glen Brittle (youth hostel, B.M.C./A.S.C.C. Memorial Hut or cottages) is a good base. Loch Coruisk (J.M.C.S. Memorial Hut) is more remote from the standard cliffs. O.S. 33 covers the mountain area. There is also a 3-inch-to-one-mile map of the Black Cuillin (new edition in two colours, 1969, 3s.) published by the S.M.C.*

* All Scottish Mountaineering Club publications are now produced by the Scottish Mountaineering Trust and distributed by West Col Productions (appendix B, 5). They may be obtained *inter alia* from the bookshops listed in appendix B, 5.

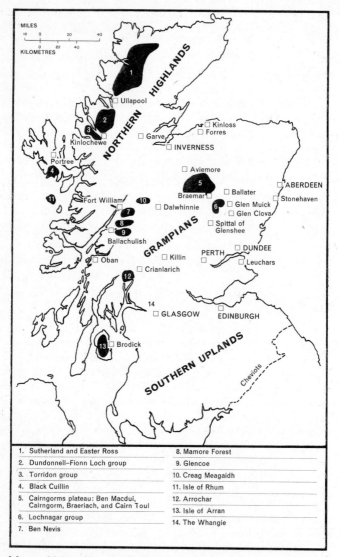

MILES

KILOMETRES

NORTHERN HIGHLANDS

□ Ullapool

1

2
3
Kinlochewe

□ Portree

4

11

Fort William

□ Garve
✕ Kinloss
□ Forres
□ INVERNESS

□ Aviemore

5
Braemar □

□ Ballater
□ ABERDEEN
□ Stonehaven

10

7
8
9
Ballachulish

□ Dalwhinnie

6
□ Glen Muick
□ Glen Clova

□ Spittal of
Glenshee

GRAMPIANS

□ Oban

□ Killin

□ Crianlarich

PERTH
□
□ DUNDEE

□ Leuchars

12

14
□ GLASGOW
□ EDINBURGH

13 □ Brodick

SOUTHERN UPLANDS

Cheviots

1. Sutherland and Easter Ross	8. Mamore Forest
2. Dundonnell–Fionn Loch group	9. Glencoe
3. Torridon group	10. Creag Meagaidh
4. Black Cuillin	11. Isle of Rhum
5. Cairngorms plateau: Ben Macdui, Cairngorm, Braeriach, and Cairn Toul	12. Arrochar
6. Lochnagar group	13. Isle of Arran
7. Ben Nevis	14. The Whangie

Map 1. *Main walking and climbing areas in Scotland.* The places shown are those referred to in §§ 100–3 (the numbers correspond to those in the text). Other areas are not shown.

BOOKS

1. *S.M.C. guide-books* (see note on p. 327).
   Northern Highlands, general guide, 1970, 42s.
   Northern Highlands, climbers' guide
   Vol. 1, *Letterewe and Easter Ross*, 1969, 26s.
   Vol. 2, *Torridon and the South*, due 1970, about 30s.
   Vol. 3, *Assynt and North-West Ross*, due 1970, about 30s.
   Western Highlands, general guide, 1964, 30s.
   Cuillin of Skye, climbers' guide
   Vol. 1, *Glen Brittle*, 1969, 20s.
   Vol. 2, *Choir' Uisg, Sgurr nan Gillean, Blaven*, 1969, 20s.

2. *Other books**
   Rock and Ice Guide to Easter Ross, Corriemulzie M.C., 1966, 7s.

RESCUE

1. *Northern Highlands*

Posts: Police, Thurso, Caithness. Tel. Police
   Police, Rhiconich, Sutherland. Tel. Police
   Inchnadamph Hotel, by Lairg, Sutherland. Grid ref. 252217
   Kintail Lodge Hotel, Kyle. Tel. Glen Shiel 275 or 248
   Glen Cottage Hostel, Torridon, by Achnasheen. Grid ref. 930565. Tel. Torridon 222
   Dundonnel Hotel, by Garve, Ross-shire. Grid ref. 090881. Tel. Dundonnell 204
   Glen Licht House, Kintail, Wester Ross (first-aid box only: at Edinburgh U.M.C. Bothy). Grid ref. 005173
   Camusrory, Loch Nevis, by Mallaig. Grid ref. 857957
Team: R.A.F., Kinloss, near Forres: via police

2. *Isle of Skye*

Posts: Glen Brittle House, Mr MacRae. Tel. Carbost 232
   Coruisk Hut: stretcher and kit. Grid ref. 487196
   Police Station, Portree. Tel. Portree 4

* By far the best books about Scottish mountaineering in general are *A Progress in Mountaineering* by J. H. B. Bell, *Mountaineering in Scotland* (Aldine paperback, Dent, 8s. 6d.) and *Undiscovered Scotland* by W. H. Murray, and *The Scottish Peaks* by W. A. Poucher (Constable, 1968, 30s.). *Munro's Tables* (S.M.C., revised 1969, 28s.) gives valuable information on the 3,000 ft mountains of Scotland, with supplementary material on the 2,500 ft mountains (Corbett's Tables) and the 2,000 ft hills of the Scottish Lowlands (Donald's Tables). The *S.M.C. Journal* has articles and details of new climbs (see bibliography).

§ 101. The Cairngorms and north-east Scotland

The Cairngorms are the whole mountain area to the east of Dalwhinnie. Cairn Gorm itself has been developed for ski-ing and tourism with a road up to Coire Cas and a cable lift almost to the summit. There is excellent hill walking on Ben Macdui, Braeriach, and Cairn Toul,[5] which together comprise the biggest area of land over 4,000 ft in Britain, and hence demand care, good equipment, and skill with map and compass. Winter mountaineering is excellent and less variable than anywhere else in Britain. There is a great deal of climbable rock and some excellent climbs. Most of the crags are, however, remote from help and demand a technique of their own; consequently it is not a good area for the novice. Lochnagar[6] gives first-class winter climbing [46] and moderately good summer climbing. There is practice climbing on the sea-cliffs from Forres to Stonehaven. Aviemore or Glenmore (youth hostel) are good bases for the northern areas; Braemar or Ballater for southern Cairngorms and Lochnagar. There are numerous bothies and several club huts and rescue shelters in the area (O.S. Tourist map *The Cairngorms*, and (planned for 1970) a special S.M.C. 1:25,000 map in three colours).

BOOKS

1. *S.M.C. guide-books* (see note on p. 327)
   Cairngorms, general guide, 1968, 40s.
   Cairngorms Area, climbers' guide
   Vol. 1, *Northern District* (the Cairngorms proper), 1961, 20s.
   Vol. 2, *Lochnagar, Broad Cairn, Glen Clova*, 1962, 18s.

2. *Other books* (see note on p. 329)
   The Cairngorms on Foot and Ski, V. A. Firsoff, Hale, 1950
   On Foot in the Cairngorms, V. A. Firsoff, W. R. Chambers, 1960, 10s. 6d.
   Glenmore, National Forest Park Guide, H.M.S.O., 1960, 8s. 6d.
   Rock Climbing Guide to the N.E. Coast of Scotland, Etchachan Club. (For the sea cliffs)

RESCUE
1. *Northern Cairngorms*

Posts: Gordonstoun School, Elgin, Morayshire (Mr Rawlings).
   Tel. Hopeman 445. (Also mountain rescue team)
   Cairngorm Mountain Rescue Team, Police Station, Aviemore.
   Tel. Aviemore 222
   Glenmore Lodge, S.C.P.R. Centre. Grid ref. 986095. Tel.
   Cairngorm 256. Also avalanche rescue equipment and dogs
   White Lady Shieling, Coire Cas, Cairn Gorm. Grid ref. 995053.
   Tel. Cairngorm 220
   Jean's Hut, Coire an Lochan. Grid ref. 981033

2. *South and East Cairngorms and Lochnagar*
Organizer: Contact police

Posts: Nature Conservancy Hut, Derry Lodge, Braemar. Grid
   ref. 041933. Tel. Braemar 678
   Police Station, Braemar. Tel. Braemar 222
   Police Station, Ballater. Tel. Ballater 222
   Spittal of Muick, Glen Muick. Grid ref. 307849. Tel. Ballater 530
   Lochnagar (first-aid box only, on top of buttress below Central
   Buttress). Grid. ref. 252855

Teams: R.A.F., Kinloss, near Forres, and Leuchars (Fife): via
   police

§ 102. Ben Nevis, Glencoe, and near-by peaks

This area is relatively easy of access. Glencoe and the
Mamores are recommendable for a first visit to Scotland.
The whole area, except Creag Meagaidh, is covered by
the O.S. Tourist map *Lorn and Lochaber*.

Ben Nevis,[7] the highest mountain in Britain (4,406 ft), can be
climbed in summer by an easy walk from Fort William, or
Glen Nevis (where there is a youth hostel). In winter, it is
usually a serious proposition, and in particular the descent
into Coire Leis from the Carn Mor Dearg Arête can be very
hazardous. A series of abseil posts (§ 66) at fifty-foot

intervals has been fixed there to try to reduce the number of accidents; the departure point on the C.M.D. Arête is marked with an aluminium notice. The north face gives all grades of rock climbing in summer but long and generally serious routes in winter [47]. These are best tackled from a base in the Allt a Mhuillin at the foot of the face preferably at or near the S.M.C.'s Charles Inglis Clark (C.I.C.) Hut. There are shelters on Carn Dearg (Grid ref. 158719), the N.W. summit (167713) and in Coire Leis (173714). A special 1:25,000 map is planned (1970) by the S.M.C.

The Mamore Forest[8] gives good hill walking, with the opportunity of claiming numerous 'Munroes' (peaks over 3,000 ft) in one day.

Glencoe[9] has good rock climbing and winter climbing, particularly on Buachaille Etive Mor. The traverse of the Aonach Eagach ridge is one of the best summer scrambles in Britain; under snow, it is a long day, with few ways off. A special 1:25,000 map is planned (1970) by the S.M.C.

Creag Meagaidh.[10] The crags of Coire Ardair give excellent winter climbing [110]; but are loose in summer. (O.S. 36).

BOOKS

1. *S.M.C. guide-books* (see note on p. 327)
   Central Highlands, general guide, 1968, 38s.
   Ben Nevis, climbers' guide, 1969, 25s.
   Central Highlands Area, climbers' guide, 1970, 26s.
   Glencoe and Ardgour, climbers' guide
   Vol. 1, *Buachaille Etive Mor*, 1959, 18s.
   Vol. 2, *Glencoe, Beinn Trilleachan, Garbh Bheinn* (including Bidean nam Bian and Aonach Eagach), 1964, 18s.

2. *Other books*
   Winter climbs: Ben Nevis and Glencoe, Ian Clough, Cicerone Press (see § 104, 2), 1969, 7s.
   The Companion Guide to the West Highlands of Scotland, W. H. Murray, Collins, 1969, 36s. The other books by W. H. Murray (see note on p. 329) are particularly good on this area.

Glencoe and Dalness, Scottish National Trust Guide
Argyll, Forest Park Guide, H.M.S.O., 8s.
Creag Meagaidh, 1967, 5s. From Graham Tiso Ltd (appendix B, 4)

RESCUE
1. *Fort William and Northern Argyll, including Creag Meagaidh*
Area organizer: contact via police: Fort William 2361

Posts: Fort William Police Station. Tel. Fort William 2361
    C.I.C. Hut, Coire Leis, Ben Nevis. Grid ref. 167723.
    Radio link to police
    Steall Hut, Glen Nevis. Grid ref. 177684 (cross river by wire
    bridge). Stretcher only
    Aberarder Farm, Lochlaggganside, by Newtonmore. Grid ref.
    479875. Tel. Kinlochlaggan 208

Team: Police Mountain Rescue Team at Fort William. Tel. Fort
    William 2361. Avalanche rescue equipment and dogs avail-
    able

2. *Glencoe*
Call on the Glencoe Mountain Rescue Team (Mr Hamish
    MacInnes), Achnacon, Glencoe. Tel. Kings House 305 and
    Ballachulish 258. Avalanche rescue equipment and dogs
    available

Posts: Altnambeitach, Glencoe. Grid ref. 140566. Tel. Police
    King's House Hotel, Rannoch Moor, Glencoe. Tel. King's
    House 259 or 260
    Scottish Ski Club, Meall Bhuiridh, Glencoe. Grid ref. 270520.
    Open in winter only

§ 103. The rest of Scotland

There is plenty of hill walking in southern Argyll, Perth-
shire, and the Southern Uplands. Rock climbing is of lesser
interest except in the following areas:

The Isle of Rhum.[11] This is a Nature Reserve, and permits
must be obtained from the M.C. of S. or the B.M.C.
(appendix B, 1). (O.S. 33.)

Arrochar[12] has some highly developed rock climbing on the Cobbler (Ben Arthur) and neighbouring crags. (O.S. Tourist map *Loch Lomond and the Trossachs*.)

The Isle of Arran[13] has excellent walking, scrambling, and rock climbing on granite. (O.S. 66.)

There is practice climbing at the Whangie,[14] eleven miles north-west of Glasgow, and on Salisbury Crags, Edinburgh.

BOOKS
1. *S.M.C. guide-books* (see note on page 327)
   Arrochar, climbers' guide, 1970, about 30s.
   Arran, Glen Rosa and Glen Sannox basins, climbers' guide, 1963, 18s.
   The Islands of Scotland (for Rhum and Arran), general guide-book, 1952, 30s.
   The Southern Highlands, general guide-book, 1949, 21s.

2. *Other books* (see note on page 329)
   Queen Elizabeth National Forest Park (for Cobbler area). H.M.S.O., 5s.
   Hillwalking in Arran, R. Meek, W. & R. Chambers, 1963, 4s. 6d.

RESCUE
1. *Dundee and Grampians and Ben Alder*
Organizer: Mr J. R. Watson, 39 Clepington Road, Dundee. Tel. Dundee 41095

Posts: Central Police Station, West Bell Street, Dundee. Tel. Dundee 23200
   Glen Doll Lodge Youth Hostel, Glen Clova. Grid ref. 278763. Tel. Clova 210 (Forestry Commission: half a mile)

2. *West of Scotland, Central Highlands and Southern Uplands*
Posts: Scottish Ski Club Hut, Coire Odhair, Beinn Ghlas, near Killin. Grid ref. 609377 (Sheet 48). Tel. Police
   Crianlarich Police Station. Tel. Crianlarich 222
   The Hawthorns, Drymen, Stirlingshire. Grid ref. 475886. Tel. Drymen 203
   Succoth Farm, Succoth, Arrochar. Tel. Arrochar 241
   Brodick Police Station, Isle of Arran. Tel. Brodick 100
   Yetholm. Tel. Police, Kelso 42
Team: R.A.F., Leuchars, Fife: via police

§ 104. The Lake District

The Lake District of Cumberland, Westmorland, and North Lancashire is one of our finest hill-walking and climbing areas. It was the birthplace of British rock climbing and is still the principal area in terms of the number of people climbing there. The rock is volcanic, either cleaved tuff which gives sharp holds, or rhyolite which is dense and hard but sometimes rather smooth. The area is roughly wheel-like in configuration with valleys radiating from the hub at Scafell. To move from one valley to another by main roads may involve long detours, and it is sometimes preferable to walk over the hills, or at least to drive over steep mountain passes. Youth hostels and camping sites are plentiful. Both the O.S. Tourist map of the Lake District and the Bartholomew's 1-inch map cover the whole area, but the former is better; the O.S. 2½-inch maps are also worth while for the more complicated parts of the area. The main climbing centres are as follows:

Langdale. The most accessible of the Lakes valleys from the south. For Bowfell, Pavey Ark, and Raven Crag [2 and 3]. Also for Gimmer Crag [38] and White Ghyll, both high-standard cliffs.

Borrowdale for numerous small cliffs such as Shepherd's Crag, for the Thirlmere Crags (Castle Rock and Raven Crag) and also for Great Gable [4] and Scafell.

Buttermere for Birkness Combe and Pillar Rock [45].

Wasdale Head. The traditional centre. In the very heart of the area and hence remote of access. For Pillar Rock, Great Gable, and Scafell.

Eskdale for Esk Buttress, various small crags, and Scafell.

Coniston for Dow Crag.

Patterdale for Dovedale, Deepdale, and Grisedale.

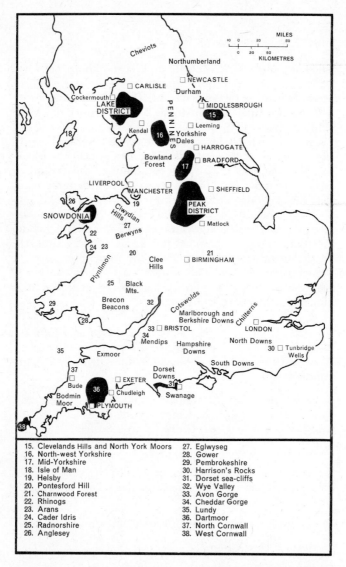

15. Clevelands Hills and North York Moors
16. North-west Yorkshire
17. Mid-Yorkshire
18. Isle of Man
19. Helsby
20. Pontesford Hill
21. Charnwood Forest
22. Rhinogs
23. Arans
24. Cader Idris
25. Radnorshire
26. Anglesey

27. Eglwyseg
28. Gower
29. Pembrokeshire
30. Harrison's Rocks
31. Dorset sea-cliffs
32. Wye Valley
33. Avon Gorge
34. Cheddar Gorge
35. Lundy
36. Dartmoor
37. North Cornwall
38. West Cornwall

Map 2. *Main walking and climbing areas in England and Wales* (§§ 104–8).

BOOKS
1. *Fell and Rock Climbing Club guide-books* (The Cloister Press Ltd,
     Heaton Mersey, Stockport, Cheshire)
     Borrowdale, 1968, 21s.
     Buttermere and Newlands Area, planned for 1970
     Dow Crag Area, 1968, 17s. 6d.
     Eastern Crags, 1969, 21s.
     Great Gable, Wasdale and Eskdale, 1969, 17s. 6d.
     Great Langdale, 1967, 21s.
     Pillar Group, 1968, 17s. 6d.
     Scafell Group, 1967, 21s.

2. *Cicerone Press Climbing Guidebooks* (16 Briarfield Road, Worsley,
     Manchester)
     Selected Climbs in North Lakeland
     Vol. 1 (Grades D–H.S.), 1969, 7s. 6d.
     Vol. 2 (Grades H.S.–X.S.), planned.
     Similar volumes for West Lakes and South Lakes are also
     planned

3. *Wainwright's Pictorial Guides to the Lakeland Fells* (Westmorland
     Gazette Ltd, Kendal, Westmorland)
     Vol 1, *The Eastern Fells*, 1955, 15s.
     Vol. 2, *The Far Eastern Fells*, 1957, 15s.
     Vol. 3, *The Central Fells*, 1958, 15s.
     Vol. 4, *The Southern Fells*, 1960, 15s.
     Vol. 5, *The Northern Fells*, 1962, 15s.
     Vol. 6, *The North-Western Fells*, 1964, 15s.
     Vol. 7, *The Western Fells*, 1965, 15s.
     These are excellent hill-walking guide-books.

4. *Other books*
     The Lakeland Peaks, W. A. Poucher, Constable, 1968, 30s.
     Walking in the Lake District, H. Symonds, Chambers, 1962, 12s. 6d.
     Fellwanderer, A. Wainwright, Westmorland Gazette, 1966, 15s.
     Lakeland Sketchbook, Wainwright, W. Gazette, 1969, 18s. The
       first of a new series of drawings with maps.
     Borrowdale, a Climber's Guide, P. Ross and M. Thompson, 1966,
       15s.
     The F. and R.C.C. Journal (see bibliography, 1) for details of new
       climbs

RESCUE

Search and rescue operations are co-ordinated by the police. Tel. Penrith 4411

Posts: Wastwater Hotel, Wasdale Head. Tel. Wasdale Head 229

Mickledore, Scafell (just below crest, Wasdale side). Grid ref. 210068

Outward Bound Mountain School, Eskdale. Tel. Eskdale 281. (Also mountain rescue team)

Sty Head Pass. Grid ref. 218095

Seathwaite Farm, Seathwaite, Borrowdale (Mr Edmondson). Grid ref. 236121. Tel. Borrowdale 284

Pillar Rock: 40 yards east of foot of Walker's Gully. Grid ref. 172124

Black Sail Youth Hostel (Easter–31 October only)

Youth Hostel, Cat Crag, High Gillerthwaite, Ennerdale Bridge, Cleator, Cumberland. Grid ref. 142141. (March–August only)

Police Station, Keswick. Tel. Keswick 72004.

Gatesgarth Farm, Buttermere (Mr Richardson). Grid ref. 194149. Tel. Buttermere 256

Old Dungeon Ghyll Hotel, Great Langdale. Tel. Langdale 272. (Also Langdale and Ambleside Mountain Rescue team)

Sun Hotel, Coniston. Tel. Coniston 248 or 262. (Also Coniston Fell Rescue team)

Dow Crag, at foot of Abrahams, B Buttress. Grid ref. 263979

Patterdale Youth Hostel, Goldrill. Grid ref. 399156. Tel. Glenridding 394. (Also mountain rescue team)

Outward Bound Mountain School, Hallstead-on-Ullswater, Watermillock. Tel. Pooley Bridge 347. (Also m.r. team)

High Street, The Knott. Grid ref. 438127

Glenridding Youth Hostel. Tel. Glenridding 269

Moor Road, Millom. Tel. Police, Millom 2207. Also search dogs

Teams (in addition to those noted above): Cockermouth Mountain Rescue Team. Tel. Buttermere 203 (Fish Hotel)

Kendal Mountain Rescue and Search Team. Tel. Police, Kendal

Patterdale Mountain Rescue Team. Tel. Police, Patterdale (Glenridding 223) or Mr Spurrett (Glenridding 293)

Penrith Mountain Rescue and Search Team. Tel. Penrith 3862

Wasdale Mountain Rescue Team. Tel. Seascale 393

R.A.F., Leeming, N. Yorkshire: via police

§ 105. Northern England and the Midlands

This region, which includes the Cheviots, the Pennines, and the Peak District – 'the backbone of England' – has plenty of good hill walking and outcrop climbing, some of it very close to big cities. As the hills are lower than those in our main mountain areas, it is a good area to start walking or rock climbing, but take care in bad weather because the distances can be considerable and route-finding difficult. The gritstone outcrops give excellent climbing – particularly crack climbing – and most of our best climbers have trained on them. Recently the limestone cliffs and disused grit and limestone quarries have also been explored and produced quite serious free and piton climbing. There are, unfortunately, quite a few access difficulties, particularly in summer, and camping is often restricted. The main climbing areas are as follows:

Northumberland and Durham. In the Cheviots, there are sizeable cliffs of volcanic rock. (O.S. 70.) The rest of the area gives mainly outcrop climbing on dolerite or gritstone, with some sea-cliffs. (O.S. 77 and 84.)

Cleveland Hills and North York Moors.[15] South of Middlesbrough. Scattered outcrops. (O.S. Tourist map *North York Moors.*)

North-west Yorkshire.[16] Several gritstone edges, including Pen-y-Ghent. Major limestone climbing at Kilnsey Crag, Gordale Scar, and Malham Cove. (O.S. 90.)

Mid-Yorkshire.[17] Very good gritstone outcrops, e.g. Almscliff, Brimham Rocks, Ilkley, and Widdop. (O.S. 96.)

The Peak District. Between and to the north and south of Manchester and Sheffield, this area has extensive gritstone edges including Laddow (north-west), Kinder (central), the Stanage–Chatsworth escarpment (east), and the Roches (south-west). There is a great deal of hard free and piton climbing in disused quarries such as Dovestones, Millstone Edge, and Lawrencefield, though some of these are still rather loose. The main limestone cliffs are near Castleton, in the Wye area (near Buxton), in Dovedale, and at Stoney Middleton. There are also numerous isolated crags such as – in the south of the Peak District, near Matlock – Black Rocks and Cratcliffe (grit), and Willersley Castle, Brassington, and Harboro (limestone). (O.S. Tourist map *The Peak District*.)

The Isle of Man[18] has short climbs on outcrops and sea-cliffs.

Helsby[19] has an excellent sandstone escarpment, convenient for Liverpool climbers.

Pontesford Hill,[20] seven miles south-west of Shrewsbury, has about fifty climbs on igneous rock, some of them 200 ft long.

Charnwood Forest[21] to the north-west of Leicester has some short climbs on volcanic rock.

BOOKS
1. *Climbs on Gritstone* (Gritstone Guide Committee)
    Vol. 1, *Laddow Area*, 1956
    Vol. 2, *Sheffield Area*, 1956
    Vol. 3, *Kinder and Roches Area*, 1951
    Vol. 4, *Further Developments in the Peak District*, 1957
    Vol. 5, *West Yorkshire Area*, 1957
    This series, which is now out of print, is being replaced and
        extended by the guide-books listed in 2 below.

2. *Rock Climbs in the Peak* (B.M.C. Peak District Committee and
        Climbers' Club. From Mountaineering Activities – see § 106)
    Vol. 1, *The Sheffield-Stanage Area*, 1964. New edition planned
    Vol. 2, *The Saddleworth-Chew Valley Area*, 1965, 15s.
    Vol. 3, *The Sheffield-Froggatt Area*, 1966, 17s. 6d.
    Vol. 4, *Chatsworth-Cromford-Brassington*, due 1970
    Vol. 5, *Northern Limestone*, 1970, 35s.
    Vol. 6, *Bleaklow Area*, planned for 1970
    Vol. 7, *Kinder Area*, planned for 1970
    Vol. 8, *Southern Limestone*, due 1970

3. *Other rock-climbing guide-books*

A Rock Climber's Guide to Northumberland, Northumbrian M.C., Dalesman Publishing Co., Clapham, via Lancaster, 1964, 11s.

Cleveland Limestone: Peak Scar and Whitestone, 3s. 6d. From Mr T. Marr, 1 Westwick Terrace, Easterside, Middlesbrough

Climbs on the North York Moors, Cleveland M.C., 1961

Yorkshire Limestone, Yorkshire M.C., 1968, 18s. 6d. From Mr P. Holt, 14 Beaufort Grove, Bradford 2

West Yorkshire Gritstone, Yorkshire M.C., planned

Lancashire Rock-climbing Guide, 1969, 12s. From *Rocksport* (bibliography, 1)

Rock Climbs on the Roches and Hen Cloud, North Staffs. M.C., 1969, 8s.

Rock Climbs at Stoney Middleton, 1967, 6s. From Mr B. Sykes, 1 High Court, Sheffield 1

Climbs on Derwent Valley Limestone, Nottingham C.C., 1966, 5s.

Rock Climbs on the Mountain Limestone of Derbyshire, Manchester Gritstone C.C., 1961

A Climber's Guide to Helsby Crags, Wayfarers' Club, 1963, 10s. Includes Frodsham

Rock Climbs in Leicestershire, Leicester M.C., 1966, 9s. From L.M.C., 33 Bedale Drive, Leicester

A Climber's Guide to Pontesford Rocks, W. Unsworth, Wilding & Son, Castle Street, Shrewsbury, 1962, 5s. 3d.

A Fell Walking and Climbing Guide to the Isle of Man, Manx Fell and Rock Club, 1961, 2s. 6d.

4. *Other books*

The English Outcrops, W. Unsworth, Gollancz, 1964, 30s.

The Pennine Way, A. Wainwright (see § 104, 3), 1968, 19s.

Walks in Limestone Country, Wainwright (as above), due 1970

The Peak and the Pennines, W. A. Poucher, Constable, 1966, 25s.

High Peak, E. Byne and G. J. Sutton, Secker & Warburg, 1966, 42s.

Pennine Way, Dalesman (see (3) above), 1965, 9s.

On Foot in the Peak, P. Monkhouse, MacLehose, 1932

Border National Forest Park, H.M.S.O., 5s.

Northumberland National Park, H.M.S.O., 5s.

Peak District National Park, H.M.S.O., 5s.

Rambles in Peakland, R. A. Redfern, 1965, 18s.

RESCUE

1. *Northumberland and Durham*

Posts: Police Station, Hexham. Tel. 999

　　Police Station, Yetholm, Kelso. Tel. Kelso 42

　　National Park Information Centre, Ingram, Northumberland.
　　　　Tel. Powburn 248

　　Scout Room, Cleveland Cottage, Middleton-in-Teesdale. Tel.
　　　　Forest in Teesdale 228

Teams: there are seven teams, obtainable via police on 999 or at
　　　　Morpeth 3131 or Durham 4929

2. *Yorkshire*

Posts: Police Station, Settle. Tel. Police, Settle 2542

　　Police Station, Grassington. Tel. Police, Grassington

Teams: Cave Rescue Organization. Tel. Police, Settle 2542

　　Cleveland Search and Rescue Team. Tel. Wainstones 462

　　Upper Wharfedale Fell Rescue Association. Tel. Police, Gras-
　　　　sington

　　Northern Rescue Organization. Tel. Police, Preston 54811

　　Swaledale Fell Rescue Organization. Mrs M. Salmon, Burn-
　　　　side, Richmond. Tel. Reeth 298

　　Holme Valley Moorland Rescue Team. Tel. Holmfirth 3642

　　Bewerley Park Centre Mountain Rescue Team. Tel. Pateley
　　　　Bridge 287

　　R.A.F., Leeming, N. Yorkshire; via police

3. *The Peak District*

Posts: Crowden Peak National Park Hostel. Tel. Glossop 3006

　　Kinder Reservoir, Filter House, Hayfield. Tel. New Mills 43117

　　Edale Information Centre, Fieldhead, Edale. (Also mountain
　　　　rescue team.) Tel. Edale 216

　　Police Station, Glossop. Tel. Glossop 3141

　　North Lees Farm, Stanage. Tel. Hathersage 317

　　White Hall Open Country Pursuits Centre, Manchester Road,
　　　　near Buxton. Tel. Buxton 3260

　　Police Headquarters, Matlock. Tel. 999

　　Police Station, Buxton. Tel. 999 or Buxton 2811

Teams: seven teams are available through police, including
　　　　R.A.F. Stafford. Tel. Police Operations Room, Ripley 3551

§ 106. North Wales (Snowdonia)

Snowdonia ranks with the Lake District (§ 104) as Britain's most developed hill-walking and climbing area. It is, however, more mountainous and the valleys are harsher. The cliffs are in general larger and often looser and more vegetated; and the hardest climbs in Wales tend to be longer and rather less easy to get off than the Lake District ones. Centres are less well defined than in the Lakes and are less necessary as several main roads run through the mountain area and make it easy to walk or climb on any mountain if private transport is available. The most popular centre is the Ogwen Valley (Nant Ffrancon) where there is plenty of accommodation, including Idwal Cottage Youth Hostel [6 and 32]. For the Snowdon massif there are farms and hostels all round from Capel Curig to Beddgelert and Llanberis, with youth hostels at the latter and at Snowdon Ranger near Llyn Cwellyn. Camping is restricted in the Ogwen, Gwynant, and Llanberis Valleys. O.S. 107 covers the whole area, but the 2½-inch maps are also useful and West Col (appendix B, 5) plan for 1970, two 1 : 25,000 sheets in three colours. The main climbing areas are as follows:

The Carneddau. These big, rounded mountains which are rather similar to the Cairngorms (§ 101), though lower, have a large number of small crags, and three important ones, Craig yr Ysfa, Llech Du, and Black Ladders.

The Glyders and Tryfan include such famous climbing grounds as Cwm Idwal, Glyder Fach, and the East Face of Tryfan. These give climbing for beginners and medium-grade climbers probably not excelled elsewhere [5 and 42].

Llanberis Pass. The climbing here is rather steeper and fiercer than in the Ogwen Valley (see, for example, [59]), and there are relatively few climbs for novices.

The Snowdon Massif includes Clogwyn du'r Arddu [39], Lliwedd, and Clogwyn y Ddysgl.

There is good climbing also on cliffs to the south of Llyn

Cwellyn (e.g. Craig y Bera), at Cwm Silyn, and at Tremadoc [41]. The last are however in a Nature Reserve and permits are required.

BOOKS

1. *Climbers' Club guide-books**

The Carneddau, 1967, 15s. 6d. Revised ed. due 1970
Tryfan and Glyder Fach, 1966, 15s. 6d. Revised ed. due 1970
Cwm Idwal, 1967, 15s. 6d.
Llanberis North, 1966, 15s. 6d.
Llanberis South, revised ed. due 1970
Clogwyn Du'r Arddu, 1968, 15s. 6d.
Lliwedd, 1966 reprint, 12s. 6d. Revised ed. due 1970
Snowdon East, planned for 1970
Snowdon South, 1966, 15s. 6d.
Snowdon West, in preparation

2. *Other books*

The Welsh Peaks, W. A. Poucher, Constable, 1963; 18s.
Rock Climbers in Action in Snowdonia, J. Cleare and A. Smythe, Secker & Warburg, 1966; 35s.
Tremadoc Area, West Col (appendix B, 5), planned 1970
Snowdonia Winter Climbs, West Col, planned 1970
Rambles in North Wales, R. A. Redfern, Robert Hale, 1968, 25s.
Hillwalking in Snowdonia, E. G. Rowlands, Cidron, 3s. 6d.
The Mountains of Snowdonia, H. R. C. Carr and G. A. Lister, 1948
On Foot in North Wales, P. Monkhouse, MacLehose, 1934.
Snowdon Biography, Noyce, Sutton, and Young, Dent, 1957; 25s.
Snowdonia, National Forest Park Guide, H.M.S.O.; 5s.
Snowdonia, National Park Guide, H.M.S.O.; 5s.
New Climbs (see bibliography, 1) for details of new routes.

RESCUE

It is asked that all reports of accidents and requests for assistance should be sent to Gwynedd Constabulary. Tel. Colwyn Bay 57171 or 999.

*All Climbers' Club guide-books are now distributed by Mountaineering Activities Ltd, Wellington Place, Liverpool Road, Manchester M3 4NQ

Posts: as noted above, contact through Colwyn Bay 57171
 Pen-y-Gwryd Hotel. Grid ref. 660558. Tel. Llanberis 211 and 368
 Ogwen Cottage Mountain School (also mountain rescue team).
  Grid ref. 650604. Tel. Bethesda 214 and 581
 Idwal Cottage Y.H.A. Grid ref. 649603. Tel. Bethesda 225
 National Mountaineering Centre, Plas y Brenin, Capel Curig.
  Tel. Capel Curig 214 and 230. (Also mountain rescue team)
 Aberglaslyn Hall, Beddgelert. Tel. Beddgelert 233
 National Park Wardens Centre, Nant Peris. Tel. Llanberis 399
 Police Station, Blaenau Ffestiniog. Tel. Blaenau Ffestiniog 250
 Foel Grach (refuge shelter; no equipment). Grid ref. 689659

Teams: Ogwen Cottage Mountain School (see above)
 Llandudno and District Mountain Rescue Team. Tel. Police,
  Llandudno
 Welsh Rescue Dog Unit. Tel. Waenfawr 249 or via police 222
 R.A.F., Valley, Anglesey: via police

§ 107. The rest of Wales

There is major climbing on the west coast of Anglesey,[26]
especially on Craig Gogarth (O.S. 106). Apart from this
the only climbing of significance is in the following areas:

The Rhinogs[22] have some long, worth-while climbs on two
cliffs, Craig Bodlyn and Craig y Cae. (O.S. 116.)
The Arans[23] have Craig Cowarch, a big rambling cliff (three
miles north of Dinas Mawddwy) and a good deal of other
rock. (O.S. 116.)
Cader Idris[24] has some quite good long climbs on three of its
cliffs, and inferior climbing on a fourth. (O.S. 116.)
Radnorshire[25] has some long climbs in the Elan Valley.

 In addition there is minor climbing on Eglywseg Mountain near Llangollen[27] (O.S. 108), and extensive new
developments on the Gower sea-cliffs[28] (O.S. 152 and 153),
and the Pembrokeshire sea-cliffs[29] (O.S. 138 and 151).

BOOKS
 West Col Coastal Climbing Guides (appendix B, 5)
 Anglesey–Gogarth, 1969, 28s.

Lleyn Peninsula, planned for 1970
Gower Peninsula, planned for 1970
Sea Stacks of the British Isles, planned for 1971

Other books
The Welsh Peaks, W. A. Poucher, Constable, 1963, 25s.
Taff Fechan, P. Leyshon and C. Jones. Supplement to *Mountaineering* (bibliography, 1), Spring 1969
'Pembrokeshire', C. J. Mortlock, and 'Rock-climbing in South Wales', Derek Ellis. Articles in *Rocksport* (bibliography, 1) April and August 1969 respectively
Interim Rock-climbing Guide to South Wales, S. Wales M.C., 1969, 4s. From Y.H.A., Park Place, Cardiff

RESCUE
1. *North Wales* (outside Snowdonia)
   Contact police. Tel. Colwyn Bay 57171

2. *Mid-Wales*
Posts: Outward Bound Sea School, Aberdovey (also mountain rescue team). Tel. Aberdovey 464
   Youth Hostel, Cader Idris. Grid. ref. 684162. Tel. Dolgellau 392
   Plas Yr Antur, Fairbourne, Merioneth. Tel. Fairbourne 282
Teams: Joint Services Mountain Training Centre, Morfa Camp, Towyn. Tel. Towyn 371. For others consult police

3. *South Wales*
Posts: Swindon Outdoor Centre, Plas Pencelli, Pencelli, Brecon (also mountain rescue team). Tel. Llanfrynach 241 and 281
   1–10 Powell Street, Penwyllt, Abercrave, Swansea Valley. Tel. Abercrave 613 or 211; or Glynneath 211
   Youth Adventure Centre, Court House, Longtown, Herefordshire. Tel. Longtown Castle 225
Teams: four teams are available through police, including R.A.F., St Athan, Barry, Glamorgan

§ 108. South and west of England

Although there are no mountains, the Downs, the Chilterns, the Cotswolds, and Dartmoor offer reasonable walking, particularly in autumn and winter. The west of England has some excellent climbing, mainly in west Cornwall. In the south-east, the only sound rock is confined to small outcrops: but fortunately, with motorway travel, it is not difficult to get to the Peak District or North Wales for week-ends. The main climbing areas are as follows:

Harrison's Rocks and other outcrops in Kent and Sussex.[30] These short sandstone outcrops are much used by Londoners. Harrison's Rocks themselves have been bought by the B.M.C. (O.S. 171 or 183.)

The Dorset sea-cliffs,[31] to the west of Swanage, give steep and fairly serious climbing on limestone. B.M.C. access regulations should be observed. (O.S. 179 for Swanage, and 178 for Lulworth.)

The Wye Valley[32] has some good limestone outcrops including Symond's Yat and Wintour's Leap (Nature Reserve). (O.S. Tourist map *Wye Valley and Lower Severn*.)

The Avon Gorge[33] gives steep climbing on limestone. (O.S. 165).

The Cheddar Gorge[34] has been climbed on in the past, but is loose and dangerous. (O.S. 165.)

Lundy.[35] This island has good granite sea-cliffs, as yet little developed. (O.S. 163.)

In Devon, Dartmoor[36] has many granite outcrops, but before climbing in the north-west part make sure that the artillery range there is not in use (O.S. 175). There is an important crag at the Dewerstone, Shaugh Prior, near Plymouth (O.S. 187), and a limestone cliff at Chudleigh, ten miles west of Exeter (O.S. 176), as well as important sea-cliff climbing on the south coast.

North Cornwall[37] has some sea-cliff climbing at, and northwards from, Bude, most of it on indifferent rock. (O.S. 174.)

West Cornwall.[38] The coast to the east and south of Land's End gives some of the best rock climbing in Britain, with good steep rock (much of it perfect rough granite) and mild weather. There are plenty of climbs of all standards. Among many good granite cliffs, Bosigran and Chair Ladder are outstanding. The greenstone at Tater Du (Lamorna) is also worth while. (O.S. 189.)

In addition, Guernsey and Jersey have some good granite sea-cliffs.

BOOKS

1. *Guide-books*

South-East England, Climbers' Club (see note in § 106), 1969, 25s.

Dorset, Climbers' Club, 1969, 17s. 6d.

Lower Wye Valley, Climbers' Club and Gloucestershire M.C., planned for 1970

Limestone Climbs in South West England, The Limestone Climbing Group, c/o Bristol U. Mountaineering C., Students Union, Queens Road, Bristol B58 1LN

Extremely Severe in the Avon Gorge, E. Ward-Drummond, 1967, 9s.

South Devon, West Col Coastal Climbing Guide (appendix B, 5) planned for 1970

Rock-climbing in Devonshire, R. Navy M.C., 1966, 15s. From R. D. Moulton, Fairmile, Woodham Road, Woking, Surrey

Sea Stacks of the British Isles, West Col Coastal Climbing Guide, planned for 1971

Cornwall, Climbers' Club (see note in § 106)

Vol. 1, *North Coast of West Penwith*, 1968, 15s. 6d.

Vol. 2, *West and South Coasts of West Penwith*, 1966, 22s. 6d.

2. *Other books*

The English Outcrops, W. Unsworth, Gollancz, 1964, 30s.

Dean Forest and Wye Valley, National Forest Park guide, H.M.S.O., 5s.

A Climber in the West Country, E. C. Pyatt, David Charles, 1969, 40s.

Dartmoor, National Park guide, H.M.S.O., 5s.

The Climbers' Club bulletin *New Climbs* (bibliography, 1) for new routes. The 1960 and 1962 numbers of the *Climbers' Club Journal* have articles about north Cornwall and Lundy respectively

RESCUE

1. *Wye Valley*

Post: Wintour's Leap; at Broad Rock, Coleford Road, Woodcroft. Grid ref. 542963. Tel. Police, Chepstow 2032

2. *Devon*

Post: Dewerstone. On wall of 'Endomoor' cottage on right fifty yards from bridge over River Plym on road to Shaugh Prior. Grid ref. 533635.

Teams: Via Dartmoor Reserve Group. Tel. Tavistock 3195 or police

3. *West Cornwall*

Posts: Count House, Bosigran, nr Gurnard's Head, St Ives. Grid ref. 422365. Tel. St Ives 5867 or Police

H.M. Coastguard Station, Tol-pedn-Penwith, Porthcurno

J. W. Smith (B.M.C. Guide) may also be able to advise and help (5 Rosewall Terrace, St Ives. Tel. St Ives 5867 or St Ives 12)

§ 109. Ireland

Contrary to popular opinion, Ireland has good rock climbing as well as hill walking. Climbers are few, and generally the climbing has not been developed nearly as fully as in England and Wales. There is scope for much further exploration. The main climbing areas are as follows:

Donegal, in the far north-west of Eire, has some of the finest granite climbing in the country. The main areas in the Derryveagh Mountains[39] are the Poisoned Glen (climbs of up to 1,000 ft), Lough Barra, and Glen Veagh. Further south, the Blue Stack Mountains[40] give some climbing around Lough Belshade. The sea-cliffs have now been fairly well explored, but only Sail Rock, a 300-ft cliff south-east of Slieve League,[41] gives good routes. O.S. $\frac{1}{2}$-inch sheets 1 and 3.

The Antrim Coast[53] has several popular basalt or limestone outcrops culminating in Fair Head, a magnificent basalt cliff with some high-grade routes.

The Mourne Mountains,[42] in County Down, thirty miles south of Belfast, are the highest mountains in Ulster (Slieve

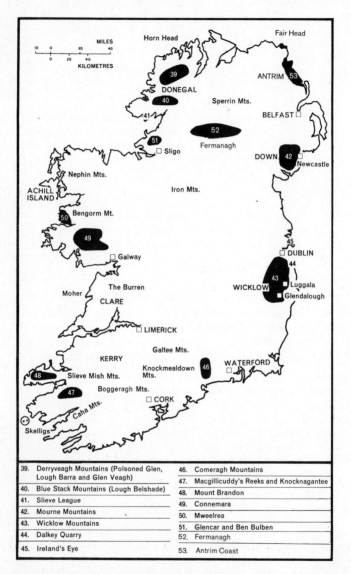

39. Derryveagh Mountains (Poisoned Glen, Lough Barra and Glen Veagh)
40. Blue Stack Mountains (Lough Belshade)
41. Slieve League
42. Mourne Mountains
43. Wicklow Mountains
44. Dalkey Quarry
45. Ireland's Eye

46. Comeragh Mountains
47. Macgillicuddy's Reeks and Knocknagantee
48. Mount Brandon
49. Connemara
50. Mweelrea
51. Glencar and Ben Bulben
52. Fermanagh
53. Antrim Coast

Map 3. *Main walking and climbing areas in Ireland* (§ 109).

Donard, 2,796 ft) and provide excellent hill walking. The climbing varies from the short delicate slab routes on Slieve Binnian and Hen Tors to the long steep routes on Eagle Mountain, Pigeon Rock and Slieve Beg. O.S. 1-inch sheet 9.

The Wicklow Mountains,[43] to the south of Dublin, give excellent climbing on the granite cliffs of Camaderry Mountain in Glendalough, and at Luggala. There is also good hill walking, especially the circuit from Glendalough, over Camaderry, Table Mountain, Lugnaquilla, and Croaghanmoira. Dalkey Quarry,[44] only ten miles from the centre of Dublin, has a great variety of climbs of all standards. There is sea-cliff climbing at Ireland's Eye,[45] north of Dublin. O.S. ½-inch sheet 16.

The Comeragh Mountains,[46] in County Waterford offer some good climbing on Old Red Sandstone and conglomerate, but are relatively unexplored.

Co. Kerry has the most extensive mountain areas in the country. The Macgillicuddy's Reeks[47] which include Carrantuohill (3,414 ft, the highest summit in Ireland) give excellent rocky scrambling and ridge walking, and climbs are now slowly being developed, for example at Lough Reagh near Glencar. Mount Brandon,[48] in the Dingle Peninsula, has rock climbing and fine ridges. There is other rock climbing at Knockagantee, on smaller buttresses scattered throughout the county and on the Skelligs. Mainly Old Red Sandstone. O.S. ½-inch sheets 20, 21, 22, 24, and 25.

Co. Clare has the huge cliffs of Moher, which are however very loose. Inland, there are small rocky hills – The Burren.

Galway–Mayo has excellent climbing in Connemara on the quartzite cliffs of Ben Corr and Ben Collaghduff, up to 1,200 ft, and also in Coum Gowlaun on Maumtrasna nearby. Further north, Mweelrea (2,688 ft) is a fine mountain rising straight from the sea, with rock climbing at

Doo Lough and good ridge walking.[50] The Achill Island sea-cliffs are probably the biggest in Britain, about 2,000 ft high, but are very unattractive.

Sligo has many vertical limestone cliffs which have hardly been touched. Glencar and Ben Bulben.[51]

Fermanagh[52] has many undeveloped limestone crags, of which Knockmore, 400 ft high, is the most notable.

BOOKS

1. *Irish Mountaineering Club* rock climbing guide-books*
   Climbers' Guide to Donegal, I.M.C. (Dublin), 1962, 3s. 6d.
   Mourne Rock Climbs, I.M.C, (Belfast), interim guide
   Climbers' Guide to Dalkey Quarry, I.M.C. (Dublin), 1964, 3s. 6d.
   Climbers' Guide to Glendalough, I.M.C. (Dublin), 1957, 3s. 6d.
   Climbers' Guide to Luggala, I.M.C. (Dublin), 1967, 1s.
   A new series of guide-books to Donegal, the Mournes and Wicklow is planned in association with the Cicerone Press (§ 104, 2)
   Climbers' Guide to Glen Inagh (Connemara), I.M.C. (Dublin), 1967, 1s.

2. *Other books and articles*
   Walking in the Mournes, E. Stanley Jones, Mourne Observer Press, Newcastle, Co. Down, 1962, 2s. 6d. New guide in preparation, 1970. From the Northern Ireland Tourist Board*

* The Irish Mountaineering Club holds stocks of guide-books, and is prepared to answer requests for information from visiting mountaineers. The addresses of the Hon. Sec. I.M.C. (Belfast) and of the Hon. Sec. of the I.M.C. Central Council may be found in the B.M.C. magazine *Mountaineering* (see bibliography, 1). On I.M.C. (Dublin) matters, write to I.M.C., P.O. Box 107, Parnell Square, Dublin 1. The Northern Ireland Tourist Board (10 Royal Avenue, Belfast 1) and the Irish Tourist Office (71 Regent Street, London W1 and Baggott Street Bridge, Dublin 2) provide general information. Maps are supplied by the Government Book Shop, 7 Linenhall Street, Belfast 2, and Government Publications Office, G.P.O., Dublin 1.

'Sail Rock', D. Scott; article in *Rocksport* (bibliography, 1), December 1968
The Mountains of Killarney, S. C. Coleman, Dundalgan Press, Dundalk, Co. Louth, 2s.
Mourne Country, E. Evans, Dundalgan Press (see above), 1968
Walking in Wicklow J. B. Malone, Helicon, 7s.
'The Hillwalkers' Guide to Ireland', Joss Lynam; article in *The Climber and Rambler* (bibliography, 1), June 1969
Irish Mountaineering (see bibliography, 1), for new climbs

RESCUE
1. *Mourne Mountains*
Post: Police Station, Newcastle. Tel. Newcastle 3583

Teams: Royal Ulster Constabulary M.R. Team, Belfast. Tel. Belfast 650222
Mourne Mountain Rescue Team. Tel. Castlewellan 256 or via police

2. *Donegal*
Posts: Gribbins Barn, Lough Barra. Tel. Police
Errigal Youth Hostel, Dunlewy. Tel. Police

3. *Wicklow*
Post: Tiglin Outdoor Pursuits Centre, Ashford. Tel. Wicklow 4169

Teams: I.M.C. (Dublin). Obtainable via Police Central Control (Tel. Dublin 52231) or any Garda station

4. *Galway*
Posts: The Twelve Bens Youth Hostel, Ben Lettery, Recess. Tel. Police
Police Station, Leenane. Tel. Leenane 2

5. *Fermanagh*
Post: Portora Royal School, Eniskillen. Tel. Police

6. *Rest of Ireland*
Post: Air Corps, Casement Aerodrome, Baldonnel, Co. Dublin. Tel. Dublin 592493
Team: An Oige, 39 Mountjoy Square, Dublin. Tel. Dublin 45734
Elsewhere: Contact Police

Part three

Alpine mountaineering

This part deals with all aspects of alpine mountaineering from the point of view of the experienced British climber. It is assumed that proficiency in the various aspects of climbing technique both on rock and on snow and ice has been achieved in Britain. Although it may not be practicable for everyone to master these techniques before going to the Alps, it is a great advantage to have done so, because you are then free to concentrate in the Alps on learning the special skills needed for safe alpine mountaineering.

Although winter alpine mountaineering is beginning to become popular among a few very experienced mountaineers, British climbers are primarily interested in summer alpine climbing (from the end of June to the middle of September), and this book does not deal with special techniques and skills needed for winter and spring ski-ing and climbing.

There is good climbing also in Spain (the Pyrenees), and Norway; these areas are lower than the Alps and have their own characteristic conditions, but the techniques described in this part can be applied there and no special mention is made of them.

The Alps can be well worth visiting for the hill walker. Most of the high alpine summits involve climbing on snow and ice, or rock, and are therefore out of bounds to him, but there is much fine walking to be done at lower altitudes, avoiding glaciers and other difficult terrain. The Dolomites and Austria are particularly suitable. Most of the lessons learned in the British hills apply equally here, and chapters 14, 16, and 19 of the present part may also be useful. The titles of the books which cover alpine walking are given in chapter 19, and the British organizations which arrange walking tours are in appendix B, 2.

Chapter 14. An introduction to the Alps

Since the Second World War, the number of British climbers visiting the Alps has increased many times over. This is no doubt partly because of the great increase in the number of active climbers, and partly because of improvements in holidays and ease of travel. But mainly it is because more and more climbers have come to realize that it is both a natural and a necessary development to go on from British mountains to the much bigger mountains of the Alps and the more complete form of mountaineering which they give.

§ 110. Essential differences between alpine climbing and British climbing

Most alpine climbs are on peaks over 9,000 ft high, and some of the longest and highest climbs reach an altitude of over 15,000 ft. As a result, alpine conditions are generally more serious than British conditions, with much snow and ice, complicated glaciers, and major objective dangers from weather, avalanches, and falling stones. Whereas British climbs are measured in hundreds of feet, alpine climbs are measured in thousands of feet, and it is necessary to think in terms of days as well as hours. Most alpine ascents are split into two stages, by going up to a hut (§ 133) on the first day, and completing the ascent and returning to the hut or valley on the second. Because of the great distances to be covered, speed is of paramount importance. Moreover, accidents, when they do occur, are usually serious because of the difficulty of holding a fall on loose rock or snow and ice, and the delays and difficulties of rescue operations in remote places. Finally, altitude reduces the body's strength and efficiency, and fatigue impairs judgement as well as speed.

On the other hand, the grandeur of the Alps is inspiring, and their scale and seriousness necessitate a singleness of purpose which is often missing from British climbing, particularly for the experienced climber who has already done most of the British climbs which really enthuse him. Moreover, the variety of alpine climbing is tremendous: there are over a dozen areas (chapter 19) and it would probably be possible to climb in the Alps every season for a lifetime without doing the same climb twice.

§ 111. Alpine skills

What are the main skills and qualities which the alpine mountaineer needs to enable him to cope safely with the greater size and difficulty of the Alps? To answer this question fully will take most of this and the next four chapters, but mainly it is a matter of common sense and experience, and a combination of fitness, route-finding skill, and rope management which taken together enable him to move fast. More specifically, he needs:

- knowledge of alpine mountains and conditions, so that he can select a route which is in good condition, and can recognize dangerous conditions of snow or weather (chapter 16);
- the ability to plan an ascent so as to pass through dangerous sections when they are at their safest (i.e., relatively free from avalanche danger) and difficult sections when they are at their easiest (i.e., when the rock is warm and free from *verglas*). An early start – often well before dawn – is the most important single factor here (§ 134);
- route-finding skill on glaciers (§ 135), snow and ice (§ 136), and rock (§ 137). A wrong choice of route can lead into great difficulties, and lose hours;
- technical ability on rock and snow and ice; and in particular, the ability to move quickly and safely on easy or moderately difficult ground. This can best be achieved by thorough training in Britain (see § 112);
- skill in rope management on snow and ice (§§ 85–9) and glaciers (§ 135) and a good understanding of crevasse rescue (chapter 18);

- good rope technique on rock, and in particular knowing how to safeguard the party while moving together (§ 137), and how to abseil safely and rapidly (§ 138). Much time can be saved by developing an automatic understanding in the party so that there is no delay due to misunderstanding or the need for explanation;
- knowledge of the equipment needed for alpine routes, and the ability to foresee what items will be required on any one climb (chapter 15);
- fitness and endurance, so that he can complete a long day safely, without getting so tired that he becomes careless or faulty in his judgement. Regular climbing and walking in Britain is the best training for this (see § 112).

The alpine *leader* must possess these qualities and skills in a high degree since it falls to him to make the major decisions, especially if the other members of the party are inexperienced. He must also understand the other members of the party and their capabilities, and be able to sense when someone is suffering an 'off day' so that he can make due allowance for it at the time.

§ 112. The importance of British training

If you wish to do climbs of any significance, you should develop your technical ability and fitness in Britain before going to the Alps, since there is so much to learn in alpine climbing that there is little time to spare for acquiring basic techniques or basic fitness there.

Rock technique. As a general rule, you should be able to lead British climbs at least half a standard harder than any alpine rock you propose to undertake. If you plan to do the easier rock routes, for example, it is suggested that you should be able to lead at least Very Difficult thoroughly competently, on bad rock as well as good; and for the harder climbs, a much higher degree of competence is required

128. *Mont Blanc and the Chamonix Aiguilles (see also 135 and 138).*

(§ 116). Too low a standard of performance will leave you with dangerously little in reserve, after the effects of fatigue and altitude have made themselves felt.

Snow and ice technique. In the Alps, skill on snow and ice is just as important as skill on rock, although to a degree you can choose between mainly rock climbs and mainly snow and ice climbs. Ideally you should master the techniques described in chapter 11 (including crampon technique) before going to the Alps for the first time. If you cannot do this, get a few days' practice with a guide or an experienced amateur, or with a colleague of the same standard as yourself, on a low glacier, before attempting a route. Some districts such as the Ötztal in Austria are very suitable for practising elementary snow and ice technique (see § 114). You owe it to your colleagues to be reasonably competent since most alpine climbs, even easy ones, involve quite delicate snow and ice climbing, and they will have to rely on you not to slip. Many British climbers who are skilled at rock climbing tend to underestimate the importance of snow and ice in alpine climbing, and there have been a number of accidents as a result. Even experienced snow and ice climbers can profit from an occasional day or so at the *école de glace*, especially as this gives a useful opportunity for practising crevasse rescue.

Fitness should be acquired in Britain by regular climbing and walking (preferably, as the time approaches, with loaded rucksacks). Hill walking to the limit of your endurance is better fitness training than any amount of outcrop climbing, though this is essential, too, for the harder alpine routes. Even if you are fit before you go out, it will take a week or so to acclimatize, and rather longer to achieve the degree of fitness needed to do the longest, hardest, and highest routes rapidly and safely. In planning an alpine programme, it is important to make allowance for this factor.

All the other skills described in § 111 above can only be acquired in the Alps themselves, though the various textbooks will give a basic grounding, and thorough study of guide-books beforehand will also help.

§ 113. The party: guided or guideless?

How to start. For the alpine novice (i.e., someone who is experienced in British climbing but has not been to the Alps before) the problem of companionship and whether to go guided is very difficult. A good solution is to join a fully experienced party, possibly as fourth man, but very few get such an opportunity, partly because experienced alpinists usually want to do difficult climbs and cannot afford to reduce their safety margin by taking an alpine beginner. Much will depend on the climber himself and his circle of friends. If he is a member of a British climbing club then it is possible that he may be able to join a club meet on which there are experienced alpinists, or the club may hire a guide or two for the whole party. The latter would give the novice an invaluable opportunity of seeing a guide in action and would enable him to appreciate the skills in which guides excel: route-finding, judgement of weather and conditions, steadiness and speed on snow and ice, etc. There can be no better and safer introduction to alpine climbing. A very sound alternative, which guarantees a minimum basic teaching, is to join an instructional course: the names of the principal British organizations running such courses are in appendix B, 2, while the Continental training organizations are in appendix D. If none of these possibilities is feasible, it may be worth hiring a guide for a few days at the beginning of the season to introduce you to glacier techniques and other basic skills. You can make contact with the guide through the local guides' bureau. Make sure that he is the sort of person who will try to pass on his knowledge to you; it is virtually useless if he is not. If you and your companions do not succeed in climbing either with experienced alpinists or with a guide, you must be very careful indeed: start off very gently and keep well within your limits. Most alpine accidents are due to inexperience – no more need be said.

Guideless parties. Nowadays *experienced* British alpinists almost always climb guideless. Guideless climbing gives much greater scope for initiative, judgement, and responsibility than guided climbing and is also, of course, much cheaper. The latter is quite an important consideration: guides' fees increase fairly steeply in proportion to the difficulty of the climb, and climbs which good British alpinists might do in their third or fourth season might each cost £30 or more. Most guides and hut guardians are prepared to give guideless parties advice about their proposed routes, and guideless climbers for their part should do what they can to foster good relationships with guides and their parties.

Size of party. Four is the ideal number for a guideless alpine party. It is preferable to travel as a foursome on a snow-covered glacier where there is danger from concealed crevasses (§ 135), and as two ropes of two on climbs themselves. This gives much greater security than one rope of two and much more speed on difficult rock than a rope of three. Moreover, the two ropes can take shares in step-cutting and in carrying common stores such as abseil ropes and pitons. A party of more than four is too cumbersome for speed, and greatly increases the danger from stonefalls. It is also difficult to control and is apt to lack the concentrated attention that is necessary for safety.

Choice of companion. Alpine climbing puts a tremendous strain on personal relationships. All the members of the party should be well known to each other, and humour and tolerance are essential. It is important that no member of the party should be dangerous or technically incompetent, since as noted above it is often necessary to move together,

129. *Alpine ice route.* The north face of Castor (Zermatt).

without belaying, over easy but dangerous ground where it could be hard to stop a slip. Alpine climbing with chance acquaintances met in huts or valleys is rarely entirely satisfactory and may possibly prove to be dangerous.

§ 114. Where to start

Each alpine area has its own particular characteristics and advantages and disadvantages. The choice between the various areas will depend on such considerations as your knowledge of the local language, distance from the U.K. (the Alps are 500 miles long and the eastern parts, such as the Dolomites, are a good deal more costly and complicated to reach than Mont Blanc or the Dauphiné), and whether you are going for the classic mountaineering (e.g. the Pennine Alps) or the more technically difficult climbing (e.g. Chamonix). Probably the best arrangement if you are climbing guideless is to start off in an easy area like Champex (§ 146), Arolla or Saas-Fee (§ 147), or the Tirol (§ 155): these will give you plenty of good climbing of moderate standard on routes of moderate length, with the opportunity to develop an all-round technique and rhythm. If you are reluctant to commit yourself on snow and ice without experience, the Tirol can be particularly recommended because the glaciers there are smaller and more even than elsewhere, and you can usually turn any icefalls (§ 125) if you wish to. If you have a guide, Mont Blanc itself (§ 146), Zermatt (§ 147) or the Oberland (§ 148) would give you better climbs. Many British climbers go to Chamonix in their first season, mainly no doubt because it is easy of access and most of the climbing is on good rock. But this is not entirely recommendable, if only because the glaciers there are usually steep and the bergschrunds and crevasses may be bad, especially late in the season: indeed, many of the 'rock routes' at Chamonix involve harder ice climbing than the 'snow routes' in Switzerland. More information about the main areas is in chapter 19.

§ 115. Guide-books and maps

Guide-books. There are guide-books to all the main areas,
published by the national alpine clubs in French, German,
or Italian as the case may be. The Alpine Club (p. 28) and
West Col Productions (appendix B, 5) have produced a
series of English language guide-books of selected climbs in
all the main alpine areas, and also in many of the lesser ones
(details in chapter 19). These translations are extremely
useful for seeing what an area has to offer, but there is
much to be said for having the original version as well,
since this describes all the routes on the mountain concerned
and therefore gives you a better appreciation of the peak
as a whole, including its ways down.

Each guide-book has general information about facilities
in the area and details of the huts and their approaches.
As with British guide-books it is best to look at the diagrams
first, and then – having picked out a route which looks
attractive – to see from the text what it (and the descent)
would involve. Guide-books should be studied in detail
before leaving this country: by this means and by reading
accounts of climbs in books and journals you can acquire a
basic knowledge of the district and the routes which will
serve you well later.

The U.I.A.A. (p. 29) has adopted a standard series of
conventional signs which is being gradually incorporated
into new guide-books.

Maps. Kümmerly and Frey (Bern) publish two good maps
showing the Alps as a whole: No. 32 *Alpine Countries*
(1:1,000,000) and No. 220 *Alpine Routes* (1:500,000). The
S.A.C. publishes an excellent 1:500,000 map showing all
its huts and the Swiss rescue posts, while the O.A.V.
produces a 1:600,000 hut map of all Austria.

The guide-books usually contain diagrams of the climbing
areas, but you will need large-scale maps in addition,
preferably in syntosil (plastic). For all-round use the
1:50,000 scale (about $1\frac{1}{4}$ in. to the mile) is best. The

1 : 25,000 maps are preferable for complicated areas but they are not available for all parts. The 1 : 100,000 maps are good for forming an overall impression of a range, but do not give sufficient detail to show a complicated route. Check the date when the map was last revised (so that you know which new roads, *téléphériques*, and reservoirs it shows), and if possible find out when the original survey was done (since a map which has merely been overprinted with new roads and other features will not show important natural changes in the topography caused by recessions of the glaciers or snow-fields). The Swiss National Landeskarte, the Institut Géographique National maps of France, and the Kompass maps of Austria are for the most part based on recent surveys. Always check the magnetic variation before using a compass as it varies from area to area (appendix E, 1).

The guide-books and maps are listed in chapter 19 and the full addresses of the publishers are in appendix D. They are usually readily available in bookshops or village shops in the areas themselves. Some good British sources are in appendix B, 5; in addition, the U.K. Branch of the Austrian Alpine Club sells German-language guide-books, and maps of Austria; while the national tourist offices of the other countries may also be able to help (appendix D).

§ 116. Standards of climbs

It takes time to understand alpine standards because the overall gradings bear very little resemblance to British rock gradings (§ 35). This is because on an average alpine route problems of all-round alpine technique are far more important than the technical difficulty of the rock, which is usually low. The position is further complicated because each of the national alpine clubs has its own system of grading climbs, and this can cause difficulty in relating the standards of climbs in the different areas.

1. *French standards.* The Vallot guides to the French Alps assess both the standard of the climb *as a whole* (based on

normal conditions but taking account of altitude, length, objective dangers, liability to bad weather, difficulty of route-finding, quality of rock, and technical difficulty), and the *technical standard* of individual rock pitches where they approach the overall standard of the climb. The overall standard is described as:

Facile	(F)
Peu difficile	(PD)
Assez difficile	(AD)
Difficile	(D)
Très difficile	(TD)
Extrêmement difficile	(ED)

and the individual pitches are described by numbers I–VI with *inférieur* ('*inf.*') and *supérieur* ('*sup.*') to indicate the lower and upper limits respectively within each number. The relationship between French and British rock pitch gradings is *roughly* as follows:

    III – Very Difficult
    IV – Severe
     V – Hard Severe/Medium Very Severe
    VI – above Medium Very Severe

Artificial pitches where pitons are used for direct aid are described as A1, A2, A3, and A4 in increasing order of difficulty. This grading assumes that all the pitons are already in place on classic routes but not on exceptional routes. It takes account of three main factors: the solidity of the pitons; the steepness and angle of the passage; and the difficulty of reaching the pitons already in place. The approximate relationship with free climbing is A1 = IV, A2 = V, A3 = VI (though, of course, if there were no pitons the rock itself would almost always be VI). Most artificial passages are A1 or A2. A1 is usually straightforward and often possible without *étriers*; A2 can be quite awkward. On A3 either the rock or the pegs will be loose (sometimes both) or it will be extremely overhanging.

On a normal D climb quite a number of the pitches would

130. *The Grandes Jorasses – Géant group* § *146.* From the Dru.

be IV and there might be a few pitches of V. On a TD climb there would normally be numerous pitches of V, some of V *sup.*, and possibly one or two of VI. Many climbs are given a high overall grading, however, although they include very few or no pitches of the corresponding technical difficulty; this is because of the general seriousness of the climbing, altitude, or loose rock. It should be noted that alpine guide-books usually assume that climbers are familiar with snow and ice, and may consequently omit to mention that a fairly good standard of snow and ice climbing is required for a particular route.

2. *Swiss and Italian standards.* These guide-books do not use the same system as the French. The Swiss give only an overall indication of difficulty without grading the individual pitches. The Italian guide-books to the Dolomites are based on a numerical system, but instead of using a separate classification for artificial sections, they describe almost all artificial passages as VI. This leads to some confusion in assessing the difficulty of the harder climbs.

The AC and West Col versions generally use an adaptation of the French system of grading, even where the original is Swiss or Italian.

Standard of the harder alpine rock routes: a warning. As noted in 1 above, the British VS and the French Grade V are roughly of the same order of difficulty, give or take half a standard. This does not necessarily mean, however, that the medium VS leader could do climbs of Grade V standard (i.e. TD). Fatigue and altitude will affect his performance: pitches which would be Very Difficult or Severe in the Lakes or Wales may feel like Very Severes in the Alps. Adverse conditions of cold, or icy rock, will also make the climb very much harder. Because of this, the possibility of the pitch being harder than it is graded, and the vital importance of avoiding even a minor fall when rescue can be so difficult and prolonged, it is advisable to climb well within your technical capacity; a reserve of at least half a standard is suggested (see also § 112). Technical ability is not by any means the only qualification for the more serious routes, which involve, for example, major problems of route-finding. Great length, great exposure, and perfect rock can combine to make such routes a paradise for the climber who is already very expert on British rock, but only if he has first acquired all-round alpine technique on the easier routes. Some climbs involve the use of pitons on a very considerable scale, e.g. East Face of the Grand Capucin du Tacul [147]. Such climbs demand a sophisticated technique and considerable endurance and should not be undertaken unless the party has extensive artificial experience elsewhere and also a good deal of alpine experience. The importance of practising artificial technique in Britain (chapter 9) until it becomes second nature, and of being thoroughly fit in the arms, cannot be stressed too much.

§ 117. Accommodation in the valley

The alpine clubs do not usually have huts or other accommodation in the valleys, and it is necessary to stay either in youth hostels (for which you must be a member of the

Y.H.A. – appendix B, 1), hotels, or pensions (some of which cater specially for climbers and are cheap), or to camp. Camping is strictly controlled in most alpine valleys, and if you are near a village you should make sure to camp only where it is permitted. A small daily charge is usually made. Unless you are camping with a party, it may be worth while to pack up your gear and leave it in the car or in a left-luggage office while you are up in the mountains. It is also advisable, and considerate for others, to leave details of your intended routes so that a search can be made if you become seriously overdue.

§ 118. Alpine huts

Most alpine climbs are done from huts three to six hours' walk ('grind') away from the valley (§ 133). These huts are provided by the alpine clubs in places convenient for the main climbs. Details of the huts and their approaches are given in the guide-books, but there are changes from time to time and it is as well to check by local inquiry. The huts range from very well-equipped hotels with accommodation for hundreds to very small refuge-bivouacs high up on major routes. Separate dormitories for men and women are the exception rather than the rule. Wide alpine bunks which take up to a dozen or so bodies at a time are usual. You will normally take up your own food for several days and either give it to the guardian to cook or – where this is permitted (not in Switzerland) – cook it yourself on your own cooker. In some cases, however (e.g. at most Austrian and Swiss huts) it is possible to buy a simple meal from the guardian. The practice varies from area to area. As noted in the introduction, membership of an alpine club entitles you to preferential treatment and reduced rates in most alpine huts.

131. *An alpine hut*. The Cabane du Mountet (Zinal), one of the finest huts in Switzerland. The north and west faces of the Ober Gabelhorn behind.

§ 119. Food

The food used for camping in Britain (§ 33) will do just as well in alpine huts; but lightness is even more important since it has to be carried a long way. The basic local food is usually cheapest: spaghetti and macaroni are both cheap and light but become difficult to cook at very high huts (e.g. the Margherita Hut on Monte Rosa). Crisp-bread and *pain d'épices* are lighter than baked bread and do not go stale. Dried soups, dried milk and dehydrated meat block are particularly useful. Certain items such as tea, coffee, tinned meat, and butter are usually cheaper in the U.K. than on the Continent and it may be worth taking supplies out with you. In the valley, it is important to eat a great deal to replenish your reserves. Unless your own cooking is completely adequate, try always to have one really large meal a day in a café or restaurant to supplement it. Restaurants are expensive by British standards, but sometimes there are workmen's cafés which suit the hungry but impecunious climber well. Eat as much fresh fruit and vegetables as possible to redress any lack of balance in your diet in the mountains. Vitamin pills may also be useful. On the climb, take plenty of lump sugar (which is cheaper than glucose) and chocolate, biscuits, and raisins, in polythene bags. Cheese has a very high food value as also does sweetened condensed milk (available in tubes). Often the need for liquid is even greater than for food – you can lose four or five pints on a long climb – but continuing excessive thirst in the valley may reflect some bodily malfunctioning or disorder. Salt helps to reduce dehydration and hence cramp; sugar-coated salt tablets are advisable on long climbs, but only if plenty of liquid is available (because otherwise the salt will merely increase your craving for water). It is worth while drinking as much liquid as you can low down on the mountain (e.g. at the hut). When going up to the mountains, take plenty of spare food in case bad weather or temporary illness delays your programme and you want to stay up for an extra day or two. Remember that shops are closed in

Switzerland (but not in France) on Sundays and adjust your programme of food-buying accordingly. If for example you want to go up to a Swiss hut on a Sunday buy your food on a Saturday (or bring it with you from the U.K. if the Sunday is the first climbing day of your holiday).

§ 120. Insurance

The cost of a rescue party in the Alps can be very high indeed, and it has to be paid by the person concerned, or his family. Doctors' bills and hospital treatment are also very expensive in the Alps, and are not covered by the National Health Service (it is usually cheaper to fly home immediately at extra expense than to stay on the Continent for treatment). Some insurance cover against both rescue and medical costs is therefore advisable, and there is also a case for insuring equipment, which can prove surprisingly expensive to replace. The Alpine Club (p. 28) gives automatic cover against rescue costs, and most of the Continental alpine clubs do likewise, together with – at extra cost – provision against medical costs; it is advisable to enquire about this when you join. Some British insurance companies will also insure you against climbing accidents, including alpine ones, but you may have to search for some time to find one which will do this at reasonable rates. It is probably easiest to make inquiries through an insurance *broker* since he will know what the different *companies* can offer. Perhaps the best arrangement of all is to have a year-round accident policy – or, at greater expense, a whole-life policy – to cover you *inter alia* against climbing accidents in Britain, with a provision that you may extend it to cover alpine countries for limited periods by arrangement.

§ 121. Mountain railways and *téléphériques*

At most of the main centres there are mountain railways and *téléphériques* (cable-cars). Use of these can save much precious time and make certain climbs much more accessible. The climbs on the south side of Mont Blanc, for example, became very much more accessible from Chamonix when the *téléphérique* Aiguille du Midi–Col du Géant was opened. Usually membership of the country's national alpine club will entitle you to cheaper rates; it is, however, not usually possible to get reduced rates on a reciprocal basis in, for example, Switzerland, if you are a member only of the French Alpine Club, and vice versa. Undue use of these aids is expensive and reduces one of the most valuable ways of getting fit – walking uphill (the spread of *téléphériques* has probably contributed substantially to the increase in the number of alpine accidents in recent years, because they make it so easy to get on to high climbs before one is fit). A good compromise on some of the shorter and more accessible ascents, such as Zermatt to the Gornergrat, is to send your pack up (or down) on the railway, but to walk yourself.

Chapter 15. Equipment for alpine mountaineering

Because of the much greater scale and seriousness of alpine climbing, and the wide variations in temperature during a single day, an alpinist needs to be more fully equipped than is normal in Britain. It is, for example, often necessary to carry equipment for snow and ice climbing as well as for rock climbing, and extra rope may be needed for abseils. It is important to avoid undue weight since this will slow the party down; hence lightweight equipment and a fair sharing of the common items (rope, pitons, and so on) between all the members of the party is essential. Nowadays most equipment can be bought as cheaply in this country as in the Alps. Indeed, the range of equipment available in Britain is greater than in many alpine centres. Of the latter, Chamonix and Courmayeur (§ 146) are notably good in this respect, while Zermatt (§ 147) at the time of writing was surprisingly bad.

§ 122. Special considerations applying in the Alps to equipment used in Britain

Clothing and footwear is basically the same as for British climbing, i.e., a windproof anorak and/or a waterproof *cagoule*, sweaters, shirt, breeches, long stockings, gloves (see chapter 3), but the following special considerations apply:

- a hat with a brim, and a neckerchief are useful for protecting your neck against the very strong alpine sun; long shirt-sleeves are also useful (glacier cream (§ 123) is of course necessary as well);
- long gaiters (§ 22) are useful for keeping out snow;
- boots (§ 23) should be rubber-soled and preferably worn in already. The soles and uppers must be in good condition, however, because a strenuous alpine season can be very punishing;

a light pair of kletterschuhe or P.A.s [51] may be taken for very
hard rock pitches;
– emergency bivouac equipment is needed for any serious routes
in case of an involuntary night out; this, and full-scale equipment for planned bivouacs, is described in § 124 below.

Crampons (§ 77), are essential on anything but pure rock
climbs; they must fit perfectly and be sharpened at the
beginning of the season and possibly again before any really
hard snow and ice climbing.

An ice-axe (§ 78) is indispensable, and it is as well to have one
short one and one long one (possibly demountable) in the
party. This gives flexibility to meet all circumstances,
ranging from steep ice in ascent (short axe) to cutting downhill or difficult probing of snow bridges (longer axe).

Rucksack. For routes which do not involve hard rock climbing, the normal frameless rucksacks used for British hill
walking are adequate [29A]; indeed, the outside pockets
can be very handy for oddments like glacier cream, guide-
books, etc., which are needed frequently during the day.
For the more difficult climbing, however, a well-designed
climbing sack [30] is essential.

Nylon or perlon rope (§ 51). There are four separate uses for
ropes in the Alps:

1. *main climbing rope, single*; a 120-ft $1\frac{3}{8}$-in. or, possibly, $1\frac{1}{4}$-in. is
   normally used. (The main rope is also used as a safety rope
   when abseiling – §§ 66 and 138);
2. *main climbing rope doubled*; this is needed for artificial climbing,
   and is also preferred by many for general use (especially on
   glaciers). Two 120-ft $1\frac{1}{4}$-in. ropes are best, though some people
   economize on weight at some risk to themselves by using the
   (weaker) $\frac{7}{8}$-in. ropes instead;
3. *abseil ropes*; $\frac{7}{8}$-in. rope is best for this. The amount depends on
   the particular descent. For most areas 120 ft is sufficient but
   240 ft is extremely useful at Chamonix or in the Dolomites. A
   continuous length has the advantage that it is less likely to catch

or come undone than two separate lengths knotted together, but the latter are often preferred because:
- each half of the rope can be carried separately (i.e. lighter and less cumbersome);
- when used for 2, both leader and second can untie if one of the ropes jams.

When abseiling with a knotted rope, check the knot after each man has used it, since the tension may loosen it;

4. *sack hauling* on hard artificial routes. A $\frac{7}{8}$-in. (or even $\frac{5}{8}$-in.) rope will do for this, but sack hauling should be avoided as far as possible because it is tiring and time-wasting.

Most British parties on *standard* routes take 120 ft of $1\frac{3}{8}$-in. nylon (or possibly $1\frac{1}{4}$-in., though this is weaker), and also, when much abseiling is involved, a 120-ft or 150-ft $\frac{7}{8}$-in. rope; a few take two $1\frac{1}{4}$-in. ropes and use them for 1, 2, and 3, as appropriate. On the *harder* rock routes, two $1\frac{1}{4}$-in. ropes are usually adequate, but many climbers prefer 240 ft of $\frac{7}{8}$-in. rope doubled, because it is lighter. A third rope may be taken as a safety rope on long abseils (i.e. when all 240-ft is needed as an abseil rope). My personal preference is a combination of a 130-ft $1\frac{1}{4}$-in. nylon (or 11-mm. kernmantel perlon) with 250-ft $\frac{7}{8}$-in. nylon. For easy climbs the $1\frac{1}{4}$-in. nylon alone need be taken, while on hard climbs it can be used in conjunction with half of the $\frac{7}{8}$-in. rope, the other half being stowed in the rucksack, ready for abseils (for which the whole length of the $\frac{7}{8}$-in. rope can be used, with the $1\frac{1}{4}$-in. rope as a safety rope).

As noted in § 51, kernmantel rope is better than hawser-laid rope for artificial climbing, and if an extended artificial campaign is envisaged, a 9–10 mm. nylon or perlon kernmantel rope may prove a good investment. Kernmantel rope is however not entirely satisfactory for prusiking either in crevasse rescue (§ 140, 2) or on overhanging rock, because the sheath tends to slip over the core under load.

When two ropes are used it is useful to dye one of them a different colour, so that they can easily be distinguished. A great deal of time can be saved by developing an automatic system in the party, by which the dyed rope is always used for the same purpose, e.g. as the standing rope in crevasse rescue (chapter 18), or as a handhold where the second decides to use one of the ropes to save time in following a pitch (§ 137).

Abseil slings and prusik-loops. Take plenty of spare new $\frac{3}{4}$-in. hemp or manila line, or $\frac{7}{8}$-in. nylon, for making abseil slings (§ 138) and prusik-loops. The latter are slings made of about 8 ft of rope, which can be attached to a standing rope with a prusik knot [153]; $\frac{7}{8}$-in. cabled nylon, or 8- or 9-mm. kernmantel nylon, is best, but hemp or manila can be used instead, though they are much less convenient in wet or freezing conditions. Prusik-loops are needed for crevasse rescue (§ 140, 2) or in the event of swinging free on over-hanging rock (so that you can climb back up the rope). Several gadgets have been made to take the place of the prusik knot; of these the Hiebeler (Schuster) 'Prusiker' is reputed to be extremely effective.

Pitons, karabiners, etc. Carry several rock pitons (§ 68) and possibly one or two ice screws or ice pitons (§ 81), according to the type of climb. A light hammer (§§ 69 and 80) may also be needed. Even on very hard artificial climbs the pitons are often in place, but on new or infrequently climbed routes this may not be so. In such a case, make inquiries as to what sort of pegs or wedges are required before you set out. Half a dozen karabiners (§ 56) will suffice for most routes, but up to thirty may be needed for really hard climbs. *Étriers* (§ 70) are useful for crevasse rescue as well as for artificial climbing.

Torch. Each member of the party needs a torch for move-ment on glaciers, etc. before dawn. A lightweight head torch is best, since this leaves your hands free. Spare batteries and a spare bulb should be taken in the party. Candle lanterns are rightly not much used nowadays, though they are still available.

§ 123. Additional items which are or may be needed in the Alps

Snow goggles are essential on snow or glaciers to prevent snow blindness (which is very painful). Surprisingly, perhaps, they are just as necessary on misty days as on sunny days. The best type is very light in weight, made of two elliptical aluminium holders with a short piece of elastic for the nose and elastic to go loosely round the back of the head. The aluminium side-pieces should have holes in them to provide the air circulation necessary to eliminate condensation. The lenses should be made of tinted glass and not of plastic (which tends to scratch and is not optically accurate), nor of plates of glass with tinted celluloid between them (as moisture can get in between the plates and distort vision). Some climbers find sunglasses (without side-pieces) quite satisfactory. There should always be at least one spare of snow goggles or sunglasses in an alpine party, in case a pair is lost or damaged.

Glacier oil or cream. Special alpine anti-sun oil or cream is necessary to protect the face or hands (and legs if your stockings are rolled down) against sunburn. There are many types available. Liquid is probably better than cream because it can be spread more evenly and is less greasy. Make sure that all exposed parts are covered: the backs of the ears, the bottom of the nose, and the inside of the arms are all too easily left out. Lip salve (colourless lipstick) should be used to protect the lips. Apply these as soon as you come into direct sunlight and repeat the process frequently throughout the day.

Water bottle or tube. It is necessary to drink large amounts of liquid in the Alps to avoid dehydration and consequent loss of strength. On most climbs there is adequate snow and melt water so that a water bottle is unnecessary, particularly if a thin rubber tube (about twelve inches long) is used to suck up what would otherwise be inaccessible trickles of water.

On some long rock climbs, however (e.g. South Ridge of the Aiguille Noire de Peuterey or in the Dolomites) lack of water is a serious problem, and one or more water bottles should be taken. Plastic or aluminium bottles are satisfactory. The addition of lemonade powder, fruit juice, or a trace of wine makes a thirst-quenching drink.

Protective headgear [144]. So many accidents have been caused by falling stones that it is sensible to use some form of protective headgear. Indeed this is now standard practice among the best climbers, and even on easy routes it is certainly recommendable where there is a known risk of stone-fall as, for example, on a long descent in a couloir (§ 136). A close fit is essential, and there should be no rim to impede the view and get in the way in chimneys. The hat must have a chin strap so that it does not drop off in a head-first fall. A hat with ribs is much stronger than a smooth dome, and fibre-glass is better than plastic since the latter shatters too easily. The B.M.C. has produced a specification (B.S. 4423: 1969) defining minimum performance levels, and only helmets meeting this are recommended.

Aneroid. An accurate, temperature-corrected aneroid or barometer can be useful, at least on very long routes, for indicating the altitude (and hence, in misty conditions, your position) or for predicting changes in the weather (§ 126).

§ 124. Bivouac equipment (including down clothing)

An alpine party should always carry a lightweight tent sack or other waterproof protection, in addition to spare clothing, on any serious route so that it can survive an involuntary night or nights out caused by bad weather or accident (§ 139). Parties without tent sacks have died from exposure in bad weather, sometimes even low down on the mountain, through not finding the hut. On advanced alpine routes it may be necessary to make one or more planned bivouacs on the mountain, and special care must be taken in choosing the equipment required and in using it. Bivouac equipment should be:

– waterproof and windproof;
– reasonably warm;
– reliable;
– easy and quick to use;
– light, so that enough can be taken without tiring the party or necessitating sack hauling.

The amount required will depend primarily on the altitude and length of the climb: more equipment would be needed high up on Mont Blanc for example than, say, in the Dolomites.

Tent sack. This is a low, two-man tent, without poles (ice-axes can be used if desired). Made of proofed nylon or perlon, it should not weigh more than one pound. It is better than one-man equipment (*cagoule* and *pied d'éléphant* – see below) because:

– it is lighter, man for man;
– it gives better protection in bad weather;

132. *Two-man bivouac sack.*

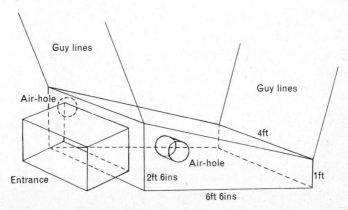

- it is warmer, because two bodies generate more heat;
- the stove can be used inside (for cooking or keeping warm) provided the sack is well ventilated to avoid carbon monoxide poisoning;
- it is more companionable – an important consideration on a big climb.

The type illustrated in [132] is very well designed, giving good protection in bad weather, with reasonable comfort and good ventilation. Unfortunately, some of the sacks available at the time of writing cannot be closed up when the climbers are lying side by side, and hence are likely to prove inadequate in a storm.

A *plastic bag or Space Blanket*, as recommended for emergency bivouacs in Britain (§§ 4 and 11), would be much better than no sack at all, but these are easily damaged, difficult to ventilate properly, and generally a good deal less satisfactory than a proper sack in bad conditions, or if more than one bivouac is involved.

A *cagoule* is a lightweight, waterproof anorak (with a hood) which is very long and can be let down below the knees. It usually has buttons inside so that the long apron can be buttoned up when it is not needed. It is made of waterproofed nylon or perlon. When bivouacking, a separate sack (*pied d'éléphant*) or, alternatively, a rucksack with a waterproof extension (§ 24), is used for the feet and legs so that the whole body can be protected. A *cagoule* has the advantage that it will enable a climber to carry on climbing in bad weather without getting wet. A party equipped with *cagoules* can also bivouac separately if need be, for example if the bivouac ledges are very small. But a *cagoule* is not as warm as a tent sack and cooking is more difficult: and as noted above is therefore not as satisfactory for extreme conditions.

Down ('*duvet*') *clothing* should be filled with very good-quality down, and should be box-pleated like a good

sleeping bag [35]. It should have a nylon or terylene covering, which is lighter than cotton; waterproofed nylon is
best since this retains heat as well as keeping out damp. It
is much lighter and warmer than conventional clothing
(sweaters, etc.). The main items are:

- *Jacket* ('*veste en duvet*'). Most alpine climbers use one of
these instead of a second sweater. It should reach to the top
of the thighs (and overlap with the rucksack extension) and
should be big enough for you to fold your arms inside it when
bivouacking. The bottom and the wrists should contain elastic
to prevent loss of heat and there should be a piece of elastic to
clip between your legs to stop it riding up. The wrist elastic
should be on the loose side to avoid restricting the blood
circulation. The front should be fastened with press studs up to
the collar. You will need a hood unless you use a balaclava.
- *Waistcoat* ('*gilet en duvet*'). This can be used instead of a light
sweater for climbing. The addition of wool or flannel sleeves
will make it warmer.
- *Short sleeping bag* ('*duvet court*'). This comes up to the lower
chest; it should have a draw tape to prevent heat loss and also
tapes to come over the shoulders to stop it slipping down. It
should not be too well filled with down since this would make it
unnecessarily cosy, given that weight is important. A *duvet
court* is a comfort on very cold bivouacs but is not normally
essential. Thick breeches, long underpants or pyjamas, and a
dry pair of socks (or *duvet* socks) in an extendable rucksack will
do almost as well.

Although *duvet* clothing – particularly a jacket – is very
useful it is also fairly expensive. An ordinary lightweight
sleeping bag can in fact be used quite satisfactorily on a
bivouac. However, unlike the *duvet* jacket, it cannot be used
for climbing in cold conditions and an extra sweater will
have to be taken as well.

A *foam rubber pad* (say fifteen inches square) can lessen the
discomfort of a bivouac appreciably without adding too
much weight. Carpet underlay foam rubber ($\frac{1}{4}$ in. thick) is
quite good enough for insulation, and can be jettisoned

afterwards. But the new waterproof sleeping pad which was introduced in 1968 is more effective – available as a 'Karrimat' from equipment stores.

Stove and pan. Some kind of lightweight cooker is desirable on a bivouac for warmth, cooking, and possibly also for melting snow for water. A solid fuel (e.g. Meta) cooker is safe and reliable (there is no possibility of a blocked jet or leaking fuel) and is also very light in weight. A small propane 'Gaz' stove is light and gives a fair amount of heat, with the added convenience that it can be lit easily for a few minutes during the night if needed. Meths stoves are also satisfactory. Paraffin stoves are too heavy, and some types of petrol stove are dangerous. A very light-weight pan is also required (see also § 32).

The technique of bivouacking is covered in § 139 (see also §§ 11 and 21).

Chapter 16. Alpine conditions and weather

§ 125. Glaciers and glacier formations

Glaciers are rivers of ice, which flow down from their sources in the upper snowfields into the lower valleys. The biggest glacier in the Alps is the Aletsch glacier in the Bernese Alps, which is twenty-two miles long and over 1,000 ft thick. The main types of glacier formations are shown in [133] and [134], and described briefly below. The left bank[A] (these references are to [133]) and the right bank[B] are always defined as if you were looking from the source.

Dry glacier.[C] In the summer, the snow on the lower reaches of the glacier melts, leaving the ice surface exposed; there is often a good deal of melt water on the surface, so the term 'dry' can be something of a misnomer. These, when not too steep and broken, are the safest glaciers for travel because the crevasses[D] are fully visible and can be avoided. A glacier is usually *snow-covered*[E] in its middle and upper reaches, and many of the crevasses may be partially or wholly concealed.

A hanging glacier is one either on a very steep face,[F] or, more accurately, one which falls over a rock face.[G] These glaciers often move rapidly and send down ice avalanches (§ 129, 4) fairly frequently.

Crevasses. These splits in the glacier ice, caused by the stresses set up by the movement of the glacier, range from minor cracks which can be stepped across,[D] to huge chasms which it may be impossible to cross[H] (see also [139] and [151]). Early in the season, even large crevasses may be completely covered by snow bridges which can be both a

help (to enable you to cross) and a danger (if it is not appreciated that there is a crevasse beneath). Where the surface stream disappears down a crevasse, this is known as a *moulin*. The very large crevasse where the glacier parts company from the *névé* (snowfield) which feeds it is known as a bergschrund or *rimaye*;[1] where it separates the glacier from the containing rock walls, it is strictly speaking a *randkluft*,[k] though the term bergschrund, like *rimaye*, is commonly used for this and any other very large crevasse. On difficult glaciers there may be several bergschrunds.[j] Often the upper lip is higher than the lower one, and this may be a serious obstacle, particularly late in the season when the bergschrunds are open and bare (§ 135).

Sérac. This is a wall or pinnacle of glacier ice. Often unstable and a cause of ice avalanches (§ 129, 4), they may collapse at any time of day or night as a result of movement of the glacier; where the collapse is due to melting or instability, it is, however, more likely to occur in the heat of the day.

Icefall. A contorted section of glacier with multiple crevasses and *séracs* in collapsed and uncollapsed state, caused by a change in the gradient of the glacier. If the icefall is short and gentle it is not serious, but long steep icefalls can be formidably complicated and difficult. All icefalls should be turned if there is a satisfactory alternative, such as a moraine.

Snout [134]. The bottom end of the glacier; often difficult because of very large crevasses. The moraine below the snout can be dangerous on account of debris sliding down, or collapsing ice. A river issues from the snout.

Moraines [134]. These are formed of boulders carried down by the glacier and may be as much as one hundred feet thick. *Terminal* moraines are at the snout of the glacier (or

133. *Main glacial features*. Lyskamm from the north-west (Pennine Alps). For key see § 125.

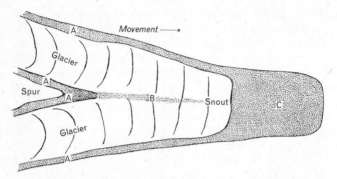

134. *The three types of moraine.* A. Lateral. B. Medial. C. Terminal.

further down the valley if the glacier has retreated).
Lateral moraines are long moraines on the edges of the
glacier,[L-M] and *medial* moraines are long moraines in the
middle of the glacier, usually formed from the lateral
moraines of two glaciers which have joined. The sides
of moraines are often unstable and tiring to walk on.
Lateral moraines are sometimes useful in avoiding difficult
sections of glacier (e.g. the moraine above Lognan on the
way up to the Argentière Hut) and will in such cases have a
path along the crest.[L] Sometimes what appears to be a
moraine may be only a thin layer of boulders on the
glacier which may conceal crevasses.

§ 126. Alpine weather

In the Alps, the weather is even more important than in
Britain and no less unpredictable. At high altitude bad
weather can be extremely unpleasant, with heavy snow and
hail and deep cold. More important than the physical discomfort of bad weather is the effect it has on the climb;
rocks quickly become sheathed in snow, ice, and *verglas*, and
it may become very difficult to move forward or even
to retreat. Mist and cloud can also make movement

dangerous, particularly on glaciers. Fortunately bad weather usually takes about six hours to develop as from the first signs. The main ways of forecasting alpine weather are described below. In interpreting them, always distinguish between general weather, which affects the whole area or even the whole of the Alps, and local weather, which applies only to your group of peaks (this is usually less permanent than the general weather). At Zermatt, for example, a storm will often concentrate on the Matterhorn and the Dent d'Hérens without involving the Obergabelhorn and the other peaks on that side of the valley.

1. *Wind direction*. As in Great Britain (§ 8) a wind from the north or north-east is usually a good sign. A wind from the west portends less settled weather; it is usually a bad sign in the long term if it continues, but is not necessarily so for the immediate future. A warm wind from the south is bad, and can quickly put avalanche-prone slopes into dangerous condition (§ 129, 2).

2. *Shape and altitude of clouds*. Small stationary black clouds forming temporarily on mountain summits, or traces of cloud moving at speed from the south or west and developing as they pass over high summits [135] are the most positive sign that bad weather is on the way. Dark, hammer-shaped thunder-clouds are also very bad. Cirrus cloud changing to cirro-stratus or to alto-stratus (particularly if it is double-layered) indicates a probability that bad weather is developing, no matter what the direction of the wind. Cumulus is a bad sign if it is developing (provided it is not merely local afternoon cloud); it is a good sign if it is dissipating. Do not be put off unnecessarily by cloud below the hut in the late evening or early morning; it will probably only be valley mist which will clear when the sun comes on to it. Very clear distant views often indicate that rain or snow is on the way (or has just gone); haze, on the other hand, is a good sign. Cold clear nights are good; warm, cloudy ones are usually bad.

135. *Bad weather brewing on Mont Blanc.* A storm usually follows the appearance of these clouds within a matter of hours. The Glacier du Brouillard is in the foreground, with the Innominata Face above it and the Peuterey Ridge on the extreme right.

3. *Barometer or aneroid.* As noted in § 123, an accurate aneroid can be very useful for showing whether a depression is on the way, or whether one is leaving the area.

The weather will vary from area to area. For example, clouds which would bring heavy snow on Mont Blanc might pass over the Zermatt peaks or at least the Arolla peaks without any precipitation. Each area has its own sensitive points which you should particularly watch: in the Mont Blanc range the main ones are the summits of Mont Blanc [128] and the Aiguille Verte, and the Col du Géant (which should be watched for cloud coming from the south). The weather forming in these places will usually give a good idea of what to expect in the rest of the area. Some areas have particular characteristics. Storms in the Dauphiné and the Bernese Alps, for example, are often sudden and serious. In the lower (and hence warmer) areas on the other hand, such as the Bernina and the Bregaglia, storms though frequent are not usually as dangerous. In the Mont Blanc chain, the tops of the Aiguilles and especially the Dent du Géant [130] are particularly prone to lightning (§ 8) which can be extremely dangerous.

Hut guardians and guides may sometimes be very expert on the local weather and give you invaluable advice; and you can telephone for forecasts in Switzerland (Tel. 162) and France (Lyon 72–05–09 for northern areas and Nice 86–57–24 for southern ones). But use your own judgement as well when your experience has developed sufficiently (see also § 134).

§ 127. Changes in conditions according to the state of the season

Generally in the early part of the season (say up to mid-July) the snow climbs are in good condition, whereas later in the season they may turn to ice; the rock faces usually get into condition in early or mid-July and stay in condition until September. The volume of winter snow and the lateness or earliness of the season may, however, throw this timetable out. Bad seasons on average outnumber good seasons. If the season is really bad, the big climbs may never come into condition at all; in the case of some high, north-facing rock climbs, for example, if they have not become free of ice by the end of July they will not come into condition that season no matter how good August is. However, even in bad seasons it is possible to achieve a good deal of run-of-the-mill climbing. In the first place, it is necessary to choose climbs which suit the conditions; in a snowy season, for example, take the opportunity of doing snow climbs once the new snow has consolidated, or choose south- and east-facing rock routes which dry quickest. Secondly, get in step with the weather. Most seasons have a rhythm of their own. Even in bad years, two or three bad days will usually be followed by one or two good ones. In such cases it is vital to be up at the hut when the good weather comes and to do this it will sometimes be necessary to be strong-willed and go up to the hut while the bad weather is still on. Although most routes will remain out of condition at least for the first day or two if the storm has brought new snow, it will usually be possible to do something fairly small.

§ 128. Changes in conditions according to the time of day

Alpine conditions vary tremendously according to the time of day. During the night, it is usually very cold; the snow freezes hard and trickles of water turn into ice or *verglas*. But when the sun comes up and the temperature rises, the snow softens and melts and the *verglas* disappears. An appreciation of the effects of these changes is essential; they affect:

- the condition of the snow for climbing; it is usually safe in the early morning but in the late afternoon when the snow is soft steps are insecure and snow bridges over crevasses are at their weakest; walking in soft snow is in any case very laborious;
- the likelihood of avalanches, which is greatest in the heat of the day (§ 129);
- the likelihood of rockfalls caused by the melting of the *verglas* and ice which cement loose rock overnight (§ 130).

The extent of the variation in conditions is however conditional on several factors:

- the altitude. Usually the higher you are on the mountain, the colder it is;
- cloud can keep the temperature up during the night or down during the day. (A warm night is usually a sign of bad weather and in any case makes snow soft and possibly dangerous);
- a cold wind will keep the temperature down, while a warm wind will keep it up;
- the direction of the face. The sun hardly touches north faces;

consequently they are usually very cold and icy and the variation in conditions there is smallest. East faces get the sun in the
morning, but on a cold day may refreeze during the afternoon.
West faces, conversely, get the sun late, and are cold in the
morning. South faces get the sun for most of the day;
– parts of a face may be in shadow when the rest is in the sun.
This is particularly important in the case of couloirs (§ 136) in
the early morning or late evening, when the upper parts are in
the sun (and hence liable to send down avalanches of rocks)
even though the lower parts are in shadow. Stonefalls are often
at their worst about an hour after the sun strikes the top of a
face.

It is because of these changes in conditions that it is
universal practice to start before dawn if much glacier or
snow and ice work is involved – for the biggest climbs at
1 a.m. or even before – so that the ascent can be completed
in the safety of the early morning, and the return journey
made if possible before the worst of the late morning or
afternoon sun or a change of weather (see also § 134).

§ 129. Avalanches and snow slides

An *avalanche* is a mass of snow or ice falling down a mountain
side. Usually it is cumulative, that is to say what starts as a
minor avalanche (a *snow slide*) may develop, given
sufficiently unstable conditions, into a very big avalanche
indeed, with many tons of snow and ice mixed up with
boulders and earth. A party involved in an avalanche may
be seriously injured or killed by:

– blows from boulders or ice blocks;
– a long fall, possibly over big drops, if the avalanche carries the
party with it;
– being buried in the debris when the avalanche comes to rest;
this is particularly dangerous in the case of a wet-snow avalanche,
since it is impossible to breathe through the snow;
– blast and suffocation from snow-filled air.

Snow slides are more common than the full-scale avalanches
on climbing routes; they are also dangerous, but a party

may escape injury provided it is not carried down by the slide.

There are four main types of avalanche:

1. New or unconsolidated dry-snow avalanches;
2. Wet-snow avalanches;
3. Windslab;
4. Unstable masses of snow or ice, e.g. *séracs* (§ 125) or cornices [142].

All of these types are most likely to occur in warm conditions though 1, 3, and 4 can occur in freezing conditions as well. In all cases, the steeper the ground the greater the risk. Judgement of avalanche conditions requires much experience, and intuition amounting almost to a sixth sense, and it is always best to err on the safe side.

1. *Dry-snow avalanche.* This is most likely to occur after a storm, before the sun has been on the face; cold north faces are particularly prone to this type of avalanche. It may occur even where the layer of snow is several feet thick. Much depends on the nature of the subsurface: downward-shelving rock at medium angle (like the tiles on a roof) may hold a considerable weight of snow, yet provide no effective support for it; where the substructure is rough or well broken up, on the other hand, the risk is diminished. A substructure of ice is always dangerous. This type of avalanche often starts with a small displacement, such as a climber's footstep, and rapidly widens and builds up [136B].

2. *Wet-snow avalanche.* This may be newly fallen snow or even old snow melting in the heat of the sun. As with 1, a great deal depends on the nature of the subsurface.

3. *Windslab Avalanche* [137]. This can occur where:

1. a layer of powder snow is formed in very cold conditions and does not consolidate on to the ice or hard snow beneath; and

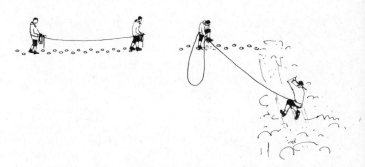

136. *Soft-snow avalanche.* These can be either 'dry snow' or 'wet snow'.

2. a layer of snow is subsequently consolidated on to the original
   layer of powder snow by the action of melting and freezing, but
   insulates it so that it does not amalgamate with the ice beneath.

Eventually, the weight of the top layers of snow builds up
so much that they are likely to slide away on the unconsolidated powder snow beneath. Windslab often occurs on
northerly or other slopes which do not get the full force of
the sun, and is especially common in winter or spring. If you
feel several feet of snow around you sink an inch or two

137. *Windslab avalanche.*

A   B

when you step on to it, or if on a slope your footsteps displace blocks of snow, this will almost certainly indicate windslab; but sometimes it is impossible to identify. The frequency of this type of avalanche depends a great deal on the snow conditions built up in the spring; usually these conditions apply throughout an area and one serious windslab avalanche should be taken to indicate that others are likely. The year 1964 was particularly bad for these avalanches, one of which killed fourteen guides and trainee guides on the Aiguille Verte. The avalanche is most likely to happen when a climber (or ski-er) traverses across a slope making deep steps; the slab of snow *above* the climber is thus severed from the lower slope on which it is resting, and slides down, starting the avalanche. It is especially dangerous because there is little chance of jumping from below the slab when it first moves.

4. *Unstable masses of snow or ice.* These avalanches are caused by the collapse of *séracs* or ice-cliffs, or by the collapse of cornices. They are very dangerous because of the immense amount of ice likely to be involved, and because of the speed and weight of the blocks of ice. Where the initial impetus is due to a shift in a glacier they can be caused at any time of day or night, but they are most likely to occur during the day because melting is also a factor.

It is suggested in various textbooks that a party involved in an avalanche should try to 'swim' along with it, so that they remain on the surface. This has been proved to be effective in some minor avalanches, but where the party is caught in a big avalanche or a fall of *séracs*, it is unlikely to make any difference. Hence the avoidance of avalanches – and shelter from them – is one of the principal considerations in alpine route-finding (chapter 17).

§ 130. Rockfalls and falling stones

Rockfalls (the collapse of a part of a rock face) are not common in the Alps; but some big falls have occurred. The summit of the Pic Sans Nom (Chamonix) for example has undergone several changes in the last century and there have been major rockfalls on *inter alia* the Col de Peuterey (1920), the East Face of the Zinal Rothorn (1929), the West Face of the Aiguille de Blaitière and the West Ridge of the Pic Nord des Cavales (early 1950s), and on the Meije, the South Face (1964) and the Brèche Zsigmondy (1965). Other, more minor, collapses have caused accidents, for example on the North-East Face of the Piz Badile in 1964.

Falling stones are a much more serious risk in the Alps than in Britain. The danger is greater on loose rock (e.g. in the Pennine Alps) than on good rock (e.g. Chamonix Aiguilles) but even on peaks where the rock is fundamentally sound, there are often sections where stonefalls occur. Much depends also on the temperature of the face; freezing conditions or a covering of new snow tend to cement the rocks in, but in warm, dry conditions falling stones are a constant risk. Stones may also be dislodged by parties higher up on the mountain; it is most important to warn parties below should even the smallest stone be sent down (see also § 7). The guide-book usually mentions places particularly liable to stonefalls. They can often be identified by dirt and debris in the snow, or by marks where stones have struck the rock. Ridges are the least exposed to falling stones; faces, and particularly couloirs and gullies, are the most dangerous (§ 136). If stones have fallen a long way their speed may be such that they are difficult to see. They will then make a shrill whistling noise – rather like a bullet – and the sooner you take cover the better (§ 134). As noted in § 123 it is advisable to wear protective headgear as a general rule, but especially where there is risk of stonefall.

Chapter 17. All-round alpine technique

§ 131. Choice of climb

As noted in § 115, there are guide-books for the main alpine areas which give adequate descriptions of the situation, length, and difficulty of the routes. In selecting a route, the principal considerations are:

- the competence, experience, and fitness of the party (§§ 111–13 and 116);
- the technical difficulty and seriousness of the climb;
- the objective dangers (avalanches and falling stones). On some routes it is necessary to accept these dangers for a short period as part and parcel of the route (e.g. on the ordinary routes on the Grépon and Grands Charmoz, which pass below the *séracs* of the Nantillons Glacier, and on the Écrins and the Dom). But some routes are open to the risk of falling stones or ice for long periods (e.g. the Marinelli Couloir on Monte Rosa). In most cases the risk varies according to the state of the season (§ 127) and the time of day (§ 128) and these considerations must influence the timing of a proposed ascent or descent, and the detailed route-finding (§§ 135–8);
- the time available;
- the difficulty of retreat should bad weather develop or the climbing prove unexpectedly difficult;
- the prevailing conditions. Never tackle a climb which is in thoroughly bad condition. New snow in particular can be exhausting and dangerous. Steep south-facing rock climbs lose their snow first after bad weather.

Much time is spent in a season in travelling up and down from huts. In easy areas you should therefore try to do at least two climbs from each hut, possibly with a rest day

138. *The Brenva face of Mont Blanc.* The climbs here are among the longest in the Alps (§ 146).

between, or traverse your peak moving from hut to hut, especially if you can save weight by buying meals from the hut guardians. As noted in § 127, it is often necessary to go up to the hut in bad weather so that you are in position when the good weather comes.

§ 132. Overall plan of the route

It is essential to form as accurate an appreciation of the route as possible before embarking on it. This can be done by very close study of the guide-book (particularly the diagrams), from reading articles in climbing journals and other publications, by discussion with guides and others who have done the climb, and by observation from other routes you have done near by. Picture postcards of the mountain can also be useful for working out the route. The main points to take into account in planning the route are:

– food (§ 119) and equipment (chapter 15);
– the time of departure from the valley (§ 133);
– details of the route to the hut;
– time of starting the route (§ 134);
– the precise point where the climbing is started ('*pointe d'attaque*');
– main technical difficulties and objective dangers on the ascent;
– the route of descent; need for abseiling (and hence abseil rope) and condition of snow or glacier (§ 138).

Allow plenty of time in case the route takes longer than expected.

§ 133. First day: the hut

In the valley. Try to make an early start with your preparations. This will enable you to check your kit and food, and get away early so that you do not have to rush up to the hut (§ 118). If you belong to a club offering reduced hut fees take your membership card with you so that you can claim them. You will also need your passport if your climb will bring you down in a different country (e.g. from France to Italy), and currency of the host country if the hut is over a frontier (money changing in huts usually proves costly). Avoid burdening your sack with extra clothes and equipment that you do not really need (though equally do not leave behind anything essential – sometimes a difficult decision to make). Hut grinds can be very long and tiring and it is desirable to avoid using more energy than strictly necessary because you will not be able to replenish it fully before the climb. At the height of the season (late July and early August) huts are often crowded, especially at week-ends, and this is an additional reason for arriving early. You must in any case ensure that you arrive before nightfall because huts are often perched high on moraines or on rocks as protection against avalanches, and the last part of the path to them can be difficult to find. Make sure that you know the exact route before you leave the valley, checking locally if there is any doubt; the tracks to most huts are marked by standard paint daubs on trees and rocks.

At the hut. When you arrive, make contact with the guardian and book your bed space. Make arrangements about the evening meal and about getting up (see § 134); arrange for breakfast also if the guardian is cooking it for you. Organize all your equipment for the climb that evening and make sure that you will be able to find it in semi-darkness in the morning, when time is precious. Fill your water bottle (for the mountain or for breakfast): in many huts the normal water supply will be frozen when you start in the morning. If possible pay your bill before you go to bed. It is very desirable to reconnoitre the early part of your route before dusk, to ensure a smooth start to the climb. Look for:

- the way out of the hut on to the beginning of your approach march. Huts are sometimes surrounded by steep ground, and you may need to fix an abseil point for the morning;
- the best place to get on to the glacier or the rock as the case may be;
- any cairns or other features (e.g. large boulders) which will

help you to follow the right route in the dark. It may be useful to build one or two small cairns of your own;

– the best place to put on the rope, and, if necessary, crampons. Sometimes (e.g. where there is difficult ground almost immediately) it will be better to put them on at the hut rather than to fumble in the dark.

§ 134. Overall conduct of the route

Time of departure. An early start is the secret of success since it gives you flexibility and a reserve of time in hand, and enables you to take advantage of the best conditions for crossing glaciers and other obstacles. The actual time of departure will depend on the time of first light, the length of the climb, and the extent of snow and ice on it. It is not advisable to embark on difficult rock climbing before dawn, but there is no reason why you should not cross scree, moraines, glaciers, or snow by torchlight. If there is much glacier and snow work late in the day, the earlier the start the better. Three a.m. would be on the early side for most normal routes; but five a.m. would definitely be late, except for the shorter rock routes. There will probably be a 'usual' time for waking for the popular climbs. It saves argument to conform to this, but if many other parties are due to get up at the same time try to get down among the first so that you are not delayed by being at the end of the queue for breakfast; a small alarm clock may be useful. I personally find that with a good meal the previous evening a cooked breakfast is unnecessary – but this is very much a matter of psychology and if you feel that you need a cooked breakfast make sure that you get it.

Speed is of vital importance because of the very great distances involved. This does not mean that the party need go faster than its normal pace; indeed, a steady rhythm is essential to avoid premature exhaustion. Speed in the Alps depends mainly on:

– physical fitness and acclimatization;
– accurate route-finding;

– quick and effective rope management;
– keeping halts and sack hauling to the minimum (it saves time to have chocolate, lump sugar, etc., readily available so that you can eat it on the move);
– resolving technical difficulties quickly.

Rope management. Because of the importance of speed, it is necessary to move together wherever possible, on rock as well as on snow and ice. Fortunately, most alpine going is fairly easy technically, and there is little need for belaying on stances in the British manner. The methods of roping up and of rope management on alpine snow and ice are substantially the same as on British snow and ice (§§ 54 and 85), but special considerations apply to glaciers and alpine rock, which are covered in §§ 135 and 137 respectively.

Objective dangers. In choosing the route, the party will often be confronted with a choice between an easy section which is potentially subject to objective dangers (e.g. falling stones, § 130) and a harder or longer (and therefore slower) section which is not. The choice between the two will depend on a careful assessment of the risks; early in the day, when objective dangers are fairly small, it will probably be worth taking the quicker, easier route, but later on the slower, safer route would be preferable. If it is impossible to avoid a dangerous section, make all speed consistent with safety. Where the passage is short (e.g. crossing a couloir) post a man as look-out to give warning of anything coming down. On a longer section, have an understanding between you as to what shelter to go for, so that you do not attempt to go in different directions. In the case of a stonefall when the party is on rock, try to take shelter under an overhang or in a crack (choose protected stances for belaying where possible); if you are caught in the open watch the stones so that at the last moment you can try to dodge them. Should you be unfortunate enough to be caught by falling ice (§ 129) on a glacier, the only refuge may be a crevasse. Couloirs are particularly liable to objective dangers and are dealt with in more detail in § 136.

Bad weather. The question may arise as to whether to go on with the route in the face of a threat of bad weather (§ 126). The decision will depend on the circumstances at the time and the degree of experience in the party. If the party is completely inexperienced, then no chances at all should be taken with the weather since a storm or even a mist could make route-finding on the return journey extremely difficult. An experienced party, however, can legitimately tackle the safer routes in doubtful conditions, provided they are prepared to turn back should it prove necessary. If there is mist around the hut in the early morning, but it is not actually snowing or raining, it is probably worth while for an experienced party to make a start and go on until the first difficulties are reached. On the other hand if you are high up and there is a serious chance that your retreat could be cut off, then it would be advisable to retreat at the first sign of bad weather. Lightning can be very dangerous and static electricity can make a compass useless. It must be remembered that to be caught in a storm on a high alpine peak is a very different thing from climbing on a wet day in Britain (though nothing can be worse than a bad Scottish winter blizzard). It can bring great difficulty and danger on what is normally an easy route (two guides, J. J. Maquignaz and A. Castagneri, disappeared in a storm on the easy route on the Dôme de Miage, and there have been many other similar cases on the Mont Blanc summit plateau). Because bad weather is such a risk, it is advisable to take a lightweight tent sack as well as a *cagoule* or a waterproof anorak on any high, serious climb (§ 124).

The special considerations applying to the descent are dealt with in § 138 below.

§ 135. Glacier technique

Most alpine routes involve at least some glacier work; even when the climb is predominantly on rock it will usually be necessary to ascend a glacier to reach the beginning of the rock and to return back down the glacier when the climb is finished. Many of the classic alpine routes, particularly at high altitude, involve long sections of glacier travel.

Need for the rope. On snow-covered glaciers, the party should be roped *at all times* no matter how easy or well trodden the route. Crevasses are no respecters of persons and can open up unexpectedly beneath even the best of us. The rope may in fact save time since you should be able to move in a more relaxed way. On dry glaciers, it is not usually necessary to rope up, since the crevasses are obvious and it should be easy to avoid them. A rope may, however, be necessary even on a dry glacier if there is a dangerous crevasse or bergschrund which cannot be avoided.

139. *Open crevasses.* The lower part of the Glacier du Dôme, on the Italian side of Mont Blanc.

Order on the rope. As noted in § 113, a foursome is the best size of party for snow-covered glaciers, though a threesome will do. A party of two cannot be entirely safe, because it may be impracticable for one member to hold the other in a fall into a crevasse or to extricate him. Descents of glaciers in the afternoon are particularly dangerous for a pair because there is little chance of the second holding the leader from above: ascents, conversely, are relatively safe because the second will not be pulled uphill as easily as downhill. In a rope of three or four, the most experienced member should normally go first so as to route-find; the next most experienced member should normally go last, as there is advantage in the party being reversible; it is particularly important that an experienced person should be last in descent, since he acts as a sheet anchor for the whole party. In the case of two climbers of unequal experience, it may be better for the more experienced member to go second, as he can make a greater contribution on the surface in the event of a mishap.

The method of roping up is much the same as in British snow and ice climbing (§ 85). Note in particular that:

- the rope interval should be forty to sixty feet, depending on the size of the crevasses. The leader needs rather more rope than the other members;
- a doubled rope (preferably differently coloured, e.g. one red, one white), is safer than a single rope because two ropes are useful in crevasse rescue. It should be clearly understood that one rope is the 'active' rope and the other is the 'standing' (or rescue) rope which is used for the various manœuvres involved in crevasse rescue (chapter 18);
- a thick ($1\frac{1}{4}$-in. or $1\frac{3}{8}$-in.) rope is much easier for crevasse rescue operations than a $\frac{7}{8}$-in. rope;
- when a single rope is used, about forty feet of spare rope should be carried by each of the end members of the party, not by one alone. Where there are two climbers on a 120-ft rope this can be done by tying on at forty feet and eighty feet respectively, leaving almost forty feet spare at each end (carried in coils as in [77]);

– each member should have a foot-loop (preferably a prusik-loop
  – [153]) so that he can relieve the strain on his waist should
  he fall into a crevasse. If the party is using the prusik system of
  crevasse rescue (§ 140, 2), each member will need three prusik-
  loops in total, of which preferably two should already be
  attached to the rope. With a doubled rope, the prusik-loops
  should be attached to the 'standing' rope. It may also prove
  useful to have several *étriers* handy (§ 140, 1);
– many climbers tie a small loop in the rope at arm's length away
  for (1) holding on to and (2) belaying in crevasse rescue,
  especially if they do not have a prusik-loop already fixed;
– a chest-loop and a thigh-loop [76] are advisable where there
  is serious crevasse danger (the chest-loop would prevent you
  slipping out of your waist-loop if you fell upside-down, and the
  thigh-loop would prevent any big load coming on to your waist
  if you were knocked unconscious and hence were unable to
  stand in your foot-loop).

Rope management. It is necessary to pay particular attention
to securing the party on the move (see also § 88). The
members of the party should keep about thirty feet apart so
that there is little chance of two of them being on the same
crevasse at the same time, and so that the load of a fall
will quickly come on to the bodies of the other members;
too many coils or too much slack in the rope may seriously
increase the length of a fall, and make it all the more
difficult to arrest. The leader will be safer if he carries no
hand coils, but some leaders carry about four feet of hand
coils in case they suddenly need to jump out of difficulty.
The second and other members should carry as few coils as
possible (say four or five feet) and should let them out and
take them in as appropriate to keep the rope taut. But on
very crevassed ground it is safer for them to carry no coils
at all.

Importance of conditions. The variations in conditions described
in chapter 16 are at their greatest in the case of glaciers.
Snow-covered glaciers are generally safest early in the
season when the snow is still plentiful and reliable, and the

snow bridges are thick and reasonably secure. As the season progresses, the crevasses become more open and the snow bridges weaker and less reliable. The time of day is also extremely important: in the cold of the early morning before the sun is on the glacier or in the late afternoon or evening an hour or so after the sun has gone off the glacier, the surface snow is frozen hard and snow bridges (and also ice-axe belays) are at their safest. In the middle of the day, on the other hand, glaciers are hot and snow bridges weak. Moreover there is a greater danger from falling *séracs*, etc. These factors must be fully taken into account in the overall plan of the day (e.g. so that sections particularly liable to falling ice and other hazards are crossed before sun-up) and also in the more detailed route-finding.

Movement on crevassed glaciers. In selecting the route the main considerations are (1) to avoid objective dangers (falling ice and rocks) as far as possible and (2) to minimize the difficulties of crossing crevasses. In respect of (2), remember that:

– the middle of the glacier is usually easiest. On bends, the outside edge of the glacier will often be more badly crevassed than the inner. Avoid icefalls if there is a suitable alternative, e.g. a lateral moraine (§ 125);

140. *Positioning the party in crevassed areas.* A and C are normal. B is necessary only on the rare occasions when the party cannot avoid travelling in the same direction as the crevasses.

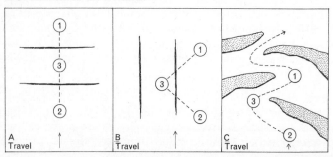

– watch very carefully for concealed crevasses and cross them at their safest point. The direction of the crevasses changes in different parts of the glacier according to the direction of the stresses in the glacier and its angle. Look to the right and left to pick up the lines of distant crevasses which may be continued under the snow ahead. Usually on snow-covered glaciers the presence of a crevasse is betrayed by a very slight lowering in the surface of the snow; although this may be only one inch or so, it can be detected by the observant eye, given good and clean snow goggles;

– a crevasse which would be safe at the beginning of the season or when frozen up in the early morning may be dangerous later on. Consequently, although existing tracks can be very useful, do not follow them blindly without having regard to changes in the conditions. (There is often a 'morning' track and an 'afternoon' track.)

The need to keep at least one member of the party on *terra firma* is the principal consideration in positioning the party. In areas where crevasses are long and concealed it is possible for the whole party, though well spread apart, to be inadvertently above the same crevasse. To avoid this the direction of the rope between the members of the party should be as nearly as possible at right angles to the direction of the crevasses [140A]. Usually in ascending or descending the middle of a glacier this is automatically the case, as the crevasses tend to be transverse; but when traversing across a glacier it may be impossible to avoid travelling in the same direction as the crevasses, and the party should then travel in two separate lines as in [140B]. There are three main ways of crossing crevasses :

– *by detouring round* – the safest, though possibly the slowest way, usually necessary in areas such as icefalls where the crevasses are very big and open [140C]. It will normally be possible to identify the wall dividing one crevasse from another crevasse in the same line, since it will be at about thirty to sixty degrees to the direction of the crevasse. The party will have to wind its way along the tops of the ice walls dividing the crevasses; they should be spread out as far as possible so that they are not all in danger of falling into the same crevasse, and should belay when standing still;

– *by jumping at a narrow point* (easiest in descent). Make sure that the take-off point is sound, and as far as possible the landing point also. Take in a few coils before you jump, and release them in mid-air if it is a long jump. Always warn the other members of the party that you are going to jump. Keep your feet well apart if you are wearing crampons, and try to land with both feet at the same time to absorb the shock. Roll forwards on landing, as in a parachute roll, if necessary;

– *by crossing a snow bridge* at a narrow part of the crevasse. Snow bridges vary greatly in thickness and reliability; as noted above, they are at their best in the early morning and at their weakest in the heat of the afternoon. The leader must prod carefully with his ice-axe to make sure that there is firm snow or ice where he is about to step. If necessary he should crawl across on hands and knees to distribute his weight more evenly. The rest of the party should be belayed (§ 86) some way away on firm ground, and should keep the leader's rope just taut. If the bridge appears insecure, the leader should belay the other members in turn, who should use exactly the same steps as he did.

Where a crevasse has a very steep upper lip, as is often the case with a bergschrund or on a steeply dropping glacier, attack it where the wall is lowest. Even so it may present serious difficulties. Ice-axes hammered in horizontally may be needed as hand- and footholds if the top lip is snow; alternatively, if the lip is ice, it will be advisable to use ice screws (preferably) or ice pitons (§ 81) as running belays or as direct aid. The techniques of inserting these are described in § 87, and the techniques needed for direct aid are basically the same as for artificial climbing on rock (§ 71). *Étriers* (§ 70) are probably worth while in that your weight is taken on the piton at not less than ninety degrees to it. If you find that full-scale artificial climbing is necessary for more than about fifteen feet, check very carefully that you have not taken the wrong route, since such climbing is extremely rare even in the Alps. In descent, it is often possible to jump a bergschrund. But make sure that the taking-off place on the upper lip is sound (it may be unsupported – like a cornice – and hence likely to collapse).

If you feel your foot go into a crevasse, throw yourself either forwards or backwards with your arms outstretched and as low as possible (keeping a tight hold on your ice-axe). By spreading your weight instantaneously in this way it will often be possible to halt an incipient fall. If you are too far in to be able to do this, keep your arms outstretched and stay still until you can be pulled out. Crevasse rescue methods are dealt with in chapter 18.

§ 136. Movement on alpine snow and ice

The techniques of movement on British snow and ice, described in chapters 2 and 11, apply equally to alpine conditions, except that in the Alps it is unusual to encounter very steep snow and ice; on the other hand conditions are more variable (this is especially important on the descent – see § 138) and the objective dangers are rather greater. Because of the latter, special considerations apply in route-finding, as follows:

Avalanche snow. As noted in § 129, the risk of snow avalanches is very serious in the Alps. These dangers can be minimized by:

– moving on the side of the mountain which is in shadow (i.e. west in the morning or east in the late afternoon). Avoid northerly slopes if there is windslab danger, since this is most common on habitually shaded parts of the mountain;
– keeping to the rocks when the snow is doubtful;
– keeping as high on a slope as possible and securing the party from a safe position when it is necessary to cross doubtful snow;
– using the trough where the surface snow has already avalanched away. This often gives a safe line, especially as the snow there is likely to be firm for step-kicking or cramponing. However, always avoid troughs made by avalanches falling from above.

Couloirs are wide gullies usually – but not always – filled with snow or ice and with rocky containing walls. They

offer a direct and short route up a face and give some very fine climbs. But on the other hand they are a natural channel for debris falling down the mountain and they usually become very dangerous when the sun warms their upper reaches. Some couloirs are permanently dangerous because they are topped by *séracs* or ice-cliffs which may send down ice at any time of day or night (e.g. the Grand Couloir on the Brenva face of Mont Blanc [138]). The following main points are relevant:

– always plan the ascent so that you can cross or climb a couloir when it is safe; as noted in § 134 this may require an extremely early start;
– climb close to the walls to take advantage of the shelter (and belays) which they provide, and in particular choose protected belay stances; avoid the middle of the couloir, especially if it contains a *rigole* (the ice channel made by falling debris);
– a layer of hard frozen snow on the ice will make progress easier; bare couloir ice may be very tough and steep, and holds on the rock walls and in the crack between the ice and the wall may then be used with advantage;
– couloir snow can be particularly treacherous when it warms up because it invariably lies on hard ice or rock. The Whymper Couloir on the Aiguille Verte is a notorious example of a couloir where the snow is usually dangerous after the early morning.

Cornices are very common on alpine ridges [142]. They are usually much bigger than in Britain (§ 18), and occasionally occur as double cornices (one on each side of the ridge); in the latter case it may be impossible to cross them safely, and it may be necessary for the party to retreat. Tracks of previous parties are useful, but use your own judgement as well because they may either have been made incorrectly by the first party, or the underside of the cornice

141. *Moving together*. On the Forbes Arête of the Aiguille du Chardonnet (§ 146).

142. *A dangerous cornice.* On the Grande Sassière (Graian Alps). The climbers have descended from the ridge to avoid being over the line of cornice break. Note that the line of break normally follows the angle of the slope overhung by the cornice (A–B), and not a vertical line. Always make a generous allowance in case the cornice takes even more of the slope with it (A–C).

may have melted, so that the steps are left on the wrong side of the line of cornice break. It is often difficult for the leader to tell the exact position of the line of cornice break, and the second and third men should warn him if it appears that he is going on to dangerous ground. If a cornice does break away the whole party may go with it. Any member of the party who is left on firm ground should throw himself in the opposite direction to act as a counter-weight.

§ 137. Technique for alpine rock

Route-finding. On rock, it is necessary to be very accurate in *detailed* route-finding because of the wide variation in technical difficulty between slightly different lines. Guide-less parties, particularly parties on their first visit to an area, are inevitably prone to errors of route-finding. Conversely, following the correct route in detail on rock is one of the most satisfying pleasures of guideless climbing. The difficulty of finding the route depends very much on the type of rock (the easier-unpegged-Dolomite rock is especially difficult) and the popularity of the climb (the 'trade routes' are usually well marked). The main requirements are:

- very detailed and thorough knowledge of the guide-book (§ 115), supported as necessary by sketches and other observations based on information from parties which have done the route. It is often instructive, particularly if the guide-book is in an unfamiliar language, to make a sketch ('topo') from it, possibly on a picture postcard of the mountain. You will need to refresh your memory on the climb and this will be easier to refer to than the guide-book;
- take the easiest line, as always in alpine climbing, avoiding unnecessary difficulties which waste precious time and effort;
- keep a careful watch on the difficulty of the climbing: if it becomes appreciably harder than it should be, it is likely that you are off-route. Correlate each section carefully with your pre-selected line, and quickly eliminate any possible alternatives before taking what seems to be the obvious line (there is often a much easier route around the corner);
- observe the route taken by any parties ahead of you;
- watch for signs of previous parties: pitons, tins, or footmarks in the snow are better indications than pieces of paper which may have been blown there;
- make sure that the previous party has not itself taken a wrong route. This is particularly likely on harder rock climbs, where pitons in place are often *pitons d'erreur*;
- check the belays (rock or piton) on stances to see whether they have abseil slings on them: although the descent route is often the same as for the ascent, sometimes it is quite different, and

blindly following abseil pitons can lead an ascending party into very great difficulties.

1. STANDARD TECHNIQUES

Easy ground: moving together. Most alpine rock is not hard technically. It is rarely necessary to climb at more than Very Difficult standard (§ 35) on an average alpine route, and most rock is Easy or Moderately Difficult, occasionally Difficult. On the other hand, the effects of altitude and fatigue make the climbing relatively more difficult, and there is a good deal of bad rock or iced rock to contend with. Because of the great distances involved, the party should move together on easy, safe ground instead of moving singly as on British rock. The ability of the party to do this safely on an average alpine climb depends on:

– all members climbing safely and within their capacity;
– judgement as to when it is safe to move together and when it is not: technical difficulty, bad rock, *verglas*, the alertness of the party, and the availability or otherwise of emergency belays must all be taken into account;
– skill in rope management so that the rope is a safeguard and not a hindrance or danger.

Rope management when moving together. The party should be tied on at intervals of about 120 ft, but the rope should be shortened [77A] to about forty to sixty feet normally. In traversing it is best to carry hand coils [77B] in the outside hand so that you can use your inside hand on holds. All members of the party must be constantly alert and must secure themselves and the other members of the party as adequately as possible at all times. This involves:

– keeping fairly close together, with the active rope almost taut so that any slip can be halted quickly; all members must be meticulous in taking in and letting out coils, so that the rope

143. *A typical alpine rock ridge.* On the traverse of the Rimpfischorn (Pennine Alps). Easy climbing, but great exposure on the left.

never lies loose or catches on rocks, thus possibly dislodging loose stones;

– passing the rope around flakes to act as natural running belays. The leader should do this as he passes by; but the second should watch the leader's rope to flick it over any convenient projections;

– a steady rhythm; do not rush on indiscriminately on easy ground when others are on a difficult few moves;

– the party positioning itself so that one member at least is always in a position to hold the others, e.g. on a ridge one person can be slightly to one side, while the others are on the other, so that all would not be pulled down on the same side of the mountain in the event of a fall;

– moving singly and belaying as necessary when a hard or dangerous pitch occurs; if the party is a threesome it will be quicker for the middleman to lead the pitch and then for the first and third men to come up at the same time with protection from above. But resume continuous movement as soon as it is safe to do so.

You can save much time in various small ways. For example, when bringing someone up on a short section take in his rope neatly so that you can hand him ready-made hand coils when he arrives at your stance; otherwise he would need to spend time coiling the spare rope himself as you move off and thus would drop behind you. Direct belays are also time-saving [145].

2. MORE ADVANCED TECHNIQUES

Harder alpine rock climbing. Although it is rarely necessary to climb hard rock on average alpine routes, some of the very best alpine climbs involve rock climbing of a very high order of difficulty, and give excellent sport to the expert rock climber who is also a proficient alpinist. This is particularly the case at Chamonix and in the Dolomites, where rock of Grade V and above abounds. The order of difficulty of these routes is discussed in § 116. As noted in § 122, a double rope is often useful. The distance between the leader and the second man should be not less than

144. *Equipment for hard alpine rock climbing.* Early morning at the Second Bivouac Bonatti on the Grand Capucin du Tacul, a major artificial climb. Note the protective helmets (§ 123).

145. *Direct belays.* Used mainly for bringing up the second man. Wherever possible make a separate belay for yourself, as in A.

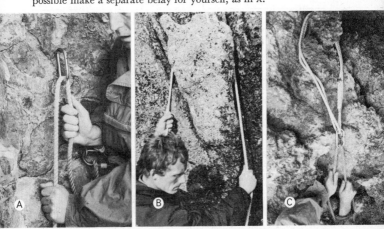

120 ft. It will often be necessary to move singly and to belay substantially as in Britain, although every opportunity should be taken of moving together as in 1 when it is safe to do so. The following adjustments to British rope technique (chapter 8) are recommended when moving singly, in the interests of speed.

Direct belays should be used for bringing up the second man wherever he can be adequately protected in this way (i.e., where the direct belay is sound, and where the second is directly protected by the rope from above so that he is unlikely to fall any distance before his weight comes on to the rope). Direct belays [145] are made by bringing in the rope:

- over a spike or flake;
- through a karabiner attached to a piton which is preferably in a horizontal crack;
- through a karabiner clipped into a sling.

The leader should be ready to leave the stance as soon as the second arrives. When the direct belay is used, the second man's rope is already on the anchor, so that all he has to do is to clip into it to form a proper belay for safeguarding the leader. Direct belays are not as safe as indirect belays for protecting the leader, and are not recommended except in artificial climbing (§ 73).

Permanent belay sling. Time will be saved if each member of the party has a heavy (1⅜-in.) nylon sling permanently attached to himself (e.g. at the main karabiner) with the loop carried over his shoulder when not in use. The loop can be placed over an anchor spike very rapidly and a proper belay can thus be made without tying any knots.

Leading through may not save as much time on alpine rock as it does on British rock. Unless the party is very fit, only about one rope length at a time can be climbed rapidly and safely at alpine altitudes. If the second has made all possible speed to join the leader he will probably be too tired to

146. *Steep Chamonix granite.* View upwards and downwards on the Rebuffat Route on the south face of the Aiguille du Midi, a *Très Difficile* rock climb. The glacier in B is about five hundred feet below.

make a good job of the next pitch immediately; nor will he have had as much time as the leader to weigh up the route ahead. Most parties will find it better to switch the lead every hour or two instead.

A shoulder for the leader is sometimes necessary at the beginning of a pitch. The second should lean his back against the rock with one knee bent. The leader puts one foot on the second's knee and the other on his shoulder (or, eventually his head), and then takes to the rock again. The second man must himself be belayed and tending the leader's rope if there is any chance of him or the leader falling off the ledge.

Assistance for the second man. It is far more important for the second man to get up a pitch quickly than to climb it prettily: he should, if necessary, use the rope. The double-rope system is extremely useful here since the second man can use one rope (there should be an automatic understanding which this should be) for his hands, while the leader brings him up on the other rope. The second should, however, *not* climb up the rope when a single rope is used because the leader cannot take it in at the same time to protect him. In a case of extreme difficulty the leader should lower a second rope (possibly the inactive part of the main climbing rope) preferably with hand- or foot-loops.

Rope throwing. On some routes it is necessary to throw the rope over a mushroom of rock or over the other side of a ridge to give direct aid. Such manœuvres usually require care and dexterity – and strong nerves.

Sack hauling should be avoided where possible: it is very time-wasting and tiring and it is better for the leader to carry his sack, perhaps with the second carrying some of his equipment for him so that it is not too heavy (a leader would rarely climb difficult rock with a sack weighing more than about ten pounds). If sack hauling is unavoidable use a separate rope; if possible tie the sack on half-way so that the second can control it from below, and put any ice-axes inside it.

Pitons. On hard climbs in the Alps, pitons and wedges are used much more freely than in Britain for belays, running belays, and direct aid. This is partly because there is much less time to spare for working out an intricate move, partly because the safety margin must be kept as high as possible on account of the great difficulty of rescue operations, and partly because it is not unusual to come across sections of rock which simply cannot be climbed

147. *Steeper Chamonix granite.* On the East Face of the Grand Capucin du Tacul. The route goes through the overhangs in the top right-hand corner of the picture.

without their aid. On most hard climbs, the pitons required are usually already in place, and can be used either for direct aid or running belays according to choice. Essential pitons which are already in place should be left there, since their removal may cause inconvenience or even danger to other parties. Should you feel the need to put in a piton, you need not ponder the moral issues unduly: safety and speed are synonymous and if it is quicker or considerably less tiring to use a piton then always do so. However, on long routes time will not permit you to place a large number of pitons. Should you find yourself needing many additional pitons on classic routes you will either have lost your way, or you will have been climbing above your standard. The technique of full-scale artificial climbing (chapter 9) is sometimes needed and the guide-book will indicate where this is so (§§ 115 and 116). On the great artificial climbs it is very important to have a smooth and rapid technique, and this ought to be developed in Britain first. As noted in § 116 the harder artificial routes involve a great deal of skill and endurance and should be undertaken only by thoroughly competent parties.

§ 138. The descent

The descent of an alpine peak needs special care, since it is the time when accidents are most likely to happen. The principal dangers to be guarded against in descent are:

- relaxation of concentration on the easy first part of the descent, with the result that the party makes errors of route-finding, or fails to halt a slip by one member;
- lack of familiarity with climbing down so that the party is unduly slow; climbing down should be practised in Britain as much as possible (§ 37, 3);
- carelessness in abseiling (see below);

148. *Dolomite verticality*. Traverse on the North Face of the Cima Ovest di Lavaredo (Cassin Route).

- poor snow conditions in the heat of the day (especially where the route of descent faces south), so that snow steps and belays are insecure, avalanches or snow slides and falling stones are likely, and snow bridges over crevasses are weak;
- renewed lack of concentration on the final easy section of the glacier, with the likelihood of falling into an unnoticed crevasse. This danger is at its greatest at the point where an obviously dangerous snow-covered glacier, on which the party has been taking special care, changes into an apparently safe dry glacier where however crevasses may be hidden under bands of old snow, or under a thin covering of moraine;
- taking the rope off while there is still a risk from crevasses.

Because snow conditions can be so bad late in the day, it is often important to get back down the mountain during the morning, and the whole plan for the day must be arranged to allow this (§ 134).

Abseiling (§ 66). This is often necessary, especially on the more difficult rock descents, and a high degree of efficiency is required in the interests of safety and speed. It is an unhappy fact that abseiling is a major cause of alpine accidents, partly, no doubt, because it is often undertaken late in the day when the party is tired and liable to carelessness. Experience has shown that the most frequent causes of accidents in alpine abseiling are:

- the abseil anchor giving way. Always check that a piton is in securely (i.e., that it is in a crack at right angles to the line of pull) and that it has not rusted or become cracked. It is often tempting to use the slings which are already in place, especially where they have been used shortly before by another party, but this is a major cause of accidents and it is far safer to take spare $\frac{3}{4}$-in. hemp or manila line, or $\frac{7}{8}$-in. nylon, so that you can make new slings wherever there is the slightest doubt about the existing slings. Take special care when abseiling from ice pegs or screws (§ 89). Always descend at an even rate, since fast braking puts an undue strain on the belay;

149. *Taking great care in descent.* On the Ober Gabelhorn (Pennine Alps).

- the abseil rope jamming when it is being pulled down. If it is necessary to get back up to retrieve the rope, on no account rely on the jammed rope for a hold, since it may give way without any warning (the great Italian climber Gervasutti was killed in this way);
- taking a wrong route and abseiling into areas of unclimbable rock where the abseil pitches are too long for the rope;
- the rope being too short, because pieces have been cut off to make slings, or it has been cut by falling stones.

These dangers can be minimized by the use of a safety rope at all times; if there is no second rope available for this arrange it with the main climbing rope in the way shown in [95]. It is also important to develop an automatic sequence. In a two-man party where separate abseiling and safety ropes are being used a possible sequence is:

1. Number one selects the safety belay, ties on and secures number two while the latter fixes the abseil belay and gets the rope down.
2. Number two abseils down (protected by number one) and belays at the bottom.
3. Number two checks that the doubled rope is not twisted and can be pulled round the belay without jamming.
4. Number one abseils down (while number two takes in the safety rope).
5. Number one fixes the abseil belay which number two has selected. As number two pulls down the double rope, number one threads it through the new abseil sling: this avoids the possibility of dropping the abseil rope, and also gets it into the correct position for the next abseil.

The sequence is then repeated except that the positions of number one and number two are reversed.

If the snaplink or *descendeur* methods of abseiling (§ 66, 2 and 3) are being used, it is best to put on a thigh-loop [76A and B] at the beginning of the abseiling and to keep it on throughout the descent; as noted in § 135, it may be worth while keeping this on for the glacier as well, in case of a fall into a crevasse.

150. *After the bivouac.* On the Aiguille Noire de Peuterey.

§ 139. Alpine bivouacs

Many climbers undertaking normal routes complete their alpine careers without ever needing to bivouac. It may, however, be necessary for a party to bivouac either on a long route which it is not normally possible to complete in one day (planned bivouac) or if bad weather or an accident delays the party so that it is compelled to stay out for the night (forced bivouac). The techniques of bivouacking are much the same as in Britain (§§ 11 and 21) except that rather better equipment (§ 124) would usually be carried by the party. It is recommended that any party undertaking a climb which is at all serious should at least take a tent sack against the possibility of a forced bivouac. The main points in alpine bivouacking are:

- the site should be protected from falling stones, snow, or ice, if possible by an overhang. Proximity of water is desirable to avoid having to use fuel to melt snow.
- select your site so that you can settle in before nightfall. Where sites are scarce, and you know that a bivouac cannot be avoided, it may be better to stop a little early at a good site rather than to have to spend the night on a bad site, or for the party to be split at nightfall on two or more inadequate sites;

- the lower your bivouac, the warmer it will be. Avoid a ridge if possible since it is likely to be draughty and exposed to lightning (§§ 8 and 126);
- if the ledge is above a drop all members of the party should be belayed overnight using pitons if necessary. Equipment should be well secured. Boots and water bottles should, if necessary, be kept close to your body to prevent them freezing.

If you are forced into an emergency bivouac high up and do not have a tent sack and other equipment your plight could be serious, especially if the weather deteriorates, as it often does. On snow use a small crevasse or possibly dig a snow-hole [25]; on rock try to find an overhang or chimney to protect you from the weather.

Chapter 18. Crevasse rescue

Although most climbers enjoy a lifetime of alpine climbing without being involved in a real crevasse rescue, all should be well versed in the requisite techniques so that no time is lost should such an emergency occur. The choice between the various methods of rescue described below is for the party as a whole to make: but it is important that all members of the party should be well versed in the one they select for rescuing an uninjured climber, and should also be familiar with the techniques needed for the much more difficult problem of rescuing an unconscious person.

Usually the victim will be able to support himself either by bridging across the crevasse or by using ledges or lower bridges within the crevasse. Sometimes, however, he will be swinging free without any hope of touching the walls (as, for example, would be the case if someone fell into the middle of the crevasse in [151]). In such a case, he must immediately take the strain off his waist and chest by standing in one or more foot-loops or prusik-loops. The human body cannot survive for more than about ten minutes suspended from the waist alone because the blood circulation through the diaphragm gets cut off; strangulation is also a danger if the rope slips up round the chest. The victim should if possible be lowered into a relatively comfortable position while the rescue operation is being mounted. The essential principles in crevasse rescue are:

- immediate, clear-thinking action; crevasses are cold places and it is vital to get the victim out quickly;
- the best man should not be afraid to take charge and organize;
- one or more belays should be established well away from the crevasse to safeguard the victim and his rescuers. If there is only

one man on the surface, prusik-loops can be used as shown in [153];
- a rucksack (tied on to a line) should be placed under the load-bearing ropes near or on the edge of the crevasse to stop them cutting through the snow or freezing in. (It is sometimes recommended that an ice-axe should be used for this purpose, but unless the party is very large the ice-axes will be required for belays);
- do not go nearer to the edge of the crevasse than necessary and take care not to dislodge masses of snow on to the victim.

As mentioned above, it is far safer to be tied on to two ropes in crevassed areas because the rescue can begin without the delay involved in getting a second rope down to the victim. The heavier the rope the better. In this chapter it is assumed that the white rope is the active rope, securing the victim, and the red rope is the standing rope, which he climbs up.

§140. Main methods of crevasse rescue where the victim is conscious and can assist himself

In a case where the victim can gain some purchase on the walls of the crevasse it may be possible for a surface party of three (or, exceptionally, two) to pull him out by sheer force. This has the merit of speed. Before attempting to do so, however, make sure that the victim is not suspended from his waist alone and that he is not likely to be forced into the underside of any overhanging lip in the crevasse. If this method is not feasible, one of the more sophisticated techniques described below may be used.

1. *Étrier system.* Two or three *étriers* (§ 70) clipped together and lowered into the crevasse can provide a rapid means of exit. The best arrangement is to attach the top *étrier* to the

151. *A huge crevasse.* Note the structure of the snow bridge. Crevasses are formed by the movement of the glacier; the accretion of snow in winter and spring forms the bridges. A. Small split. B. Covered by snow. C. Reopens. D. More snow. E. Mature crevasse.

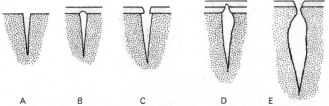

red rope, or to a spare rope if the party is climbing on a single rope, leaving the main (white) rope round the victim's waist. He can then climb up the *étriers* and when he reaches the top rung of the topmost *étrier* have his weight taken momentarily on the main rope (possibly with a foot-loop) while the red rope and the *étriers* are pulled up further. The process is then repeated. *Étriers* are particularly useful for surmounting the lip of a crevasse because they do not bite into the lip to the same extent as a rope.

2. *Prusik-loop system* [152A]. Two prusik or, preferably, Penberthy [153] loops are needed for the feet and – even when two ropes are used – a third one for the chest. As noted in § 122, there are specially designed implements available (e.g. the Hiebeler 'Prusiker') for use instead of prusik-loops; these are much more convenient, but are an additional item to carry. Kernmantel rope may prove unsatisfactory for this method since the sheath may slip over the core under load. The technique is as follows:

1. The victim pulls out the lower prusik-loop from his pocket; it is already attached to the red rope. He then passes it behind his knee and places his foot in it. It is a matter of personal preference whether he passes the loop through his waist-band *en route*: the advantage is that this holds him in a more vertical position and thus increases stability and relieves the strain on his waist, chest, and arms; the disadvantage is that it makes the arrangements rather more complicated.
2. He then warns the surface party (who have by now secured the red rope) and transfers his weight on to the foot-loop. The surface party take in the white rope.
3. He then passes the higher prusik-loop behind his other knee and places his other foot in it. He also takes out his third (short) loop and attaches it to the rope above the two longer ones; ideally he should be able to clip it into a chest- or shoulder-loop already in place [76c] or else slip his head and shoulders through it. If this loop is not too long, he will be able to take the weight of his upper body on it.
4. He then stands in the upper foot-loop, moves the lower loop up,

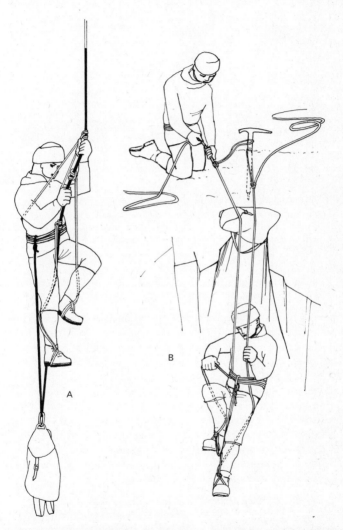

152. *Crevasse rescue.* A is the prusik method. The weight of the rucksack makes it easier to move the bottom loop. B is the double foot-loop system.

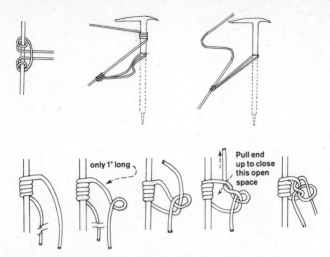

153 *Friction knots for crevasse rescue.* The prusik knot (above) is traditional, but the new Penberthy knot (below) is easier to move after
loading and less likely to kink the rope. With both knots the axe can
be used as a windlass to take in the rope, the knot to hold it.

and transfers his weight to it while he moves the upper loop
again. He also moves the chest-loops, as necessary.

He continues as in 4 until the operation is completed. The
exit may be very difficult if the standing (red) rope has
bitten into the lip of the crevasse. It will then be necessary
either to take the whole of the victim's weight on the white
rope and pull the red rope up to a better position, or to
lower another rope with a foot-loop (see method 3 below) or
alternatively to lower an *étrier* or two as in method 1. The
white rope is taken in as the victim moves up, but there is
little point in trying to pull on it, since this is very tiring for
the surface members and is unnecessary if the victim is
using a third loop for his chest. *Étriers* can be used in
conjunction with prusik-loops if desired.

3. *Double foot-loop system* [152B]. If this system is used there
should be loops in the white and the red rope at about an
arm's length from the waist when travelling on glaciers.
The procedure is:

1. The victim, suspended from the white rope, pulls the loop in the red rope down (the rescuers hold the white rope and slacken the red rope to allow this), passes it behind his knee and places his foot on it. As with method 2 (1), the loop may be passed through the waist-loop if desired.
2. He then warns the surface party and stands in the red rope which is held tight.
3. He then draws down the loop in the white rope (the surface party holds on the red rope and slackens the white rope to allow this), passes it behind his knee, and places his other foot on it.
4. The victim then takes his weight on the white rope, while the red rope is drawn in about three feet by the surface party and temporarily secured.
5. The victim then stands in the red foot-loop, and the process is repeated.

In this way the victim can eventually climb out of the crevasse. It should be noted that the victim must be in a position to give instructions to the surface party at each movement. This system cannot be used very satisfactorily with nylon rope less than $1\frac{1}{4}$-in. thick since the stretch is too great to allow the victim to make much progress with each movement. It may be advantageous to tie on about four feet from the end of the rope, and to make a foot-loop in the end itself which you can carry in your pocket. The advantage of this is that the victim can immediately stand in the loop without waiting for the surface party to slacken the red rope as in 1. It is the normal method of making a foot-loop also for when a single rope is used for glacier travel.

4. *The pulley system* [154]. This can be used where the victim can get purchase on the walls of the crevasse and it is not too steep. Its great advantages are that it makes use of the pulley principle so that it requires less strength in the rescuers and victim than some of the other methods, and that both the surface party and the victim can contribute to the total effort. There are many variations, but the two main methods are:

1. where the party is climbing on a single rope, a spare length is

needed on the surface. One end is secured firmly (x) and the other (y) is held by one or more of the rescuers; the middle of the spare rope is then lowered to the victim, who clips it through his waist karabiner. The rescuers then pull on (y) while the victim pulls on the fixed end (x).

2. where the party is climbing on a doubled rope, the easiest arrangement is to pass the red rope through a karabiner suspended from a loop on the edge of the crevasse. The spare end is then lowered back to the victim who can either pull it to raise himself up, or can alternatively clip it through his waist karabiner as in 1, so that a double pulley is formed.

If there are two or more rescuers it is best to do the haulage from the surface; this is certainly preferable where the victim is weak or has freezing hands.

§ 141. Crevasse rescue where the victim is unconscious

This is an operation of great difficulty which will require a surface party of at least three. One of the members of the surface party will have to go into the crevasse to:

– give first aid to the victim (§ 98);
– tie the victim on to the haulage rope or ropes (see below);
– direct operations and escort the victim to the surface.

Some sort of pulley (double or triple) is advisable (see § 140, 4). It is particularly important to tie the victim on to the haulage rope in such a way that he cannot slip out or turn upside-down. As in all rescue operations, a principal consideration is to avoid injuring the victim further, and the method chosen will have to take full account of the nature of his injuries. There are two main methods:

The triple bowline [166]. This may be used if there are no serious back injuries. It is advisable to tie an additional loop round the victim's shoulder and clip it in high up on the rope.

Stretcher. If there are serious injuries some form of stretcher is required to move the man safely. If the crevasse is not very cold, it may be possible to wait until a rescue

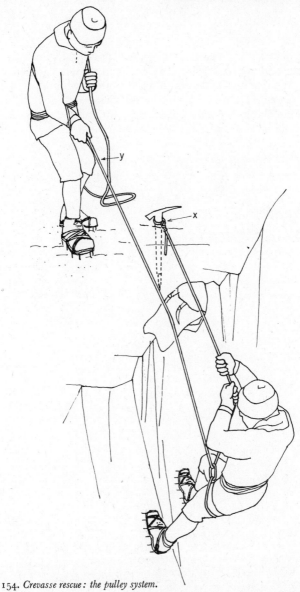

154. *Crevasse rescue: the pulley system.*

stretcher can be brought (e.g. by helicopters). If, however, the accident occurs high up, the cold and the delay involved will probably necessitate raising the victim with improvised arrangements. Unless by chance ski sticks and skis happen to be available, ice-axes passed through holes made in the climbing sacks may be the best that can be done.

Chapter 19. Where to climb in the Alps

As with chapter 13, I can do no more here than describe the areas briefly, and list useful maps and books for you to study. The areas are described from west to east and, where necessary, from south to north. Map 4 (pp. 442–3) shows their approximate positions. The major ones for the climber are the Dauphiné (§ 143), Mont Blanc (§ 146), the Pennine Alps (§ 147), the Bernese Alps (§ 148), the Bregaglia and Bernina (§ 151), some of the Austrian groups (§ 155), and the Dolomites (§ 156). These offer an enormous amount of climbing, and few British climbers go outside them. I have however thought it worth while to include most of the lesser-known, minor areas as well, partly because they may appeal to novices or hill walkers, and partly because some of them have very good rock climbing at relatively low altitudes and consequently can be recommended to experienced alpinists also in bad seasons when there is nothing to be done in the high areas. It will be evident from previous chapters that the higher areas in particular may involve quite serious mountaineering, and alpine novices should proceed cautiously, preferably starting in one of the easier areas suggested in § 114. Walkers will find plenty of scope below the snow line in all the areas.

Accommodation. There is usually good accommodation in the valleys in the form of *pensions*, youth hostels, or camping grounds (§ 117), and in the mountains in the form of alpine huts run by the alpine clubs (§ 118); details are usually given in the guide-books and no regular mention is made of them here. The Swiss Alpine Club publishes a list of all its huts and Swiss mountain rescue posts (*Clubhütten Verzeichnis*, 1967, 25s. with map), while the French Alpine Club has its own *Refuges des Montagnes Françaises et Zones Limitrophes* (1967, about 60s.) with useful sketch maps.

Books. Many of the books listed in the bibliography give information about individual alpine areas or climbs incidentally, but there are few modern books describing the Alps as a whole from the climber's or walker's (as distinct from the ski-er's) point of view. The following deserve special mention:

The Alps, Wilfrid Noyce, Thames and Hudson, 1964, 63s. A beautifully produced picture book, with commentary.

World Atlas of Mountaineering, Wilfrid Noyce and Ian McMorrin, Thomas Nelson, 1969, 90s.

On Rock and Ice. A. Roch, Black, 1947. Many excellent photographs of good alpine climbs.

The Alps, R. L. G. Irving, Batsford, 1947. A good descriptive book, though its views on harder mountaineering are distinctly dated.

Selected Alpine Ice-Climbs, J. Cleare, West Col. Planned for 1970, probably as the first of a series of narrative guides to classic rock and ice routes.

Salute the Mountains,* W. Pause, Harrap, 1962, 45s. An excellent guide to one hundred walks and easy climbs.

Im Steilen Eis,* E. Vanis, B.L.V., Munich, 1964, 45s. Fifty ice climbs.

Guide-books (§ 115) and other books relating to particular areas are listed in the relevant sections below. The prices vary somewhat from shop to shop but those included should serve as a rough guide. Many of the titles given are out of print at present (in which case no price is given), but they have been included to give as complete a picture as possible: they may still be obtainable from libraries or second-hand, and most of the guide-books are likely to come into print

---

* These are typical of a half a dozen books in this series, which give brief details and a photograph of each route, with a diagram of the surrounding area. With the exception of *Salute the Mountains* they are all in German, but the presentation is so simple that even non-German speakers will usually be able to understand the essentials.

again in the future. In addition the magazines or journals published by the Continental alpine clubs and by the Alpine Club and Alpine Climbing Group (see bibliography, 1) are invaluable sources of up-to-date information, and the back-numbers are very useful for areas where the guide-books are out of date. The Continental alpine clubs and State Tourist Offices (appendix D) usually issue short brochures on request. The Michelin Green Guides (in English) to the French Alps, Switzerland, and Austria give useful background information, though they are for the tourist, not the mountaineer. The old Baedeker's guides for walkers are still extremely useful, though unfortunately long out of print.

Maps (§ 115). The relevant large-scale maps are listed in the appropriate sections, the best size being 1 : 25,000 which is now becoming more widely available, especially in Switzerland. As usual, the abbreviations used are in the index; the full addresses of the publishers are in appendix D.

§ 142. Western subsidiary Alps (France, Italy, and Switzerland)

To the south and west of the main alpine areas of Mont Blanc (§ 146) and the Dauphiné (§ 143) there are extensive smaller mountains, including the Maritime Alps, the Ligurian Alps, the Cottian Alps (which have however a major peak – Monte Viso, 3,841 m.), the Préalpes du Nord, and the Hautes Alpes Calcaires. These give a great variety of rock climbing, ranging from the Calanques (the sea-cliffs near Marseille) to the Salève (just south of Geneva). The cliffs of Vercors (between Aspres and Grenoble) and the Chartreuse (between Grenoble and Chambéry) afford very steep limestone climbing, similar in character to the Dolomites (§ 156) or the Kaisergebirge (§ 155) though shorter. Some of these subsidiary mountains (but especially the Maritime Alps) may be worth visiting when bad weather puts Mont Blanc and the Dauphiné out of condition.

Map 4. *Main alpine climbing areas.*

GERM

SWITZERLAND

☐ Zurich

☐ Bern

18

19

UPPER
ENGADINE

12
URI ALPS
11   13

☐ Grindelwald

17   ☐ St Moritz

ORTLE

10
BERNESE ALPS

LEPONTINE
ALPS

9   ☐ Brig   14   15 16   ADAMELL

☐ Geneva

NORTHERN
PRE-ALPS

3   ☐ Zermatt

☐ Chamonix   PENNINE ALPS   GRIGNE

MONT   7   8
BLANC   ☐ Courmayeur

2   5   6

☐ Grenoble   GRAIANS   ☐ Milan

1   ITA

☐ Turin

DAUPHINÉ
4

COTTIAN
ALPS

FRANCE

MARITIME
ALPS

MEDITERRANEAN SEA

WESTERN SUBSIDIARY ALPS (§1
1. Vercors
2. Grande Chartreuse
3. Hautes Alpes Calcaires

DAUPHINÉ (§143)
4. Barre des Écrins

GRAIANS (§§144 and 145)
5. Grande Casse
6. Gran Paradiso

MONT BLANC RANGE (§146)
7. Mont Blanc

PENNINE ALPS (§147)
8. Monte Rosa

BERNESE ALPS (§147)
9. Western areas
10. Bernese Oberland

URI ALPS, etc. (§149)
11. South of Susten Pass
12. Engelberg
13. Tödi

LEPONTINE ALPS (§150)
14. Rheinwaldhorn

VAL BREGAGLIA AND UPPER ENGADINE (§151)
15. Bregaglia
16. Bernina
17. Albula

GRIGNE (§152)

ADAMELLO-PRESANELLA (§153)

ORTLES (§154)

AUSTRIA (§155)
18. Rätikon
19. Silvretta
20. Ötztal
21. Stubai
22. Karwendelgebirge
23. Kaisergebirge
24. Zillertal
25. Glockner
26. Lienz Dolomites

DOLOMITES (§156)
27. Brenta
28. Catinaccio
29. Sassolungo-Sella
30. Marmolata
31. Pala
32. Civetta
33. Cinque Torre
34. Tofana
35. Sorapis
36. Tre Cime

JULIAN ALPS (§157)
37. Triglav

MILES

50   0   50

50   0   50
KILOMETRES

MAPS

I.G.N. 1:50,000, 1:25,000, and 1:20,000 series
I.G.M. 1:100,000 and 1:25,000 series
L.K. 1:50,000 series and 1:25,000 (Dents du Midi)
DIDIER ET RICHARD (special walkers'/climbers' maps –
appendix D, 3) 1:50,000 series including Vercors, Chartreuse–
Sept Laux, Alpes Maritimes, and (1:25,000) Belledone-
Taillefer
Cartes Paschetta des Alpes Maritimes, 1:50,000. By Girard et
Barrière, 17 rue de l'Ancienne Comédie, Paris 6

BOOKS

1. *Alpine Club – West Col guide-books* (appendix B, 5)
   Dents du Midi Region (the Hautes Alpes Calcaires), 1967, 18s.
   Selected Climbs in the Dauphiné (see § 143) *and Vercors*, 1967, 28s.
   Maritime Alps – Vésubie basin and Argentera, 1968, 25s.

2. *Escalades Choisies du Léman à la Méditerranée*, G.H.M., Arthaud
   (in French)
   Vol. 1, *Alpes du Nord*, 1947
   Vol. 2, *Alpes du Sud*, 1947

3. *Guide des Varappes du Salève*, 1965, 20s. (Available from
   Rother, Munich)

4. *Guida dei monti d'Italia*, C.A.I.–T.C.I. (in Italian)
   Alpi Marittime, 1934

5. *Guides des Calanques*, C.A.F., Provence (from 1 rue des Feuillants,
   Marseille, France) (in French). A series of short guide-
   books

6. *Guide-book by F.F.M.* (in French)
   Guide des escalades du Vercors et de la Chartreuse, S. Coupé, 1963,
   25s.

7. *Guides Paschetta (Randonnées et Alpinisme) des Alpes Maritimes*,
   (3 vols.). C.A.F. and Tourist Office, 15 Avenue de la Victoire,
   Nice, 1965

8. *Guida da Rifugio a Rifugio*, C.A.I.–T.C.I. (in Italian). Walks and
   easy climbs
   Alpi Liguri e Marittime, 1958, 80s.
   Alpi Cozie, 1959, 80s.

§ 143. The Dauphiné (France)

The Dauphiné, to the south-east of Grenoble, is a compact area with climbs of all types and standards. The mountains are big and, like those in other major areas, pose difficult problems of route-finding and weather. Some of them are rather loose. The easier routes, however, given care, can provide good first- or second-season climbs. The two highest peaks are the Barre des Écrins (4,101 m.), which is fairly easy by the normal route on its north face and west ridge, and the Meije (3,983 m.), the traverse of which is one of the finest alpine classics, for experienced alpinists only. The Pic Coolidge (3,774 m.), by its south ridge, is one of the easiest climbs in the area. The Aiguille Dibona is a popular subsidiary peak, with good rock. La Bérarde is the best single centre (there is a C.A.F. hut), but the area is complicated and no one base serves all the climbs.

MAPS

    I.G.N. 1:50,000, *Orcierès, La Mure, St Christophe en Oisans, Briançon,* and *La Grave.* 1:20,000 series as eight subdivisions of each of these

    DIDIER ET RICHARD (special walkers'/climbers' maps – appendix D, 3) 1:50,000, *Haut Dauphiné*

BOOKS

1. *Alpine Club – West Col guide-book* (appendix B, 5)
   Selected Climbs in the Dauphiné and (see § 142) *Vercors,* 1968, 28s.

2. *Guide Vallot du Massif des Écrins,* G.H.M., Arthaud (in French)
   Vol. 1, *Meije–Écrins,* 1969, 70s. (North and east of La Bérarde)
   Vol. 2, *Ailefroide, Pelvoux, Les Bans, l'Olan,* 1951. (South of La Bérarde). Revised ed. due 1970

3. *Kleiner Westalpenführer,* Rother (in German)
   Haut Dauphiné (Devies/Laloue), 1961, 16s.

4. *Other books*
   High Heaven, Jacques Boell, Elek, 1947
   La Barre des Écrins, H. Isselin, Arthaud, 1954 (in French)

La Meije, H. Isselin, Arthaud, 1968 (in French)
Haut Dauphiné, F. German, Arthaud, 1955 (in French)

§ 144. Western and central Graians (France)

These mountains, the Maurienne, Vanoise, and Tarentaise,
to the north of the Dauphiné (§ 143), give plenty of high
walking and some climbing, usually quite easy and suitable
for novices. The Grande Casse (3,852 m.) is perhaps the best
peak, the north face being a classic climb. There is some
hard rock climbing on the Aiguille de Vanoise. Pralognan
is a good centre for the Vanoise, and Val-d'Isère for the
Tarentaise. The whole area is relatively unfrequented.

MAPS

    I.G.N. 1:50,000, *Lanslebourg, Tignes, Moûtiers, Modane,* and
       St Foy–Tarentaise. 1:20,000 series as eight subdivisions of
       each of these

    DIDIER ET RICHARD (special walkers'/climbers' maps –
       appendix D, 3) 1:50,000 *Vanoise*

BOOKS

1. *West Col guide-book* (appendix B, 5)
    Graians West (Tarentaise and Maurienne)

2. *Guide Vallot* (in French)
    Guide de la Tarentaise et Maurienne (2 vols.)

3. *Guide Gaillard* (in French). From Imprimeries Réunies de
      Chambéry, 3 rue Lamartine, Chambéry 73, France
    Le Massif de Vanoise, au nord du Col de la Vanoise, 1969, 40s.

4. *Other books*
    Mountain Holidays, Janet Adam Smith, Dent, 1946
    Savoy Episode, H. Merrick, Hale, 1946

§ 145. The eastern Graians (Italy)

These mountains, to the south of Aosta, are mostly easy and
are thus suitable for novices, or when bad weather puts
Mont Blanc (§ 146) and the Pennine Alps (§ 147) out of
condition. The Gran Paradiso (4,061 m.) is the principal

peak, extremely easy by its ordinary route. The Grivola and the Herbetet give some difficult climbs.

MAPS

Bottega d'Arte, Courmayeur, 1:120,000 *Carte Touristique de la Vallée d'Aosta*

I.G.M. 1:100,000 No. 41 *Gran Paradiso*. 1:25,000 series as sixteen subdivisions of this. Main ones are: *Gran Paradiso, Torre del Gran San Pietro, La Grivola, Cogne* and *Ceresole Reale*

KOMPASS 1:50,000 No. 86

BOOKS

1. *West Col guide-book* (appendix B, 5)
   Graians East (Gran Paradiso area), 1969, 32s. 6d.

2. *Guida dei monti d'Italia*, C.A.I.–T.C.I. (in Italian)
   Gran Paradiso, 1963

3. *Guida della Valle di Cogne* (in Italian). Edizioni S.P.E. di Carlo Fantin, Turin

4. *Kleine Führer*, Rother (in German)
   Gran Paradiso, Gegenfurtner, 1966, 10s. With 1:100,000 map

5. *Guida da Rifugio a Rifugio*, C.A.I.–T.C.I. (in Italian). Walks and easy climbs
   Alpi Graie, 1963, 100s.

§ 146. Mont Blanc range (France, Italy, and Switzerland)

The Mont Blanc massif provides climbing second to none both on rock and on snow and ice. The discriminating can find easy routes, but in general the standard of the climbing is high. The rock is mostly granite and usually very rough and reliable; the cracks take pegs well. The rock climbs tend to be steep and strenuous, with cracks, chimneys, and *dièdres* (§§ 45–6) predominating. Although there are some climbs which do not require a high level of rock technique, it is necessary to be able to lead at Severe, and preferably Very Severe, standard to do most of the usual rock climbs well. Many of the climbs involve mild rope manœuvres and there is a good deal of abseiling.

Chamonix is the main centre on the north side (France). Cheap accommodation is available at the Refuge des Amis de la Montagne, the Chalet-Refuge Premier de Cordée and a special Alpine Centre at Argentière, opened in 1972. Most British climbers however camp at Les Houches, Les Praz, or Argentière. Chamonix has very good equipment shops (English is spoken at Snell Sports) and there is also a local Club Alpin Français office. Courmayeur, which is rather smaller than Chamonix, is the main centre on the south side (Italy) but it is cheaper and easier to stay at La Palud, or at the good camp site at Purtud. In Courmayeur, a very good equipment shop is that of the late Toni Gobbi.

The Mont Blanc massif has a road tunnel (Chamonix–Courmayeur) and also several important *téléphériques* (e.g. Chamonix–Aiguille du Midi–Col du Géant–Courmayeur) which bring all parts of the massif except the south-west side of Mont Blanc (from the Peuterey ridge to the Miage glacier) and the south-easterly peaks (Mont Dolent, etc.) within fairly easy reach of Chamonix, albeit at some expense. The main areas in the massif, from west to east, are as follows:

Mont Blanc (4,807 m.; 15,770 ft). The highest mountain·in western Europe. It is not technically difficult by the normal routes, but it is very vulnerable to bad weather and bad conditions. The south face routes (the Brenva face climbs, and the Peuterey, Innominata, and Brouillard ridges) are among the longest and highest climbs in the Alps. There is excellent hard rock climbing on the subsidiary peaks, such as the Aiguille Noire de Peuterey and Mont Blanc du Tacul [147].

Géant–Rochefort–Grandes Jorasses [130]. The ordinary routes are not hard, but these also are big mountains and require experienced judgement. The Grandes Jorasses has some of the greatest climbs in the Alps on its north face (which includes the famous Walker Spur) and on its east face. The

Courmayeur side of the Rochefort group has given some new routes to British climbers recently.

The Chamonix Aiguilles [146], which include the Grands Charmoz, Grépon, Blaitière, and Plan, give superb rock climbing, and also hard ice climbing. Most climbs are 2,000–4,000 ft long.

The Aiguille Verte group includes the Droites and the Courtes which have some fairly easy ridges. The Aiguille Verte itself is a magnificent peak with no really easy routes: its Whymper Couloir has been the scene of many accidents in descent (§ 136). The Dru has excellent long rock climbs of all standards above Severe. The Moine, which is relatively low, offers a good first acquaintance with the group.

Chardonnet–Argentière. The Chardonnet has the Forbes Arête [141], one of the best of the easier mixed climbs in the range. The north faces of both mountains give an introduction to the harder ice climbing.

Triolet, Leschaux, and Mont Gruetta. Perhaps the most remote and least frequented peaks in the range and hence for experienced parties only.

The Aiguilles Dorées and du Tour, and Mont Dolent, are on the Franco–Swiss–Italian border at the east end of the range. The area gives easier climbing than the rest of the range and is very suitable for a first season. There is a climbing school at La Fouly, near Champex in the Swiss Val Ferret (appendix D, 9).

MAPS

I. L.K. I : 100,000 No. 46 covers the whole area except for the extreme west, for which see No. 45

    I : 50,000 No. 5003 (Mont Blanc–Grand Combin). Nos. 292 (for Western areas) and 282 (for N.E. areas). No. 292 is also available in syntosil by Kümmerly & Frey

    I : 25,000 No. 1344 (*Col de Balme*) and 1345 (*Orsières*). No. 1364 (*Mont Blanc*) in preparation

2. I.G.N. 1:50,000, *St Gervais les Bains, Mont Blanc* and *Chamonix*.
1:20,000 series as eight subdivisions of each of these. Main
ones are: *St Gervais les Bains Nos. 4* and *8, Mont Blanc Nos. 1*
and *2,* and *Chamonix Nos. 5* and *6.* This series is not as clear
as the L.K. 1:25,000 because of its reliance on contours
instead of hachuring. 1:10,000 series of *Mont Blanc* now being
introduced in twenty-four sheets, of which about ten cover
the main climbing areas; those for Aiguille du Midi and
Aiguille Verte now published

3. DIDIER ET RICHARD (special walkers'/climbers' maps – appendix D, 3) 1:50,000 *Mont Blanc–Beaufortin*

4. I.G.M. 1:25,000 Carte del Monte Bianco (six sheets)
1:25,000 Nos. 27 (*Mt Bianco–Courmayeur*) and 28 (*La Vachey*)

5. T.C.I. 1:50,000 No. 12 *Gruppo del Monte Bianco*

BOOKS

1. *Alpine Club – West Col guide-book* (appendix B, 5)
Selected climbs in the Mont Blanc Range
Vol. 1, *Col de la Seigne to Col du Géant,* 1967, 35s.
Vol. 2, *Col du Géant to north-east end,* 1967, 28s.

2. *Guide Vallot: La Chaîne du Mont Blanc,* G.H.M., Arthaud (in
French)
Vol. 1, *Mont Blanc-Trélatête,* 1956
Vol. 2, *Aiguilles de Chamonix–Grandes Jorasses,* 1956
Vol. 3, *Aiguille Verte–Dolent–Argentière–Trient,* 1967

3. *Guide Vallot,* Librairie Fischbacher (in French)
Les Aiguilles Rouges de Chamonix, 1946, 25s.

4. *Kleiner Westalpenführer,* Rother (in German)
Montblanc-Gruppe, Königer, 1967, 18s.

5. *Guide Vallot,* Arthaud (in French). For walkers
Chamonix–Mt Blanc–St Gervais, 55s.

6. *Guida dei monti d'Italia,* C.A.I.-T.C.I. (Italian)
Monte Bianco, Vol. 1, Col de la Seigne–Col du Géant, 1963, 85s.
Vol. 2, Col du Géant–Col de Grapillon, 1968, 90s.

7. *Constable Alpine guide-book* (general information and walking)
Chamonix–Mont Blanc, Collomb, 1969, 30s.

8. *Guide Pédestre*, Kümmerly & Frey. For walkers
   Vol. 1 (International series), *Tour du Mont Blanc* (French and
   German editions)

9. *Other books*
   Mont Blanc and the Aiguilles, C. D. Milner, Hale, 1955, 30s.
   Mt Blanc and the Seven Valleys, R. Frison Roche, Kaye, 1961, 45s.
   Mont Blanc: an Anthology, Claire E. Engel, Allen & Unwin,
      1965, 54s.
   Mountaineering Holiday, F. S. Smythe, Hodder & Stoughton, 1950
   Brenva, Dr T. Graham-Brown, Dent, 1944
   Les Aiguilles de Chamonix, H. Isselin, Arthaud, 1961 (in French)

§ 147. The Pennine Alps (Switzerland and Italy)

This is the whole range between the Grand St Bernard Pass
and the Simplon. It has more mountains over 4,000 m. than
any other alpine group, and includes the highest summit in
Switzerland (Monte Rosa, 4,634 m.). On the ordinary
routes, the technical difficulty of the rock climbing is not
great and it is rarely necessary to climb at over Very
Difficult standard. On the other hand the length of the
climbs necessitates a good deal of moving together in
exposed positions on rock and snow and ice, and the higher
routes tend to be serious. Most British climbers base themselves in the Swiss – as distinct from the Italian – valleys
because of their easier access. The main bases from west to
east are as follows:

Arolla. An excellent area for beginners, perhaps the best in
Switzerland, with a mountain school. The peaks are not
very high, nor are they difficult or complicated. The Pigne
d'Arolla (3,796 m.) is an easy snow climb and Mont Blanc
de Cheilon offers an attractive traverse. The Petite Dent de
Veisivi and the Aiguilles Rouges d'Arolla (longer) give
pleasant rock climbing. Most people camp while in the
valley.

Zinal has some easy climbs, such as the popular Besso
(3,667 m.), and also a circle of bigger and more difficult

mountains, e.g. the Ober Gabelhorn (4,063 m.) the Zinal Rothorn (4,221 m.), and the Weisshorn. The north ridge of the Rothorn is a most attractive climb of moderate difficulty.

Zermatt is overlooked by the Matterhorn, and surrounded by 4,000 m. peaks: indeed, most of the major peaks of the Pennines are easily accessible. There is little at low altitude, but several of the high peaks are not difficult (e.g. Allalinhorn, Rimpfischhorn, Strahlhorn, and Breithorn). It is the only centre in the Pennines ranking as an international holiday resort, with all that that entails in high prices. Many British climbers stay at the Bahnhof Hotel, which is cheap and has cooking facilities. There is a camp site just below the village, with access for cars; many climbers however leave their cars at St Niklaus and take the train.

The Saas Valley gives good access to some of the east Zermatt peaks (Allalinhorn, Alphubel, Lenzspitze, Nadelhorn) and also has a range of peaks of its own including the Weissmies. There are several useful rock climbs at lower altitude such as the Jagigrat and the Portjengrat. Quite a good area for beginners. Saas-Fee is the best-known centre, but Saas-Almagell and Saas-Grund are better placed for some of the climbs.

Macunagna (Italy) is ideal for the climbs on the Macunagna face of Monte Rosa, which are comparable with those on the Brenva face of Mont Blanc [138], but they are also accessible in a long day from Zermatt.

MAPS
1. L.K. 1 : 100,000 Nos. 46 (for Chamonix–Zermatt) and 47 (for Monte Rosa).
   1 :50,000 Nos. 282 (for Grand Combin), 283 (for Arolla–Zinal), 284 (for east of Zinal, Zermatt, and west of Saas-Fee), and 285 (for Saas-Fee). The Italian side is covered by Nos. 293 (*Valpelline* – south of Arolla) and 294 (*Gressoney* – south of Zermatt)
   1 :50,000 special series Nos. 5003 (for western Swiss areas) and

5006 (for eastern Swiss areas). No. 5006 also available in syntosil by Kümmerley & Frey

1 : 25,000 Nos. 1326 (*Rosablanche*), 1346 (*Chanrion*), 1328 (*Randa*) and 1348 (*Zermatt*). Others planned include: Nos. 1366 (*Mt Vélan*), 1347 (*Matterhorn*) and 1329 (*Saas*)

2. I.G.M. 1 : 100,000 Nos. 28 (western Italian areas), 29 (central Italian areas), and 30 (eastern Italian areas). 1 : 25,000 series as sixteen subdivisions of each of these. Main ones are: *Prarayer, M. Cervino, Breithorn, M. Rosa, Macunagna*, and *Pizzo Bottarello*

3. T.C.I. 1 : 50,000 No. 3, *Il Cervino et il Monte Rosa*

BOOKS

1. *Alpine Club – West Col guide-book* (appendix B, 5)
   Selected Climbs in the Pennine Alps
   Vol. 1, *Saas Fee, Zermatt and Zinal*, 1968, 37s. 6d.
   Vol. 2, *Arolla and Western Ranges*, 1968, 28s.

2. *Guide des Alpes Valaisannes*, S.A.C. (in French: published also in German as *Walliser Führer*)
   Vol. 1, *Ferret to Collon*, 1963, 35s. Reprint of 1937 ed. with supplement
   Vol. 2, *Collon to Theodul*, 1947, 35s.
   Vol. 3a, *Theodul to Monte Moro*, 1952 } Sold together for
   Vol. 3b, *Strahlhorn to Simplon*, 1952 }   45s.

3. *Guida dei monti d'Italia*, C.A.I.–T.C.I. (in Italian)
   Monte Rosa, 1960, 65s.

4. *Kleiner Westalpenführer*, Rother (in German)
   Walliser Alpen, Königer, 1966, 15s.

5. *Constable Alpine Guide* (general information and walking)
   Zermatt and District, Collomb, 1969, 30s.

6. *Guides Pédestres: Wanderbücher*, Kümmerly & Frey. For the walker
   Vol. 17 (Swiss series), *Val de Bagnes et d'Entremont* (in French). For western Pennines
   Vol. 12 (Swiss series). *Val d'Anniviers, Val d'Hérens* (in French and in German). For Arolla and Zinal
   Vol. 8 (Swiss series). *Vispertäler* (in German). For Zermatt and Saas-Fee

7. *Guida da Rifugio a Rifugio*, C.A.I.–T.C.I. (in Italian). Walks and
   easy climbs
   Alpi Pennine, 1951

8. *Other books*
   Man and the Matterhorn, Gaston Rébuffat, Nicholas Vane, 1967,
   63s.
   Walking in the Alps, J. H. Walker, Oliver & Boyd, 1951
   The Matterhorn, G. Rey, Blackwell, 1946
   Zermatt and the Valais, Sir Arnold Lunn, Hollis & Carter, 1955
   La Haute Route, André Roch, Marguérat, Lausanne, 1963, 75s.

§ 148. The Bernese Alps (Switzerland)

This range, to the north of the Rhône Valley, is rather lower
than the Pennine Alps (§ 147) but has much to commend it.
The climbing is not technically hard on the standard routes,
but the highest peaks are serious, largely because they get
some of the worst weather in the Alps. The region is in two
main parts.

The western Bernese Alps. This area, from St Maurice to the
Lötschberg Tunnel, gives fairly gentle climbing, mostly at
about 3,000 m. The main peaks are the Diablerets (3,209 m.),
the Wildstrubel (3,244 m.), and the Balmhorn (3,709 m.).
There is low-altitude rock climbing in the Argentine, to the
east of Bex, near St Maurice. It is a good area for a first
season.

The eastern Bernese Alps ('*The Bernese Oberland*')* has mainly
4,000 m. peaks, including the Finsteraarhorn (4,274 m.),
the Aletschhorn, the Jungfrau, and the Mönch. The Eiger
is only slightly lower. The area is bounded on the north by
the huge wall from Scheidegg to Meiringen which gives the
extremely impressive north-face climbs on the Jungfrau,

* Strictly, the Bernese Oberland is the whole area between Lake
Thun and Canton Valais, but mountaineers often refer to it in this
limited sense.

Mönch, Eiger, and Wetterhorn. The Engelhorner, south of
Meiringen, have plenty of very steep rock climbing, mostly
limestone. Grindelwald is perhaps the best centre, but it is
also possible to enter from the south through the Lötschental
or up the Aletsch glacier from Fiesch. The Baltschiedertal
has some fine rock climbing above Visp. There are mountaineering schools at Rosenlaui, Meiringen and at Fiesch
(appendix D, 9).

MAPS

1. L.K. 1:100,000 Nos. 41 (for western areas), 42 (for southern
   Oberland), and 37 (for northern Oberland)
   1:50,000 Nos. 272 and 263 (for western areas), 264 (for southern
   Oberland), 265 (for south-east Oberland), and 254 and 255
   (for northern Oberland)
   1:50,000 special series Nos. 5009 (for N.W. areas) and 5004
   (for N.E. areas)
   1:25,000 includes Nos. 1285 (*Les Diablerets*), 1266 (*Lenk*), 1267
   (*Gemmi*) and 1286 (*St Leonard*). Others in preparation
   Nos. 37, 41 and 255 are also available in syntosil by Kümmerly
   & Frey

2. KUMMERLY & FREY. 1:75,000. No. 20 *Berner Oberland:
   Lötschberg: Oberwallis*

BOOKS

1. *Alpine Club – West Col guide-books* (appendix B, 5)
   Selected Climbs in the Bernese Alps, 1968, 32s. 6d.
   Engelhörner and Salbitschijen, 1968, 25s.

2. *Bündnerführer*, S.A.C. (in German)
   Vol. 2, *Oberland und Rheinwaldgebiet*, 1951, 30s.

3. *Höchgebirgsführer durch die Berner Alpen*, S.A.C. Bern, A. Francke
   (in German)
   Vol. 1, *Diablerets bis Gemmi*, 1951, 25s.
   Vol. 2, *Gemmi bis Petersgrat*, 1966, 25s.
   Vol. 3, *Bietschhorn, Breithorn, Nesthorn, Aletschhorn*, 1948, 25s.
   Vol. 4, *Petersgrat–Finsteraarjoch–Unteres Studerjoch*, 1964, 31s. For
   Jungfrau, Eiger, and Mönch
   Vol. 5, *Grindelwald–Meiringen–Grimsel–Münster*, 1964, 35s.

4. *Bergsteiger Führer*, Rother, Munich (in German)
   Berner Alpen, Königer, 1967, 38s.

5. *Guide-book by S.A.C.* (in French)
   Guide de l'Argentine, 1944, 10s.

6. *Guide des Alpes Vaudoises*, S.A.C. (in French)
   Dents de Morcles–Sanetsch, 1946, 15s.

7. *Guide-book by Akademischen Alpen Klub, Bern*, A. Francke (in German)
   Engelhornführer, 1954, 25s.

8. *Guides Pédestres: Wanderbücher*. Kümmerly & Frey. For the walker

   Vol. 3 (Bernese series), *Passrouten in Berner Oberland: À travers les cols de l'Oberland bernois*, German and French editions respectively

   Vol. 21 (Swiss series), *Valais Central* (for southern half of western areas). French

   Vol. 17 (Bernese series), *Obersimmental–Saanenland* (for northern half of western areas). German

   Vol. 15 (Swiss series), *Lötschberg* (for S.W. Oberland). German

   Vol. 19 (Swiss series), *Brig–Simplon–Goms* (for S.E. Oberland). German

   Vol. 11 (Bernese series), *Kandertal* (for N.W. Oberland). German

   Vol. 6 (Bernese series), *Lütschinertäler* (for northern Oberland). German

   Vol. 19 (Bernese series), *Oberhasli* (for N.E. Oberland). German

§ 149. Uri Alps and neighbouring areas (Switzerland)

These areas, to the east of the Oberland (§ 148) and to the north of the Lepontine Alps (§ 150) are rather lower than the main alpine areas, and hence may be worth a visit for novices or in a bad season. Much of the climbing is fairly easy snow and ice, but there is also a great deal of rock climbing, some of it of very high quality. There are plenty of huts, but in any case many of the rock climbs can be reached from the road. The main areas from south-west to north-east are as follows:

South of the Susten Pass. The Dammastock (3,630 m.) and other peaks to the north-east of Gletsch give snow and ice climbing, and also some very good rock climbs similar to those of the Chamonix Aiguilles (§ 146) though on a smaller scale. Further east, there is excellent low-altitude rock climbing near Göschenen, north-west of Andermatt, of which the best known is the Salbitschijen (2,950 m.) with its classic south ridge (T.D. *inf.*) and numerous harder climbs on good granite.

North of the Susten Pass (including the Engelberg). The main peak is Titlis (3,239 m.) which though fairly easy by its ordinary route also has hard limestone climbing. Engelberg is a central base.

Tödi Range. To the north-east of Andermatt is a considerable range of fairly easy peaks of which the highest is Tödi (3,620 m.).

MAPS

L.K. 1:100,000 Nos. 42 (for south of Susten Pass), 37 (for north of Susten Pass), and 38 (for Tödi)

1:50,000 Nos. 255 (for south of Susten Pass and Titlis), 245 (for north of Susten Pass), 246 and 256 (for Tödi group)

1:50,000 special series Nos. 5001 (for south of Susten Pass and Titlis) and 5008 (for north of Susten Pass)

1:25,000 includes Nos. 1211 (*Meiental*), 1231 (*Urseren*), 1232 (*Oberalppass*) and 1193 (*Tödi*)

Nos. 37, 255, 5001, 5008, 1193, 1231 and 1232 are also available in syntosil by Kümmerly & Frey

BOOKS

1. *West Col guide-books* (appendix B, 5)
   Central Switzerland (*Furka, Grimsel, Susten*), 1969, 38s.
   Engelhörner (see § 148) and *Salbitschijen*, 1968, 25s.

2. *Urnerführer*, S.A.C. (in German)
   Vol. 1, *Kaiserstock–Windgällen–Oberalpstock*, 1954, 26s.
   Vol. 2, *Urner Alpen West* (Gotthard–Titlis), 1966, 46s. Includes the main rock-climbing areas.

3. *Hochgebirgsführer Durch die Glarner Alpen*, S.A.C. (in German)
   Glarnerführer mit Skiführer, 1964, 35s. For Tödi

4. *Wanderbüch*, Kümmerly & Frey. For the walker
   Vol. 29 (Swiss series), *Uri*, in preparation

§ 150. The Lepontine Alps (Switzerland and Italy)

This is the large area to the north-east of the Pennines
(§ 147), between the Simplon Pass and the Splügen Pass,
(including the Ticino Alps). The highest peak is the
Rheinwaldhorn (3,398 m.) in the Adula district, south-east
of the St Gotthard Pass. In general there is not much of note
for the climber, but the scope for the hill walker is tremendous.

MAPS
   L.K. 1:100,000 Nos. 38 (for northern areas) and 43 (for
      southern areas)
   1:50,000 Nos. 265 (for areas west of the St Gotthard Pass), and
      266–7 (for areas east of the St Gotthard Pass)

BOOKS

1. *Guide des Alpes Valaisannes*, S.A.C. (in French: published also in
   German as *Walliser Führer*)
   Vol. 4, *Simplon–Furka*, 1920, 17s.

2. *Guide-books by S.A.C.*
   Alpi Ticinesi, 1932; 20s. (in Italian)
   Tessinerführer mit Skiführer, 1931 (in German)

3. *Bündnerführer*, S.A.C. (in German)
   Vol. 2, *Oberland und Rheinwaldgebiet*, 1951, 32s.

4. *Guida dei monti d'Italia*, C.A.I.–T.C.I. (in Italian)
   Alpi Lepontine Occidentali. In preparation
   Alpi Lepontine Orientali. In preparation

5. *Guida da Rifugio a Rifugio*, C.A.I.–T.C.I. (in Italian). Walks and
   easy climbs
   Alpi Lepontine, 1956
   Vol. 5, *Alpi Lepontine*, 1956, 55s.

6. *Other books*
   Walking in the Alps, J.H. Walker, Oliver & Boyd, 1951

§ 151. The Val Bregaglia and Upper Engadine (Switzerland and Italy)

This part of south-east Switzerland, to the south and north of St Moritz, is lower and warmer, and usually has better weather, than the Pennine Alps (§ 147) or the Oberland (§ 148). The Bernina and Albula groups are suitable for a first or second season since the climbing is fairly easy and the routes are not very complicated. The Bregaglia is more difficult, with many hard rock climbs. Details of the main groups from south-west to north-east are as follows.

Bregaglia. The Sciora cirque includes the north-east face of the Piz Badile, one of the classic harder routes of the Alps; but the other areas to its east, notably the Forno, Albigna and Allievi cirques, give excellent climbing too, sometimes on snow as well as rock.

Bernina. In this area, to the south of St Moritz, the main snow peaks are the Piz Bernina (4,049 m.: the most easterly alpine 4,000 m. peak), Piz Roseg, Piz Zupo, Bella Vista, and Piz Palu. Separate from the main group is Monte Disgrazia (3,678 m.). Pontresina is a good centre, and has a mountaineering school (appendix D, 9).

Albula. To the north of St Moritz and east of the Lepontine Alps (§ 150), this area, of which Piz Kesch (3,418 m.) is the principal summit, has plenty of easy climbing and glacier travel. It is, however, probably more worth while for the walker than for the climber.

MAPS
s.l.k. 1:100,000 No. 44
   1:50,000 Nos. 278 (for Bregaglia and Disgrazia), 268 (for Bernina), and 258 (for Albula)
   1:25,000 includes Nos. 1296 (*Sciora* – for the Piz Badile etc.), 1276 (*Val Bregaglia* – the valley only), 1277 (*Piz Bernina*) and 1237 (*Albulapass*). No. 1277 is also available in syntosil by Kümmerly & Frey

2. I.G.M. 1 : 100,000 No. 18 (for Badile and Disgrazia). 1 : 25,000
   series is much better value here. Main ones are *Pizzo Badile*,
   M. Disgrazia, *Passo del Muretto*, and *Pizzo Bernina*
3. F.B. 1 : 100,000 No. 51

BOOKS

1. *Alpine Club – West Col* guide-books (appendix B, 5)
   Bregaglia West (*Sciora, Badile, Cengalo*), 1967, 16s.
   Bregaglia East (*Maloja, Forno, Albigna, Disgrazia*), planned for
      1970
   Bernina Alps, 1968, 30s.

2. *Bündnerführer*, S.A.C. (German)
   Vol. 4, *Südliche Bergellerberge und M. Disgrazia*, 1966, 35s.
   Vol. 5, *Bernina-Gruppe*, 1954–5, 32s.
   Vol. 6, *Albula*, 1934, 28s.

3. *Guida dei monti d'Italia*, C.A.I.–T.C.I. (Italian)
   Masino–Bregaglia–Disgrazia, 1936
   Bernina Alps, 1968, 30s.

4. *Bergführer*, Rother (in German)
   Bergell, Nigg/Philipp, 1968, 20s.
   Bernina, Flaig, 1967, 22s.

5. *Guida da Rifugio a Rifugio*, C.A.I.–T.C.I. (Italian). Walks and
      easy climbs
   Alpi Retiche Occidentali, 1953, 55s.

6. *Wanderbüch*, Kümmerly & Frey, Bern (in German). For the
      walker
   Vol. 28 (Swiss series), *Bergell*
   Vol. 3 (Swiss series), *Oberengadin*

7. *Other books*
   Walking in the Alps, J. H. Walker, Oliver & Boyd, 1951

§ 152. The Grigne (Italy)

This very small area of low peaks, to the east of Lecco, has
some short rock climbs on good steep limestone. Useful in
bad weather or as training climbs.

MAPS

1. L.K. 1:100,000 No. 48

2. T.C.I. 1:20,000, *Gruppo delle Grigne*

3. KOMPASS 1:50,000 No. 91. In preparation

BOOK
    Guida dei monti d'Italia, C.A.I.–T.C.I. (Italian)
    Grigne, 1937

§ 153. Adamello–Presanella (Italy)

This range, south of the Ortles (§ 154) and immediately west of the Brenta Dolomites (§ 156), has easy climbs and glaciers. Interesting mainly for novices or hill walkers.

MAPS

1. I.G.M. 1:100,000 No. 20. 1:25,000: *Monte Adamello, Care Alto, Temu,* and *Cima Presanella*

2. F.B. 1:100,000 No. 50

3. T.C.I. 1:50,000 No. 14

4. KOMPASS 1:50,000 No. 71

5. O.A.V. 1:25,000 No. 49

BOOKS

1. *Guida dei monti d'Italia*, C.A.I.–T.C.I. (in Italian)
    Adamello, 1954, 65s.

2. *Kleiner Führer*, Rother (in German)
    Adamello–Presanella, Gatti, 1969, 10s.

3. *Guida da Rifugio a Rifugio*, C.A.I.–T.C.I. (in Italian). Walks and
      easy climbs
    Alpi Retiche Meridionali, 1954

4. *Other books*
    Walking in the Alps, J. H. Walker, Oliver & Boyd, 1951

§ 154. Ortles Group (Italy)

This area, to the east of St Moritz, reaches as far as Bolzano. The Ortles (3,899 m.) is the highest peak, but the valleys radiate from a central hub at Monte Cevedale (3,764 m.), further south. The climbs are mostly easy, comprising long ridge traverses and easy glaciers.

MAPS

1. I.I.G.M. 1 : 100,000 No. 9, and 1 : 25,000 series

2. F.B. 1 : 100,000 No. 46

3. T.C.I. 1 :50,000 No. 13

4. O.A.V. 1 :50,000 No. 48

BOOKS
1. *West Col guide-book* (appendix B, 5)
   Ortler Alps (*Ortles, Zebru, Trafoier wall, Cevedale*), 1968, 25s.

2. *Bergsteiger Führer*, Rother (in German)
   Ortler–Gruppe, Drescher, 1969, 38s.
   Also shorter version by same author, 1969, 12s.

3. *Guida da Rifugio a Rifugio*, C.A.I.–T.C.I. (in Italian). Walks and
      easy climbs
   Alpi Retiche Meridionali, 1954

4. *Other books*
   Walking in the Alps, J. H. Walker, Oliver & Boyd, 1951

§ 155. Austria

Austria has a great deal of snow and ice mountaineering, mainly in the Tirol; it is usually of a not very difficult kind, and hence is suitable for a first or second season. The Rätikon, Karwendelgebirge, and Kaisergebirge give excellent rock climbing on steep limestone, often exposed and strenuous; they come into condition early, and can conveniently be visited for training on the way to the Dolomites (§ 156) or when the higher peaks are out of condition. The scope for the hill walker is very considerable in all the areas; the days need not be long as the huts are plentiful and provide food. Austria has several climbing schools (appendix D). The main areas from west to east are as follows:

Rätikon. Between Klosters (Switzerland) and Feldkirch. This area has extensive hard limestone climbing.

Silvretta group. This gives easy climbing. The glaciers are mostly small and not difficult.

The Ötztal group, south-west of Innsbruck, culminates in the Wildspitze (3,774 m.). The glaciers are the biggest in the eastern Alps; although they are sometimes badly crevassed, the difficulties can usually be avoided, and they are thus suitable for novices.

The Stubai group, between the Ötztal group and the Brenner Pass, is mainly walking country, but there are also fairly easy snow and rock traverses.

Karwendelgebirge. About ten miles north of Innsbruck almost on the Austro-German frontier. There are plenty of short III and IV climbs, while the famous Lalider Wall (about 2,500 ft high) has many long, hard ones. Pegs are used, but free pitches are often long.

Kaisergebirge. About forty-five miles east of Innsbruck. There are two main areas, the Zahmer Kaiser and the Wilder Kaiser, of which the latter gives the better climbing; best approached from St Johan. The rock is excellent although there is a good deal of rubble on ledges and in gullies, especially on the easier routes. Most climbs are 1,000–1,500 ft long. The best ones are V and VI, mainly free climbing.

Zillertal. This area, to the east of the Brenner Pass, has some of the best snow and ice climbing in Austria, including some long and fairly difficult routes. It is perhaps more suitable for experienced alpinists than for novices. The main peaks are the Hoch Feiler (3,510 m.), Moesele, Schwartzenstein, and Grosser Löffler.

Glockner group. This gives easy climbing but includes the highest mountain in Austria (Grossglockner, 3,797 m.).

Lienz Dolomites. These give limestone climbing of a not very difficult kind.

MAPS

1. O.A.V. 1:600,000 Hut map of all Austria
   1:25,000 Nos. 26 (*Silvretta*), 30/1–4 (*Ötztal*), 31/1–2 (*Stubai*), 5/1–3 (*Karwendelgebirge*), 8 (*Kaisergebirge*), 35/1–3 (*Zillertal*), 40 (*Glockner*), and 56 (*Lienz Dolomites*)

2. KOMPASS 1:50,000 Nos. 32 (*Rätikon*), 41 (*Silvretta*), 43 (*Ötztal*), 36 (for Stubai), 26 (*Karwendelgebirge*), 9 (*Kaisergebirge*), 37 (*Zillertal*), and 39 (*Glockner*)

3. F.B. 1:100,000 Nos. 37 (*Rätikon-Silvretta*), 25 (*Ötztal*), 24 (*Stubai*), 32 (*Karwendelgebirge*), 30 (*Kaisergebirge*), 15 (*Zillertal*), 12 (*Glockner*), and 18 (*Lienz Dolomites*).
   1:50,000 Nos. 371 (for Rätikon) and 373 (for Silvretta).

4. L.K. 1:50,000 Nos. 238 (for Rätikon) and 249 (for Silvretta)
   1:25,000 Nos. 1136 and 1156 (for Rätikon) and 1198 (for Silvretta)

BOOKS

1. *Austrian Alpine Club* (O.A.V.) (appendix B, 2)
   Taschenbüch (in German), annual, 5s. Details of huts etc.

2. *West Col guide-books* (appendix B, 5)
   Silvretta Alps, planned for 1970
   Ötztal Alps, 1968, 33s.
   Kaisergebirge, planned for 1970
   Zillertal Alps, planned for 1970

3. *Felix Austria guide-books*. Tallantire. Hut to hut touring and climbing up to Grade III. From Austrian A.C. (appendix B, 2)
   Vol. 1, *Venediger region*, 1965, 11s.
   Vol. 2, *Zillertal Alps*, 1966. Reprint due 1970
   Vol. 3, *Niederen and Hohen Tauern*, 1968, 31s.

Vol. 4, *Pitztal – East and West*, 1966, 16s.
Further volumes in preparation

4. *Alpenvereinsführer*, Rother, Munich (in German)
   Rätikon (Flaig), 1966, 38s.
   Silvretta (Flaig), 1966, 41s.
   Ötztaler Alpen (Klier/Prochaska), 1968, 37s.
   Stubaier Alpen (Rabensteiner/Klier), 1967, 41s.
   Wettersteingebirge (Pfanzelt), 1966, 38s.
   Wettersteingebirge 2 (Spindler/Trautman), 1958, 19s.
   Karwendelgebirge (Klier/März), 1969, 41s.
   Kaisergebirge (Leuchs/Nieberl), 1967, 30s.
   Zillertaler Alpen (Klier), 1966, 41s.
   Glockner-Gruppe (Lienbacher/Peterka), 1969, 38s.
   Venediger (Peterka), 1969, 41s.

5. *Kleiner Führer*, Rother, Munich (in German)
   Silvretta (Flaig), 1968, 8s.
   Ötztaler Alpen (Lienbacher), 1967, 14s.
   Stubaier Alpen (Klein), 1968, 14s.
   Karwendelführer (Klier/März), 1966, 14s.
   Wetterstein (Volk), 1965, 12s.
   Kaiserführer (Schmitt), 1967, 10s.
   Zillertaler Alpen (Raitmayr), 1967, 12s.
   Glockner–Venediger (Lienbacher), 1967, 16s.

6. *Bündnerführer*, S.A.C. (in German)
   Vol. 7, *Rätikon*, 1936, 25s.
   Vol. 8, *Silvretta und Samnaun*, 1934

7. *Other books*
   Walking in the Alps, J. H. Walker, Oliver & Boyd, 1951. For
   Ötztal and Stubai groups
   Over Tyrolese Hills, F. S. Smythe, Hodder & Stoughton, 1936

§ 156. The Dolomites (Italy)

The limestone of the Dolomites gives rock climbing of all
standards, both free and artificial. It is usually very steep –
indeed often overhanging – with massive exposure. On most
of the easier routes the rock is good, but it is often doubtful
on the harder ones. There is a lot of rubble in the gullies
and on the ledges. Pitons are used extensively both for
belays and for artificial climbing; the rock takes them well,

but the pegging on the harder routes is often insecure because of the poor quality of the rock. Route-finding is complex on the easier routes (which usually involve a good deal of traversing) but may be more straightforward on climbs with a greater number of pitons in place. The almost complete absence of snow and glaciers makes it unnecessary to start before dawn, but in hot weather it is as well to complete south-facing climbs early to avoid the fierce midday sun. Contrary to popular opinion, the weather is no better in the Dolomites than in the higher alpine areas; June and September are the best months. Huts are plentiful and luxurious, but there are no 'self-cooking' facilities. Of the many areas in the Dolomites, the following are perhaps the main ones, from west to east. The focal points are Trento, Bolzano, and Cortina d'Ampezzo.

The Brenta group, to the north-west of Trento, is by far the most extensive, and also the most westerly, of the Dolomites, bordering on the igneous Adamello–Presanella group (§ 153). It has quite a number of short III and IV routes on good rock (as well as harder ones) and is thus suitable for a first visit. There are some small glaciers and ice couloirs. The weather tends to be worse here than in the rest of the Dolomites.

Catinaccio. This group is relatively low and has numerous short but worth-while routes. Good for a first visit or bad weather.

Sassolungo and Sella includes the famous Sella Towers, which give mostly short climbs of III and IV. Sassolungo is more serious.

Marmolata. The highest peak in the Dolomites (3,344 m.) with a glacier on top. Has some extremely long, hard climbs. The ordinary route on the south face of the Marmolata is a Grade IV classic.

The Pala group is relatively unvisited, but has worth-while climbs of all standards.

The Civetta group has a very large number of long hard climbs, mainly free climbing on good rock. This is the main centre of Dolomite climbing.

The Cinque Torre, south-east of Cortina, have short climbs of all standards. A good introductory area.

Tofana group, to the north-west of Cortina. Fairly long climbs.

Sorapiss, to the south-east of Cortina. Long climbs, with some snow and ice.

The Tre Cime Di Lavaredo. Perhaps the most famous of the Dolomites, this group has a great deal of climbing of all types and qualities (including the north face of the Cime Grande, one of the classic north faces of the Alps). As with most other Dolomite areas, much of the rock is not good. The area becomes extremely crowded in July and August.

MAPS

1. I.I.G.M. 1:100,000 Nos. 20 (Brenta), 11 (W. Dolomites, including Marmolata), and 12 (E. Dolomites, including Tre Cime). 1:25,000 series as sixteen subdivisions of each of these numbers

2. F.B. 1:100,000 Nos. 50 (Brenta), 16 (W. Dolomites), and 17 (E. Dolomites)

3. T.C.I. 1:50,000 Nos. 15 (Brenta), 5 (Sella–Catinaccio–Marmolata), 10 (San Martino and Pala), and 1 (Cortina d'Ampezzo and Dolomiti Cadorine)

4. O.A.V. 1:25,000 Nos. 51 (Brenta), 52/1b (Catinaccio), 52/1bb (Sella), 52/1c (Marmolata), 52/1cc (Pala)

5. KOMPASS 1:50,00 Nos 53 (Brenta), 54 (Catinaccio and Sassolungo), and 55 (Marmolata and eastern groups to Tre Cime). 1:15,000–30,000 No. 565 (Brenta)

BOOKS

1. *Alpine Club – West Col guide-book* (appendix B, 5)
   Selected Climbs in the Dolomites
   Vol. 1, *East*, 1970, 40s.
   Vol. 2, *West*, 1970, 38s.

2. *Guida dei monti d'Italia*, C.A.I.–T.C.I. (in Italian)
   Dolomiti di Brenta, 1949
   Sassolungo–Catinaccio–Latemar, 1942
   Odle–Sella–Marmolata, 1937
   Pale di San Martino, 1935
   Dolomiti Orientali, Part 1, 1950
                          Part 2, 1961, 70s.

3. *Dolomiten–Kletterführer*, Rother (in German)
   Part 1a, *Rosengarten–Schlern, Geisler- und Puezgruppe, Langkofel,*
      1969, 33s.
   Part 1b, *Sella, Marmolata, Pala*, 1969, 33s.
   Part 2a, *Nordöstliche Dolomiten* (Langes), 1964, 34s.
   Part 2b, *Civetta, Monfalcone, Schiara* (Hiebeler), 1964, 40s.
   Part 3, *Brenta-Gruppe* (Wels), due 1969

4. *Guida da Rifugio a Rifugio*, C.A.I.–T.C.I. (in Italian). Walks and
      easy climbs
   Alpi Retiche Meridionale (for Brenta), 1954
   Dolomiti Occidentali, 1953
   Dolomiti Orientali, 1955

5. *Wanderbüch* (in German). For the walker
   Dolomiten–Wanderbüch, Delago, Freytag-Berndt, 1967, 36s.
   Dolomiten–Bergwanderführer, Hager, Rother, 1968, 19s.
   Brenta, Gatti, Rother, 1969, 12s.
   Pala, Gatti, Rother, 1960, 8s.
   Vom Rosengarten zur Marmolata, Hager, Rother, 1966, 12s.

6. *Other books*
   The Dolomites, C.D. Milner, Hale, 1951; 25s. Many pictures

§ 157. The Julian Alps (Yugoslavia and Italy)

This range, to the north of Trieste, gives good limestone
climbing similar to the Dolomites (§ 156). The highest peak

is Triglav (2,863 m.), a spectacular and beautiful mountain. Many of the ordinary routes are made easy by an abundance of fixed ropes and cut-out holds, but there is a good deal of hard climbing on the faces. It is a fine area for those who prefer to be off the beaten track, but in 1964 the huts were not good.

MAPS

F.B. 1:100,000 No. 14

OESTERR. WANDERKARTE 1:50,000 No. 210 (for Triglav)

BOOKS

1. *Bergsteigerführer*, Rother (in German)
   Julische Alpen, Schöner, 1966, 38s.

2. *Guida dei monti d'Italia*, C.A.I.–T.C.I. (in Italian)
   Alpi Giule. In preparation

3. *Other books*
   Alpine Pilgrimage, J. Kugy, Murray, 1934
   Die Julischen Alpen im Bilde, J. Kugy, 1951 (4th ed.), 35s.
      Excellent photographs and descriptions. The best general book on the Julian Alps, by their greatest pioneer. In German
   Die Bergwelt Jugoslawiens, Lucic-Roki, Rother, 1969, 65s.
   Jugoslawisches Hüttenverzeichnis, 1957, 20s. Details of huts. In German

Appendix A. Glossary of Gaelic, Norse, and Welsh words in British place-names

1. Gaelic

In Gaelic the stress accent falls on the first syllable except in compound names, where the chief stress falls on the qualifying word. The aspirated diagraphs 'bh' and 'mh' are represented by 'v' in English; 'fh' is silent; 'ch' is equivalent to the guttural sound heard in the German word *Nacht*.

In the respelt word the vowels have the following phonetic values: 'a' as in 'father', 'ā' as in 'shake', 'â' as in 'all', 'e' as in 'pen', 'ē' as in 'feet', 'ê' as in 'where', 'i' as in 'tin', 'ī' as in 'time', 'o' as in 'cot', 'ō' as in 'mote', 'oo' as in 'foot', 'ow' as in 'cow', 'u' as in 'tub', and 'ū' as in 'tube'. Of the consonants 'g' is always hard as in 'gate'. (Pronunciation is given in parentheses after each entry.)

The definite article varies according to gender, number, case, and the initial letter of the noun to which it is prefixed; its forms are am, an, an t-, a', na, na h-, nam, nan.

Aber, Abar, Obar, mouth or confluence of a river
Abhainn, Amhuinn (av'-uin), river. Usually **Avon**
Airidh (ar'-ē), sheiling
Allt (âlt), brook, burn, stream. Conventional forms: **Ald, Alt, Auld, Ault**
Amhach (avuch), a neck
Aodann (eu (as in French) -dun), a face
Aoineadh (uen'-a), a steep promontory or brae
Ard, Aird, a high point, promontory
Ath (ah), a ford; also a kiln
Avon, conventional form of **Abhainn,** q.v.
Bad (bât), a thicket, tuft
Ban, white, fair. **Ban-Righ,** Queen
Bard, a poet; a dike, enclosure, ward
Barr, a point, top, extremity
Beag (bāk), little, small. Conventional form: **Beg**
Bealach (byall'ach), breach, pass, gap
Beinn (byān), a mountain. Conventional form: **Ben**
Beith (bā), a birch tree

Beithir (bay'-ir), gen. **a bheithir** (a vay-ir), a monster
Bidean (bee'-tjan), small pointed top, pinnacle
Binnean or **Binnein** (bin'-en), a pinnacle, little mountain
Bo, plural **Ba,** cow, cows
Bod, male organ
Bodach (bott'-ach), an old man, hobgoblin, spectre
Bog (bok), soft, miry, damp
Bord, gen. **a bhuird** (a voord), a table
Both, Bothan (bo, bo'-han), a hut, booth, or bothy
Braigh (brai'-h), top, summit. Usually **Brae, Bread**
Brat, Brot, a veil, a cover
Bratach, gen. **a bhrataich** (a vrataich), a flag
Breac (brechk), spotted, piebald, speckled, trout
Breatann (bray'-tann), gen. **bhreatainn** (vray'-tann), Britain
Brochan, gen, **a brochain** (a vrochann), porridge
Brod, gen. **a bhroid** (a vroj), a goad, a sting, an awl
Bruaich (broo'-ach), a bank, brae, brim, steep place
Buachaille (bu'-ach-il), a herdsman
Buidhe (boo'-i), yellow, golden coloured
Buiridh (boory), gen. **a bhuiridh** (a voory), bellowing
Burn, a stream. *Anglo-Saxon:* Burne
Cadha (ka'-a), a pass, steep path
Cailleach (kyl'-ach), a nun, old woman
Camas (ka'-mas), bay, bend, channel
Caoir (keur), a mountain torrent, plural **caoirean**
Caol (kaol), strait, firth, narrow. Other form: **Kyle.** Alternative Gaelic
  form: **Gaolas**
Caor (keur), rowan; gen. plural **nan caoran,** of the rowans
Caora (keura), gen. **caorach,** plural **caoraich,** sheep
Carn, a heap of stones, cairn
Carr, broken ground
Cas, a foot, stem, handle, steep (adj.)
Ceann (kyenn), head, headland. Usually **Ken, Kin**
Ceathramh (keruv), fourth part, a quarter
Cill (kil), a cell, church. Usually **Kil**
Cioch (kioch), a pap, woman's breast
Cir (kēēr), a comb, coxcomb, gen. **chir**
Clach (klach), a stone. **Clachan,** stones, hamlet
Clais, a hollow
Cleit (klājt), a ridge, reef, rocky eminence
Cluain, a field, pasture, green plain, meadow
Cnap (krap), a knob, hillock
Cnoc (knochk, krochk), a knoll. Usually **Knock**
Coill or **Coille** (kolyi), a wood, forest
Coire (kor'-e), a cauldron, kettle, circular hollow. Other form: **Corry**
Con, dogs; gen. plural **nan con**

Creag (krāg), a rock, cliff
Crom, bent, sloping, crooked
Cruach (kroo′-ach), stack, heap, haunch
Cuinneag (koon′-yak), a wooden milking bucket
Cul (kool), the back, a nook
Da, two
Dail (dal), a field. In Norse, a dale
Damh (day), a bullock, heifer
Darach, oak, oak wood
Dearg (jer′-ek), red
Diollaid (jee-ol-adj), a saddle
Doire, groove, hollow
Druim, the back, ridge. Usually **Drem, Drom, Drum**
Dubh (doo), black, dark. Other form: **Dhu**
Dun (doon), a fort, castle, heap
Each, Eich, a horse
Eagach (aikach), notched, place of notches
Eaglais (āklash), a church, temple
Ear, east
Eas (es), a waterfall. Other form: **Easach** (es′-ach), a cascade
Eididh (ay′-je), garment, mantle
Eighe (ay), a file; **Beinn Eighe,** the serrated Ben
Eilean (ēl′-an), an island
Etive (**Loch**), from 'foul' or 'horrid one' (Watson, *Celtic Place Names of Scotland*, p. 46)
Eun (ee-un), a bird; plural **eoin** (yawn), birds
Fad, long, e.g. **Beinn Fhada,** long mountain
Fada (fatta), **Fem fhada** (atta), e.g. **Ben Attow,** long
Feadan, narrow glen
Fear (fer), a man, husband, individual
Fearn (fern), an alder tree
Feith (fā), bog, sinewy stream, a vein
Fiacaill (fee′-ach-cal), a tooth
Fiadh (fee′-ugh), a deer
Fionn (fyoon), white, clear, bright
Fitheach (fee′-ach), gen. **an fhithich** (a-nyee-ich), a raven
Frith (free), gen. **frithe** (free′-u), deer forest or hunting ground
Fuar (foo′-ar), cold
Fuaran (fou-ar′-an), a perennial spring, well
Gabhar or **Gobhar** (go′-ur), a goat
Garadh (ga′-ra), a fence, dike, garden
Garbh (gar′-v), rough. Other spelling: **Garve**
Geal (gel), white, clear, bright
Geodha (goe), a narrow creek, chasm, rift, cove
Gille (geel′-yu), boy, youth, manservant
Glac, a hollow, dell, defile

Glas, grey, pale, wan; green. **Glais,** a stream
Gleann (glyan'), narrow valley, dale, dell. Usually **Glen**
Gob, point, beak
Gorm, blue, sometimes green
Greadadh (great'-ag), gen. **a ghreadaidh,** torment, blast, whip
Gru (groo), **Gruamach** (groo-amach), gloomy, forbidding, grim
Gruididh (groo-ji), gritty or gravelly
I (ē), an island
Inbhir (in'-ver), confluence, place at the meeting of river and sea. Other
    form: **Inver,** cf. **Aber**
Innis (in'-ish), island, meadow. Usually **Inch**
Iolair (yol-ar), an eagle
Ken, Kin. *See* **Ceann**
Kil. *See* **Cill**
Knock. *See* **Cnoc**
Kyle. *See* **Caol**
Ladhar (leu-ur), hoof, prong
Lag (lak), a hollow in a hill. Usually **Lagan, Logan, Logie**
Lairig, the sloping face of a hill, a pass
Laogh (lao-g), a calf
Leac (lechk), **Lic** (leechk), a slab
Leacann (lechkan), a sloping hillside
Leathad (le'-ud), a slope, declivity
Leathan (lyā'-un), broad
Leis (laish), a thigh
Leitir, a slope
Liath (lēa), grey
Linne (lyĕn'-a), a pool, sound, channel
Loch, a lake, arm of the sea. **Lochan,** small loch
Machair (mach'-ar), a plain or extensive beach
Madadh (mat'-a), a dog
Madadh allaidh (awlee), fierce dog (= wolf)
Madadh ruadh (roo'-a), red dog (= fox)
Maighdean (mey'-jen), maiden; **a mhaighdean** (a vey'-jen), the maiden
Mairg, pity
Mam, a round or gently rising hill, e.g. **Mam Sabhal** (mam soul),
    rounded hill of barns
Maol (mull), headland, bald top, cape
Meadhon (me'-un), middle, central
Meall (myal), knob, lump, rounded hill
Merrick, 'The Merrick', from 'Meur', a finger – the pronged, branching
    hill-range
Monadh (mon'-a), moor, heath, hill, mountain
Moine or **Mointeach** (mo'-en-tyach), moss-land, mossy
Mor, great, large, tall. English form: **More**
Muc (moocht), a sow, pig. Usually **Muck, Muick**

Muileann (mool'-an), gen. **a mhuilin** (a vool-in), a mill
Mullach (moolach), top, summit
Nevis, may be from O. Irish 'neim' = venom, the 'venomous one' (Watson, *Celtic Place Names of Scotland*, p. 472)
Ob, a bay, creek, haven. Other: **Tob**
Odhar (ŏ'-ur), dapple, drab, dun-coloured, sallow
Or, gold
Ord, a round steep, or conical hill
Os (ōs), outlet of a lake or river
Pit or **Pet**, farm, hollow
Poll (poul), a pool, pond, pit
Rathad (ra'-ud), a road, way
Reidh (rā), plain, level, smooth
Riabhach (rē'-ach), drab, greyish, brindled, grizzled. Other form: **Riach**
Righ (rē), a king. Other form: **Ree**
Roinn, a point, headland, peninsula
Ros, a point, promontory. Other form: **Ross**
Ruadh (roo'-a), red, reddish
Rudha (roo'-a), promontory. Usually **Ru, Rhu, Row**
Ruigh, a run for cattle, sheiling, land sloping
Sail, a heel
Sean (shen), old, aged, ancient
Seileach (shāl'-ach), a willow
Sgeir (skeir), a reef, sea-surrounded rock
Sgorr or **Sgurr** (skor, skoor), a peak, conical sharp rock. Sometimes **Scaur**
Sith (shē), a fairy. **Sithean** (shee'-an), a fairy hillock or knoll
Slioch (slee'-och), from **Sleagach** (slay'-gach), armed with spears, from **Sleagh**, a spear
Slochd, a deep hollow
Sneachd (snyachg), snow
Socach (sochk'-ach), snout, point of land
Sput (spōōt), a spout of water, dim. **Sputan**
Srath (stra), a valley, plain beside a river, strath
Sron, nose, peak, promontory. Other form: **Strone**
Sruth (stru), a stream, current. Usually **Struan**
Stac (stak), a steep rock, conical hill
Steall (styall), a spout of liquid, a cataract
Stob (stop), a point
Stuc (stook), a pinnacle, peak, conical steep rock
Suidhe (sooi'-ye), sitting, resting place
Taigh or **Tigh** (ty), a house. Usually **Tay, Ty**
Tairbeart (tar'-pyart), an isthmus. Other forms: **Tarbet, Tarbert**
Tarmachan, ptarmigan
Teallach (tyallach), a forge, hearth

Tir (tyēr), country, region, land. Other form: **Tyr**
Tobar, a well, spring, fountain. Usually **Teber**
Toll (towl), gen. **tuill** (tooyl), a hole
Tom (tōm), a hillock, mound
Torr, a mound, heap, hill
Tulach (tool'-ach), knoll, hillock, eminence. Anglicized forms: **Tilly,**
   Tully, Tulloch, dim. **tulachan,** plural **tuilachean**
Uachdar (ooach'-ur), upper-land. Usually **Auchter, Ochter**
Uaine (ooin'-e), green
Uamh (oo'-av), a cave, a grave
Uig (ooēg), a nook, bay
Uisge, water, rain

2. Norse

A, Ay, A, island, e.g. Soa, sheep isle, Pabbay, priest's isle
Bard, extremity, point, headland
Beck, a brook
Bogha or **Bodha,** a sunk rock
Brochs, circular dry-stone supposed Pictish buildings
Ey, an island. *See* **Ay**
Fell, Field (*Norwegian,* **Fjeld**), mountain
Firth, Frith (*Lat.* **Fretum**), strait, estuary of a river
Gill, a ravine
Gio, a chasm, rift
Grind, a gate
Holm, an island in river or sea near the shore
Hope, an inner bay. **Gob,** e.g. Oban
How (**Haugr**), a burial mound
Law, a conical hill
Lax, a salmon
Mol, shingly beach.
Nab (*Norwegian,* **Knab**), a rock projection
Ness, a point, headland
Papa, spiritual father, a prefix to several of the Orkney and Shetland
   Islands
Skerries, isolated rocks or islets
Stack, a columnar rock
Stor, Stour, big, large, great ·
Thing, Ting, a provincial parliament
Vik, Wik, a creek
Voe, a little bay, inlet
Whal (*Norwegian,* **Hval**), a whale

3. Welsh

The pronunciation of Welsh is greatly simplified by an understanding of the following points:

(a) The language is almost completely phonetic.

(b) The accent falls almost invariably on the penultimate syllable as in English 'moment'-ous'.

(c) The seven vowels, a, e, i, o, u, w, y, each have their own sounds, which they retain with a slight slurring effect when joined together as diphthongs.

a long as in English 'half'
  short as in English 'hat'
e long as in English 'wait' (North-Country)
  short as in English 'wet'
i long as in English 'seat'
  short as in English 'sit'
o long as in English 'coat'
  short as in English 'cot'
u almost the same as long i
w long as in English 'tomb'
  short as in English 'foot'
*y obscure as English u or o in 'undone'
  long as the Welsh u
  short as the short Welsh i

(d) All consonants are pronounced and always in the same way. Of the consonants, the following alone need comment.

c always hard as in 'cat'
ch as in Gaelic or German 'ach' or 'och', never as in 'church' or 'ache'
dd as English 'th' in 'this'

---

* Of these three sounds the first is the most common. The second and third are only met in words of one syllable and in the last syllable of longer words. Exceptions are the definite article 'y' or 'yr', the preposition 'yn' meaning 'in' and the possessive adjectives 'fy' and 'dy' meaning 'my' and 'thy', all of which have the so-called obscure sound as 'uh', 'err', 'un', 'vuh', and 'duh'.

f   always as English 'of'
ff   always as English 'off'
g   always hard as in 'gun'
ll   no parallel in English
r   always trilled slightly, e.g. a Welshman would emphasize
     the difference in pronunciation between English 'father'
     and 'farther'
s   always strong as in 'sister', never as in 'busy'
th   as English 'th' in 'think'

(e) Certain initial consonants of words undergo mutation
    according to fixed laws. The types likely to be met in place-
    names are:

c	softens to g	e.g.	**carreg** to **garreg**
p	softens to b		**pont** to **bont**
t	softens to d		**tre** to **dre**
g	disappears		**gallt** to **allt**
b	softens to f		**bach** to **fach**
d	softens to dd		**dysgl** to **ddysgl**
ll	softens to l		**llyn** to **lyn**
m	softens to f		**moel** to **foel**
rh	softens to r		**rhyd** to **ryd**

Aber, estuary, river mouth
Aderyn, plural **adar,** bird
Adwy, pass
Ael, brow, edge
Afanc, beaver, fabulous monster
Afon, river
Aig, plural **eigiau,** herd, multitude
Aran, high place, eminence
Arddu, very black; or black height, probably
Bach, fem. **bechan,** little
Bala, lake outlet
Ban, peak
Barcut, kite
Bedd, grave
Bedwen, plural **bedw,** birch
Bera, stack
Beri, kite
Betws, chapel
Beudy, cowhouse (this is the prevalent form in Caernarvonshire but
    elsewhere in Wales the word takes different forms)

Blaen, point, top; plural **blaenau,** upper reaches
Boch, cheek
Bod, dwelling, abode
Braich, arm
Bran, crow
Bras, thick, rich
Brith, fem. **braeth,** pied, speckled
Broga, frog
Bron, breast
Brwynog, rushy, marshy, sad
Bryn, hill
Bual, bugle, buffalo
Bustach, bullock, ox
Buwch, cow
Bwlch, col, gap
Cadair, chair
Cae, field
Caer, camp, fort
Cafn, trough, canoe
Cam (n.), step
Cam (adj.), bent, wrong
Canol, middle
Capel, chapel
Carn, Carnedd, cairn, hill
Carreg, plural **cerrig,** stone, rock
Carw, deer, stag
Caseg, mare
Castell, castle
Caws, cheese
Ceffyl, horse
Cefn, ridge, back
Cegin, kitchen
Celli, grove, copse
Celynen, plural **celyn,** holly
Cesail, armpit
Chwarel, quarry
Ci, plural **cwn,** dog
Cidwm, wolf
Cigfran, raven
Cilfach, nook, recess
Clawdd, ditch, embankment
Clip, bluff
Clogwyn, cliff, precipice
Cludair, heap, pile
Clyd, warm, sheltered
Cneifio, shearing; plural **cneifion,** flocks, clippings

Coch, red
Coeden, tree, plural **coed,** trees, wood
Collen, plural **cyll,** hazel
Corn, Cyrn, horn, trumpet
Coron, crown
Cors, bog, swamp
Crach, dwarf, scab, pimple
Craig, rock, crag
Criafolen, rowan
Crib, comb; used figuratively for a toothed ridge
Cribin, rake; used figuratively for a toothed ridge
Crochan, cauldron, pit
Croes, cross
Cromlech, megalithic standing stone(s)
Cwm, combe, valley
Cwrwgl, coracle
Cyfrwy, saddle (of a horse)
Cymer, confluence
Cyngor, plurals **cynghorion,** counsel, advice, **cynghoriau,** council
Cythraul, demon
Dau, fem. **dwy,** two
Derwen, plural **derw,** oak
Diffwys, worthless
Dinas, city, fortress
Dol, meadow
Drws, door
Du, black
Dwfr, Dwr, water
Dyffryn, valley
Dylif, flood
Dyn, man
Dysgl, dish
Eglwys, church
Eigion, bottom, depth
Eilio, to plait, weave
Eithinen, plural **eithin,** gorse
Erw, acre
Eryr, eagle
Esgair, leg, ridge
Fford, road
Ffridd, enclosed rough grazing (intake, heaf)
Ffynnon, spring, well
Gafl, plural **gaflau, geifl,** fork
Gafr, plural **geifr,** goat
Gallt, hill slope, hill on road (N. Wales), wood (S. Wales)
Gardd, garden

Garth, enclosure, ridge
Gefail, smith
Glan, bank, shore
Glas, blue, grey, green, light-coloured
Glyn, valley, glen
Golau, Goleu, light
Gorffwys, rest
Grug, heather
Gwalch, hawk
Gwastad, level, smooth
Gwaun, meadow, moorland
Gwennol, swallow
Gwernen, alder; plural **gwern,** alders, alder-swamp or meadow
Gweryd, moss, sward
Gwrach, hag, witch
Gwrhyd, fathom
Gwryd, chain; manliness
Gwy, water, stream (usually as suffix – wy)
Gwyddfa, tomb
Gwyliwr, watchman
Gwyn, fem. **gwen,** white
Gwynt, wind
Hafod, summer dwelling (shieling)
Hanner, a half
Haul, sun
Hebog, hawk
Helygen, plural **helyg,** willow
Hen, old
Hendref, winter dwelling
Hir, long
Hydd, stag
Hyll, ugly, wild, gloomy
Isaf, lowest
Lon, lane
Llan, enclosure, church, village
Llech, flat stone
Llithrig, slippery (slope)
Lloer, moon
Llug (n.), light, gleam, blotch
Llug (adj.), gleaming, dawning, tending to appear
Llwybr, path
Llwyd, grey
Llwyn, bush, grove
Llyn, lake
Llys, court, palace
Ma, Man, place (usually as suffix – fa)

Madog, fox
Maen, stone
Maes, open field
Main, narrow
March, stallion
Marchog, knight, horseman
Marian, moraine
Mawnog, peat bog
Mawr, big, large
Meillionen, plural **meillion,** clover
Melin, mill
Melyn, fem. **melen,** yellow
Merch, woman
Miliast, greyhound bitch
Mochyn, plural **moch,** pig
Moel, hill (usually bare or rounded)
Mor, sea
Morfa, salt marsh, marsh near the sea
Mur, wall
Mynydd, mountain
Naddyn, chipper
Nant, brook, glen, gorge
Newydd, new
Niwl, mist
Nodded, refuge, protection
Nyth, nest
Oen, plural **wyn,** lamb
Oer, cold
-og, suffix converting a noun to an adjective
Ogof, cave
Onnen, plural **onn, ynn,** ashtree
Pair, cauldron
Pant, hollow, valley
Parc, park, enclosure
Pen, head, top
Penmaen, rocky headland
Pentref, village
Pererin, pilgrim
Perfedd, middle
Person, parson, person
Pistyll, waterfall
Pont, bridge
Porfa, pasture
Porth, gate, port
Pren, tree, wood
Pwll, pool

Rhaeadr, waterfall
Rhigol, groove, trench
Rhisgl, bark, rind
Rhiw, hill, slope
Rhos, moor, heath
Rhyd, ford
Saeth, arrow
Sarn, causeway
Serth, steep (brant)
Taith, journey
Tal (n.), front, forehead
Tal (adj.), high, tall
Tan, under, as far as
Tarw, bull
Teg, fair, warm, pretty
Tomen, heap, mound
Trafel, slate-trimming blade
Tref, town, township, homestead, hamlet
Trem, look, sight, view
Trewern, township, homestead
Tri, three
Tro, turn, corner
Troed, foot
Trum, ridge, summit
Twll, hole
Twr, tower
Ty, house
Tyddyn, small farm
Uchaf, highest
Un, one
Y, Yr, the
Ych, ox
Yn, in
Ynys, island, hill surrounded by bog
Ysbyty, hospital, hospice
Ysfa, sheepwalk, consumed spot, craze, itching
Ysgawen, plural **ysgaw,** elder tree
Ysgol, school, ladder, peal
Ysgyfarnog, hare
Ystrad, dale
Ywennol, foaming

Appendix B. British organizations and addresses

This appendix lists all the organizations and firms mentioned in the text, with the exception of Continental organizations, which are in appendix D.

1. National organizations

ALPINE CLUB, 74 South Audley Street, London W1Y 5FF

ASSOCN. OF SCOTTISH CLIMBING CLUBS (A.S.C.C.) (page 29). Replaced by Mountaineering Council of Scotland * (see below).

BRITISH MOUNTAINEERING COUNCIL (B.M.C.) (page 29), Crawford House, Precinct Centre, Manchester University, Booth Street East, Manchester M13 9R2

BRITISH RED CROSS SOCIETY (B.R.C.S.) (§ 90), 14 Grosvenor Crescent, London SW1

CAMPING CLUB OF GREAT BRITAIN AND IRELAND LTD, 11 Lower Grosvenor Place, London SW1 (there is a Mountaineering Section)

CENTRAL COUNCIL OF PHYSICAL RECREATION (C.C.P.R.), 70 Brompton Road, London SW3 1HE

MOUNTAIN RESCUE COMMITTEE (M.R.C.) (§ 90)
England and Wales: H. K. Hartley, Esq., 9 Milldale Avenue, Temple Meads, Buxton, Derbyshire SK17 9BE
Scotland: H. MacInnes, Esq., Achnacon, Glencoe, Argyll

MOUNTAIN BOTHIES ASSOCIATION, D. W. Howe, Esq., 3 Greenfoot, Mealsgate, Carlisle CA5 1DF

MOUNTAINEERING COUNCIL OF SCOTLAND (M.C.S.) (formerly A.S.C.C.)* A. G. Cousins Esq., 11 Kirklee Quadrant, Glasgow G12 0TS

NATIONAL SKI FEDERATION OF GREAT BRITAIN, 118 Eaton Square, London SW1

NATURE CONSERVANCY, 19 Belgrave Square, London SW1

RAMBLERS' ASSOCIATION, 1 Crawford Mews, London W1

SEARCH AND RESCUE DOG ASSOCIATION, K. MacKenzie, Esq., 1 Canal Road, Inverness

---

* This change occured in mid-1970, too late to make consequential changes throughout the whole of the text.

M. O. Hammond, Esq., 11 Avenue Close, Stoney Middleton, near Sheffield S30 1TA

J. Ellis Roberts, Esq., Tan y Marian, Waenfawr, Caernarvonshire

SKI CLUB OF GREAT BRITAIN (S.C.G.B.),
   118 Eaton Square, London SW1 W9AF

YOUTH HOSTELS ASSOCIATIONS (§ 27),
   England and Wales: Y.H.A., Trevelyan House, St. Albans, Herts.
   Scotland: S.Y.H.A., 7 Bruntsfield Crescent, Edinburgh 10 (see also 2 below)
   Northern Ireland: Y.H.A., 28 Bedford Street, Belfast
   Ireland: An Oige, 39 Mountjoy Square, Dublin 1

2. Main organizations arranging mountain training or holiday courses

AUSTRIAN ALPINE CLUB (Austria and Dolomites only: liaison with Austrian mountaineering schools),
   U.K. Branch, Wings House, Bridge Road East, Welwyn Garden City, Herts.

C.H.A. (Britain and abroad),
   Birch Heys, Cromwell Range, Manchester M14HU

HOLIDAY FELLOWSHIP (Britain and abroad),
   142 Great North Way, Hendon, London NW4

MOUNTAIN LEADERSHIP TRAINING BOARD (§ 2),
   c/o B.M.C. (see p. 485)

MOUNTAINEERING ASSOCIATION – see Y.H.A. Travel (below)

OUTWARD BOUND TRUST (see 3 (5, 7, 16, and 18) below),
   73 Great Peter Street, London SW1

RAMBLERS' ASSOCIATION SERVICES LTD (Britain and abroad),
   124 Finchley Road, London NW3 5JA

SCOTTISH COUNCIL OF PHYSICAL RECREATION (S.C.P.R.),
   4 Queensferry Street, Edinburgh EH2 4PB (see 3 (2) below)

SCOTTISH Y.H.A. (see e.g. 3 (3) below),
   7 Glebe Crescent, Stirling FK8 2JA

SCOUT ASSOCIATION (Britain and abroad),
   25 Buckingham Palace Road, London SW1

Y.H.A. ADVENTURE HOLIDAYS (includes former Mountaineering Assn.),
   Trevelyan House, St Albans, Herts.

YOUTH ADVENTURE TRAINING (Britain and abroad),
   19 Moorfields, Liverpool 2

Y.T.B. TRAVEL SERVICE (abroad only: liaison with some Continental mountaineering schools),
   Knightsbridge Station Arcade, Brompton Road, London SW3
   In addition some education authorities arrange training at local level, as do certain organizations such as the Y.H.A. and the Girl Guides' Association (for members only).

3. Mountain schools and instructional centres

SCOTLAND
   (1) West Highland School of Adventure, Applecross, Ross-shire
   (2) Glenmore Lodge, S.C.P.R. Centre, Aviemore, Inverness-shire
   (3) Glenbrittle Youth Hostel, Isle of Skye. (Summer courses only)
   (4) Glencoe Mountaineering School, Glencoe, Argyll

LAKE DISTRICT
   (5) Outward Bound Mountain School, Eskdale, Cumberland
   (6) Brook House Mountain Centre, Boot, Eskdale, Cumberland
   (7) Outward Bound Mountain School, Hallsteads on Ullswater, Penrith, Cumberland
   (8) Brathay Hall, Ambleside, Westmorland
   (9) Lakeland Mountaineering School, The Boathouse, Clappersgate, Ambleside, Westmorland

PEAK DISTRICT AND YORKSHIRE
   (10) Yorkshire Dales Adventure Centre, Gildersleets, Giggleswick, Settle
   (11) Centre for Open Country Pursuits, White Hall, Manchester Road, Buxton
   (12) Birchfield Lodge, Hope via Sheffield, Derbyshire
   (13) Kyndwr Scwd, Fox House Corner, Hathersage Road, near Sheffield
   (14) Edale Centre for Outdoor Pursuits, c/o Lea Farm, Edale, Sheffield

SOUTH AND WEST OF ENGLAND
   (15) Bowles Outdoor Pursuits Centre, Eridge, near Tunbridge Wells, Kent
   (16) Outward Bound School, Ashburton, Devon

WALES
   (17) Plas y Brenin, National Mountaineering Centre, Capel Curig, near Betws-y-Coed, North Wales. Book through the Sports Council (Dept. B), 70 Brompton Road, London SW3 1EX
   (18) Outward Bound Girls' School (Wales), Rhowniar, Towyn, Merioneth

NORTHERN IRELAND
(19) Tollymore Mountain Centre, Co. Down (applications to
    C.C.P.R., 49 Malone Road, Belfast BT9 6RZ
    In addition, a number of local education authorities have their
own mountain schools (e.g. the Birmingham Education Authority
centre at Ogwen Cottage, North Wales).

4. Some mountaineering equipment suppliers

THE ALPINE CENTRE,
    193 Church Street, Blackpool
ARVONS,
    Ogwen Terrace, Bethesda, near Bangor, North Wales
ALLAN AUSTIN MOUNTAIN SPORTS,
    4 Jacob Street, Manchester Road, Bradford 5
BERGHAUS LTD (and LD MOUNTAIN CENTRE),
    34 Dean Street, Newcastle upon Tyne NE1 1PG
THE BIVOUAC,
    56 North Parade, Matlock Bath, Matlock, Derbyshire
BLACKS OF GREENOCK,
    Industrial Estate, Port Glasgow, Renfrewshire PA14 5XN
    Ruxley Corner, Sidcup, Kent DA14 5AQ
    22–4 Gray's Inn Road, London WC1
    53 Rathbone Place, Oxford Street, London W1
    250 High Street, Sutton, Surrey
    Shakespeare Street, Nottingham NG1 4FD
    86 Broad Street, Birmingham 15
    40 Marsh Street, Hanley, Stoke on Trent
    263 Deansgate, Manchester 2
    18 Corporation Street, Sheffield SR3 8RN
ELLIS BRIGHAM,
    6–14 Cathedral Street, Manchester M4 3FU
    162 Whiteladies Road, Bristol
    73 Bold Street, Liverpool 1
    Capel Curig, near Betws-y-Coed, North Wales
    Market Jew Street, Penzance, Cornwall
JOE BROWN,
    Menai Hall, High Street, Llanberis, North Wales
    Capel Curig, near Betws-y-Coed, North Wales
THE DALES OUTDOOR CENTRE LTD,
    Coach Street, Skipton, Yorkshire BD23 1LH
FRANK DAVIES,
    Compston Corner, Ambleside, Westmorland

7 Colmore Circus, Snowhill Ringway, Birmingham 4

40 Woodhouse Lane, Leeds 2

BENJAMIN EDGINGTON LTD,

144 Shaftesbury Avenue, London WC2

2A Eastcheap, London EC3

18 Arwenack Street, Falmouth

18 Lloyd Street, Albert Square, Manchester 2

FISHERS (MOUNTAIN EQUIPMENT),

17 Lake Road, Keswick, Cumberland

2 Borrowdale Road, Keswick, Cumberland (Postal Department)

HELLY HANSEN (UK) LTD,

Ronald Close, Kempston, Bedfordshire

HIGHRANGE SPORTS,

5 Dalmally Street, Glasgow

KARRIMOR PRODUCTS LTD,

Avenue Parade, Accrington BB5 6PR

ROBERT LAWRIE LTD,

54 Seymour Street, London WIH 5WE

MOAC PRODUCTS,

12 Corn Exchange, Manchester 4

DON MORRISON,

343 London Road, Sheffield

MOUNTAIN SAFETY RESEARCH INC. (M.S.R.),

c/o Field and Trek (Equipment) Ltd, 25 Kings Road,
Brentwood, Essex

NEVISPORT,

261 Sauchiehall Street, Glasgow

131 High Street, Fort William, Inverness-shire

PINDISPORTS LTD,

14 Holborn, London EC1

373 Uxbridge Road, London W3

1098 Whitgift Centre, Croydon, Surrey

27 Martineau Square, Birmingham 2

JO ROYLE HIGH PEAK OUTDOOR CENTRE,

22 High Street, Buxton, Derbyshire SK17 6EV

P & S OUTDOOR SHOPS,

71A Godwin Street, Bradford

4 Allerton Road, Four Lane Ends, Bradford

THE SCOUT AND GUIDE SHOP,

17 Turl Street, Oxford

14 Goodramgate, York

BRYAN G. STOKES,
   9 Charles Street, Sheffield
TEBBUTT BROS.,
   35 Market Place, Wednesbury, Staffordshire
TERRY'S FESTERHAUNT,
   Groombridge, Sussex
GRAHAM TISO LTD,
   13 Wellington Place, Leith, Edinburgh 6
ROGER TURNER MOUNTAIN SPORTS,
   105 London Road, Leicester
   120 Derby Road, Nottingham
ULTIMATE EQUIPMENT LTD (tents, helmets, clothing),
   Warkworth, Morpeth, Northumberland
VANGO (SCOTLAND) LTD,
   356 Amulree Street, Glasgow G32 7SL
Y.H.A. SERVICES LTD,
   29 John Adam Street, London WC2N 6JE
   35 Cannon Street, Birmingham B2 5EE
   36 Fountain Street, Manchester M2 2BE
   Other addresses are advertised in climbing magazines (see bibliography, 1).

5. Mountaineering books and maps

Most of the shops and mountaineering schools listed above supply guide-books, periodicals, recent instructional books, and maps. Any good bookseller will also supply them. The following booksellers carry good stocks of mountaineering books or maps.

GASTON'S ALPINE BOOKS (new and secondhand: all British and foreign guide-books),
   134 Kenton Road, Harrow, Mddx. HA3 8AL
AUDREY SALKELD (new and secondhand; also O.S. maps),
   11 Tone Road, Clevedon, Somerset
EDWARD STANFORD LTD (all maps and guide-books),
   12–14 Long Acre, London WC2
J. B. WYLIE & CO.,
   406 Sauchiehall Street, Glasgow C2
WEST COL PRODUCTIONS (Alpine Club, Scottish Mountaineering Trust and West Col guides; alpine and certain British (S.M.T. or West Col) maps),
   1 Meadow Close, Goring, Reading RG8 0AP, Berkshire

The main publishers or distributors of British guide-books are given with the guide-books in chapter 13. Publishers of Continental guide-books and maps are in appendix D.

Appendix C. British mountaineering clubs

The following clubs are members of the B.M.C. or M.C.S. (see pages 29–30). The addresses of the secretaries of the university clubs are usually c/o The Students' Union, and Service and hospital clubs have permanent addresses of this type also. Most of the other clubs do not have permanent addresses. The addresses of all secretaries are available from the B.M.C. (appendix B, 1).

The Climber and Rambler (bibliography, 1) publishes meeting arrangements for local clubs, monthly. Some Irish clubs are listed at the end. The addresses of the Continental alpine clubs (pp 30–31) are in appendix D.

1. Clubs which are members of the British Mountaineering Council

Achille Ratti C.C., Aldermaston M.C., Alpine Climbing Group (page 31), Alpine Club (page 28), Anabasis Club, Army Mountaineering Association, Association of British Members of the Swiss Alpine Club (A.B.M.S.A.C.).

Barnsley M.C., Barrow Mountaineering and Ski Club, Birmingham Athletic Institute M.C., Black and Tans M.C., Blue Peter Club, Bowline C.C., Bristol Aeroplane Company Aces Rucksack Club, Bristol College of Science and Technology, Bristol Exploration Club (Climbing Section).

Cambridge University M.C., Carlisle M.C., Cave and Crag Club, Ceunant M.C., Chester M.C., Cleveland M.C., Climbers' Club, Clwb Dringo, Pothmadog, Cockermouth M.C., Coventry M.C.

Derbyshire Pennine Club, Dunstable and District M.C., Durham University M.C.

East Yorkshire M.C., Exeter and District C.C.

Fell and Rock C.C. of the English Lake District (F. and R.C.C.), Fylde C.C.

Gloucestershire M.C., Gritstone Club, Guy's Hospital M.C.

Harrow M.C., Hyperion M.C.

Ibex M.C., Irish M.C. (Belfast Section).

Junior M.C. of Scotland (J.M.C.S. London Section).

Karabiner M.C., Keele M.C., Keswick M.C., King's College Newcastle M.C.

Ladies' Alpine Club, Lancashire Caving and Climbing Club, Leeds University Union C.C., Leicestershire Association of Mountaineers, Lincoln M.C., Liverpool and District M.C., Liverpool University M.C., London Graduate M.C., London M.C., London School of Economics M.C.

Manchester Gritstone C.C., Manchester University M.C., Merseyside M.C., Middlesex Hospital M.C., Midland Association of Mountaineers, Mountain Club, M.C. of North Wales, Mountaineering Section of the Camping Club, Mynydd C.C.

North London M.C., North Staffordshire M.C., Northumbrian M.C., North West M.C., Nottingham Climbers' Club, Nottingham University M.C.

Oread M.C., Oxford M.C., Oxford University M.C.

Parnassus C.C., Peak C.C., Peterborough M.C., Phoenix M.C., Pilkington Recreation Club, Mountaineering Section, Pinnacle Club, Polaris M.C., Preston M.C.

Queen's University M.C.

Reading M.C., Reading University M.C., Rimmon M.C., Rock and Heather Club, Rock and Ice C.C., Rockhoppers (S.W. London M.C.), R.A.F. Mountaineering Association, Royal Artillery Alpine Club, Royal Engineers Mountaineering and Exploration Club, Royal Military Academy Sandhurst M.C., Royal Navy Ski and M.C., Rucksack Club, Rugby M.C.

St Mary's Hospital M.C., Sandstone Climbing Club, Scottish M.C. (S.M.C.), Sheffield University M.C., Southampton University M.C., Southern Mountaineering Association, South Essex C.C., South Wales M.C., Summit M.C.

Tricouni Club, Tuesday C.C.

University College of N. Wales M.C., University College of Wales Aberystwyth M.C., University of Birmingham M.C., University of Bristol M.C., University of Hull M.C., University of Leicester M.C., University of London M.C.

Vagabond M.C.

Wayfarers' Club, Wellington M.C., Wessex M.C., West Cumberland M.C., Whitchurch M.C., Wolverhampton M.C.

Yeti Club (London), York M.C., Yorkshire M.C., Yorkshire Ramblers' Club.

2. Clubs which are members of the Mountaineering Council of Scotland

Aberdeen University Lairig Club

Cairngorm Club, Carn Dearg M.C., Creagh Dhu M.C.

Etchachan Club, Edinburgh University M.C.

Falkirk M.C., Ferranti M.C.

Galloway M.C., Glasgow University M.C., Glasgow Glenmore M.C., Glenmore M.C., Grampian Club, Greenock M.C.

Hall Russell and Alexander Russell Recreation Club (Mountaineering Section)

Inverness M.C.

Junior M.C. of Scotland (J.M.C.S.) (this club has sections in Glasgow, Edinburgh, Perth, Lochaber, and London)

Kirkcaldy and District M.C.

Ladies' Scottish C.C., Lomond C.C.

Moray M.C.

Royal College of Science and Technology, Glasgow Athletic Club (Mountaineering Section), Rucksac Club

St Andrews University M.C., Scottish M.C. (S.M.C.), Scottish M.C. (Western District).

3. Mountaineering clubs in Ireland

Dublin University C.C.

Glenfofany C.C. (Belfast)

Irish M.C. (Belfast), Irish M.C. (Dublin) (see footnote in § 109)

North West M.C.

Queen's University M.C.

Tralee M.C.

Appendix D. Continental organizations and addresses

This appendix lists the addresses of the main Continental organizations useful to the mountaineer, including all those referred to in chapter 19. Although the publishers of maps and guide-books are included it will probably be easier to obtain these from the British sources in appendix B, 5. Similarly, for mountaineering holidays or courses abroad, it may be better to deal with the British organizations in appendix B, 2, several of which have a liaison with the mountaineering schools in Austria, France, and Switzerland listed below.

1. Austria

AUSTRIAN ALPINE CLUB (Österreichischer Alpenverein; O.A.V.),

   U.K. Branch: Wings House, Bridge Road East, Welwyn Garden City, Herts.

   Headquarters: Wilhelm-Greil Strasse 15, Innsbruck, Tirol, Austria

   The U.K. Branch deals with all matters, including membership, training courses, holidays, maps and guide-books, and advisory services. The O.A.V. is not to be confused with the Österreichischer Alpin Klub (O.A.K.), a select climbing club.

AUSTRIAN STATE TOURIST DEPARTMENT,

   16 Conduit Street, London W1

BERGSTEIGERSCHULE HEILIGENBLUT (mountaineering courses), Heiligenblut, Carinthia, Austria

BURO FÜR STUDENTENWÄNDERUNGEN (walking and climbing courses),

   Schreyvogelgasse 3, Vienna 1, Austria

FREYTAG-BERNDT U. ARTARIA (makers of F.B. maps of eastern Alps),

   Wilhelm-Greil Strasse 15, Innsbruck, Tirol, Austria

   Schottenfeldgasse 62, Vienna, Austria

HOCHGEBIRGSSCHULE GLOCKNERGRÜPPE (mountaineering courses),

   Berghaus Mooserboden, Post Kaprun, Salzburg, Austria

HOCHGEBIRGSSCHULE TIROL (mountaineering courses),
  Altes Landhaus (Zimmer 365), Innsbruck, Tirol, Austria
KOMPASS-VERLAG (publishers of Kompass maps of Austria and
    Dolomites),
  Prinz Karl Strasse 47, Starnberg am See, Austria

2. Czechoslovakia

CZECHOSLOVAK TRAVEL BUREAU (Čedok),
  45 Oxford Street, London W1
CZECHOSLOVAK ALPINE CLUB (Ustredni Sekce Horolezectvi),
  Na Porici 12, Prague 1, Czechoslovakia

3. France

FRENCH GOVERNMENT TOURIST OFFICE,
  178 Piccadilly, London W1
FRENCH ALPINE CLUB (Club Alpin Français: C.A.F.),
  Headquarters: 7 rue la Boétie, Paris 8e, France
  Branch: rue de la Gare, Chamonix Mt-Blanc, Haute-Savoie,
    France
  Join at either address. Apply to H.Q. for information about
  C.A.F. training courses, and addresses of sections.
ARTHAUD, B. (publishers of guide-books to the French Alps),
  6 rue de Mézières, Paris 11e, France
  23 Grande-Rue, Grenoble, France
CHALETS INTERNATIONAUX DE HAUTE MONTAGNE
    (mountaineering courses),
  212 Boulevard St Germain, Paris 7e, France
FÉDÉRATION FRANÇAISE DE LA MONTAGNE (F.F.M.),
  7 rue la Boétie, Paris 8e, France
GROUPE DE HAUTE MONTAGNE (G.H.M.),
  7 rue la Boétie, Paris 8e, France
INSTITUT GÉOGRAPHIQUE NATIONAL (makers of I.G.N. maps
    of France),
  107 rue la Boétie, Paris 8e, France
DIDIER ET RICHARD (makers of special walkers'/climbers' maps
    for mountain areas based on combinations of I.G.N. maps.
    Available in paper or plastic),
  9 Grande Rue, Grenoble, France

LIBRAIRIE DES ALPES (for all French mountaineering books),
6 rue de Seine, Paris 6e, France

UNION NATIONAL DES CENTRES DE LA MONTAGNE (U.N.C.M.),
(mountaineering courses),
45 rue Raffet, Paris 16e, France

4. Germany

GERMAN TOURIST INFORMATION BUREAU,
61 Conduit Street, London W1

GERMAN ALPINE ASSOCIATION (Deutscher Alpenverein:
D.A.V.),
Praterinsel 5, Munich 22, Germany

BERGVERLAG RUDOLF ROTHER (publishers of *Alpenvereins-führer* and other guide-books),
Postfach 67, Munich 19, Germany

B.L.V. VERLAGSGESELLSCHAFT (publishers of books in note on
p. 442)
Munich, Germany

BERGSTEIGERSCHULE (mountaineering courses),
Schwalbenstrasse 5, 81 Garmisch-Partenkirchen, Germany

5. Italy

ITALIAN STATE TOURIST OFFICE,
201 Regent Street, London W1

ITALIAN ALPINE CLUB (Club Alpino Italiano: C.A.I.),
Via Ugo Foscolo 3, Milan, Italy
Via Barbaroux 1, Turin, Italy

ITALIAN TOURING CLUB (Touring Club Italiano; makers of
T.C.I. maps),
Corso Italia 10, Milan, Italy

MILITARY GEOGRAPHIC INSTITUTE (Istituto Geografico
Militare: makers of I.G.M. maps),
Viale F. Strozzi 14, Florence, Italy

CARTO-LIBRERIA BRIVIO (for all Italian maps),
Place E. Chanoux 30, Aosta, Italy

6. Norway

NORWEGIAN NATIONAL TOURIST OFFICE,
20 Pall Mall, London SW1

NORWEGIAN ALPINE CLUB (Norsk Tindeklub),
  Mr Per Sendresen, c/o Wilhelmsen, Roald Amundsensgt. 5,
  Oslo, Norway
NORWEGIAN TOURING CLUB (Den Norske Turistforenig),
  28 Stortingsgaten, Oslo, Norway
NORWEGIAN CLIMBING SCHOOL (Den Norske Klatreskole),
  Johannes Drægni, Turtagrö Hotel, Turtagrö, Norway
NORWEGIAN SCHOOL OF MOUNTAINEERING (Den Norske
  Fjellskole),
  Terje Vigerust, Hövringen, Norway
'VARDEN' SCHOOL OF MOUNTAINEERING ('Varden' Fjell-
  skole),
  Eilif Sulheim, Spiterstulen, Böverdalen, Norway

7. Poland

POLISH TRAVEL OFFICE 'ORBIS',
  313 Regent Street, London W1
POLISH ALPINE CLUB (Klub Wysokogórski),
  Sienkiewicza 12/439, Warsaw, Poland

8. Spain

SPANISH NATIONAL TOURIST OFFICE,
  70 Jermyn Street, London SW1
SPANISH MOUNTAINEERING FEDERATION (Federación
  Española de Montanismo),
  Barquillo 19, Madrid 4, Spain

9. Switzerland

SWISS NATIONAL TOURIST OFFICE,
  Swiss Centre, 1 New Coventry Street, London W1
SWISS ALPINE CLUB (Schweizer Alpen Klub – S.A.C.; Club
  Alpin Suisse – C.A.S.),
  Membership: Swiss National Tourist Office (see above)
  Guide-books and maps: Verkaufszentrale des S.A.C., Zollikon,
  Zürich, Switzerland
  Mountaineering courses: Central Committee S.A.C., Laubegg-
  strasse 70, 3000 Bern, Switzerland
ASSOCIATION OF BRITISH MEMBERS OF SWISS ALPINE CLUB
  (A.B.M.S.A.C.),

Membership: Hon. Treasurer, A.B.M.S.A.C., c/o Swiss National Tourist Office (see above)

Other matters: Hon. Secretary at address in *Mountaineering* (see bibliography,1)

FEDERAL TOPOGRAPHICAL SERVICE (Eidgenössische Landestopographie: Service Topographique Federal. Publishers of 'L.K.': 'C.N.' official Swiss maps)
  Bern, Switzerland

KÜMMERLY & FREY A.G. (publishers of K.F. maps and walkers' guide-books to Switzerland – the *Wanderbüch: Guide pédestre* series)
  Geographischer Verlag, Bern, Switzerland

VERLAG A. FRANCKE A.G. (publishers of guide-books to the Bernese Alps),
  Bern, Switzerland

CENTRE D'ALPINISME ET DE SKI (mountaineering courses),
  La Fouly, Val Ferret, Valais, Switzerland

CENTRE D'ALPINISME (mountaineering courses),
  Arolla, Valais, Switzerland

CENTRE D'ALPINISME (mountaineering courses),
  Pontresina, Grisons, Switzerland

INTERNATIONAL SCHOOL OF MOUNTAINEERING, LEYSIN
  c/o 2 Woodcote, Frith Hill Road, Godalming, Surrey

ÉCOLE DE VARAPPE (climbing courses),
  3984 Fiesch, Switzerland

SWISS MOUNTAIN CLIMBING SCHOOL (mountaineering courses),
  Silvretta, Klosters, Grisons

SWISS MOUNTAIN CLIMBING SCHOOL (climbing courses), c/o
  Martin Epp, Andermatt, Switzerland

SWISS MOUNTAINEERING INSTITUTE (mountaineering courses),
  Rosenlaui, Meiringen, Switzerland

MAX EISELIN (mountaineering tours),
  Stampfenbachstrasse 138, 8006 Zurich, Switzerland

10. Yugoslavia

YUGOSLAV NATIONAL TOURIST OFFICE,
  143 Regent Street, London SW1

YUGOSLAV ALPINE CLUB (Planinska Zveza Slovenije),
  Postni Predal, Ljubljana, Yugoslavia

Appendix E. How to use a map and compass

This appendix deals with the essential principles of map and compass work, which should be learned in your home area before going to the mountains proper.* Although map reading may appear rather dry, it can in fact be extremely interesting. Time spent in browsing over maps of mountain areas will also give you a thorough basic knowledge of them and stimulate ideas as to where you might walk or climb.

While it is not necessary for easy hill walking *in good weather* to master map and compass work, you will find an altogether freer pleasure if you have a basic understanding so that you can be sure of getting to your destination at the right time. In any case, the time is bound to come sooner or later when the mountains will test your route-finding skill to the hilt; and it is not going too far to say that the ability to pass this test successfully could make the difference between your getting back to the valley and being forced to spend the night in the open, with all the consequences that might involve. The application of map and compass work to route-finding in the hills is dealt with in chapter 1 (especially §§ 6 and 9).

As noted in §§ 25 and 26, the 1-inch Ordnance Survey maps and a compass of the Silva type with base-plate are recommended as the best all-round combination for the British hills. Although the 1 : 50,000 Ordnance Survey maps are now becoming available, most mountaineers are still using the 1-inch series and this appendix is based mainly on them. The same general principles apply in the case of Continental maps, except that there is no comparable grid system.

1. The three norths

The three norths are shown in [155]. They are:

* The subject is covered more fully in the books listed in the bibliography, 6.

True north. This is the direction of the North Pole. It is shown on the bottom or side of the O.S. map by an arrow, but it is of no more than academic interest to the mountaineer in this country since, when using O.S. maps, it is far easier to use grid north.

Grid north. An important advantage of the grid system (see next section) is that the vertical grid lines run almost exactly north–south (for example, in the Snowdon area the grid lines average about one and a half degrees west of true north). These lines enable bearings to be taken direct from the map, and it is recommended that these grid bearings should always be used in preference to bearings using true north (see sections 7–9 below).

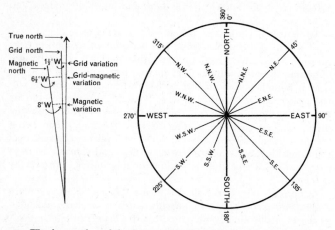

155. *The three norths and the sixteen main points of the compass.* The amounts of the variations between the norths vary from place to place, and, except for the grid variations, from year to year.

Magnetic north. This is the direction in which the compass needle points. The Magnetic North Pole is in the north of Canada and moves slightly from year to year. The difference between magnetic north and true north (the 'magnetic variation') varies from place to place and is shown at the side or bottom of most alpine and other maps. In the case of modern O.S. maps, however, grid north is always used instead of true north and consequently the figure of variation given is the 'grid-magnetic' variation – the difference between magnetic north and grid north ([155]). In Europe the Magnetic North Pole lies to the west of true and grid north, and it follows that magnetic bearings are always greater than true and grid ones; consequently, the respective variation always has to be *deducted* from the magnetic bearing to arrive at a true or grid one, or of course *added* if the conversion is from true or grid to magnetic. In the Snowdon area in 1962, for example, the grid-magnetic variation was 8°W so a magnetic bearing of 263° would give a grid bearing of 255° (page 506).

The main points of the compass are shown in [155]. These are convenient for describing an approximate direction, but when using a compass it is usual to work in degrees. These are always measured *clockwise* starting at north (360 or 0 degrees).

2. The grid system and grid references

The latitude and longitude are stated on the margins of the map, but to give greater accuracy in defining positions the Ordnance Survey has covered the whole of the British Isles with an imaginary rectangular grid made up of one-kilometre squares. Every point in Britain can thus be defined as so many kilometres east and

156. *Six-figure grid reference.* The six-figure reference is 643579; the four-figure reference for that grid square would be 6457.

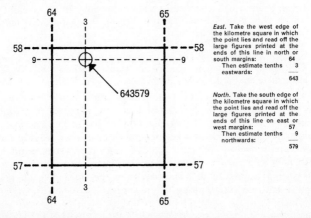

East. Take the west edge of the kilometre square in which the point lies and read off the large figures printed at the ends of this line in north or south margins: 64
Then estimate tenths eastwards: 3
———
643

North. Take the south edge of the kilometre square in which the point lies and read off the large figures printed at the ends of this line on east or west margins: 57
Then estimate tenths northwards: 9
———
579

north of the imaginary zero point in the Atlantic, west of Cornwall. In practice, mountaineers are interested only in defining locations on a particular map and for this purpose the system of four-figure or six-figure grid references is used. The four-figure grid references are correct to one kilometre and are therefore quite adequate for defining the position of important crags, lakes, or villages. The six-figure reference is correct to about one hundred metres and is therefore better for specifying a camping place or a meeting point.

The method of calculating a grid reference (in this case for the summit of Glyder Fawr, O.S. Sheet 107) is shown in [156]. On the same basis the summit of Snowdon is at grid reference 609544. Always take 'eastings' or 'horizontals' (the figures along the top and bottom edges of the map) before 'northings' or 'verticals' (the figures on the upright sides of the map). One way of remembering this is that if you go into a house you will walk inside (i.e. 'eastings') before you go upstairs (i.e. 'northings'); another is that the 'E' and 'H' of 'eastings' and 'horizontals' come alphabetically before the 'N' and 'V' of 'northings' and 'verticals'.

3. Scale

All maps bear a set relationship to the distance on the ground, i.e., they are drawn to 'scale'. There are two main ways of describing scale:

– it can be described as so many inches to the mile. In the case of the 1-inch O.S. map, for example, one inch on the map exactly represents one mile on level ground.
– alternatively, it can be described as a fraction of the corresponding distance on the ground. For example, again in the case of the 1-inch O.S. map, the fraction (the 'representative fraction') is $1/63,360$ since there are 63,360 inches in one mile.

With the exception of the 1-inch maps, most maps are drawn on the second basis, with scales of $1:20,000$, $1:25,000$, $1:50,000$, $1:100,000$, and so on. The $2\frac{1}{2}$-inch O.S. map is in fact a $1:25,000$ map, though '$2\frac{1}{2}$-inch' is a fair general description as it is almost the same (a true $2\frac{1}{2}$-inch map would be $1:25,344$). When using the 1-inch O.S. map it is often convenient to use the grid lines for measuring approximate distances, since the sides of each grid square are 1,000 metres long.

4. Conventional signs and contours

For reasons of space and clarity, maps use standard signs to depict all that is significant on the ground. These 'conventional signs' are usually shown on the bottom of the map. An hour or two spent in learning the signs on a 1-inch map would be well worth while. The signs on other maps are broadly similar.

Contours. For the mountaineer, the most important signs are the contour lines, which are brown lines drawn on the map at a set height above sea level. These show the shape of the mountains.

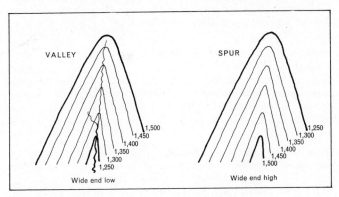

157. *Watch the contours to avoid confusing a valley with a spur.*

On the standard 1-inch O.S. maps they are at fifty-foot intervals (i.e. the 'vertical interval' between contours is fifty feet). The heights are marked only occasionally on the fifty-foot contours, but at every 250 feet there is a thicker line with the height marked on it, and the height of any fifty-foot contour can be worked out by counting up or down from this. On some of the Tourist Editions, the contours are at a vertical interval of one hundred feet and the height is given in each case. In certain mountain areas some contours have not been surveyed on the ground, but have been sketched in by eye between the surveyed contours; hence there may be inaccuracies in detail which can be misleading where the mountain shapes are complicated or have small-scale features.

Layering. On the Tourist Editions of the 1-inch O.S. maps (and also on the Bartholomew ½-inch maps and some foreign maps) the land at different heights is tinted differently. On the 1-inch maps, for example, land between sea level and 500 feet is green, with different shades at one hundred feet and 300 feet; above 500 feet it changes progressively from very light to dark brown, with a change every 500 feet. Layering shows at a glance the areas of high and low land, and hence the shape of the mountains.

Hachuring is a method of showing hill features by short lines drawn in the direction of the slope, thicker at the top of the slope than at the bottom. It is not used on O.S. maps (though some of the Tourist Editions use shading to similar effect) but it is common on the Continent.

Cliffs. A cliff is too steep to be shown by contours and a conventional sign (the same as for a quarry) is used – a black irregular edging with black markings on the side of the cliff. The edge itself is shown by the black line, and you will see the contours ceasing at this line, and other contours resuming at the bottom of the cliff; the difference between their heights is, of course, the height of the cliff.

Triangulation pillars are rectangular pedestals of concrete or natural stone used in the survey of Britain; they have brass fittings on top to take survey instruments. They are found on many summits and provide a positive means of identification in bad weather. They are shown on the map by a small triangle followed by the height. If there is a height on the map but no triangle shown, then that is simply a spot height not marked on the ground.

Youth hostels are indicated by a small red triangle and G.P.O. telephone boxes by a 'T'. Mountain Rescue Posts where stretchers and other rescue equipment are available (see chapters 12 and 13) are spelt out in full. Footpaths and tracks are shown thus – – – –. It is important not to confuse these with county boundaries (– — — —) or parish boundaries (.................) since these boundaries sometimes go over cliffs or along river beds!

5. The shape of mountains

As noted above, the Ordnance Survey uses contours (and sometimes layering) to show the shape of hills and mountains. For a

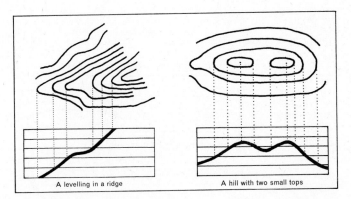

A levelling in a ridge   A hill with two small tops

158. *Careful study of changes in the slope of the ground, reflected in the contours, will often enable you to fix your position.*

mountaineer, the ability to read contours accurately is one of the most important map-reading skills. Where the contour lines are close together, the hill-side is steep, and where they are far apart the gradient is slight. Contours will therefore enable you to select the least tiring line on a mountain, and will warn you if you are on the wrong route; for example by showing that the ground is sloping in a different direction from what it should be. A skilful reading of contours will often give your exact position on a route; for instance, if you are walking up Moel Siabod (grid reference 705547 on O.S. Sheet 107) in mist by the west ridge (from grid reference 677543) you will come on a definite levelling off in the ridge, and you can tell from this that you must be at grid reference 690545. A similar example is shown in [158]. Indeed, many mountaineers are so good at following the shape of the mountain from contours that they rarely find a compass necessary.

The gradient is calculated by dividing the rise (the vertical interval) between two points into the horizontal distance between them. Thus if the rise is one hundred feet and the horizontal distance is 500 feet, the gradient is one in five (quite a steady pull). For the purpose of calculating gradients on the one-inch map, one mile can be taken as about 5,000 feet, giving the following rough gradients:

Distance between successive fifty-foot contours	1 in.	0·5 in.	0·1 in.	0·01 in.
Approximate gradient	1 in 100	1 in 50	1 in 10	1 in 1

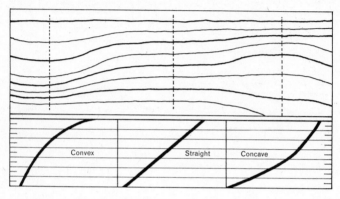

159. *The three types of slope.*

6. Setting the map

Before you can read off from the map the names of the features around you, it is necessary for the map to be set. This means that the map is facing in exactly the same direction as the ground, i.e. that a pencil laid on the map from your position to any other position on the map will also point to that position on the ground. There are two methods.

1. *By eye.* Where visibility is good and the country is not totally unfamiliar it is easy to set the map simply by identifying points on the ground and on the map and rotating the map until it exactly matches the countryside around.

2. *By compass.* In bad weather or in unfamiliar or featureless country the compass method is the only reliable way. With a transparent-base compass put the base over the Magnetic North Pole symbol on the map, and rotate the map until the symbol points in the same direction as the compass needle [160]. With a prismatic compass put the hair-line along the symbol and rotate the map until the needle points along the hair-line (and symbol).

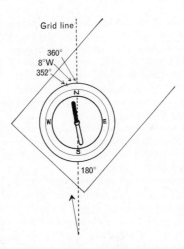

160. *Setting the map by compass, where the grid-magnetic variation is 8° W.*
(See 155).

7. Using a compass

Once your map is set, you may in good weather be able to find
your route without using your compass, since you will be able to
find all you need either from the map or by direct observation.
But in bad weather when visibility is very restricted a compass is
essential to find your way off the summit or on to the next one.

What does the use of a compass entail?

First, it needs a basic understanding of the compass as an
instrument so that it can be used accurately. The magnetized end
of the needle, which points to the Magnetic North Pole, is always
marked, and usually has luminous paint on it so that it can be seen
at night. North on the compass scale is also luminous, and so is the
direction of travel on the Silva compass. When using the compass,
make sure that there is no ferrous metal (e.g. an ice-axe, a karabiner,
or barbed wire) or a photo-electric exposure meter near by, since
this might disturb the needle. Carelessness here can lead to serious
errors. The compass should also be tested occasionally for accuracy.
Subject to this, the compass needle can be relied on in all parts of

the British Isles, with the exception of certain areas where there is local deflection. These include the Cuillin ridge in the Isle of Skye and, by repute, parts of Stob Coire Nan Lochan (Glencoe) and Bowfell (Langdale). Where there is local deflection, the compass needle can swing wildly within a few feet: the deflection is worse the closer the compass is to the ground.

Secondly, it requires an understanding of grid north and magnetic north (section 1 above).

Thirdly, it involves the measurement of the angles between grid north (on the map) or magnetic north (on the compass) and the direction of travel. These angles are called 'grid bearings' and 'magnetic bearings' respectively.

Fourthly, it is necessary to know where you are on the mountain, since you cannot take any useful bearings unless you have a fixed point to start from. If in good weather you notice that visibility is deteriorating, get a fix of your position while you still can. If the clouds clear later, much can be done to establish your position by back bearings (see below), but it is far simpler and safer to know where you are in the first place.

8. Bearings: map to compass

You can work out the direction of the next part of your journey in three stages [161]:

STAGE ONE. CALCULATE FROM THE MAP THE GRID BEARING BETWEEN YOUR PRESENT POSITION AND THE DIRECTION YOU WANT TO GO.

The method of working out grid bearings depends on whether you use a protractor or a compass, thus:

Grid bearing with a protractor. Work out the position of your next objective on the map, and draw a thin line to it from your present position. Place the centre point of the protractor over your present position, and the base of the protractor parallel with a grid north line, and read off the bearing of your direction of travel on the protractor scale.

Grid bearing with prismatic compass. Place the 360-degree and 180-degree marks on the compass parallel with a grid north line (with 360 degrees to the north). The direction of the compass needle does not matter. Then place the hair-line along the line of travel. The grid bearing can be read off on the dial.

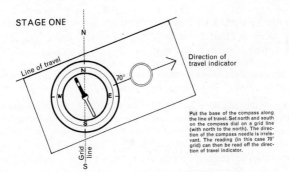

STAGE ONE

Line of travel

Direction of
travel indicator

Put the base of the compass along
the line of travel. Set north and south
on the compass dial on a grid line
(with north to the north). The direction of the compass needle is irrele-
vant. The reading (in this case 70°
grid) can then be read off the direction of travel indicator.

STAGE TWO

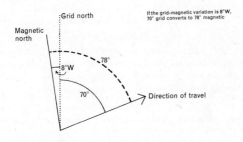

If the grid-magnetic variation is 8°W,
70° grid converts to 78° magnetic

Grid north

Magnetic
north

8°W

78°

70°

Direction of travel

STAGE THREE

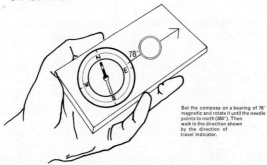

Set the compass on a bearing of 78°
magnetic and rotate it until the needle
points to north (360°). Then
walk in the direction shown
by the direction of
travel indicator.

161. *A bearing: map to Silva compass.*

Grid bearing with Silva compass. The same as with the prismatic compass except that it is much more accurate because you can see through the base on to the map.

STAGE TWO. CONVERT THE GRID BEARING INTO A MAGNETIC BEARING, BY ADDING THE GRID-MAGNETIC VARIATION.

This is necessary to take account of the difference between grid north (as used in stage one) and magnetic north (as used in stage three). As explained in Section 1 above, the grid-magnetic variation is arrived at by deducting the grid variation from the magnetic variation; it varies in different parts of the country, and from year to year. A convenient way of remembering whether to add or subtract this variation according to whether it is west or east of north is:

Variation west, compass best (i.e. greater numerically);
Variation east, compass least (i.e. smaller numerically).

As in Britain magnetic north will remain to the west of grid and true north for many years to come, the magnetic bearing in degrees will always be greater than the grid and true bearings. Hence to arrive at the magnetic (or 'compass') bearing, always *add* the grid-magnetic variation to the grid bearing obtained in stage one. For example:

Grid bearing (in degrees)	Grid-magnetic variation (in degrees west)	Magnetic bearing (in degrees)
70	6	76
255	8	263
355	8	363 (i.e., 3 deg.)

If you have difficulty in working out whether to add or subtract the variation to convert a bearing it may be helpful to remember that:

Grid to magnetic ADD (i.e. there are more letters in 'magnetic' than in 'grid');
Magnetic to grid SUBTRACT (i.e. there are fewer letters in this conversion).

STAGE THREE. PUT THE MAGNETIC BEARING ON TO YOUR COMPASS.

To do this, put the direction-of-travel indicator (Silva compass) or the hair-line (prismatic compass) against the number of the magnetic bearing on the compass dial, then rotate the compass until the compass needle points to 360 degrees (i.e. to north). Then march in the direction shown by the direction-of-travel indicator or the hair-line, if possible selecting a point *en route* (a boulder, or a fence) to help you keep direction. As noted in § 9, it is often necessary to make deviations, and these must be compensated for.

Short cuts. There are two possible ways of avoiding stage two:

– using a compass such as the Silva Ranger compass which has an adjustment to enable the meridian lines in the base to be reset to allow for the grid-magnetic variation;
– compensating for the grid-magnetic variation temporarily on the compass by pointing the compass needle at 360 degrees less the grid-magnetic variation instead of at 360 degrees as in stage three. If the variation is 7 degrees west, the needle would be pointed at 353 degrees (the variation is *subtracted*). The compass dial remains set as in stage one, i.e. at the grid bearing obtained from the map.

9. Bearings: compass to map

There are two sets of circumstances in which you may need to take bearings with the compass (as distinct from applying known bearings to the compass as in the previous section).

1. *To identify another peak, where this cannot be done from the map directly.* This involves:

   (1) rotating the compass until the needle points to 360 degrees (this, however, is not necessary with the prismatic compass);
   (2) turning the direction-of-travel indicator (or the sighting line if there is one) until it points to the peak, and reading off the magnetic bearing;
   (3) converting the magnetic bearing into a grid bearing. As noted in stage two of the previous section, the magnetic bearing is always greater in Britain than the grid bearing. It is therefore necessary to *subtract* the grid-magnetic variation from the magnetic bearing to arrive at the grid bearing. For example:

Magnetic bearing (in degrees)	Grid-magnetic variation (in degrees west)	Grid bearing (in degrees)
243	8	235
4	6	—2 (i.e. 358 deg.)

The grid bearing can then be drawn in from your position, and with any luck should pass through the peak concerned.

2. *To identify your own position by back bearings.* This can be very useful if you are not sure where you are. Possibly the mist will clear for a moment and enable you to see into a neighbouring valley or across to near-by peaks. Obtain grid bearings on to two points in the same way as in 1 (except, of course, that the points must be identifiable). The idea then is to draw lines from the position of the points on the map back along the grid bearings: where the two lines cross must be your position. To do this you must convert the grid bearings into grid back bearings by adding or subtracting 180 degrees (if an object is S.E. of you, then you must be N.W. of it). For example:

Grid bearing (in degrees)	Grid back bearing (in degrees)
135	315
195	15

The method is explained in [162].

The two 'short cuts' referred to in section 8 can also of course be used in these cases to avoid converting the bearings from magnetic to grid.

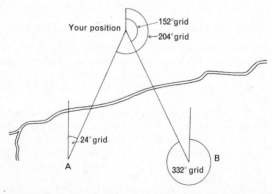

162. *Back bearings to identify your own position.* If the compass bearings from your own position to A and B are 211° and 159° magnetic respectively, the grid bearings are 204° and 152° respectively (assuming that the grid-magnetic variation is 7°W.). The back bearings must therefore be 24° and 332° respectively (obtained by adding or subtracting 180°). When these grid back bearings are drawn from A and B on the map, the point where they cross will be your position.

Appendix F. Knots for mountaineers

This appendix shows how to tie the common knots and refers to their main uses. Useful books on knots and splices are in the bibliography, 6.

Make absolutely certain that you can tie the knots correctly in all circumstances, including times when you are tired or cold and thus likely to make mistakes. An incorrect knot could easily lead to an accident. Always take special care to ensure that knots do not work loose. Finish off each one with an overhand knot (see below) or two half hitches [163D] and leave sufficient spare rope to allow the knot to tighten up under load. These precautions are especially important with some kernmantel nylon ropes which tend to resist bending to the shape of the knot, and hence are liable to spring open in use and slip under load. Check your main knots frequently on a climb.

1. Knots for tying on to the main climbing rope

Until recently, the bowline [163 and 164] and the Tarbuck [168] knots were standard end man's knots, but with the increasing popularity of kernmantel rope, in much of which it is impossible

163. *The bowline.* 'The rabbit (i.e. the end of the rope) comes out of its hole, round the tree, and back in again.' All climbing knots should be secured with two half hitches, as in D, or an overhand knot (thumb knot), as in 80C, to prevent them working loose.

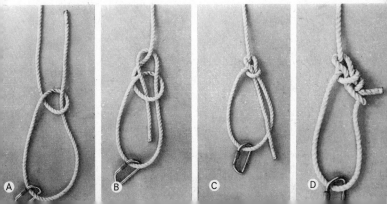

A   B   C   D

164. *A quick way of tying the bowline.* This method has the advantage that the knot is tied close into your waist without any need for adjustment, and that it can become completely automatic to tie.

to tie either knot properly, *the figure-of-eight knot loop* [167] is now (1967) recommended generally for tying on. It may be tied either as a closed loop for use with a karabiner or looping over the body, or it may be formed by threading. Its advantages are:

– it does not work loose, even with kernmantel rope;
– it is stronger than the bowline and not much weaker than a Tarbuck in those ropes that will take one;
– it does not pull through under load because the two parts of the rope in the knot are forced in opposite directions against each other.

This knot can also be used:

– for the middle man to tie into the main climbing rope;
– for tying an anchor knot into the waist-loop in a belay [81B and c].
– in the figure-of-eight knot belay [82]; and in the ice-axe belay (§ 17).

165. *The bowline on the bight.*

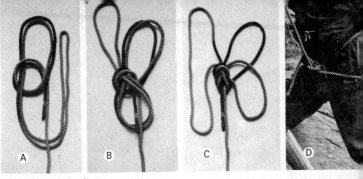

166. *The triple bowline.*

The single bowline. Although the figure-of-eight knot loop is pre-ferred, this knot can be used for the end man in hawser-laid rope of sufficient flexibility. Whereas it is then reliable if the load comes on the main axis of the knot (i.e. along the main climbing rope), it can turn into a slip knot under heavy sideways loading (e.g., where a main belay karabiner is clipped direct into a waist-loop which is tied with a bowline).

The bowline on the bight and the triple bowline give extra loops which can be used as thigh-loops or chest-loops to relieve the strain which

167. *The overhand knot (A–B) and the figure-of-eight knot (C–D).* The method of tying the overhand knot doubled, for nylon tape or webbing slings (p. 205), is at E–H, though sewing is preferable (p. 535).

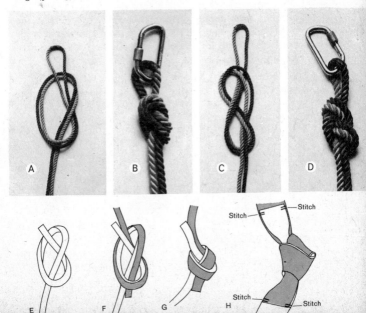

a single bowline puts on a suspended climber's waist. For example:

– in artificial climbing (§ 67) or on crevassed glaciers (§ 135);
– in rescue work, where someone has to be lowered (§§ 94 and 141).

The triple bowline is the better knot because it is easier to tie (it is simply a standard bowline tied in a double rope), and because its extra loop gives increased comfort and security.

The overhand knot [167] is useful for:

– securing the end of any knot which is likely to work loose [80c];
– the Pigott rope stretcher [125].

The Tarbuck knot. This is a sliding friction knot specially developed by Mr Kenneth Tarbuck for hawser-laid nylon rope, used in conjunction with a waist-band and karabiner (§ 54, 2). Like the devices used in tent guy-ropes, it can be freely moved up or down the standing rope, but will resist any ordinary load imparted from the two ends. Under heavy load, however, it closes up, thus providing a cushioning to the shock of a fall, reducing the risk of injury to both man and rope. Although this cushioning could be valuable in a fall where the leader's rope jams a few feet from his waist, since the whole of the force of the fall is then concentrated in a short length of rope which may not otherwise be able to stretch sufficiently to absorb the shock, the knot cannot be unreservedly recommended, except for experienced climbers using flexible hawser-laid rope, because:

168. *The Tarbuck knot.* To get this knot tight, tie it against pressure from your foot, as in D. Do not use it with kernmantel rope.

- it can either not be tied, or comes undone, in kernmantel and, to a lesser extent, in the stiffer modern hawser-laid rope;
- it is easy to tie it incorrectly;
- its energy-absorbing properties have become less important with the wider use of double ropes and heavy nylon rope.

If you use it, make sure that you tie it in the correct sequence and that it is always tight. The leader's knot should normally be extended to nine to fifteen inches in length and he should check this before he starts a pitch. For the second held directly from above there is no reason why the knot should not be closed against the karabiner, which is less cumbersome. It is also useful for:

- guy-ropes on tents (§ 30);
- adjustable cows' tails in artificial climbing (§ 67);
- adjustable ice-axe slings [106B and 107A].

2. Knots for joining two ropes

The fisherman's knot is the best knot for joining two ropes of equal thickness since it is small and does not easily work loose in use, but can be undone after it has been under load. The double fisherman's is rather more bulky, but is even more secure and is recommended in preference to the single version wherever there is any chance of it tending to work loose. These knots are used for:

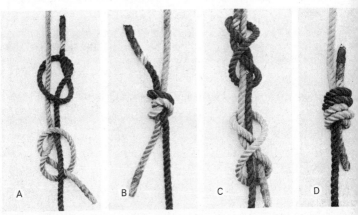

169. *Fisherman's knots.* A and B show the single knot, C and D the double version. Note that the two sides of the knot match each other.

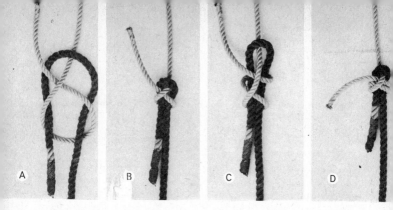

170. *Sheetbends*. A and B show the single version, and C and D the double.

- joining two ends of a sling (§ 55);
- joining two climbing ropes, though this practice is not recommended except in unusual circumstances (§ 54);
- joining two ends of a waist-band (§ 54, 2) though they are rather more bulky than the reef knot (see below) for this purpose.

The sheetbend is often used in place of the fisherman's knot, but it is bulkier and probably more likely to work loose; the double sheetbend is safer than the single variety. This is quite a useful knot for joining up abseil slings (§ 66) as it can be adjusted rather more easily than the fisherman's knot. It is usually recommended for joining two ropes of markedly unequal thickness as it does not distort.

The reef knot is a flat knot which should be used only in cases where it lies on a surface and not freely in the air. It distorts dangerously when the load is not along the main axis. It is recommended for:

- bandaging (§ 98);
- the middle and end knots of a waist-band (§ 54, 2).

It can also be used for abseil slings (§ 66) though the double sheetbend or the double fisherman's is better.

3. Other knots

The round turn and two half hitches is a slip knot used for:

- tying a rope on to ice-axes or rucksacks to be hauled up a difficult pitch;
- belaying on to a tree with the main climbing rope (§ 60).

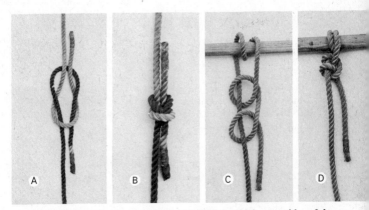

171. *The reef knot and a round turn and two half hitches.* If the two sides of the reef knot do not correspond exactly, it is a dangerous 'granny knot'. The reef knot is tied 'left over right, and right over left'.

The clove hitch can sometimes be used for tying on to a piton [86].

The prusik and Penberthy knots are sliding friction knots used for attaching a sling to a standing rope [153], for:

– crevasse rescue (§ 140, 2) both for the victim and on the surface;
– in mountain rescue when the stretcher escort needs a chest-loop to support his shoulders (§ 94);
– for climbing up the rope on overhanging rock pitches (§ 76);
– for tying on to the main climbing rope where the second needs to be able to adjust his position on the rope without untying; in this case a short sling is used with a prusik knot on to the main rope at one end and clipped into the waist karabiner at the other.

The use of the prusik knot for climbing up a standing rope has to some extent been superseded by the advent of special devices such as the Hiebeler 'Prusiker' and the Clog 'Ascender'; the Penberthy knot is also claimed to be more effective than the prusik.

Bibliography and films

For reasons of space, this list is selective. Some out-of-print books are included (without prices) since they will probably still be available second-hand, or from libraries. Prices of foreign publications are approximate only.

1. Periodical publications (available direct or by subscription through *e.g.* Gaston's Alpine Books – appendix B, 5)

Alpine Journal. Alpine Club; annual, £2·75 (soft cover); £3·50 (hard cover). Comprehensive coverage of mountaineering developments, including expedition reports, worldwide, with annual surveys of climbing in Britain; equipment and technical reports; book and journal reviews. Profusely illustrated. From West Col Productions (appendix B, 5)

Alpine Climbing. Alpine Climbing Group; annual, about 40p. Latest developments in the Alps with technical notes on major routes, and pull-out supplements on various areas. From the Alpine Club (appendix B, 1)

Alpinismus. Reitmorstrasse 21, Munich 22, West Germany; monthly, £4 a year; mainly in German

The Climber and Rambler. Holmes McDougall Ltd, 36 Tay Street, Perth PH1 5TT; monthly, 20p

Mountain. 30 Collingwood Avenue, London N10. £3·30 annually (ten issues).

Mountaineering. Replaced in 1972 by *Mountain Life.* British Mountaineering Council (appendix B, 1); every two months, £1·90 for six. From Chris Brasher, The Navigator's House, River Lane, Richmond, Surrey, TW10 7AG. National coverage of mountain activity; news about B.M.C. activities (see p. 29) and about expeditions and equipment; details of guidebooks and club journals. The B.M.C. publishes a separate handbook with up-to-date address lists of secretaries of member clubs, guides and training organizations; and it also has an annual publication, *New Climbs,* giving details of new routes throughout the country.

Rocksport. Every two months, 20p each from T.I.M. Lewis, 23 Farndale Close, Long Eaton, Notts.
Rucksack. Ramblers' Association (appendix B, 2); quarterly, 1s.

Most of the British mountaineering clubs publish journals, some of which make an important contribution to mountaineering literature (see, for example, the extracts in the anthologies by Ward and by Pyatt and Noyce listed in the next section). The journals most likely to interest non-members are given below.

Climbers' Club Journal. Annual, 12s. 6d. From Mrs M. F. Walker, 22 Asmuns Hill, London NW11
Fell and Rock Journal. Annual, about 12s. 6d.; from the Cloister Press Ltd, Heaton Mersey, Stockport, Cheshire; includes details of new climbs in the Lake District.
Irish Mountaineering (see footnote in § 109). Occasional, 5s.; includes details of new climbs in Ireland.
Scottish Mountaineering Club Journal. Annual, 10s. 6d.; from West Col Productions (appendix B, 5); includes details of new climbs in Scotland.

The Continental alpine clubs (appendix D) publish the following journals which include information about the Alps:

Austrian Alpine Club (O.A.V.), *Mitteilungen* (monthly);
    Der Bergsteiger (monthly, 70s. a year)
Austrian Alpine Club (O.A.K.), *Österreichische Alpenzeitung* (every two months), 20s. a year. From O.A.K., Getreidemarkt 3, Vienna 1060, Austria
French Alpine Club, *La Montagne et Alpinisme* (five times a year), 40s.
Groupe de Haute Montagne, *Annales* (yearly)
Italian Alpine Club, *Rivista Mensile* (bi-monthly)
Swiss Alpine Club, *Les Alpes: Die Alpen* (quarterly). Also a monthly bulletin

2. General books and mountaineering in Britain (see chapter 13 for guide-books and other books dealing with particular British areas)

BONINGTON, CHRISTIAN, *I Chose to Climb*, Gollancz, 1966, 30s.
BROWN, JOE, *The Hard Years*, Gollancz, 1967, 42s.
CLARK, R. W., *Mountaineering in Britain*, Phoenix House, 1957, 45s.
    A Picture History of Mountaineering, Hulton Press, 1956

COXHEAD, E., *One Green Bottle*, Collins (Fontana), 1955

LUNN, SIR ARNOLD, *A Century of Mountaineering*, Allen & Unwin, 1957

MILNE, M., *The Book of Modern Mountaineering*, Arthur Barker, 1968, 63s.

MILNER, C.D., *Rock for Climbing*, Chapman & Hall, 1950. Many photographs

MOFFAT, GWEN, *Space Below My Feet*, Hodder & Stoughton, 1961

MORIN, NEA, *A Woman's Reach: Mountaineering Memoirs*, Eyre & Spottiswoode, 1968, 50s.

MURRAY, W.H., *Mountaineering in Scotland*, Dent, 1962, 30s. *Undiscovered Scotland*, Dent, 1954

NOYCE, WILFRID, *The Climber's Fireside Book*, Heinemann, 1964, 30s.

NOYCE, WILFRID and MCMORRIN, IAN, *World Atlas of Mountaineering*, Thomas Nelson, 1969, 90s.

POUCHER, W.A., *The Scottish Peaks*, Constable, 1964, 21s. (see also §§ 104 and 106)

PYATT, E.C., *Where to Climb in the British Isles*, Faber, 1960, 20s. *Mountains of Britain*, Batsford, 1966, 25s. (see also § 108)

PYATT, E.C., and NOYCE, WILFRID, *British Crags and Climbers: an Anthology*, Dobson, 1952

RICHARD, COLETTE, *Climbing Blind*, Hodder & Stoughton, 1966, 21s

SMYTHE, F.S., *Spirit of the Hills*, Hodder & Stoughton, 1946, 20s.

STYLES, SHOWELL, *Mountaineers' Weekend Book*, Seeley Service, 1960, 15s. *Rock and Rope*, Faber, 1967, 25s.

UNSWORTH, W., *Because It Is There: Famous Mountaineers, 1840–1940*, Gollancz, 1968, 21s.

WAINWRIGHT, A., *The Fell Walker*, Westmorland Gazette (§ 104), 1966, 15s. The story behind the hill-walking guide-books

WARD, MICHAEL, *The Mountaineer's Companion*, Eyre & Spottiswoode, 1966, 50s.

WRIGHT, J.E.B., *Rock Climbing in Britain*, Kaye, 1964, 16s.

3. Mainly instructional books

BELL, J.H.B., *A Progress in Mountaineering*, Oliver & Boyd, 1950

B.M.C. (appendix B, 1), *Safety on Mountains; The Mountain Code*

CREW, P., *An Encyclopaedic Dictionary of Mountaineering*, Constable, 1968, 30s.

DISLEY, J., *Tackle Climbing This Way*, Stanley Paul, 1968, 18s. or paperback 7s. 6d.

Educational Publications, *Rock Climbing* (Know the Game Series), 1968, 4s.

EVANS, C., *On Climbing*, Museum Press, 1956, 30s.

FRANCIS, G.H., *Mountain Climbing* (Teach Yourself series), E.U.P., second ed., 1964, 8s. 6d.

FRASER, COLIN, *The Avalanche Enigma*, Murray, 1966, 42s.

GREENBANK, A., *Instructions in Rock Climbing*, Museum, 1963 *Instructions in Mountaineering*, Museum, 1967, 17s. 6d.

KIRKUS, C.F., *Let's Go Climbing*, Nelson, 1960, 2s. 6d.

LANGMUIR, ERIC, *Mountain Leadership*, S.C.P.R. (appendix B, 2), 1969, 10s. Official handbook of M. L. Training Boards (§ 2)

MACINNES, HAMISH, *Climbing*, S.Y.H.A. (appendix B, 1)

MARCH, BILL, *Modern Snow and Ice Techniques*, Cicerone Press (§ 104, 2), 1973, £1.

Mountaineering Association (appendix B, 2), *A Short Manual of Mountaineering Training*, Kaye, 5s.

NOCK, P., *Rock Climbing*, Foyle, 1963, 4s.

RÉBUFFAT, G., *On Snow and Rock*, Kaye, 1963, 42s. Many photographs

SELIGMAN, G., *Snow Structure and Ski Fields*, privately printed, second ed., 1963, 75s.

UNSWORTH, W., *The Book of Rock-Climbing*, Arthur Barker, 1968, 25s.

WEDDERBURN, E.A.M., *Alpine Climbing On Foot and With Ski*, Countrygoer, 1954, 12s. 6d.

WILSON, KEN, *Hard Rock*, Hart-Davis, MacGibbon, 1974, £6.95

WRIGHT, J.E.B., *Technique of Mountaineering*, Mountaineering Association (appendix B, 2) and Kaye, 1964, 17s. 6d.

YOUNG, G. WINTHROP, *Mountain Craft*, Methuen, 1949. The classic on the fundamental principles

4. Mainly alpine mountaineering (see chapter 19 for guide-books and other books dealing with particular alpine areas)

ALLAIN, P., *Alpinisme et Compétition*, Arthaud, Paris

BONATTI, W., *On the Heights*, Hart-Davis, 1964, 35s.

GEIGER, H., *Geiger and the Alps*, Oscar Bucher, Stollberghalde 16, Lucerne, 1966. Many photos of routes

GERVASUTTI, G., *Gervasutti's Climbs*, Hart-Davis, 1957

GILLMAN, P., and HASTON, D., *Eiger Direct*, Collins, 1966, 36s.

HARRER, H., *The White Spider: The History of the Eiger's North Face*, Hart-Davis, 1965, 35s.

HECKMAIER, A., *Les Trois Derniers Problemes des Alpes*, Arthaud, 1952

LUKAN, K., *The Alps and Alpinism*, Thames & Hudson, 1969, 90s.

MUMMERY, A.F., *My Climbs in the Alps and Caucasus*, Blackwell, 1936, 9s. 6d.

REBUFFAT, G., *Starlight and Storm*, Dent, 1956

ROCH, A., *Climbs of My Youth*, Dent, 1956

On Rock and Ice, Black, 1947. Many photographs

SCOTT, DOUG, *Big Wall Climbing*, Kaye & Ward, 1974, £4.75

ULLMAN, J.R., *Straight Up: John Harlin, The Life and Death of a Mountaineer*, Doubleday, N.Y., 1968, 63s.

WHYMPER, E., *Scrambles Amongst the Alps*, Murray, 1954, 25s.

YOUNG, G. WINTHROP, *On High Hills*, Methuen, 1947

5. Greater ranges (mainly Himalayas)

BARKER, R., *The Last Blue Mountain*, Chatto & Windus, 1959, 21s.

BRASHER, C., and HUNT, SIR JOHN, *The Red Snows*, Hutchinson, 1960. The Caucasus

BUHL, H., *Nanga Parbat Pilgrimage*, Hodder & Stoughton, 1956

CLARK, S., *The Puma's Claw*, Hutchinson, 1959. The Andes

DYHRENFURTH, G.O., *To the Third Pole*, Werner Laurie, 1955 (later edition in German). A survey of Himalayan climbing

EVANS, C., *Kangchenjunga: The Untrodden Peak*, Hodder & Stoughton, 1956

GRANT, R.H., *Annapurna II*, Kimber, 1961, 30s.

HILLARY, SIR EDMUND, *High Adventure*, Hodder & Stoughton, 1955

HUNT, SIR JOHN, *The Ascent of Everest*, Hodder & Stoughton, 1954, 25s.

MASON, K., *Abode of Snow*, Hart-Davis, 1955, 25s. A survey of Himalayan climbing

MORDECAI, D., *The Himalayas*, 1966, 27s. Lists peaks over 20,000 ft. From R. A. Redfern, Old Brampton, Chesterfield, Derbyshire

NOYCE, WILFRID, *Climbing the Fish's Tail*, Heinemann, 1958
   To the Unknown Mountain, Heinemann, 1962
SCARR, JOSEPHINE, *Four Miles High*, Gollancz, 1966, 36s.
SLESSER, M., *Red Peak*, Hodder & Stoughton, 1964, 30s.
   The Andes are Prickly, Gollancz, 1966, 40s.
SMYTHE, F.S., *Camp Six*, Black, 1956, 6s.
TERRAY, L., *Conquistadors of the Useless*, Gollancz, 1963, 30s.
   (with J. Franco) *At Grips with Jannu*, Gollancz, 1967, 42s.
ULLMAN, J.R., *Americans on Everest*, Michael Joseph, 1966, 50s.

6. Related subjects

Astronomy
MOORE, P., *The Observer's Book of Stars*, Warne, 1962, 5s.

Flora and fauna
BARNBY, T.P., *European Alpine Flowers in Colour*, Nelson, 1967, 30s.
PEARSALL, W.H., *Mountains and Moorlands* (New Naturalist), Collins, 1960, 30s.
STOKOE, W.J., *The Observer's Book of Wild Flowers*, Warne, 1963, 5s.
   The Observer's Book of British Ferns, Warne, 1951, 5s.

Camping
BASILLIE, M., and WESTWOOD, J., *'Mid moor and mountain*, Boy Scouts' Association (see appendix B, 2), 1960, 7s. 6d.
COX, JACK, *Camp and Trek*, Lutterworth, 1964, 15s.
   Camping for All, Ward Lock, 1958, 15s.
   Camping Sites in Britain, Cade (see § 105, note), 3s. 6d.

Caving
BARRINGTON, N., *Caves of Mendip*, Dalesman (page 340); 10s. 6d.
CULLINGFORD, C.D.H., *British Caving*, Routledge & Kegan Paul, 1962, 75s.
Britain Underground, Dalesman (p. 341)
MYERS, J. O., *Underground Adventure*, Dalesman, 8s. 6d.

Geology
DURY, G., *The Face of the Earth*, Penguin Books, 1966, 6s.
EVANS, I.O., *The Observer's Book of Geology*, Warne, 1956, 5s.

TRUEMAN, A.E., *Geology and Scenery in England and Wales*, Penguin Books, 1949, 5s.

Knots and splices
ASHLEY, C.W., *Ashley's Book of Knots*, Doubleday, 1960, 84s.
FRANKLIN, E., *Tying Knots*, Pearson, 1960, 8s. 6d.

Mountain rescue and first aid
Mountain Rescue Committee (appendix B, 1), *Mountain Rescue and Cave Rescue*, 25p.
MACINNES, HAMISH, *International Mountain Rescue Handbook*, Constable, 1972, £3·25
MARCH, BILL, *Improvised Techniques in Mountain Rescue*, Jacobean Press, 58 Grove Street, Edinburgh, 1973
MARINER, W., *Mountain Rescue Techniques*, U.K. Branch Austrian Alpine Club (see appendix D, 1), 1964, 8s. 6d.
MOFFAT, GWEN, *Two Star Red*, Hodder & Stoughton, 1964, 21s. The story of R.A.F. Mountain Rescue
British Red Cross Society (appendix B, 1), *A.B.C. of First Aid First Aid* (official manual of the B.R.C.S., St John Ambulance Association, and the St Andrew's Ambulance Association)
Royal Air Force, *Mountain Rescue*, (PAM Air) 299 (2nd edition). H.M.S.O., 1968, 12s. 6d.
Fédération Française de la Montagne (appendix D, 3), *Secours en Montagne de France* (rescue methods), 1967, 20s.; and *Secourisme en Montagne* (medical aspects), 1969, 20s.

Navigation
PICKLES, T., *Map Reading*, Dent, 1963, 5s.
Ramblers' Association (appendix B, 2), *Map Reading for the Countrygoer*, 6s.
War Office, *Manual of Map Reading* (Part One), H.M.S.O., 1956, 8s. 6d.

Orienteering
PIRIE, G., *The Challenge of Orienteering*, Pelham Books, 1969, 30s.
Scottish Orienteering Association, *A Short Guide to Orienteering*, 1969, 1s. 6d. From H. Philip, 47 Corslet Road, Currie, Midlothian

Ornithology

FISHER, J., *Bird Recognition*, four vols., Penguin Books, 1948
PETERSON, R., MOUNTFORT, G., and HOLLOM, P.A.D., *A Field Guide to the Birds of Britain and Europe*, Collins, fourth ed., 1961, 15s.

Photography

DE MARÉ, ERIC, *Photography*, Penguin Books, 1957, 5s.
MILNER, C.D., *Photography of Scenery*, Focal Press, 1961, 35s.
   Mountain Photography, Focal Press, 1945
   All About Taking Pictures in the Hills, Focal Press, 2s. 6d.

Ski-ing

Austrian Association of Professional Ski Teachers, *The New Official Austrian Ski System*, Kaye, 1961, 35s.
FIRSOFF, V.A., *On Ski in the Cairngorms*, W. & R. Chambers, 1964, 6s.
HUNTER, J.K., and GULBRANSEN, O., *Ski-ing in Britain*, Nelson, 1963, 12s. 6d.
JOUBERT, G., and VUARNET, J., *How to Ski the New French Way*, Kaye & Ward, 1968, 40s.
Scottish Ski Club (appendix B, 1), *Ski-ing in Scotland*, 5s.
Ski Club of Great Britain (appendix B, 1), *Handbook on Ski-Touring and Glacier Ski-ing*, 1961, 4s. 6d.

Weather

LESTER, R.M., *The Observer's Book of Weather*, Warne, 1955, 5s.
SUTTON, O.G., *Understanding Weather*, Penguin Books, 1964, 3s. 6d.
BARTLETT, D., and BARTLETT, K., *Signpost to the Weather*, Stanford (appendix B, 5), 1949, 3s. 6d.

7. Films on mountaineering and rescue

TITLE	SUBJECT	FROM
Going to the Hills	Introduction to hill walking	Educational Foundation for Visual Aids, 35 Queen Anne Street, London W1

Rock Climbing	Basic principles by Royal Marine Commandos	Royal Navy S.N.S.O., H.M. Dockyard, Portsmouth
Climb When You're Ready	Instructional film on rope management	C.C.P.R. (appendix B, 2)
Hazard	Safety while climbing in the Dolomites	British Steel Corporation, 33 Grosvenor Place, London SW1
Mountain Rescue	Rescue equipment and operations (M.R.C. film)	N. F. Kirkman, Esq., 16 St John Street, Manchester M34EA *(8 mm. version)* National Audio Visual Aids Library, 2 Paxton Place, Gipsy Lane, London SE27 *(16 mm. version)*

The British Mountaineering Council (appendix B, 1) will supply on request a comprehensive list of films on mountaineering and rescue which are available on hire or loan from distributors and film libraries.

Addendum One
Belaying on snow: the deadman*

As noted in §§ 17 and 86, the ice-axe rarely gives a safe belay because it tends to pull through the snow, or even (if wood-shafted) to break under load. There have been accidents on snow and ice climbs as a result of which the whole party has been taken down. For this reason, it is strongly recommended to belay on rock by natural or artificial means wherever possible, for example on the wall of a gully or on rock outcrops on a wider slope.

In the later 1960s, however, the 'deadman', which was originally devised for tethering dogs in the Antarctic, has been developed to a degree where it now provides a reliable and recommended anchor in a wide variety of snow, including poor quality unconsolidated snow which would be quite unsafe for an ice-axe belay.

Test results have shown that a deadman *correctly placed* can sustain loads of about one ton in firm, crystalline snow; even in poor snow consistently high results were obtained, though in some cases the deadman was pulled through it for several feet until eventually the snow in front was built into a hard compressed mass capable of sustaining a considerable load. With *poor placement*, however, the results dropped to a much lower level (around 600–800 lb.) comparable with normal ice-axe or snow stake belays.

1. Types of deadman

Essentially, the deadman is an 8-in. by 10-in. plate of $\frac{1}{8}$-in. alloy, with a hole in the centre to take a five foot length of

---

* This note is based on material in *Mountain Leadership* (bibliography, 3) and in research notes by Peter Crew in *Mountain*, September 1969.

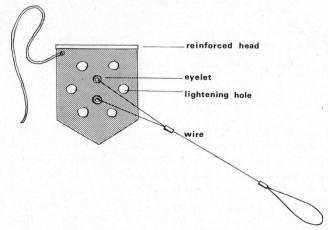

reinforced head

eyelet

lightening hole

wire

172 *An improved deadman.* A smaller version, the 'deadboy', is also available. This diagram, and 174–5, by Robin Day.

nylon rope secured with a barrel knot at one end and a loop at the other for belaying.

Various improvements have however been devised as shown in [172]. Note in particular:

– the wedge-shaped bottom helps to cut into hard snow;
– the flat top of hard metal gives rigidity and resistance to hammering;
– the two holes for the belay rope spread the load more evenly over the whole surface area;
– the wire sling is relatively stronger and more durable than nylon; and its thinness helps it to cut through the snow to adopt a 'normal' attitude to the belayer and the deadman regardless of how far the latter has been hammered or stamped in;
– the 1-in. diameter holes reduce weight without any loss of efficiency in normal snow, though they could possibly reduce holding power in the extremely light powder snow encountered in the polar regions or in the Alps in winter;
– a karabiner clipped through one of these holes and the belay loop enables the deadman to be carried conveniently over the shoulder like an ordinary sling;
– a light cord may be attached to one corner to assist in withdrawing the deadman.

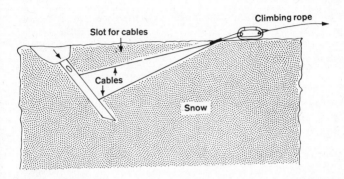

173 *The snow-fluke.*

In addition, M.S.R. (p. 489) have produced the *snow-fluke*, which automatically adjusts to the correct position under load, even when being pulled through soft snow (an action which is claimed to give a valuable dynamic braking effect) [173]. It is, however, not yet established whether this is as satisfactory as the normal deadman in average circumstances; some tests have suggested that it may come out of the snow more easily.

2. Use of the deadman on slopes

In principle, the deadman is embedded in the snow in such a way that its entire surface resists movement through the snow when a load is applied to the rope: i.e. it acts as an anchor. First select a position at least ten feet above the stance and cut a T-shaped slot in the snow (the cross-bar to take the deadman, and the upright to take the wire). The deadman should be buried about 1 ft and bedded down by tapping firmly with the shoulder of the ice-axe shaft near the spike; the wire sling is accommodated in the upright of the T and because of its cheese-cutting action it will adopt a normal position between the deadman and the load. The belayer ties his sling or rope into the wire sling (as in [83 A–B]), taking care that the depth of the slot is great enough to accommodate it. He can then give an indirect belay round his waist (as in [175 and 82]). The whole system should then be tested to ensure that it is bedding down properly.

To achieve full security, it is *absolutely essential to place the deadman correctly* since otherwise it may start slipping or cutting through the snow under load, or even, as shown in [174 c], flick out. In particular, observe the following points:

- the cross-bar of the T must be at least 1 ft deep and angled into the snow in such a way that the direction of the expected load forms an internal angle with the deadman of 50°;
- the upright of the T should point exactly to the stance and should be at right angles to the plate. It should be cut to the same depth as the cross-bar initially, but tapering off to nothing towards the stance. It is important that the upright is deep enough throughout its length to accommodate the rope between the deadman and the belayer at the correct 50° angle to the deadman without bending it upwards (which would alter the direction of force applied to the deadman and possibly flick it out under load). The channel should be as narrow as possible and should not disturb the lip of the cross-bar hole;

174. *The correct angle for use of the deadman.* Too large or too small an angle could cause it to come out under load.

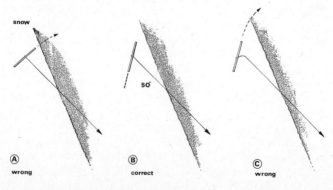

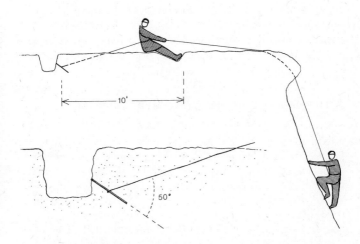

175. *Use of the deadman on flat ground.* The deadman should be put in at the bottom of the pit, at the correct 50° angle to the belayed leader, who remains well back from the cornice.

– the deadman can be stamped or hammered into the cross-bar but special care must be taken in slabby snow not to fracture the whole retaining mass. The rule is that if the snow has good natural cohesion (e.g. very hard or slabby), disturb it as little as possible, but if it lacks cohesion (e.g. soft or wet), then stamp the deadman well in. In either case, make sure to avoid disturbing the snow in front of the deadman (except to cut the slot for the rope) since this may break the snow's cohesion with the result that it gives under load.

3. Use of the deadman on flat ground

Many snow climbs finish on flat ground on a ridge or on the edge of a plateau, where it is often difficult to find an existing belay. Fortunately, the deadman is just as efficient buried in a horizontal position as in any other [175]. Dig a small pit approximately 12–18 in. deep according to the type of snow; and cut a vertical slot into the pit on the side where the stance will be taken, for the rope. The deadman can then be pushed or hammered at the correct relative angle into the snow at the bottom of the pit, and the climber ties on to the sling in the normal way.

4. The ice-axe as an alternative to the deadman

Where no deadman is available, the ice-axe can be used as an anchor by burying it in a cut-out slot in the snow at right angles to the direction of pull. The rope is attached some three inches towards the head from the middle of the shaft by a tight clove hitch [86 F], which will not slip along the axe in the event of it moving under load. A slot for the rope should be cut as for the deadman, to avoid the risk of the axe flicking out (see (2) above). The axe must then be well stamped in and tested. While this is not as satisfactory as the deadman, it is a good deal stronger than the normal (upright) ice-axe belay shown in [21].

5. The deadman strongly recommended

All in all, the advent of the deadman and now the snow-fluke has led to a fundamental improvement in the security of belays. The smaller deadboys in particular can be used in a very wide variety of situations, including where the snow cover is thin, and can also be carried easily. The use of these new aids is therefore strongly recommended, provided it is practised until the correct method of placement is unfailingly achieved.

Addendum Two
Webbing loops for mountaineering*

A climber was killed in 1970 when the knot in a webbing loop that was used to secure an abseil rope became untied. It is believed that the knot had been tied as a double-overhand but there is no conclusive evidence whether the knot was imperfectly formed or whether it had become loosened in use. The case draws attention to the vital need for reliable joins in webbing loops used for belaying and similar purposes. It is strongly recommended that webbing loops be formed by sewing wherever possible. When sewing to the necessary standard is not possible, it is recommended that webbing be knotted by means of a double-overhand knot [167 E–H], though this is substantially weaker. *The knot should be regularly and frequently checked for security, and sewing carefully examined for any sign of wear.* Advice is given below on sewing and knotting webbing and on the choice of webbing for mountaineering purposes.

1. Sewing

Loops should be formed by sewing the overlapping ends of the webbing in such a way that the tensile strength of the join is not less than 80 per cent of that of the webbing itself. A lockstitch machine must be used and the sewing securely finished off by back-sewing. Specimens of the sewn join should be tested to verify that the strength requirement is met. Guidance on sewing joins in webbing is given in a number of British Standards, e.g. B.S. 1397 – Industrial safety belts and harnesses. *Domestic sewing machines are not*

* This note was issued by the Equipment Sub-Committee of the B.M.C. in *Mountaineering*, Vol. 6, No. 4, and it is reprinted with minor amendment, by kind permission.

*suitable for this work and sewing must be done by a specialist webbing
product manufacturer.*

A suitable design of sewn join that has been found to meet
the strength requirement is shown in [176]. (This design of
join is the subject of patent application by RFD-GQ Ltd.)
Each end of the overlap is bound with 1-in.-wide nylon tape
and the sewing extends beyond the ends of the webbing,
which have been previously cut square with a hot knife.
The thread is of nylon of not less than 27 lb. breaking load.
The stitches are at a pitch of approximately five per inch to
give a total of approximately 110 stitches in all in addition
to the back-stitching. The stitches are distributed over a
total length of about $3\frac{5}{8}$ in. Sewing should not be closer than
$\frac{1}{8}$ in. to the edge of the webbing.

A simple overlapped join is unlikely to meet the strength
requirements given above.

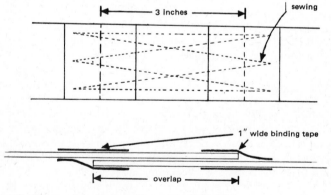

176. *Recommended method of sewing nylon webbing.*

2. Knotting

The only known safe knot for joining webbing is the double-
overhand knot which can only retain about 60 per cent of

the strength of the webbing. The procedure for tying this knot is shown in [167 E–H], and care should be taken that it is tied correctly and pulled tight. At least two inches of webbing should be allowed to protrude from each end of the knot and, after securely tightening the knot, the ends may be taped or hand-stitched to the main loop to prevent them from working back through the knot. Regular inspection is necessary to ensure that the knot has not worked loose during use. It should be noted that the stiffer types of webbing are more difficult to tie securely and extra care must be taken.

3. Choice and strength of webbing

Whenever possible, it is recommended that tubular nylon webbing with a breaking load of not less than 4,000 lb. be used for belay loops. Even when loaded under unfavourable conditions, loops of this material, when properly sewn or knotted, may be expected to have a breaking load in excess of 4,400 lb. This is adequate to withstand the heaviest loads likely to be imposed in emergency after a reasonable amount of use. Lighter-weight nylon tubular webbing with a breaking load of not less than 2,200 lb. may be acceptable for less exacting uses, such as anchorage for an abseil rope, where the maximum loads will be less. Two-ply webbing of similar load ratings is acceptable with sewn joins but is less satisfactory for knotting.

Index

More about Penguins
and Pelicans

Annapurna South Face

Chris Bonington

In 1970 Chris Bonington and his team successfully
battled up a seemingly impregnable mountain in the
Himalayas. It was a magnificent triumph for mountaineering and good teamwork. *Annapurna South Face* tells
how it was done.

'I am left . . . with a sense of wonder at this feat; of
admiration for the men who dared and did it'–Lord
Hunt in the *Sunday Times*.

'He writes as well as he climbs'–*Times Literary
Supplement*.

'This is a very good book indeed, exciting,
psychologically illuminating and honest, and I read it
entranced'–C. P. Snow in the *Financial Times*

Not for sale in the U.S.A.

Don Whillans: Portrait of a Mountaineer

Don Whillans and Alick Ormerod

This is the story of a Mancunian plumber who climbed his way to fame.

In the company of Joe Brown, Chris Bonington and others Don Whillans has thrilled the world with his spectacular and heart-stopping climbs.

Adapted from his diaries this vigorous, humorous account tells how it all happened–from the early beginnings in the Derbyshire Peak District to his triumphant ascent of Annapurna in 1970.